I0016217

Speaking Geek

The ABC's of Technology

by Bob Cohen

www.bobology.com

Speaking Geek

The ABC's of Technology Terms

Why This Book?

The language of technology is changing how we communicate. To follow the plot on television shows it's necessary to understand an increasingly technical vocabulary. The average dinner conversation includes technology terms and job skills require a working knowledge of the language of technology.

News reports cover technology product announcements as major events. As an instructor of adult education programs, I explain a wide range of technology to people of all ages and technical backgrounds. Students taking my classes often ask me to explain a technical term when it's introduced in the lesson.

Learn More with the Free Weekly Newsletter

It's because of this need that I write a weekly newsletter (to subscribe go to www.bobology.com and sign up for the email newsletter) where I explain a technical term of the week. It's impossible to cover all the technical terms used in the English language, but this book will help you understand many of the most important ones, explained in as non-technical a language as possible. The email newsletter is completely free and you can always unsubscribe at any time by clicking on an unsubscribe link.

The Basics

Computers, Networks, and the Internet

Computer Hardware and Software

Computers are electronic devices that can perform calculations using instructions from software.

The computer is the hardware, while software is the instructions which tell the computer what to do. If you were in your kitchen making a meal, you would be the computer and the recipe which you're following would be the software. The recipe tells you what ingredients and utensils you need to use to physically prepare the meal. Follow one recipe and you might have a sandwich, follow a different one and you'd end up with a salad. You're the same person, but you're following different instructions for each meal.

Networks

For computers to communicate with each other they need to connect to each other. When computers connect to other computers it's called a network. Networks make it possible for us to visit websites using the Internet. These websites are on computers located somewhere on the Internet and a network allows the computer that has the website to communicate with our computer. The Internet is one of the best know networks, since almost everyone with a computer uses it.

Wireless and Mobile

A network that doesn't need physical cables is called a wireless network. Wireless networks make it possible to move around with computers, and that's called mobile computing. You might use a form of computer called a smartphone, which is designed from the ground up to use wireless networks. Wireless networks eliminate the need to use a cable to connect a computer to a network. But wired, or wireless, it's still a network.

World Wide Web

While you and I use personal computers and other personal electronic devices, there are companies, governments, and educational organizations that use large computers and networks. When these computers and networks are connected to a public network called the Internet, they become part of the World Wide Web. The World Wide Web consists of every computer and network connection to the Internet. Since it's public, it's possible to send messages across the Internet from one computer to another. In contrast, a private network would only connect specific computers to each other and a private network would require the approval of the organization that owned the network in order to connect to it.

Social Media

With the World Wide Web making connections between computers easier, people can connect with each other using websites specially designed for this purpose. Since human beings are social by nature, Social Media has become a popular use of the World Wide Web.

The Cloud

The cloud is a way of referring to computers that you can't see, but that you can connect to from your computer. They are somewhere up in the "sky," in the cloud. In fact they are in computer rooms somewhere on the ground, but you don't really know, or care where they are. As long as you can connect to them, it's possible for your computer to ask them to do things for you. All of these "things" have been lumped together in the term "the cloud." So as a result it's a bit confusing.

In reality, if you get directions from a website, use an online shopping cart to make a purchase, or use a backup service over the Internet, you're already using the cloud.

Companies and Standards

Companies make products and offer services, and their goal is to make a profit for their investors. Governments and industry organizations create standards. These don't always go well together.

Companies

Companies are in the business of trying to attract and retain customers and make as much profit as possible. Without profit, they can't continue to survive and grow. In our society, companies can create products, offer services, and attract customers. Build a better mousetrap and people will buy it. The more unique the product, the greater the opportunity to make a profit, since no other company has anything similar to offer to customers. This is capitalism and it's baked into our economic system.

When one company offers a smashing success, other companies see an opportunity to make money if they can come up with a better idea. As a result, competition between companies is created. Competition offers consumers choices, and it forces companies to continually innovate and offer new and better products and services to customers.

Proprietary Standards

One way companies try to hold on to customers is by offering products and services that create a lasting relationship, rather than a one-time purchase. If a customer invests in learning and using one company's products or services, the customer has made an investment that may cause them to think hard before switching to a competitor. In addition, there may be an investment of money in resources to use the product that would be lost if the customer switched to another brand of product or service.

An example of this is a razor blade. Buy one and you're usually committed to using replacement razors from the manufacturer of the blade handle. The money you'll spend on razor blades during the time you own that brand is many times more than the cost of the original blade. And if you buy and stock up on replacement blades, you're unlikely to switch until you use up any supply you have on hand. Another product that is like this is a computer printer. The profit is in the replacement ink and toner for the manufacturer. So what's this have to do with anything?

When a company is the only source of a product or service, they stand to make all the profit. When a company's product becomes so widely used, it can become a standard by which all other products are measured. However, since no other company can offer it, the product or service is called "proprietary." There is nothing inherently wrong with a proprietary standard, but it means one company has all the control. This kind of standard is often called a "defacto" standard as well, since one company has control of the product that sets the industry standard.

Industry Standards

In contrast, when a group creates a product specification and allows many companies to manufacture products or offer services, this is considered an industry standard. Sometimes companies co-operate and get together to set standards when they see that they would benefit more from having an industry standard, rather than compete and have products that might not work together from different manufacturers.

Your Role as Chief Information Officer

The job title of people who keep information technology working at large organizations is often the "Chief Information Officers," or CIO. If information technology is responsible for a missed payroll, having to stop the manufacturing line, or shut down a service, the Chief Information Officer often is blamed. In our homes and small businesses, we are our own Chief Information Officers since we write the checks that pay the bills.

Just like the Chief Information Officer of a large organization, we depend on the companies who make our technology products and services. Something breaks, and we have to pay the bill and spend the time trying to figure out how to fix it. I suspect that some of you have spent some time trying to make technology work and it can be very frustrating. So what does this mean to you?

There's a valuable lesson about personal technology that can be learned from people who spend large amounts of money on technology. They try to minimize risk by using proven products and by keeping their technology as simple as possible. When there is a defacto standard or an industry standard, they often use that product or service, since it's got a large customer base. A large customer base means better support. CIO's also check out the support and resources of the company before they make any purchase.

Connecting products together from one company and making them work can sometimes be frustrating, but when you start connecting products and services from different companies together, you have a new job. The professionals in technology who make different company's products work together are called Integrators. And when you use products or services from different companies, you have become an Integrator. That means that if there is a problem where two different company's products don't work with each other, it's your job to fix it, or find someone who can.

Simplifying your technology is one way to make your life easier, and using products and services from companies who offer better support can make the difference between hours of frustration and going about your day. Chief Information Officers invest a lot of time learning about technology and the companies involved in them, and if you're reading this book, you're on the path to making better choices and opening up new possibilities.

What are Computers?

When you think of a computer you might think of a box with cables coming out of it, with a display monitor screen, a keyboard, and a mouse. These devices are commonly referred to as personal computers or PC's.

What's Inside?

All personal computers include electronic components connected via cables and electronic connections using boards that hold the components, called Printed Circuit Boards, or when used with a computer, a Motherboard (explained later). The major parts of a computer include a processor chip, called a Central Processing Unit, that performs the calculations. It's a complicated electronic circuit that is on a single silicon chip. The CPU is the "brain" of the personal computer and runs everything.

In order to perform calculations, a computer needs a place to store it's work, which is memory. Different types of storage technologies are used to make the most of price versus speed. Faster speed usually cost more when you're dealing with technology. The fastest memory is called RAM (explained later), while the hard disk drive is the slower memory, but it's much less expensive.

So inside we have a board, a CPU, memory, and a hard disk drive. The connections to the outside world include various connectors where cables can be plugged in to let devices communicate with the computer.

Just as a note, desktops usually have additional slots for connecting add-on circuits. This is used to extend the capability or enhance the performance. Common add-on circuit cards include graphics cards for faster game performance, cards with special connectors, and sound cards for more sophisticated audio recording and playback.

A laptop is a form of personal computer that is portable and includes a built-in screen, keyboard, and mouse. It's essentially the same type of device as a personal computer but is more portable.

What's Outside?

The connectors include ways to connect an external display device, usually the monitor. Monitors are made in various sizes and display ratios. A traditional screen has a ratio of 4 units wide to 3 units high, like an older model TV. Since many users now use computers to play movies and video, many monitors have a widescreen ratio, which is 16 units wide by 9 units high. This is the standard ratio for High-Definition TV.

In addition to the monitor, a personal computer has a keyboard and a mouse. These are called Human Interface Devices and are necessary for a person to use a personal computer. The computer doesn't really need them, but people do.

Peripherals

Additional connectors are usually available which allow connections to external devices, called peripherals. They are called peripherals because they aren't inside the personal computer case, they are peripheral to it. Common peripherals include printers and speakers, but there are thousands of devices made that will connect to a personal computer.

The ability to connect peripherals to a personal computer can change an average everyday computer into a point-of-sale cash register with a credit card swiper and a cash drawer. The ability to connect peripherals to a personal computer has been one of the reasons they have become so widely used.

OK, so this is a personal computer, and you probably own one or have at least used one. But lately you might be hearing the term "devices." In fact, Microsoft announced that it was reorganizing its whole organization recently and one part of the organization includes "devices."

What are Devices?

A device is a computer that simply isn't a personal computer. It includes a CPU, memory, and a way for a person to use the device. A device can do many, if not all, of the things a personal computer can do because it is a computer by any other name. It's called a device because it just doesn't have the traditional case, monitor, keyboard, and mouse we often associate with a personal computer. In a way, devices are to computers like breeds are to dogs.

Your already probably familiar with what a dog is, so let me draw a little comparison between computers and dogs. Dogs are four legged mammals with fur that are all descendants of a type of wolf. Humans, through breeding, have created all kinds of breeds of dogs in an amazing assortment of sizes, shapes, colors, and temperaments. But chances are you can recognize a dog when you see one, regardless of what breed it is. Devices are like the different breeds of dogs, only they are different breeds of computers, and we haven't stopped making up new ones.

Common Devices

Some of the most common devices are tablets and smartphones. But devices can also come in other forms. Let's take on tablets and smartphones and look at some other "devices." Tablets Apple is credited with making the tablet popular with its iPad product, and now there are other manufacturers of tablet devices since they have become a popular form of computer. Tablets are a computer, with a CPU, storage, and a screen. The screen uses a technology called a "touchscreen" (explained later in the mobile section) and a person uses the tablet by touching the screen. The touch causes the device to respond.

What's happened is that your fingers have become the mouse and your taps are the equivalent of mouse clicks. The keyboard is part of the display, and when it appears, your fingers can make contact with the display to enter text. So tablets have all the major parts of a personal computer, which include a CPU, memory, storage, along with a display, keyboard, and "mouse" which is your finger contact. If this sounds a lot like a personal computer, you've got the right idea since a tablet is at it's most basic definition, another physical form of a computer.

Smartphones

Smartphones (explained in more detail later in the mobile section) are phones that do more than just make phone calls. The popular definition of a smartphone is a device with a CPU, storage, a touchscreen, and includes it's own phone number for making and receiving phone calls. It's actually just another type of computer. These are smaller than a tablet (so you can hold it up to your ear to make a phone call), and include a built-in phone. Think of a smartphone as a portable computer with a phone function built-in and you've got the right idea. So maybe you know about tablets and smartphones and are willing to accept that they are "devices" that are really just a different size and shape. But there are more devices out there.

Other Devices

There are other types of devices besides smartphone and tablets which are computers. They don't fit the traditional definition of a personal computer, and they aren't a tablet, or a smartphone, but they have the basics of a computer. Often these are computers dedicated to a specific function or a type of activity. Game consoles, which are pretty common, are one type of device you might know about, and these are computers designed specifically to play games. The Sony Playstation, Microsoft XBox, and the Nintendo Wii are common Game Consoles. They have a CPU, memory, use game controllers instead of a keyboard/mouse, and typically use a television as a display.

As the power of computing hardware improves, devices sometimes cross over into other functions and this is blurring the lines of computing. Devices can include forms of computers that might already exist such as a game console, but you might be hearing about "wearable" computers. Google already has produced a set of glasses with a computer built-in, and Apple has created the Apple watch device.

I visited a dog show recently and was amazed at the number of breeds of dogs. All of the sizes, shapes, colors, and temperaments of different dogs. You can probably recognize a dog when you see one. Computers are a lot like dog breeds. Remember, as long as it has a CPU, memory, and it does calculations of some sort, it's a computer by any other name.

1-10

3D Printer

A 3D printer is an automated computer printer that builds solid objects using instructions from a computer file. The computer file includes three dimensions of length and width and depth to create the 3rd dimension needed for a solid object instead of a printed diagram.

Adding and Subtracting to Make Solid Objects

3D printers create objects by "printing" many thin layers made of liquid material that dries to a solid shape. These layers are printed one at a time, but when added together, can create a 3 dimensional solid object. Adding layers together is called an "additive" process for creating an object. You might be familiar with wood carving, where the wood carver removes wood to create the sculpture. The carving removes material to create the object and it's called a "subtractive" process. Much of our manufacturing has been subtractive, where we use tools and machines for removing material to create the shape of the object we want. 3D printers add many thin layers one at a time to create and build an object.

Add enough layers together and you can create a solid object. If you need to make something thicker, adding layers to it is a way to make something that is thin, thicker. Think of a sheet of paper, since it's pretty thin. Add 500 sheets together in a stack (which, by the way makes a ream of paper) and you've got a thick object. Instead of keeping each sheet of paper separate, imagine that they are glued together into a solid piece of material, and you've got a block, not 500 sheets.

Making Deposits with a Printer

Ink-jet printers use tiny nozzles to spray a thin layer of ink on paper. Using instructions from a computer, the ink-jet printer deposits tiny dots of ink in all the right places to print letters and photos. If you've ever sliced any food in your kitchen, you know that large objects can be sliced into layers, like a tomato. While your skills in slicing may be pretty good, a computer with the right software can take any solid object and "slice" it into really thin layers. If you could put the slices of your tomato back together, you've got a whole tomato. So now let's use slices to create something new.

Printing an Object

Let's say you want to create a chess piece. If you can create a computer diagram of the chess piece made up of slices so that when all the slices are added together you get a chess piece, you've got some idea of how the software for 3D printing works. It's not too different from your kitchen slicing, just finer and more precise (no offense at precision kitchen slicers meant here). Each time the printer prints a layer, it moves itself left, right, and for a 3D printer, it can also move move up and down in the 3rd dimension. Instead of printing each slice with ink, the 3D printer uses a liquid material, like a plastic, for each layer of the chess piece. Moving up just a fraction of an inch for each layer, the printer deposits an additional layer of material one layer at a time. Each layer of plastic is liquid enough to keep it's shape and join with the next layer as the plastic cools. So when all the layers are "printed," you've made a complete chess piece.

Types of 3D Printers

3D printers are made in a wide range of process, sizes, and for use with different printing materials. They range in size from desktop models slightly larger than a typical desktop printer to large industrial models that can print large solid objects at high speeds. Different models make use of different materials for the solid printed object. Some models use plastics and others use liquid metals and can be used for manufacturing industrial products.

Prices are coming down on 3D printers all the time and there are models now available for under $500.00 from a company called Solidoodle (solidoodle.com). As a result, more people are buying them and more product plans and are being created all the time. Websites are available to obtain designs for 3D printers. A popular one is Thingverse (www.thingiverse.com) created by Makerbot, one of the most popular 3D printer brands. At Sulpteo (http://www.sculpteo.com) you can create and publish designs for objects that people can order on the Web for printing at Sculpteo and then have it shipped to their home or office.

The Future of Manufacturing and 3D Printing

While 3D printing isn't ready yet to replace low-cost assembly and manufacturing, it's getting closer all the time. Instead of stocking replacement parts for an item like cars and household products, they can be printed on demand and shipped. With no need to keep inventory on hand, it's possible to manufacture parts for products that have no spare parts inventory. Items that were un-repairable before because of a lack of a part can become repairable and last longer if the design is available for a 3D printer.

With 3D printing, custom made products will be more common. Instead of having to rely on manufacturing a product in large volumes to lower costs, someday you will be able to order your product with customized options manufactured just for you. Complex objects with unusual shapes and patterns won't be a problem with 3D printers, so designers can try new and creative approaches.

3D printing isn't just changing products, it's also changing medicine. A new company, Organovo (www.organovo.com) is developing bioprinted human tissue for therapeutic and research uses. I'm sure we haven't seen all the uses for 3D printing. As 3D Printing becomes more widely available you might even be able to order your coffee in a custom mug that's manufactured while you wait.

4K TV

4K TV is an ultra-high definition television, also known as UHDTV (Ultra High Definition TV) or simply UHD (Ultra High Definition), which is the latest in consumer television image quality.

A 4K television offers four times the resolution of a standard 1080p HDTV, with twice the number of pixels both horizontally and vertically. This means that picture clarity is dramatically increased since there are more pixels, and therefore, more detail, on the screen. 4K TVs also boast a broader color palette, allowing for a richer range of colors improving the vibrancy of each image.

In case you were wondering, a 1080p TV has 1,080 pixels along the width of the screen. If you own a flat screen TV that you've bought in the past 6-7 years, chances are it's a 1080p resolution TV, also known as HD. These HD TV's were a large improvement over the standard resolution screen TV"s.

A pixel is a dot on the screen. Since resolution is made up of tiny dots called pixels, improving television resolution required not only developing screens capable of displaying the increased number of pixels, but also necessitated the development of cameras capable of recording such high quality images. When these special cameras record Ultra HD images for a movie or television show, the large amount of digital data is compressed for transmission to an Ultra HD viewing device, like a 4K TV. This digital transmission is received by the compatible television and then decompressed to restore the image to its original Ultra HD format. 4K televisions can even intelligently fill-in missing pixels so standard 1080p HD data can be viewed with the spectacular image quality provided by Ultra HD.

4K TVs are currently available with either LCD or LED displays, and now OLED technology. OLED stands for organic light emitting diode and offers a clear, vivid image at a wider viewing angle than current LCD or LED technology. OLEDs are more lightweight and can be used in super thin displays. 4K TVs are also equipped with passive 3D viewing technology. Passive 3D technology works differently than active 3D technology by providing a full 1080p image for each eye. This passive 3D technology results in increased detail and less eye fatigue when viewed through the lightweight 3D glasses. Passive 3D glasses are also less expensive than their active 3D counterparts.

The 4K TV viewing experience is relatively new, and the content available in the current market is expanding. In addition to many Blu-ray discs released in the later half of 2013 that were optimized for Ultra HD viewing, marked as "Mastered in 4K", Netflix now has videos available in 4K resolution.

I might add that since Ultra HD broadcasting takes a lot more bandwidth than standard HD broadcasting, television stations will take a little longer to catch up. However, almost all of the 4K TVs are equipped with intelligence to fill-in images for missing pixels so the quality of television viewing will be improved even before network stations change their broadcast technology.

Should you rush out to buy one?

Just between us, there's no need to replace your TV. In fact, if unless your TV is larger than 40", you may not even notice the difference between 4K and 1080p TV's since the pixels are smaller on smaller screen sizes. To be honest, when I was at the Consumer Electronics Show last January, I didn't notice any difference in the quality of the image in smaller screen sizes. However, I did have a chance to see a large screen projector with a 4K resolution image, and that was pretty impressive. In fact, 4K is the resolution used in digital projectors in movie theaters, which gives them the ability to replace the old film projectors and reels of film.

A

Accelerometer

When you rotate your smartphone or tablet, and the screen flips, a small circuit called an accelerometer detects your movement and tells your smartphone to swivel the screen. Almost every smartphone has an accelerometer built-in which makes gestures like "shake" and apps like the level possible since your smartphone knows how fast it's moving and in what direction because of this useful electronic circuit.

The accelerometer in your smartphone (and in most electronic devices) is a semiconductor material like most other electronic components. The difference is that the material acts like a small spring that detects changes in mechanical motion, then converts the motion into electrical signals used by software applications.

What is Acceleration?

To understand acceleration you only need to know if the speed or direction of an object is changing. Velocity measures speed and bearing at any one point. Change direction, speed, or both and you create acceleration. It's called acceleration whether you're speeding up, slowing down, or changing direction. Let's take a look at what happens when you move your smartphone from your desk or table.

When your smartphone is sitting on the surface, it has no velocity and no acceleration. Lift it up to your ear and you've got acceleration because it went from being at rest to moving. As you bring it closer to your ear, your hand moves slower until you stop. Your movement caused acceleration and the circuit inside your smartphone detects and measures the motion.

So what's the deal with direction?

Like most people, you don't always move your smartphone in a straight line. When you lift it up from a table or desk to your ear, your arm moves in an arc, or circle, not in a straight line. As your smartphone moves in a circle, the changing movement causes acceleration.

A frequently used smartphone motion that causes a change in direction occurs when you rotate your smartphone from a vertical position to a horizontal position. This pivot movement is often used to enlarge a web page or turn a photo for a larger view. The speed of the smartphone doesn't change much in this example, but the direction does, which is acceleration, and can be measured by the accelerometer.

Using this information, your smartphone knows it's moving from one position to another and needs to rotate the screen to match the final position when the smartphone comes to rest.

How smartphones use acceleration

In addition to the screen rotation that the accelerometer causes when the orientation of your smartphone changes, there are several other ways your smartphone uses this circuit.

The "shake" gesture

Apple iPhones and Android smartphones recognize the shake gesture as a command to make something happen. When you grab your device and shake it rapidly, the accelerometer is telling your device that you did a "shake" and sent a command to the software to make something happen.

Motorola's Moto-X uses the shake gesture to turn on the LED light, which makes uses like the flashlight easy.

Apple uses the shake gesture as an "undo" function. Type out a word, phrase, or sentence in an app like notes and then shake your iPhone or iPad (it's a little easier with the smaller iPhone). A menu pops up on your screen with the option to "undo" your last action. When typing a note in the Notes app, a text message, or email, the Shake gesture can be used to open the undo button. Whether it's entering text, doing a cut or paste or deleting, shake your iPhone or iPad and you'll see the undo button appear. Tap "undo" to confirm, or tap Cancel to go back.

In the Mail app, you can use shake to move an email to a folder after moving it or restore an email to the inbox after deleting it.

Urbanspoon

An app called Urbanspoon uses the shake gesture to spin a roulette wheel listing of restaurants nearby in case you can't decide where to go out. It's great for finding new options for dining and is a very popular app for both iOS and Android. It's available for free on the Apple App Store and the Google Play store for Android.

Driving and Game Apps

Driving game apps use the accelerometer to sense changes in velocity so you can turn your smartphone as a steering wheel while playing the game. Some games don't even require that you touch the screen and use the accelerometer to track the movement of your hand and use that motion to control the play of the game.

Health App Pedometer

If you carry your iPhone in a pants pocket while you walk, the Health app uses the accelerometer as a pedometer to count your steps. By measuring the movement of your leg, the accelerometer counts each step, and the app uses the data to calculate the total number of steps you've taken in a day.

Level

The Compass app has a built-in level option that makes your iPhone into a compass and electronic level. If you need to hang a picture on a wall or know which way is North, this app will do it for you. It's included with the iOS operating system and located in the Utilities folder. The app opens to the compass function, to access the level, swipe from right to left.

To my way of thinking

Accelerometers help us with tracking steps, rotating screens, playing games, useful gestures and make electronic devices like smartphones and tablets easier and with more to use. In fact, accelerometers are used in many electronic devices like cameras to help you keep it level and in drones to stabilize flight.

While you don't need to know that an accelerometer is the electronic circuit making all of this possible, you'll now have a better appreciation for what this technology does to make your life a little easier.

Ad Blocker

An ad blocker is a software application that blocks advertisements from appearing on web pages. Ad blockers are available for desktop web browsers and with Apple's release of version 9.0 of iOS for iPhones and iPads, Apple now allows the installation of ad blocker apps to block ads from appearing when using the built-in Safari web browser.

Why do websites have ads?

Many websites generate revenue by allowing ads to appear on their web pages. Ads can appear in the form of text, graphic, video, or an audio file. Since the website is a form of publication that's viewed and read by people, displaying an ad on a website offers the website owner a means to generate income whenever people click on the ads.

Some ads just take up space on the page when you view a webpage, while others like a video or audio file may start playing when you open the webpage on your desktop, laptop, smartphone, or tablet. Others "pop-up" ads appear as a window that covers the content of the webpage, requiring you to click on some icon like an "X" in the corner to remove the pop-up.

A website owner has every right to make money, and if the website publishes useful information that people often view, a percentage of the people visiting the website are bound to click on the ad. Many websites support themselves with revenue from advertising much like a newspaper, magazine, or television show receives payment from advertisers. Since people spend a lot of time viewing webpages on their computers and mobile devices, advertisers are willing to pay to reach people when they are browsing the web.

How are ads displayed?

Displaying ads is typically done using automated software provided by ad networks. An ad network is a business that works with advertisers who want their ads displayed on webpages and connects the advertisers with website owners willing to display ads. The systems are automated so that the ads are displayed and "rotate," or change in a specific space on the website. And the ads change depending on the budget and type of website.

You might see one ad on a website for cosmetics, and when you visit it later, you might see an ad for a hotel in the same location on the webpage. These automated ad networks include Google ads as well as others who work with advertisers who want to use the Internet for advertising. It's similar to a television network that has many shows and time slots for advertisers and sells the time. On the Internet, it's space on a webpage that's sold.

Since there are so many websites on the Internet, it would be time-consuming for an advertiser to contact dozens or even hundreds of website owners, so ad networks offer a convenient way for an advertiser to place their ad across many websites with one advertising contract.

Why block ads?

When using a desktop and laptop computer to browse web pages, the screen is large enough to display ads and the information at the same time without the ads taking up too much space. They're visible, but as a reader you'll still be able to read the content and view any pictures and images. Whether you find them intrusive or not is a matter of personal choice, after all, some people watch full-length ads like informercials on television.

One issue with ads displaying on a webpage is that tracking software is usually by the ad network that places the ad on the website. Tracking can include what ads you see, what ads you click on, and what web pages you view. While your personal identity may not be known, the ad network knows that it's your computer, smartphone, or tablet that views the webpages and ads. As a result, you may want to block ads for privacy reasons if you don't want to be tracked.

Another issue with ads is that ads can slow down your web browser and use additional data. Ads are usually "pulled" from a different computer than the one that runs the website you're viewing.

Here's what happens when a webpage is displayed.

When you view a webpage, the text, images, video and audio are displayed on in your web browser. Your web browser is an application that knows how to open up a webpage, and it also knows how to pull information from other locations using the instructions in the webpage that hidden from your view. Webpages have the capability to display a picture from a file on a computer. However, the picture doesn't need to be located on the same computer as the web page. You don't see the "code" displayed on your screen, you only see the finished webpage.

When a webpage has to pull information from several different computers, it can slow down how long it takes the webpage to finish appearing or "loading" on your computer or device. It's simply a case of storing information in two or more places like you do at home. If you have something handy like salt or pepper on the kitchen counter, it's easy to get to fast. Even if it's in a kitchen cabinet, you can open a drawer, but it's still fast to get to it when you're in the kitchen. But if you kept a container or special plate in the garage or storage, it just takes longer to locate it and bring it to the kitchen where you can use it. So how does this relate to webpage ads?

Webpages that display ads don't store the ads on the same computer as the webpage content. The ads are given a placeholder, and when you view the webpage, the ad is pulled from a different location, much like going to storage when you need to get that special plate or container you need in the kitchen. If the ad were part of the webpage, like your salt and pepper containers are in the kitchen, it would be fast to get to it. Put it in another location on the Internet, and it just takes a little longer to bring it over and display it on the webpage you're viewing.

Ads are simply additional files that are displayed on webpages, so at home, with a fast Internet connection, you may never notice the fraction of a second it takes for the ad to display and you'll usually see the whole webpage appear quickly. With a smartphone, it might be little different.

When using a smartphone to browse the web, you're often using your cellular data plan, so you're Internet speeds may not be as fast as they are at home, and you're using your cellular data plan bandwidth quota. As a result, webpages with ads may display slower than those without ads and the ads increase the amount of data you use in your data plan. As a result, Apple decided to allow ad blocker apps for iPhones and iPads. As you can imagine, advertisers are concerned about people with smartphones being able to block their ads, it's like being able to block ads from appearing while you're watching a television show.

There're a few other reasons smartphone users may want to block ads: the size of a smartphone screen and the space an ad takes up when it appears. Since smartphone screens are smaller than desktops and laptops, information on a webpage is smaller and anything that blocks the view of the information (like an ad) can be frustrating and annoying. Clicking on a small "X" to remove the ad often requires more finger dexterity than using a mouse to school over an "X" on a desktop or laptop screen.

How do I block ads?

To block ads, you'll need to install an ad-blocking application on your computer, smartphone, or tablet. The ad blocker software is usually available from the add-ons or the extensions menu in your web browser. Most desktop ad blockers are free.

Websites

Some popular ad blockers for desktop browsers such as Internet Explorer, Chrome, Firefox, and Safari are these:

Adblock Plus - an open source ad blocker

https://adblockplus.org/

Ghostery

https://www.ghostery.com/en/our-solutions/ghostery-add-on/

Adblock - a donation supported ad blocker

https://getadblock.com

For smartphone and tablet users, only Apple users have access to ad blockers on the Apple App Store. Google doesn't make ad blocking apps available for Android users to download. However, you can download the Firefox browser for Android and install a plug-in for the smartphone version.

After downloading the ad blocker app for iOS, you'll need to go to Settings, then choose Safari in the menu. Scroll until you see the menu for Content Blockers, then slide the switch button to the ON position, and it will change to green. Your ad blocker now active and ads will be blocked when using Safari to open webpages.

Apple users can try these out, all of which have excellent reviews:

- Crystal
- Blockr
- Purify Blocker
- Block Future

To my way of thinking

While many websites generate income from ads, users of smartphones (with smaller screens) are rightfully frustrated with the appearance of ads that block content on websites they visit. Apple has opened the door, giving users a choice with the ability to block ads using an app or simply leave well enough alone.

Adobe Flash

Adobe Flash is a software program that is used to create and play sound, video, and graphics on computers and the Internet. Often referred to as just "flash" for short, it's a software product that is developed and owned by Adobe, one of the largest software companies in the world.

Flash allows you to watch video, listen to music and play games on your web browser. This can be on a Web site over the Internet, or on a computer file in a program, such as a game or video. These types of files are often referred to as "media files" and Adobe Flash is often referred to as a "media" program. Video, audio, music, and games are often referred to as media because they take time to play back. Think of when you listen to a song. You could listen to just one point in time, but it wouldn't be music. It's the fact that it does take time to play that makes it "media."

Just a tip since you'll come across this when reading about Flash.

To be clear, I'm not referring to flash memory, which is a type of memory hardware. In this article, I'm discussing Flash software and media files. Someone might use the word flash in conversation to refer to flash memory, not Flash software or media files, so don't be afraid to ask them to clarify. In the process you'll impress them with your expertise and technical knowledge.

Some Specifics About Flash

Flash refers to two types of software. The first type is the Flash software program used by developers to create Flash files. The other is the Flash player software, which is needed to display and playback any file created in Adobe Flash. The player program is free while the content creation program requires the purchase or licensing from Adobe.

Developed in the mid 1990's, Flash became a popular way for Web sites to display and play videos on the Internet. The reason is that video files are much larger in size than files with just text or photos. Flash takes the original video file and creates a smaller video file from which takes less time to send over the Internet from the Web site to your computer. As a result, a Flash video can be played faster since it's a smaller file. At the time, Flash solved a real problem and allowed many Web sites to use video. Since that time, however, other formats for video have been developed and Internet speeds have become faster. As a result, Flash isn't the only solution available now.

Games

Adobe Flash has also become important when playing online games. Many Web sites allow users to play games, and there are thousands of games for computers and dedicated game player devices. Since games use moving graphics and video, the game developers often use Flash to create the game, so Flash is required to play it. Game developers use Flash because in addition to video, it provides animation to text, drawings and still images. Flash media files can be developed which allow communication from the viewer. By using this capability, a Flash media file can respond to feedback like a mouse click. In fact, what makes Adobe's Flash software unique is this capability to create media that can respond to a mouse click, keyboard stroke, or game controller command.

Flash and Apple

Flash can also be used on many mobile devices with the notable exception of Apple's iPhone and iPad. Apple devices will not play Flash files. If you see a large black space on a Web site while viewing it with an Apple iPhone or iPad, you are looking at a Flash video. It just won't play. Sometimes you'll see an error message instead, or in addition to this, telling you that you need Adobe Flash to playback and view the Web site. There's nothing you can do about this, except wait until you can access another computer. Apple's Mac computers will play Flash files, just not the mobile devices.

Here's what happened. When Apple developed the iPhone and iPad, they decided that allowing flash to play on their devices was not the best way to playback video or media files. Although Flash was used on many Web sites, Apple took a chance that people would want their devices more than they cared about playing flash video from Web sites. So what happened?

Apple managed to do OK in selling iPhones and iPads. Flash use on Web sites has been declining, and new Web standards have been developed in the meantime that don't require the use of Flash. Apple probably had lots of reasons, but it's not that important.

To accommodate Apple mobile devices, Web sites often use both Flash video and another copy of the video in a format that plays back on Apple devices. Web sites are capable of identifying your device's hardware and software, then sending your device or computer the best version for playback. So you might play a Flash video from YouTube on your computer because YouTube can tell that you are using a computer that can run Flash. While the video file that YouTube sends to your iPhone or iPad would be a different format that plays on Apple devices.

Android devices will play flash, so if you have an Android device, you can play flash and enjoy many of the same features that are accessible from the Internet version of websites.

Flash Player and Updates

In order to display a Flash file on your computer or from a Web site, you'll need to install the Adobe Flash player software, which is free. Adobe will periodically require downloads of updates to Flash in order to work properly with the latest improvements to Web sites using Flash media. Adobe Flash is right there to help you experience the site to its fullest.

So What's the Future?

For browsing the Web, it's becoming less important to have Flash, but it's still used on a fair number of Web sites. If you want to use a Web site that uses Flash, you'll need Flash. Since so many Web sites are offering Apple friendly alternatives in addition to Flash, it's less of a problem, and you may never come across the need for Flash at all.

Software developers that become familiar with a software program just don't like to give it up, since they can usually work faster and include capabilities that might not be available in other software. Adobe Flash is still used when Web site and software developers feel that Flash's capabilities and features will create a better solution than another software program. Because

Adobe Flash has many developers, as long as Adobe continues to add capabilities and features, Flash will be around. Rather than emphasizing Flash's use for video, Adobe's Web site promotes Flash as an animation tool for creating games, where it's a popular software development tool among game developers.

Advanced Search on Google

Advanced search is a built-in feature of Google (and most search websites) which allows a user to specify additional requirements for a search. When used for searching the Web, an advanced search gives additional information to Google, which helps refine the search.

You might remember a time when you took lessons at your school library about how to use the card catalog to find specific books by an author, title or subject, and knowing how to use that card catalog made it easier for you to locate books about specific subjects. Knowing how to use the advanced search on Google will make you better at finding what you are looking for on the web.

An example

For example, you might enter the words "auto" and "repair" in the search box when you type in a search. After you start the search, Google interprets what you were looking for to determine the results to show you. The search results will include any website that has to do with the words auto and repair. Some of the websites might just be about autos, some websites listed in the list will be about mechanics and others will be about auto repair.

If you put the words in quotes using "auto repair" you've told Google you want websites that use the words in that combination instead of any website that has to do with the word auto and the word repair. Using a phrase in quotes is a way to limit your search to words used in a specific order.

Google is pretty good at interpreting what you are likely to be searching for when you enter a search term, but if you know how to use the advanced search features, you can save yourself time and find more relevant results. There are a couple of ways to access these additional features for advanced search, using specific characters like the parentheses, which are called "operators," and using Google's advanced search web page, which does a lot of the work for you and can be easier to use for beginners. Let's look at both.

Using Punctuation and Operators in the Search Box

The text area where you enter your search term on Google or other search sites is called the "search box." When you enter characters in that box and click or tap to search, Google uses whatever you entered to search its database of websites and return website listings relevant to your request.

Certain punctuation marks can be used to provide additional instructions to Google's search. I mentioned putting a phrase in quotes earlier, and this punctuation limits the search to websites that use that specific word order and combination. You can include multiple words in quotes to search for some very specific information such as a website that refers to a line in a song like, "a little help from my friends." Google will search for websites that include that specific phrase and ignore websites that simply include the words.

Another common punctuation mark is the minus or dash sign. When you place a minus or dash sign in front a word like this in the search box "fruit -apples" Google will produce results that include the word fruit but exclude any website that includes the word apples. Using the dash for exclusion is useful for words with multiple meanings like jaguar, which is the name of an animal and a car. Using the word car in the search with a dash sign in front of it "jaguar -car" will exclude websites that include the word car in their content.

An operator is a specific word that when added to a search gives Google specific instructions on your search. An example of an operator is the word "OR" which when added between two words will produce results for websites that include either word. If you were searching for a website that could use the word shop or the word store, you could add the word OR in between the two words like this "shop OR store." Your results will include websites that include the word store as well as websites that include the word shop.

Another type of operator is a word with a colon after it. For example using the word "site" with a colon and then your search term can limit the results of your search to a specific website directly from the Google search box. Other operator terms exist which can be used to find pages that link to a specific website and find websites related to a specific website.

If you're interested in more ways to use punctuation for your searches you can read this web page by Google on how punctuation and operators work to produce specific search results.

Using the Advanced Search web page

Knowing a few of the punctuation marks and operators that I described can be helpful and will help you search the web faster. But, there's actually an easier way to use all of these advanced search features without the need to remember any of them and that's the advanced search web page on Google.

This web page includes several search boxes where you can enter your search. Each box explains how it will find web pages or narrow your results and automatically starts the search just as though you had entered the punctuation or operator to conduct that specific type of search.

In addition to the explaining what happens when you use a specific box on the advanced search page, you'll find an explanation of the punctuation and operators you can use on the main Google search page to help you learn how to use the advanced search features you use most often. As you become familiar with them through repetition, you can use the correct punctuation or operator and save time, or if you don't care to remember them, always use the advanced search web page. Here's the link.

Websites

https://support.google.com/websearch/answer/2466433?
p=adv_operators&hl=en&rd=1

http://www.google.com/advanced_search

To my way of thinking

Since we all access the web and receive more of our news and information from websites, learning how to search the web to find information is a helpful and possibly an essential skill for using the Internet. While we can let Google and other search sites interpret our broad general requests, there are times when we want something very specific and knowing how to use Google's powerful search software to help find something specific will make the technology work for you.

Adobe Flash

Adobe Flash is a software program that is used to create and play sound, video, and graphics on computers and the Internet. Often referred to as just "flash" for short, it's a software product that is developed and owned by Adobe, one of the largest software companies in the world.

Flash allows you to watch video, listen to music and play games on your web browser. This can be on a Web site over the Internet, on a computer file in a program, such as a game or video. These types of files are often referred to as "media files" and Adobe Flash is often referred to as a "media" program. Video, audio, music, and games are often referred to as media because they take time to play back. Think of when you listen to a song. You could listen to just one point in time, but it wouldn't be music. It's the fact that it does take time to play that makes it "media." Just a tip since you'l come across this when reading about Flash.

To be clear, I'm not referring to flash memory, which is a type of memory hardware. In this article, I'm discussing Flash software and media files. Someone might use the word flash in conversation to refer to flash memory, not Flash software or media files, so don't be afraid to ask them to clarify. In the process you'll impress them with your expertise and technical knowledge.

Some Specifics About Flash

Flash refers to two types of software. The first type is the Flash software program used by developers to create Flash files. The other is the Flash player software, which is needed to display and playback any file created in Adobe Flash. The player program is free while the content creation program requires the purchase or licensing from Adobe.

Developed in the mid 1990's, Flash became a popular way for Web sites to display and play videos on the Internet. The reason is that video files are much larger in size than files with just text or photos. Flash takes the original video file and creates a smaller video file from which takes less time to send over the Internet from the Web site to your computer. As a result, a Flash video can be played faster since it's a smaller file. At the time, Flash solved a real problem and allowed many Web sites to use video. Since that time, however, other formats for video have been developed and Internet speeds have become faster. As a result, Flash isn't the only solution available now.

Games

Adobe Flash has also become important when playing online games. Many Web sites allow users to play games, and there are thousands of games for computers and dedicated game player devices. Since games use moving graphics and video, the game developers often use Flash to create the game, so Flash is required to play it. Game developers use Flash because in addition to video, it provides animation to text, drawings and still images. Flash media files can be developed which allow communication from the viewer. By using this capability, a Flash media file can respond to feedback like a mouse click. In fact, what makes Adobe's Flash software unique is this capability to create media that can respond to a mouse click, keyboard stroke, or game controller command.

Flash and Apple

Flash can also be used on many mobile devices with the notable exception of Apple's iPhone and iPad. Apple devices will not play Flash files. If you see a large black space on a Web site while viewing it with an Apple iPhone or iPad, you are looking at a Flash video. It just won't play. Sometimes you'll see an error message instead, or in addition to this, telling you that you need Adobe Flash to playback and view the Web site. There's nothing you can do about this, except wait until you can access another computer. Apple's Mac computers will play Flash files, just not the mobile devices.

Here's what happened. When Apple developed the iPhone and iPad, they decided that allowing flash to play on their devices was not the best way to playback video or media files. Although Flash was used on many Web sites, Apple took a chance that people would want their devices more than they cared about playing flash video from Web sites. So what happened?

Apple managed to do OK in selling iPhones and iPads. Flash use on Web sites has been declining, and in the past year it went down from 24% of Web sites to 18.5% (http://w3techs.com/technologies/details/cp-flash/all/all). New Web standards have been developed in the meantime that don't require the use of Flash. Apple probably had lots of reasons, but it's not that important.

To accommodate Apple mobile devices, Web sites often use both Flash video and another copy of the video in a format that plays back on Apple devices. Web sites are capable of identifying your device's hardware and software, then sending your device or computer the best version for playback. So you might play a Flash video from YouTube on your computer because YouTube can tell that you are using a computer that can run Flash. While the video file that YouTube sends to your iPhone or iPad would be a different format that plays on Apple devices.

Android devices will play flash, so if you have an Android device, you can play flash and enjoy many of the same features that are accessible from the Internet version of websites.

Flash Player and Updates

In order to display a Flash file on your computer or from a Web site, you'll need to install the Adobe Flash player software, which is free. Adobe will periodically require downloads of updates to Flash in order to work properly with the latest improvements to Web sites using Flash media. Adobe Flash is right there to help you experience the site to its fullest.

So What's the Future?

For browsing the Web, it's becoming less important to have Flash, but it's still used on a fair number of Web sites. If you want to use a Web site that uses Flash, you'll need Flash. Since so many Web sites are offering Apple friendly alternatives in addition to Flash, it's less of a problem, and you may never come across the need for Flash at all.

Software developers that become familiar with a software program just don't like to give it up, since they can usually work faster and include capabilities that might not be available in other software. Adobe Flash is still used when Web site and software developers feel that Flash's capabilities and features will create a better solution than another software program. Because Adobe Flash has many developers, as long as Adobe continues to add capabilities and features, Flash will be around. Rather than emphasizing Flash's use for video, Adobe's Web site promotes Flash as an animation tool for creating games, where it's a popular software development tool among game developers.

Advanced Search

Advanced search is a built-in feature of Google (and most search websites) which allows a user to specify additional requirements for a search. When used for searching the Web, an advanced search gives additional information to Google, which helps refine the search.

You might remember a time when you took lessons at your school library about how to use the card catalog to find specific books by an author, title or subject, and knowing how to use that card catalog made it easier for you to locate books about specific subjects. Knowing how to use the advanced search on Google will make you better at finding what you are looking for on the web.

An example

For example, you might enter the words "auto" and "repair" in the search box when you type in a search. After you start the search, Google interprets what you were looking for to determine the results to show you. The search results will include any website that has to do with the words auto and repair. Some of the websites might just be about autos, some websites listed in the list will be about mechanics and others will be about auto repair.

If you put the words in quotes using "auto repair" you've told Google you want websites that use the words in that combination instead of any website that has to do with the word auto and the word repair. Using a phrase in quotes is a way to limit your search to words used in a specific order.

Google is pretty good at interpreting what you are likely to be searching for when you enter a search term, but if you know how to use the advanced search features, you can save yourself time and find more relevant results. There are a couple of ways to access these additional features for advanced search, using specific characters like the parentheses, which are called "operators," and using Google's advanced search web page, which does a lot of the work for you and can be easier to use for beginners. Let's look at both.

Using Punctuation and Operators in the Search Box

The text area where you enter your search term on Google or other search sites is called the "search box." When you enter characters in that box and click or tap to search Google uses whatever you entered to search its database of websites and return website listings relevant to your request.

Certain punctuation marks can be used to provide additional instructions to Google's search. I mentioned putting a phrase in quotes earlier, and this punctuation limits the search to websites that use that specific word order and combination. You can include multiple words in quotes to search for some very specific information such as a website that refers to a line in a song like "a little help from my friends." Google will search for websites that include that specific phrase and ignore websites that simply include the words.

Another common punctuation mark is the minus or dash sign. When you place a minus or dash sign in front a word like this in the search box "fruit -

apples" Google will produce results that include the word fruit but exclude any website that includes the word apples. Using the dash for exclusion is useful for words with multiple meanings like jaguar, which is the name of an animal and a car. Using the word car in the search with a dash sign in front of it "jaguar -car" will exclude websites that include the word car in their content.

An operator is a specific word that when added to a search gives Google specific instructions on your search. An example of an operator is the word "OR" which when added between two words will produce results for websites that include either word. If you were searching for a website that could use the word shop or the word store, you could add the word OR in between the two words like this "shop OR store." Your results will include websites that include the word store as well as websites that include the word shop.

Another type of operator is a word with a colon after it. For example using the word "site" with a colon and then your search term can limit the results of your search to a specific website directly from the Google search box. Other operator terms exist which can be used to find pages that link to a specific website and find websites related to a specific website.

If you're interested in more ways to use punctuation for your searches you can read this web page by Google on how punctuation and operators work to produce specific search results.

Using the Advanced Search web page

Knowing a few of the punctuation marks and operators that I described can be helpful and will help you search the web faster, but there's actually an easier way to use all of these advanced search features without the need to remember any of them, and that's the advanced search web page on Google.

This web page includes several search boxes where you can enter your search. Each box explains how it will find web pages or narrow your results and automatically starts the search just as though you had entered the punctuation or operator to conduct that specific type of search.

In addition to the explaining what happens when you use a specific box on the advanced search page, you'll find an explanation of the punctuation and operators you can use on the main Google search page to help you learn how to use the advanced search features you use most often. As you become familiar with them through repetition, you can use the correct punctuation or operator and save time, or if you don't care to remember them, always use the advanced search web page.

Websites

https://support.google.com/websearch/answer/2466433?
p=adv_operators&hl=en&rd=1

http://www.google.com/advanced_search

To my way of thinking

Since we all access the web and receive more of our news and information from websites, learning how to search the web to find information is a helpful and possibly an essential skill for using the Internet. While we can let Google and other search sites interpret our broad general requests, there are times when we want something very specific and knowing how to use Google's powerful search software to help find something specific will make the technology work for you.

Algorithm

An algorithm is, in the most basic sense, a procedure for performing a certain task. Computers use algorithms as step-by-step sets of instructions for achieving a goal. However, algorithms are not only used by computers.

How people use algorithms

People use algorithms all the time. Counting the change in your purse or pocket is an algorithm, since you're using a procedure, it's addition. When I was in Sweden visiting my son recently, I had to convert Swedish Kroner to U.S. Dollars, so I was using an algorithm to do the conversion. While the steps for performing a simple math problem may not seem like a procedure, it is. But there are many complex procedures that people do every day, we just know them so well that we don't have to think of all the steps.

Following a recipe for making a meal is a procedure, and it involves more than just math for the steps. To follow a recipe, you might have to do procedures like "pour" water or "chop" an onion. Pouring and chopping are procedures that we recognize and have learned how to perform. If these tasks are described in enough detail, they can be broken down into steps which can be described in mathematics. And here's where computers come in.

Computers and Algorithms

Computers have two distinct advantages over human beings that make them great for performing algorithmic tasks: they have fast processors that allow them to do mathematical computations very quickly, and they have lots of memory available for storing information. Because of their calculating speed, computers can accomplish difficult, tedious tasks in fractions of a second, ones that would take a person hours.

Computers are pretty good at taking tasks that are repetitive and routine. Sorting lists of data like numbers or letters is such a task. The algorithms is the procedure that provides instructions to the computer so it knows how to sort a list. Since computers understand the language of software, the algorithm is written in software.

There's more than one way

There's almost more than one way to do anything, and if that's the case, then there is more than one algorithm for any task. Here's an example of how a better algorithm can make sorting numbers in a list faster.

The natural way for a sorting algorithm to work would be to go through the list, find the largest or smallest number, write that down, find the next smallest or largest, and to keep going until the list is sorted. It is pretty clear that a long list would take ages to sort.

A better method, for people and computers alike, is called Quicksort. It's like dividing a big project for one person and dividing it into two smaller projects so two people can work on it at the same time. In this algorithm, the computer chooses a random number called the "pivot" out of the list and creates two sub-lists: one that has all the numbers larger than the pivot, and the other with all the smaller numbers. Then, it does the same thing to each sub-list, repeating this until each sub-list only has one member in it. At this point, everything will be sorted because each member of the list has been checked and organized as smaller or larger than a pivot at some point.

Sorting is just one of a wide variety of tedious tasks that computers can solve quickly but people cannot.

Knowing how to work with algorithms will let you apply them to your life and to your computer work. Algorithms can save immeasurable amounts of time, so knowing how to apply them is a very worthwhile skill.

Amazon Cloud

Amazon was one of the earliest players in cloud computing, having started with a cloud storage system in 2006. For a number of reasons, Amazon has never had the lead in cloud based storage services, as you might think early participation would have earned the company. Amazon just added the ability to synchronize files across various devices and computing platforms. This now allows them to compete with Apple, Google, and Microsoft online data cloud storage solutions.

Amazon Cloud has a Drive Sync app working for Windows or Mac OS X. As with other cloud services, the Amazon app puts a virtual folder on your PC desktop. Files placed in that folder are automatically synced to the Amazon Cloud Drive. This makes them accessible from any device that has access via the Internet to the Amazon Cloud.

By default the Amazon virtual cloud drive folder that appears on the Windows or Mac OS X desktop includes sub-folders from all types of files and documents, except a music file or selection. Also, some files, for example a video, are filed under documents. That means the video type of file is not stored in the same type of folder from one device to another. Quite a few users have complained about this inconsistency. These inconsistencies are not even consistent from one type of file to the next, and this problem has caused problems for many first time users. There is a different scheme for uploading and storage placement for music.

Overall, the Amazon Cloud is about the same as other cloud storage and synchronization services. Amazon provides 5 gigabytes of storage, just as most of the other cloud data storage services do provide. At this time it can be said that for Kindle users, who use the Kindle Fire or make a lot of content purchases from Amazon, the Amazon Cloud data storage service could be the service of choice.

Android

If you are at all familiar with smartphones, you no doubt have heard the term "Android" plenty of times. However, if you are not all that tech savvy, you may wonder exactly what it refers to.

Android is an operating system designed for use on mobile devices like smartphones and tablets. It was developed by a company called Android, which was purchased by Google in July of 2005. With more people using mobile devices for accessing the Internet, Google certainly made a pretty smart decision.

Android Plays Nice With Others

An important aspect of Android is that Google allows and encourages other companies to use Android in their products. This process is called licensing, and when you purchase a smartphone or tablet with Android, the manufacturer has obtained a license from Google to install it on their device. This means that the operating system can be found on phones and tablets made by Samsung, LG, HTC, Sony and other manufacturers.

Google's licensing of Android also allows manufacturers to customize the look of their smartphone or tablet with a unique design. As a result, while all Android devices use the Android operating system, each one can be a little different based on the customization the manufacturer did for their device.

Like any software product, Android is updated regularly. Google uses both numbers and names for their versions of Android, using a dessert or candy for each major version. The current version is the 4.2 Jelly Bean operating system, and 5.0 Key Lime Pie is expected to be released later this year.

Google also runs a few Web sites and services that just happen to work well with Android devices. Services you like gmail and Google Calendar are easy to setup and use with an Android device. And Google has it's own cloud storage and apps for documents, spreadsheets, and presentations. So for anyone already using Google services, Android is a very nice fit.

Not all Android devices use the same version of Android since the choice of which version to use is up to the manufacturer. As a result, the smartphones and tablets using the most recent version of Android, have all the newest features. But the devices using older versions of Android are limited to the features available in the Android version used on the device.

Keep this in mind if you're considering an Android device. Be sure to check to see what version of Android uses, and if it can be updated, because some devices don't support updates. Often the free or less expensive devices cost less because they use older versions of Android.

Apps for Android

The ability of manufacturers to customize and choose which version of Android they use on a device has made Android the world's most popular mobile operating system for smartphones.

As a result, Android apps are readily available and there are now almost as many apps available for Android as there are for Apple's iOS operating system.

Google runs an app marketplace called Google Play, where Android owners can browse and purchase apps, but Google also allows others to sell apps for Android devices. Amazon, which uses a version of Android in their Kindle Fire product, has an app marketplace, and several cellular providers run their own app marketplaces.

Is Android Right for You?

With Android being a very capable mobile operating system you now have more competition and choice, which is good for the consumer. Some of your choices to change from one mobile operating system to another will have more to do with the content and apps rather than the device itself. If you have a lot invested in music, apps, or other content you've purchased for an iPhone, you'll have to replace all of that investment, with the possible exception of music. If you like using iTunes on your computer, or have been an iPod user, then an Apple device is probably the way to go since you're already familiar with Apple products.

If you are going to use a mobile device for email, messaging, social networks, taking pictures, or browsing the Web, and don't need the hand-holding support available from Apple, then Android is a good solution, as many have discovered.

For tablets, however, Android still lags behind Apple in the number of apps specifically built for the iPad, and the content available for movies, TV, and other media on Apple is second to none, which is why iPads still are the leading tablet sold worldwide.

API

Computer programming can be a complex and time-consuming task. Fortunately, in many cases, successful programs may be used to help speed up the process of creating new ones. An application programming interface, or API, describes the parts of a program which are accessible for use by others in this way.

Most programs consist not simply of a stream of successive instructions but also of relatively small collections of these which encapsulate a particular behavior or calculation and are meant to be reused many times. Called "functions," "procedures" or "methods" depending on the programming language which is used, these relatively self-contained pieces of behavior help programmers create more modular, robust programs.

Even a relatively simple computer program, in fact, might contain hundreds of these pieces. When programmers decide to make programs useful not just to end users, but also to other programmers in their own work, they must decide which of these makes the most sense to expose.

Not all of the pieces that a good program contains will be candidates for such reuse; some might, for example, depend too closely on assumptions made within the particular computer program they are part of. Furthermore, simply making all of the functions a program contains available for outside use will complicate the job of those who would use a few of them, as they will need to figure out which are most valuable for a particular purpose.

In designing an application programming interface, then, programmers serve as curators of sorts, selecting and making available those parts of their programs that should be most useful to others. Even a program which consists internally of hundreds or thousands of such pieces might be reduced to a mere handful in this way, with the pieces that are so exposed being those deemed to have the most value to programmers who might want to reuse them.

A piece of software which is designed to compress digital image files, for example, would probably make use of hundreds of functions in order to do its work. Its application programming interface, on the other hand, might consist of a few well-documented functions with helpful names like "compressImageFile" and "decompressImageFile." In other cases, an API might instead allow programmers to reuse such software or services over the Web, with function names being replaced by variations on the URLs that most are familiar with from Web browsers.

App Store

An app store is a resource on the Internet that allows software applications, also known as apps, to be downloaded and installed on a computer, smartphone, tablet, or another device. While Apple, Microsoft, Google, and other companies include many applications with their different operating systems, the availability of apps developed by other people and companies, called "app developers," provides the owner of a computer, or device, the ability to add optional apps which make the device more useful.

Within the computer industry, hardware makers know that people buy a computer or device for the application they use it for, not the hardware itself. After all, it's the software application that provides the functionality such as email, Internet browsing, map directions, and others. A wide variety of apps available for any device makes the device more useful for the owner.

Each app store is different

There is no single app store, as each operating system, computer, or device uses the app store provided by the manufacturer of the device. For example, Apple's iPhone, iPad and Apple Watch use the Apple App Store, Apple Mac computers use the Apple Mac App Store, Android devices use the Google Play store, and Microsoft Windows 10 users use the Windows 10 App Store.

How app stores work

An app store includes two pieces. There is a repository of apps on the Internet, which is the storage location of the app software available for download. The second piece is the app store application that runs on the computer, smartphone, tablet, or device. The local app store application automatically connects to the app store library. Once on the app store, the user can see the apps available and download or purchase the app of their choice.

There are now over one million apps available on Apple's App Store and a similar number in the Google Play store for Android. There are apps that help people with their finances, video game apps, picture apps, social media apps, apps that help you maintain your apps, and pretty much anything else under the sun that is imaginable.

Apple was the first; others copied

The Apple App Store was introduced in 2008 shortly after the iPhone was launched. iPhone users could download different application software onto their smartphones using the App Store app built into the iPhone. Before this, when computer users installed applications, the user would purchase a CD or download a file from the Internet. Apple changed this process by requiring all app developers to submit their app to the Apple App Store for review. In addition, the iPhone software only allowed users to install apps from the Apple App Store.

iPhone users and app developers both benefited from this change. Every iPhone owner had access to a wide range of applications, available for download from a safe and secure location managed by Apple. Same goes for the Apple Watch. If any purchase was necessary, the purchase was made using a credit card that Apple kept on file, not a third party. As a result, Apple built trust and security with iPhone users. When the iPad came out, the App Store was just opened up to iPad users.

App developers also benefited from the Apple App Store. For the first time, there was a store included on the iPhone, which the user could use to browse and search for apps. Using a simple, standard and secure connection to Apple made the installation of apps on iPhones a simple and easy process. As a result, app developers rushed to offer apps on the Apple App Store, making the iPhone a more versatile smartphone than any other one in the market. App developers also benefited.

App developers make money from placing their app in the Apple App Store since Apple collects any money for app sales directly from the user, keeps about 30% and pays the app developers the remainder. Since the Apple App Store first opened in 2008, $13 Billion has been paid by Apple to app developers and Apple during July-August 2013 Apple paid $25 Million a day to app developers. As a result, other computer companies are copying the Apple App Store approach.

To my way of thinking

Regardless of what kind of hardware you use, it's the software application that makes it useful. App stores operated by the same company that make your hardware or operating system create a simpler, safer, and more reliable way to install additional applications for your device. As a result, there are more apps available from app developers. Apps make your hardware more useful, and if a piece of hardware isn't useful, it's commonly called junk and ends up collecting dust on the shelf.

So if you haven't explored the library of apps available through your hardware's app store, it's time to visit the store and try a few out.

Apps

An "app" is short for a mobile application. It comes from the word application, which describes software that runs on computers. Since mobile devices are smaller than desktop and laptop computers, the term application become commonly shortened when referring to an application that works on a mobile smartphone or tablet and has stuck.

Why Do We Need Apps?

Your smartphone or tablet or wearable device (if you own one) is just another type of computer. Your hardware needs software in order to be useful; otherwise you've got a pretty high-priced paperweight.

About 90% of all smartphones, tablets, or smart watches sold around the world use either Apple or Android software. Apple's mobile operating system, iOS, is included on every Apple mobile device, and they are all made by Apple. Android is made by Google and is used by many different manufacturers of mobile devices. The operating systems, iOS and Android are the equivalent of Windows or Mac OS on a desktop or laptop.

Apps Included on Your Device

Like your desktop of laptop, you need the operating system to make the hardware work. But to accomplish more with your computer, you add software applications. Just like desktops and laptops, smartphones and tablets include some commonly used apps as standard when you open up your device. What are these?

Some examples of commonly included apps are a browser for surfing the Web, an email app for reading, sending, and receiving emails, a calendar for appointments, and a contacts list. There's also usually a camera app for using the camera and an app for storing and managing your photos. Maybe you use some, all, or none of these apps.

If you have a smartphone, the phone app is what makes your device function as a phone. It almost makes more sense to think of a smartphone as a handheld computer that also has a phone app, rather than just a smartphone. The capability of your device depends not only on the hardware, but on the software, or apps that you use on your device.

If you have an Apple Watch, the apps are located on the main screen of your device and function similar to that of your iPhone. You are able to sync your smartwatch apps and customize your Apple Watch with the watchOS2 update and download apps available to you through the Apple Store. The apps on your Apple Watch are more limited than the apps you use on your other Apple devices.

Add-on Apps

In addition to the standard apps included on your device, there are literally hundreds of thousands of additional apps that can be installed. The categories of add-on apps include banking, weather, games, shopping, productivity, travel, fitness, and more.

Almost everything you can do on a Web site is available in the form of an app. In fact, you often see Web sites displaying information about their mobile app. Good examples are travel Web sites like Travelocity, Kayak, Hotels.com, and Priceline. All of these services have Web sites, and all of them also have a mobile app. The mobile app gives you the functionality of the Website from your mobile device.

By using a mobile app, you're no longer tied to being in front of your computer or opening up your laptop in order to accomplish a computing task. Using the app on your mobile device is often as good as, and sometimes better than using a computer.

Let's take one more example. I often ask people in my classes when the last time was that they bought a paper map. Most people laugh when I ask this because they use their computers for directions and printing maps. And people with mobile devices hardly ever use the Web sites for maps or directions any longer. Since smartphones are almost always connected to the cell tower signals that they use, it's possible to open up a map app on your smartphone. Many people use their smartphone app instead of their car navigation system since the smartphone app is updated and can usually display traffic conditions.

Where Do You Find Add-on Apps?

Where you can find apps and how to get them on your phone or tablet depends on what mobile device you use. Since over 90% of all mobile devices are Apple or Android, these two types of devices have the largest selection of mobile Apps.

Apple Users

Users with iOS devices (those made by Apple) can find apps from the App Store located on their device. If you haven't used the App Store you'll have to register with your email address and a password to create an Apple ID.

The App Store is also available within the iTunes desktop application (free from Apple). Be sure to as you use the same Apple ID on both your desktop and your iOS device since you can update and manage your Apps from iTunes on your computer or from your mobile device. If you download an app directly from your mobile device, the app will immediately show up on the device. If you download an app through your computer, you will have to sync your phone to your computer for the application to be transferred.

Android Users

Individuals who use Android phones can find Apps in the Google Play Market (play.google.com) or through the Amazon Appstore for Android (http://www.amazon.com/mobile-apps). Both app markets have an App for your Android device in addition to a Web site where you can download and purchase Apps.

Both the Google Play store and the Amazon Appstore for Android have a link where you can register your mobile device and any App you choose in the stores, and the app will automatically be installed on your device when it's connected to the Internet.

Registering your Android device in the stores is also helpful to find Apps that work on your specific Android device (it's not necessary for Apple users since the Apple App Store recognizes your device automatically). Since Android is used by many different manufacturers, not all apps work on all devices. Registering and letting the app markets know what kind of device you have will give them the ability to let you know if the app you're considering will work on your model and make of hardware.

Future of Mobile Apps

As with many other types of technology, apps have rapidly become a large part of our world. When Apple ran the ad campaign "there's an app for that," there were 20,000 apps on the App Store. Now there are over 900,000. Adding Apps can help you make your life easier with the convenience of having these Apps in the palm of your hand or on your tablet.

Artificial Intelligence (AI)

Artificial Intelligence is the ability of a machine to process information and ideas like a human brain. A more scientifically appropriate definition says that artificial intelligence is the ability of a machine to perceive its environment and then act to achieve success.

History of Artificial Intelligence

Alan Turing first coined the term in the middle of the 20th century. Alan Turing was a mathematician whose work on cracking the German Enigma code was the basis of the movie "The Imitation Game." The movie is highly rated by critics and audiences alike (I also recommend it) and has won several awards. Many people aren't familiar with the pioneering work Alan Turing did on computers and the influence he had on the new science of information technology. Turing is a significant contributor to the development of computer science as we know it today, and his work is in use today in AI.

In 1950, Alan Turing wrote a paper "Computing Machinery and Intelligence" which opens with the question "Can Machines Think?" The paper goes to speculate on the idea that a machine can imitate the human brain, which he called the "imitation game" (which is why the movie has the title.) The test Turing developed to see if a machine is capable of imitating the human brain became known as the Turing Test, and has become the basis of many other tests of artificial intelligence.

Popular Fiction

Artificial Intelligence is featured prominently in science fiction. Isaac Asimov popularized AI as a concept in the fiction of with his Robot Series in which robots with AI can help humans lead a better life. Other popular culture examples also commonly use AI. The HAL computer aboard the 2001 Space Odyssey ship possessed artificial intelligence. The android known as Data on Star Trek The next Generation had an extremely advanced degree of AI. And, of course, the machines of the Terminator movie franchise or either Battlestar Galactica series exhibited some of the most advanced fictional AI of all. Popular fiction and movies have caused many people to wonder if humanity will be replaced by AI machines.

The Reality of AI

Of course, that's all speculative fiction, and when it comes down to the reality, AI has proven to be tremendously difficult to realize by even the best scientists in the field. Creating technology that can learn and adapt to its environment is very complex and computing intensive. In addition, any machine that needs to "sense" the environment needs technology that can do what the human senses of touch, sight and hearing can do, and with the sensitivity we take for granted all too often.

It's important to note that artificial intelligence is not an all or nothing concept. A machine can possess it to varying degrees, from the chess-playing computer Deep Blue that first beat a world chess champion, to the far from realized fictional examples above.

So what's keeping us from realizing the remarkable feat of true artificial intelligence, despite all our other advances in technology? The main issue is that machines just don't have common sense. Human beings can deduce a lot of facts based on known data.

One example of AI suggests that the average human, when made aware that the President is in Washington, will deduce that the president's legs are also in Washington. The problem with machines is that they can only determine this fact if they have been programmed to know that when the President is in Washington, his legs are also in Washington. The lack of common sense in a machine precludes it from being truly intelligent, so far.

For AI to be truly realized, a machine must be able to learn independently of its human programmers. In other words, it has to be able to adapt and learn, and possibly even create it's own programming, much like humans do every day. Unfortunately, the field of AI has proven to be far more complex than early speculation would have led us to believe. The machines that have been made in the field of artificial intelligence today have problems with simple tasks like navigating a room. So robots that can respond to many tasks around a house aren't here yet.

To my way of thinking

While AI may seem like a remote possibility, the pursuit of machine intelligence often results in the invention of simpler, but very useful tools and ideas. The idea of a self-driving car seemed like science fiction just a few years ago. Vehicles today, however, are commonly equipped with collision avoidance systems and other technology to aid the driver as we develop laws and regulations for computer driven automobiles. Often, these types of technologies come about as the result of research into AI.

So while a machine can't do everything a human can do, machines have always been used to do some of the things that people can do. From the earliest lever that was used to lift a weight heavier than a human could lift, people are always seeking ways machines can make our lives better, and sometimes we just can't anticipate the changes caused when a machine takes on a new task.

Augmented Reality

Augmented Reality is the enhancement of perception through the use of technology. What we see, hear, touch, or smell with our senses is "reality." Adding additional information enhances what our own senses can perceive, and "augments" our real world perception.

How technology enhances our senses

We use technology to augment our reality almost every day. For instance, we can enhance our perception of the world by simply lighting candles at a dinner party. While looking at our world through a flickering flame, we see our world differently, we might feel something new as our experience has changed: by adding a candle to our experience, the candle augments the natural light. A candle is pretty basic technology, but you probably get the idea about how any technology can change what our senses perceive, so what happens when we apply computing technology, which is what most people mean when they refer to the term augmented reality.

Computer-based augmented reality

One example of augmented reality is already in modern automobiles. Some new cars come equipped with rear-view safety monitors mounted on their dashboards. While backing-up, cameras directed at the driver's rear-view provide a more effective view of the world than the simple use of mirrors can accomplish. But there is more to this system than merely a rear-view display: sophisticated sensors supplement a driver's perceptions as the dashboard display offers sounds (flurries of beeps) and flashing graphics if the vehicle gets too close to a solid object. The additions of audio and graphical warnings to the dashboard display enhance a driver's perception of the world: that's Augmented Reality.

Smartphone augmented reality apps

With sophisticated cameras, Internet access, location sensors, and high-resolution displays, it was only a matter of time until someone started creating augmented reality apps for smartphones. A common use of augmented reality in smartphones is for travel and location information. By accessing the Internet, smartphone apps can retrieve information about almost any location and overlay it on your screen; all you need to do is point your smartphone camera at a building, store, or street location, and additional information from the Internet appears on your display.

Wikitude is widely considered the leading augmented reality app available today and is available for both Apple iOS and Android smartphones. While at a location, point the app at a building, and it will display additional information about the building overlaid on top of the image.

Authentication

Authentication is how someone (often a website) verifies you are who you say you are, also known as your "identity." The basic idea goes back thousands of years – any time a sentry said, "Halt! Who goes there?" he was taking the first step of authentication. Websites use authentication when you "login" using your username and password, which is how a website essentially asks the same question "halt, who goes there?" Enter the correct information and you are "authenticated" and can access the website.

What Identifies You

Authentication requires some way to prove you are you. In general, there are three pieces of information that are commonly used to verify someone's identity, 1. what you know, 2. what you have, and 3. what you are.

So what exactly are these things, and how can they be used to prove you are you? They are:

1. What you know: This is the most common type of authentication. It is something you know. A password, a specific date, the pin you create for your ATM, or anything else you know works for 'what you know.' The primary advantage of 'what you know' is that it is hard to steal. The primary disadvantage is, you can forget it.

2. What you have: Exactly what it says, this is things like car keys, key cards, ID badges – anything you can carry with you could be used to authenticate you. The obvious disadvantage of using something you have is that it can be lost or stolen. The advantage is that, unlike 'what you know' as long as it's with you, it will work.

3. What you are: Fingerprints, retina patterns, genetic makeup – anything about you that does not change, and under normal circumstances, cannot change. The big advantage with 'what you are' is that you cannot lose it or forget it. It is also difficult to steal. The potential disadvantage stealing this type of identification requires removing from you. For genetics, that can mean some hair. For a fingerprint or retina print, it could mean removing the part that identifies you. You might have seen this type of identify theft used in movies.

Some authentication methods use one of these things (like a retinal scan or a fingerprint) to prove a person is who she says she is, some use two (like an ATM card and a passcode).

How authentication is used

Today most people have had experience using authentication requiring one thing and authentication requiring two things. If you use a house key, you have used authentication requiring one thing. Most websites that require a login use one thing to authenticate. The username says who you are, and the password is used to verify you are who you say you are. Most people are familiar with debit cards. Most of the time using a debit card requires two things to authenticate – something you have, the card, and something you know, the pin code. Swiping the card says, "I own this account". Entering the pin code says, "yes, I own this account."

To my way of thinking

Authentication is not something that people think about often, but it is something many of us use every day. From logging onto social media to using debit cards, authentication is a normal, but important, part of our lives. A credit card with a magnetic swipe isn't a very good way of authenticating someone's identity, and online purchases don't even require a physical signature. A signature on a receipt isn't a form of authentication at the time of purchase, and is mainly used for backup documentation

This one-step authentication (possession of the card) has made credit card theft from hacking a profitable venture for criminals. But adding a second way to authenticate someone when they make a purchase and credit cards become more secure.

However, add another way to verify someone's identity besides the magnetic card, such as a pin code, and it becomes much harder for someone to impersonate you. This two-step authentication (because it requires two forms of identification) is why we use pin codes with ATM cards, and why the US is moving to a system that will require pin codes on credit card purchases, similar to the system used in Europe. Most bank cards have moved on to using chips inserted in the credit cards as well.

Make it difficult for someone to impersonate you, and you have more security for websites and online accounts. That's why you see so many websites asking for complicated passwords that require numbers, both uppercase and lowercase characters, and special characters. The harder it is for someone else to guess your password, the harder it is to impersonate you.

Using fingerprints is becoming easier, and Apple has used the fingerprint sensor to authenticate the iPhone user, and recently launched Apple Pay, where your fingerprint and iPhone can be used to make a purchase at a retail location with the new iPhone 6.

Authentication can make everyday activities easier too. When I took a vacation out of the country recently, I pre-enrolled in the U.S. Customs and Border Protection program Global Entry. After a live interview at a customs office, a fingerprint scan and a small fee, I was approved. Now, when re-entering the U.S., I can use a customs kiosk which scans my passport, fingerprints and takes a photo. When authenticated this way, I received a ticket from the kiosk and used the Global Entry express lines to present my ticket to go through customs and bypassed the lines.

Auto Responder

An auto-responder is a computer program that automatically sends a pre-written message in response to a person's inquiry. It's usually used with email lists in order to send a confirmation message or scheduled email after a person signs up for a subscription or makes a purchase on any website.

The auto-responder is the software program that instructs the email program to respond with a pre-written message once individuals submit certain personal information. Auto-responders can be setup to send not only one auto-response message, but several responses at pre-determined scheduled intervals.

How to recognize an auto-responder

Forms on web pages often exist where an email address and name are entered, for example, when making a purchase, so the purchase confirmation email is sent. The form for entering an email address is visible on a web page as a stand alone square or rectangular box design. By entering the email address and name, you provide the information that triggers the auto-response message on another computer. Once the "submit" or "click here" button is pressed or selected, your name and email address are used by the program to send an email. Usually within moments, a pre-written message from an auto-responder arrives in your email Inbox.

Why Use An Auto-Responder

Auto-responders help website owners or web designers gather information from a web visitor that can be used later in a mailing list. The information normally gathered is the name of the person and their email address. Auto-responders may include a request for additional information, such as a zip code, or check boxes to indicate specific interests. Many times a space exists for typing in questions or comments the person may need to make. The use of an auto-responder eliminates the need to have a person respond manually to inquiries on a 24/7 hourly basis.

Anyone who receives an auto-responder message receives confirmation that they correctly entered their name and email address and often the email received includes additional information. Since the auto-response message is simply an automated email, it can be pre-written to include any text, or graphics desired.

How Are They Used and Who Uses Them

Seen on almost every website on the Internet, web owners, web designers and especially Internet marketers, set up auto-responders as part of their website coding for various functions. Here are some examples.

The automated response can provide notification or confirmation email to a customer that their purchase order was received at an online store. Auto-responders are also used to provide customers with welcome messages on enrollment in some newsletter subscription, membership program or organization. Other examples of their many practical functions are that they provide instant support, information and referral information on an around the clock basis--without any human intervention.

To my way of thinking

The best part of using auto-responders is that they are fully customizable to the particular need of their users, the people and businesses who need to reply to many emails and request. And people receive responses with helpful and valuable (usually!) information faster than waiting for a person to respond.

After all, if computers aren't making our lives a little better, they just aren't being useful tools.

Autosave

Autosave is a software function in any program or application that saves an in-progress file automatically in order to prevent accidental data loss. One place you may have seen auto-save is in Microsoft Office applications, such as Microsoft Word, but the function is also used on other computers, applications and in web applications such as Google Docs among others.

Why autosave is helpful

Autosave is a convenient feature since accidents happen with technology. Losing power, a computer failure, a loss of your Internet connection or spilled coffee on a keyboard (an example from my real life) can all cause your technology to stop working. When the technology stops working, it's possible that any one application program you've been working with may not save your current activity, such as when you're working on a document.

Imagine that you are working on a lengthy, multi-page document and the electricity in your house suddenly cuts out. Your computer loses power in the middle of your work. If you haven't saved the file – you haven't created a permanent copy of your work on your computer since you began working on it – your work is lost completely.

How Autosave works

In order to prevent this, autosave creates a copy of your work periodically while you are working on it. If your work was autosaved, when you power your computer on again, you can load the application that you were using, and the application will ask you if you want to restore the lost information. Because the autosave feature has made a copy automatically while you were working, it will be able to restore your work from the most recent autosave file.

Autosave isn't perfect in saving work-in-progress. Some programs autosave once every several minutes or even every five minutes. If your computer's power is interrupted between one autosave and the next, you will lose all of the work made after the last autosave. It is possible in some programs to change how frequently you want autosave to take place, and other programs do not have any Auto Save function at all. Review the documentation for the software you are using to clarify these details.

Autosave and Versions

Autosave is not the only solution to saving your progress. Apple Mac computers using their OS X operating system have a built-in software application called "Time Machine," which creates many copies of the same file at different points in the file's progress. This allows the user to reopen copies of the file they were working on at many different points in the file's history.

For example, imagine that you are writing a lengthy business letter and you have made many revisions since you began. Time Machine would have created copies of the letter at different times since you began revising, so you can conveniently reload older revisions of the letter if necessary.

Saving multiple copies of a file allows you to manage different versions of the same file, so you can go back to a previous version to review what it was like and compare the changes made in each version. This type of version management feature is often used in teamwork applications so different people can work on the same document or file and track the document or file as new changes are made. Each time the file or document is opened and edited, the previous version is automatically saved as a "version" for review if necessary.

Some useful tips on Autosave

While Autosave is a useful feature and will let you recover work from a certain point in time, it is much safer instead to manually save files at your own pace. Because autosave typically creates files separately from your original file, you can save files manually and take advantage of autosave simultaneously and have the best of both methods.

Autosave doesn't replace the need for a backup to your data, since your autosave files are usually in the same location as your original files for any application. You should use a backup disk and application for any files on your local computer hard drive, backup your smartphone, and even consider using a cloud file storage service since the cloud service (Microsoft, Apple, Google, Dropbox, etc.) makes backups of all of your files.

B

B2B

What is B2B?

Often coined a marketing term, B2B or business-to-business, is a way for a company to market their product or services to another company. It involves the direct sell from one business to another. B2B (business-to-business) has one of the largest markets and is made up of products and services that aren't usually used by consumers, but mainly for other businesses to purchase.

How it works

B2B marketing is similar to that of consumer marketing (B2C) because they use the same strategies. The only real difference is that consumers buy products and services based on their special interest, whereas, B2B buyers make decisions based on profit margins.

Strategies

The reason for B2B marketing is to help the companies efforts in bringing in more revenue. Strategies to achieve this would include a high concentration in the sales department, a well as advertising, public relations, direct mail, trade shows, and other tactics to market a particular product or service from one business to another business.

To my way of thinking

For an organization or for individuals that have a business looking to sell products of services to another business, B2B can help you to understand better the markets differences from business to consumer (B2C). However, for the average person, looking to purchase or sell a product or service to an everyday user, B2B might not be as adequate a tool to use, so I don't recommend B2B marketing in that case. B2B or business to business is a market where sales would flourish best with a good marketing strategy to help sell among large companies.

Bandwidth - see Mbps

Battery Life

Battery Life means the amount of time your mobile device's battery will last on a single charge. The term "battery life" comes from the importance that people put on mobile devices such as smartphones, tablets, and laptops. Since all portable devices use internal batteries, it's important when using them to know how long a single charge will last and when it's necessary to find a power outlet to recharge the battery.

How much battery life a device has on a full charge depends on a variety of factors including how the device is used and the size of the battery. Let's take a look at how a mobile device is frequent used to see what can affect battery life. If your smartphone or tablet is connected to a Wi-Fi connection and you are sending or receiving data, the battery is being used to power the processor and the communications. When your smartphone or tablet screen is on, the backlighting that illuminates the screen uses the battery.

For laptops, an internal hard disk drive requires battery power to operate the drive. Smartphones and tablets don't use hard drives, and some laptops, like the Macbook Air and Microsoft Surface don't use hard drives, so they have much longer battery life than laptops with a hard drive. All of these demands for power affect battery life for any mobile device.

As a result, battery life is typically measured in terms of the device's usage. Smartphone specifications provide information on the battery life for talk-time, Internet use, video playback, audio playback, and standby time. Since people tend to use a smartphone for many uses, it's difficult to make an accurate prediction of how long a single charge will last for a specific user's needs.

One of the hardware improvements that manufacturers focus on is the battery life of their devices, particularly smartphones since they are the most mobile of devices. Each manufacturer uses a balance of cost, size and weight to provide a battery life that most users would find acceptable. In addition to the physical aspects of the battery, device makers can also improve battery life by using an efficient operating system that maximizes the battery life and the demands the applications place on the battery.

The battery life of a tech gadget can deteriorate over time because each battery is meant to endure only a certain number of charges as charging degrades a battery over time. However, you may never see this happen because mobile batteries often have a long life-span of operation.

How a battery's capacity is measured

A battery's capacity to supply current over a period of time is measured in milliamp hours (mAh). The current a battery produces is usually directly related to its physical size so that a large battery will have a higher mAh capacity than a smaller one. The capacity of larger batteries may be stated in Amp/hours instead of milliamp hours for especially large ones. Comparing the mAh capacity of similar size batteries can be useful when weighing factors like expected life or cost.

An ampere, or amp for short, is a measure of current, while milliamps are thousandths of an amp. An automotive battery can supply hundreds of amps for a short period, for instance, but a flash light battery may be capable of only one or two amps. Measuring battery output with milliamp hours allows for comparisons in specific applications.

As an example, consider a circuit that needs ten milliamps to operate. If a 500 mAh battery is connected to it, the battery should last 50 hours. If a 1000 mAh battery were connected, it would last 100 hours. Simply divide the mAh capacity by the current needed to determine the time.

Milliamp hour capacity varies considerably by battery type. Also, batteries lose capacity as they age. While it may seem that a 1000 mAh battery could deliver an amp for an hour in an application, such a high output will generate internal heat that will reduce the current output prematurely. A better choice for the application may be a battery with a larger mAh capacity in order to limit heat effects. Heat is always the enemy of battery output and service life.

Tips to Maximize battery life

Virtually all of the manufacturers of mobile devices use Lithium Ion batteries in their devices, so battery life tips apply to almost any mobile device. An Internet search for how to improve battery life for your specific model of the device will typically yield a good selection from well know technical publications.

Here's the general advice from Apple on their page on maximizing battery life performance:

- Update to the latest operating system for your device. Updating is important regardless of what brand of device you use since many performance improvements are included with the operating system software for your device.

- Avoid extreme temperatures. Exposure to very high temperatures can damage the battery and permanently affect the battery life of the charge. Typically, batteries on smartphones are designed to operate above freezing and below 95 degrees Fahrenheit. The interior of a car on a warm sunny day can easily reach 95 degrees, so avoid leaving your smartphone another mobile device in a locked car. Exposure to cold temperatures doesn't create any permanent damage but does affect the battery life temporarily when the battery is below it's recommended operating temperature. Laptop batteries often have a higher minimum operating temperature than smartphones or laptops.

- Your case could be damaging your battery. Certain cases don't allow your device to stay cool while charging (which is when it's likely to get hotter) and could cause the mobile device to operate at too high a temperature. If you notice that your mobile device gets hot when you charge it, just remove it from the case for charging.

- If you don't use your mobile device often, keep the battery at about 50% charged. If a mobile device is stored for more than six months without a charge, it can cause the battery to go into a deep sleep and incapable of holding any charge.

In normal daily use, it's OK to charge your battery anytime since the charging adapters and circuits will prevent it from overcharging.

Two easy things you can do in addition to updating to the latest operating system for an iPhone (or almost any smartphone) are these tips:

- Dim your screen as much as comfortable since a brighter screen setting uses more power. Access the dimmer slider on iPhones with a swipe up to open the Control Center, change it in settings on other mobile devices.

- For smartphones, leave WiFi on all the time. Your device uses less power to access the Internet communicating over WiFi when compared to using it's cellular signal. With WiFi on, your device will use a WiFi network when one is available and automatically send and receive data over WiFi instead of cellular data.

Websites:

Here's Apple's link on maximizing battery life for iPhones and iPads.

https://www.apple.com/batteries/maximizing-performance/

Here's Samsung's webpage with information on extending battery life.

http://techlife.samsung.com/tips-extending-life-smartphone-battery-1303.html

One more solution

Another solution to extending battery life is to purchase an external battery that can be used to charge your device. Small, portable battery packs and cases are available that function as a portable charger for your device. You charge your spare battery the same way you charge your mobile device, then when you need a charge, plug your charging cable from your device into a portable battery pack.

Binary Code

Chances are, even if you are not a technically savvy individual, you have heard the term "binary code" used in reference to technology. But what is binary code, and what does it do? Simply put, binary code is a type of code that translates into information or instructions for computers.

Binary code consists of two values, either 0 or 1. From this simplistic type of coding, different text characters, numbers, or processing instructions can be derived and translated by computers. The manner in which this is done is mathematically fairly simple. For any place in a binary number, there are are two possibilities, 0 or 1, for holding that place. This means that a 1 digit binary number can represent either of two possible value, a 2 digit binary number can represent any of 4, and so on and so forth. Any series of binary code can, because of this, represent a wide range of possibilities, and which possibility is determined by the exact order of the 0s and 1s in that series. Computers understand different binary values to represent different numbers or text characters. By translating these values, computers can turn these binary representations into more understandable language.

Binary code is based on the binary number system, which employs the same principles to represent numbers as a series of 0s and 1s. Its modern usage is mostly in the realm of computer programming, although other technologies do employ it. In addition to binary numbers, a binary alphabet, based on different values of binary numbers, has been developed as a universal guideline for how computers translate binary code into text. This is the manner in which both numbers and text characters can be derived from the same coding system. It is this flexibility which makes binary code so useful in computer science and programming.

While binary code is a fairly advanced technological concept, it can be very useful to learn, particularly for someone who is thinking about learning programming skills. Understanding binary code gives a great insight into how computers really do the things that they do, and can be both interesting and helpful.

Binge Watching

Binge watching is the practice of viewing multiple episodes of a television series or a series of movies consecutively, either in one sitting or a short period.

How streaming services made binge watching popular

Viewers often binge using online streaming services such as Netflix, Hulu Plus or Amazon that allow users to watch multiple seasons of a television show or multiple movies in a series at any time. With a service like Netflix, binge watching is not only easy to do, but often encouraged.

When one episode finishes, Netflix automatically begins to play the next episode without any input from the viewer. The automatic start of the next episode often leads to watching many episodes in one sitting, known as binge watching.

Binge watching is not limited to television shows. The content being watched can also refer to any similar video series, such as a movie series with sequels, such as the Harry Potter series or Lord of the Rings, or a series of YouTube videos. The term Binge watching just applies to anything you'd watch. But while streaming services have made binge watching easy, they aren't the only way to binge watch.

The evolution of binge watching

Before such streaming services, binge watching was not quite so accessible. Binge watching a television show meant buying an entire season's worth of episodes in a boxed set to watch them all in a row within a short period. For example, the cost of the first season of Friends, the hit sitcom, is around ten dollars; the entire series costs upwards of one hundred dollars.

Another alternative to buying box sets was to record the show as episodes played at the scheduled time on television, using a VCR, which today seems an out-od-date technology. Traditionally, television shows follow a release schedule of one episode per week, so several episodes or a whole season can be recorded using a VCR, and then binge watched all at once. New recording devices and video-on-demand services make the task of binge watching easier than ever.

Devices like digital video recorders from cable or satellite television providers are capable of recording shows, and movies and television shows are available to download and watch anytime with services such as iTunes, Google Play, and Amazon Video. A download of the video lets you carry it with you on a portable device so you can watch anytime, even without an Internet connection.

Why do people like to binge watch?

Binge watching satisfies the desire that often accompanies finding an entertaining, new television show: the desire to consume as much of that show as possible. For example, a friend of mine who likes the TV series 24 would never watch the weekly episodes during a regular broadcast season. He said he got too caught up in the show and wanted to see next weeks episode so he could find out what happened. So each year he waited for the season tom come out on DVD, then purchased it and watched the whole season in a few sittings.

Then there are people who find a TV show they like, but haven't watched the series from the beginning. As the series Breaking Bad became more popular, people started watching it well into the series when characters and plot-lines were playing out. After they had discovered the series, binge watching allowed them to watch previous seasons and catch-up, and even watch the entire show from first to last episode, even after its production of new episodes ended.

To my way of thinking

With today's video-on-demand and streaming services, binge watching is easier than ever. It can be a relaxing, fun way to spend an evening enjoying a favorite new show, without the need to be a captive to the original weekly or annual schedule of shows. Technology is at it's best when it gives you new choices for entertainment and the freedom to manage your time.

Bit and a Byte?

The terms bit and byte refer to the value of information used in a computer. Digital computers use data in which each piece of information has a value of one or zero. You can think of these values as the position of a switch.

The number one represents the switch when it is on; the zero represents the switch when it is off. In fact, computers use miniature circuits, which are actually tiny switches. Computers can turn many switches on and off at a single time, which is why it can count faster than your fingers by using light switches.

Computers Know Two Numbers

Computers (and when I say computers I mean any type of computing device) use this system of counting with only two numbers, called binary, because a number can only be a zero or a one. It just doesn't know any other numbers. You're most familiar with using a decimal system, where a single digit can be 0 through 9. The 10 possible ways to write a single piece of information, 0, 1,2,3,4, 5, 6, 7, 8,and 9 represent the 10 digits.

Combine more than one decimal place, and you've got a lot of possible number combinations. To a computer's way of thinking a binary number is a bit, and it calculates using combinations of bits.

Since a computer can change a bit from a zero to one and back again so fast, it's able to perform calculations without even knowing that there's a number larger than 1.

Bits and Bytes

Since one digit is a bit of information, like a zero or one, more than one digit of information creates what's called a byte of information. In our familiar decimal counting system using 0 through 9, when you count to ten you need to add a second digit. Since bits can only be zeros or ones (off and on to a computer), to count beyond 1, another digit is necessary. Then you create a combination of two digits which can be either zeros or ones. For example, 01 or 10. Since we're talking bits, 10 is not 10, but the rules of counting with zero and one, called the binary number system, tell us that 10, in decimal numbers, is the number 2. Add more places and it's possible to create larger numbers to be used in calculations.

This is what a byte does for a computer, it combines more than one place, or bit, to create a combination of zeros and ones that represent a larger number. Combining eight bits together creates a byte consisting of eight bits. Bytes allow computers to calculate faster since the byte is more complex information that just a single bit.

Software is a Translator

Software is the secret sauce that takes bits and bytes and translates them so that more information can be represented by zeros and ones. When software is used, it can translate a document on a computer screen into complex combinations of zeros and ones that the computer can understand and manipulate. Software combines bits and bytes to make something better. Just like you have ingredients in your kitchen like milk, bread, jelly, and peanut butter, when they are combined you make a sandwich. Software combines the zeros and ones together to create documents, display videos, send email, and more, but it's all done in zeros and ones.

It's a Digital World

Counting in binary is easy for a computer because a computer can do basic detections of the numbers 0 and 1 extremely fast. For humans, this is quite tedious. It was necessary to come up with other ways of hand writing information that utilized both letters and numbers to represent the data put into a computer. The fact is that still, today, one BIT of data represents one single piece, or a bit, of information.

Bitcoin

Bitcoins are a form of currency used on the Internet, with no physical format, and that are not backed by any government. Bitcoins can be used by anyone around the world with access to the Internet for any type of transaction. In order to conduct a transaction using bit coins, someone who wants to pay in Bitcoins has to find another person willing to accept Bitcoins as payment. But that's becoming easier as bit coins are becoming an accepted form or currency.

Where is Bitcoin?

Bitcoin uses decentralized software that's managed by a community of users. The software doesn't run on a single computer, but works on many computers at once, communicates between them, and duplicates functions across the network of computers. This feature of the software is called peer-to-peer. The Bitcoin software on one computer is smart enough to know how to connect to other computers running Bitcoin using the Internet. Since no single computer is running Bitcoin, it can cross borders, and no single person or computer can control it. It is because of this network that there is no central authority that controls Bitcoin, or owns the software that makes it work.

People who volunteer to run Bitcoin software on their computers create a network consisting of thousands of computers around the world. By the way, people who let bitcoin use their computers are rewarded by "earning" Bitcoins.

This is very different from how the United States government or any other country controls it's currency. There is no "backing" for a Bitcoin since it's value is determined by what people are willing to trade for it. But when you think about it, that's how most transactions take place, two people agree on what something is worth and then trade, either in goods, services, or currency.

How do you use Bitcoins?

Transactions take place when people transfer Bitcoins between themselves. A software application called the "wallet" is used to hold and transfer Bitcoins for users. Several wallets exist that are available for free at the Bitcoin website, bitcoin.org. Transactions use two types of encryption to prevent fraud or "double spending" of Bitcoins. You can make and receive payments in 10 minutes, which is the time it takes the Bitcoin software to confirm the transaction since more than one computer has to "agree" that the transaction is confirmed. There's no one computer running all of Bitcoin, so it's a pretty resilient software.

There's no transaction fee required, but some Bitcoin services charge a small transaction fee to pay for their computers and will process a transaction faster. The Bitcoin software tracks all Bitcoin transactions, so it's always clear which account owns a specific Bitcoin. Bitcoin is not totally anonymous, like cash since there is a digital record of every transaction.

How are Bitcoins made?

A person who goes by the pseudonym "Satoshi Nakamoto" originally created the technology as a way to trade cash outside the existing financial system. Bitcoins are created in a process called "mining" by the people in the network that host Bitcoin software. A Bitcoin is created when a computer solves a complex mathematical equation, and the equation changes each time it's solved. And it becomes more difficult to solve.

When a computer solves the math problem, a new Bitcoin is created. There's a limit to the number of Bitcoins that can be mining which is 21 million. After that no new Bitcoins can be created. While this might seem like a problem, Bitcoins are designed to be broken up into pieces so you can buy and sell using a fractional Bitcoin.

Value of Bitcoins

While Bitcoins were once worth less than $1 per coin, their value has increased as awareness and use of Bitcoins has increased. You can check the current value at Bitcoin Exchange Rate (http://www.bitcoinexchangerate.org). When I'm writing this article on November 2013, a Bitcoin is worth about $900 U.S. Dollars. Bitcoin value is volatile right now, but more common use will result in what experts predict will be more stable exchange rates.

Investments in Bitcoins

Bitcoins have become an investment. Just like the stock market, increased interest causes the price of each Bitcoin to go up. Similarly, prices have gone up as it has become more difficult for computers to complete the math problems that create Bitcoins. Bitcoin creation has slowed over time, which increases the price. While prices have fluctuated over the last four years, they're currently at an all-time high.

Bitcoins have become accepted by some online sellers, including dating site OkCupid, blog and community WordPress, and Chinese Web services company Baidu. This is due to the fact that fees for processing orders with Bitcoin cost less than traditional credit card processing fees.

The future of Bitcoin

Currency is really just a form of trading. Before currency, people traded in goods and services. Cattle, goats, grain and other goods had a value. Currency made trading easier since the first currency, in the form of coins, were more portable. A coin was essentially neutral form of "value" that could be traded for a goat or wine. Bitcoins are a form of digital currency exist in a computer, and can be moved using the Internet. They can be converted into other forms of currency at public exchange rates, so they are establishing a place as a global form of payment. While using digital currency might seem a strange idea, we use it every day when we swipe a credit card or pay a bill online.

Bloatware

Bloatware refers to the many pieces of add-on software that come pre-installed by device makers on a new computer or phone. For a computing device to work, it needs an operating system, but it doesn't need bloatware.

While typically harmless, bloatware can eventually prove quite annoying, and very well may be the reason behind poor device performance. Let's look at how operating systems and bloatware are different.

Operating Systems and Add-On Software

Common examples of operating systems include Microsoft's Windows, Apple's Mac OS X, Google's Android, and Apple's iOS. If there is an application or software function contained in the operating system, it's considered part of the operating system.

The operating system software provided by these companies often includes a few commonly used applications, such as email or a web browser. Bloatware is software that manufacturers add-on to the operating system, usually to make their hardware different from other manufacturers, or as a way to make additional money when you

So what's all the fuss?

We've all been there. Our new laptop or phone boots up, and we eagerly start exploring its installed software to discover just what it can do. Then we become overwhelmed, wondering why our new gadget can play games, serve up sports schedules and edit Word documents when all we wanted to do was make phone calls.

For instance, perhaps the phone you bought for business purposes comes pre-installed with Angry Birds. You may have no interest in playing games, and indeed might find their presence distracting. These additional applications are referred to as bloatware due to how they bloat otherwise slim, highly functional devices.

Why is bloatware installed?

Bloatware is appealing to device manufacturers for many reasons. If a manufacturer sells you a computer pre-installed with Microsoft Office, for instance, then they have purchased it for you as part of the retail price, and can justify charging more. They can then advertise their systems as being tailored to office professionals. Further, if Office comes pre-installed, consumers who purchase the system aren't likely to investigate competitors since they already have software that meets their needs. Finally, Microsoft will likely enjoy increased sales of add-on products that improve Office's effectiveness for specialized tasks.

Another common reason bloatware is pre-installed is due to incentives offered to the manufacturers by the add-on software companies. A very effective way to advertise a software product is to get it placed on the home or start-up screen of a computer or mobile device. Often the installed add-on software is a free version or trial version, with an option to purchase upgrades or a subscription. Since computer and device makers make very small profits on the hardware, they find the incentives offered by the software companies an attractive way to increase their profits.

What are the drawbacks?

Unfortunately, bloatware isn't always best for those of us who use the computers or phones. Purchasing computers and devices with lots of software already installed can be a source of confusion if that software starts doing things we don't expect. A mysterious anti-virus program might mean well if it blocks certain apps from starting, but if we've not installed the anti-virus program to begin with, we have no way of knowing why things aren't working as expected. Most disturbing, though, is that some Android phones don't let users remove bloatware. While it can be disabled, how to do so is not immediately obvious.

To my way of thinking.

Fortunately, many of bloatware's annoyances can easily be countered by removing or disabling the offending apps. Even so, many computer and phone issues are caused by its presence, and it can be difficult to diagnose strange problems when they can't be traced to specific applications that were installed by choice.

For Android users, it's possible to buy an Android device directly from Google (their Nexus brand) with the current version of Android installed and no bloatware.

Visit this website to learn more:

https://play.google.com/store/devices

The only maker of devices that use the Apple operating systems is Apple, so Apple devices are sold only with the operating system provided by Apple and the applications included in the operating system. It doesn't matter where you buy an Apple device, they are all the same out of the box.

For Microsoft users, any computer purchased at a retail store is almost guaranteed to have bloatware installed on it. It's estimated by computer experts that it can take from 3-4 hours to remove the bloatware that comes installed on a typical Windows consumer PC. Here are several solutions for how to buy a Windows computer without bloatware.

One is to buy a computer through the business website. Dell, HP, Toshiba, and even retail sites like Tiger Direct and Best Buy have business areas of their websites. On these web pages you can specify the exact software you want installed on your computer.

Another option is to find a local computer repair technician and ask them if they can set-up a system for you the way you want it customized.

And a third option is to purchase a computer directly from Microsoft. Microsoft sells models of major manufacturer's PC's called the Microsoft Signature Experience with no bloatware and support directly from Microsoft. These are available at Microsoft retail and online stores.

For more information go to this link:

http://www.microsoftstore.com/store/msusa/html/
pbpage.MicrosoftSignature

Blu-ray

Blu-ray is a type of information medium used to store digital information that can be played or read through a specialized Blu-ray player or a computer. Today, the most common application of Blu-ray disc technology is to store movies and video games.

Blu-ray discs are round, flat plastic discs and measure about 5 inches in diameter. One side of the disc is usually labeled with information about what is contained on the disc. The other side is highly reflective; this is the side that is read by the computer or Blu-ray player.

Blu-ray is an optical disc medium. This means that the information is read using a special laser that scans the disc and read the information on it. Other types of optical discs include CDs and DVDs. Blu-ray players are available that let you watch Blu-ray discs on your TV. Many modern computers can also read and write Blu-ray discs if they have a Blu-ray drive.

Blu-ray disks will not work on a drive unless is specifically capable of supporting Blu-ray. However, Blu-ray drives will play other types of DVD's and CD's.

History of Blu-ray

Blu-ray was introduced by Sony in 2006. As high-definition televisions were becoming more affordable, there was a need for a newer alternative to the DVD disc, which was limited to about 9 Gigabytes of storage space and could not store a full-length high-definition film. Blue-ray discs can store 5 times that amount or more.

Around the same time Sony introduced the Blu-ray, another medium was released as a direct competitor called HD-DVD (High Definition DVD). The competition was close for several months, and you could readily find new movies being released in both formats. In the same way VHS conquered Beta-Max for the home video cassette market in the 1970s, Blu-ray won the battle when HD-DVD manufacturers ended production in 2008.

Blue-ray is now an industry standard. The Blu-ray Association of over 180 companies (http://www.blu-raydisc.com) manages the trademark and technology standards so products are standard across manufacturers.

Why is it called Blu-ray?

The name 'Blu-ray' comes from the color (blue-violet) of the laser that is used to read and write the discs in Blu-ray devices. Traditional optical disc lasers are red. The Blu-ray laser can read more information compared to other types of lasers; this is one of the reasons that a Blu-ray disc can store so much information.

A blue-ray disk can store up to 25 Gigabytes of data on one layer, and some disks and readers can use two layers, which will double the storage to 50 Gigabytes. This works out to about 9 hours of high-definition video, so any feature length movie will fit on a single disk.

The Future of Blu-ray

You may have noticed that many new computers don't include a CD or DVD drive. Increasingly, computer users download files and media from the Internet. With a high-speed Internet connection in your home, you can download a movie in a matter of minutes. And you can buy one from Amazon, Apple, and Google. So the need for physical media like a DVD to store a lot of information, just isn't as great.

In addition to buying a movie, services like Netflix make it easy to watch a video on-demand and send it to your computer or TV over your high-speed home connection.

Because it's possible to obtain large files like movies over the Internet, there is less need for a physical copy, except for sale as a retail item.

Do you need to go to Blu-ray?

If you've got a TV screen smaller than 42 inches, you probably won't notice the difference between a high-definition movie or TV show and the Blu-ray version. And there's another new technology called 4K, which dramatically increases the image quality on a large screen.

For many people, high-definition is good enough, and constantly upgrading a media library to newer formats is costly. So the on-demand approach of Netflix or Amazon is appealing since you don't have to invest in media at all. Something to think about when you look at all those old cassette tapes and VHS movies you might have stashed around.

Bluetooth

Bluetooth is a wireless communication standard that connects electronic devices to each other. If you're wondering what those things are that resemble large hearing aids in so many people's ears, those are Bluetooth receivers. The receiver communicates with a cell phone using Bluetooth.

Bluetooth creates a great way to communicate between an automobile, a computer, or an earpiece, to a cellular phone. It's a high tech, wireless way to exchange digital or voice data over a short distance, which is 10 meters, or about 32 feet.

The Reason Bluetooth Exists

Bluetooth was originally invented for use with cell phones. A wireless communications technology was needed that wouldn't use much of the battery power in a cell phone, could be used in very small devices, like earpieces, and was as low cost as using a cable connection. Lower power, however, translates into low range, and that's why there's a limit of 10 meters, which is about 32 feet.

Bluetooth was invented by Dr. Jaap Haartsen while he worked at Ericsson, the Swedish electronics company. The name Bluetooth is from a 10th century Danish king, Harald Blåtann Gormsson. According to legend, Harald was well known for getting different tribes to communicate with each other. He also had a love of blueberries, which stained his teeth, and was nicknamed King Blåtann, which translates into English as "Bluetooth."

The Bluetooth logo consists of the Nordic runes for his initials, H and B (since my wife is Norwegian this has to be mentioned in the article).

One advantage of Bluetooth is that it's a worldwide industry standard, and it is a low-cost, easy to manufacture technology. As a result, there are an estimated 2 billion Bluetooth devices in use around the world made by over 17,000 companies that are members of the Bluetooth. To use Bluetooth with a device, who belong to the Bluetooth Special Interest Group, which oversees the qualifications and specifications of Bluetooth devices, and protects the Bluetooth trademark. In order to manufacture and sell a piece of Bluetooth equipment, the device must meet the standards set by this group.

Bluetooth devices are always looking for another Bluetooth device that's nearby. They broadcast a signal that searches for any other Bluetooth device nearby, a lot like when kids yell "Marco" when they are playing Marco-Polo with each other. When another device answers "Polo," the two devices are ready to be connected. Connecting Bluetooth devices is done using a technique known as "pairing," which is like introducing one person to another by name.

Once the two Bluetooth devices learn each other's "names," they become paired, and will automatically connect when they are within the range of each other. This is how your Bluetooth headset automatically connects to your cell phone when it's within the range of your cell phone, and how your cell phone will automatically connect up to your car's hands-free connection when you start your car. The requirement for pairing creates a secure connection and keeps Bluetooth devices that are strangers from communicating with any of your devices.

Some Bluetooth Examples

Bluetooth is a great technology for our mobile world, where so many devices rely on battery power. In addition to earpieces, there are Bluetooth keyboards for use with tablets, and Bluetooth speakers for tablets and smartphones. New Bluetooth devices are being introduced frequently, and with some creative uses. There's a Bluetooth scale that uses Bluetooth to send your weight to a smartphone app that keeps track of your weigh-ins, and a grill thermometer that displays the temperature of your steak on your smartphone as it cooks on the grill.

Bookmarks

A bookmark is an Internet browser feature used to mark web pages for quick, easy future reference. It is accessible on all browser types, including, but not limited to, Google Chrome, Internet Explorer, Safari, Firefox. On Internet Explorer, bookmarks are called Favorites.

How bookmarks work in web browsers

Once a person accesses a page, there is a button that they can press on the top of their web browser that allows them to "bookmark" a page. Usually, there is a "bookmark" tab at the top of any web browser that the user can click. Once he or she clicks that button, they will want to look for the "add bookmark" option that comes up under that tab. Once they add the bookmark, the visible page is saved for quick future access. From that point forward, the user can click the "bookmarks" tab on the top of the browser, select the bookmarks that are available in the drop down menu that appears, and choose the web page they would like to view.

While each web browser is slightly different, most browsers use a menu bar that appears along the top that allows the user to save a bookmark in the list that appears on their browser. Often this list appears automatically, but in the settings for most browsers there is usually an option to display the menu bar, which will display these bookmarks.

Bookmarks are sometimes also identified with a "star" button or "bookmark" button, which looks like a bookmark one would put in a physical book, in all other website browsers. Web browsers can even keep track of frequently visited web pages and start an automatic list of bookmarked web pages based on your Internet browsing.

How bookmarks started

Bookmarks, which have also been called "favorites" and "hotlists," have been around since the Mosaic web browser was first introduced in 1993. Ever since then, users have implemented the use of bookmarks in their daily web browsing to allow them to re-access the pages that they frequent with ease and speed.

Social bookmarking

There are social networking websites where users can share a list of bookmarked web pages with other users of the social network. One of the most popular social bookmarking social networks is Pinterest. Pinterest is a social network where users create accounts and "pin" pictures that appear on web pages to their account. The pinned pictures link back to the web pages where the picture appears. The user's account is a collection of photos that are "pinned" (which is the same as being bookmarked) from web pages on the Internet. The pictures are publicly available to view on the user's Pinterest account so anyone can view the pictures and click on the picture to go the specific web page where the picture appears.

While Pinterest is one of the most well know social bookmarking social networks, others have been around for a while such as Reddit, SumbleUpon, and Digg. In fact, when you post a link to a Facebook,

Twitter, or LinkedIn account, you're sharing that web page link in as a social bookmark with your connections. So you may not have even realized you're using social bookmarking already!

To my way of thinking

Browsing the web is one of the most frequent activities people do while using the Internet, it often helps to be able to find and locate specific web pages and websites. Using bookmarks is the web's version of placing a card or note in the book to help you locate a specific place.

Broadband

Broadband describes any physical network connection that can carry multiple types of signals at the same time. When referring to broadband, the technologies include coaxial cable, fiber optic cable or Digital Subscriber Line technologies.

Broadband technologies have the capacity to carry information and data so video, voice and large amounts of data (like computer files) can move across a single cable at the same time. This capacity makes it possible for many users of a single connection to enjoy a television show, play video games and browse the Internet all at the same time.

Do you have broadband at home or work?

Chances are you already have a broadband connection to your home or office from your Internet Service Provider, which is probably a cable or phone company. Cable and phone companies have typically been the companies that install wired connections to homes and workplaces. Cable companies install a coaxial cable that is used for your television connection while telephone companies, which used provide wires called "twisted pair" for telephone lines, now use fiber optic cable.

AT&T calls their fiber optic connection U-Verse while Verizon refers to their fiber connection as FIOS. Compared to twisted pair wiring, fiber optic has a significantly larger capacity for data and information. Coaxial wire, which is what is used to carry television signals, always had the capacity to carry large amounts of information such as a television signal, so cable companies have used technologies that allow the same cable to carry data for your Internet connection.

What kind of signals does broadband carry?

Broadband doesn't describe a specific capacity or type of signal for a connection, just the type of physical connection so homes with the same type of physical broadband connection could have different capabilities. Let's look at a few examples.

One home, home "A," has a fiber optic broadband connection from a phone company and another home, home "B," has a coaxial broadband connection from their cable company. Home A uses their broadband connection for a phone number and Internet access but subscribes to television through a satellite provider. Home B with a cable broadband connection uses the service for television and Internet and uses the local phone company for a home telephone line.

If this sounds familiar, it's because the lines have blurred for where you obtain your services as a result of broadband connections to the home. You can usually obtain your choice of telephone and television service, as well as Internet service from any company that runs a broadband connection to your home.

There is one exception, however, and that's Digital Subscriber Line broadband technology, also known as DSL. DSL was used by the telephone companies to carry a digital signal over a standard telephone wire. Using DSL technology allowed telephone companies to use their existing twister-pair wires to carry both voice and data on the same line. However, DSL capacity is a little too slow for video or television signals, so DSL use has been declining as a type of broadband connection, and many telephone companies are investing in fiber optic cable connections.

When a broadband connection provides you Internet access, the company that's providing your connection uses a pricing arrangement where you'll typically pay for a maximum data capacity. Often the minimum capacity you can purchase is more than sufficient for downloading videos for a single user but as more people start to share the connection and use it for browsing the Internet and accessing large files on Internet services like Netflix or YouTube, the minimum capacity may not be sufficient and you might have to purchase a higher capacity service tier.

Your Internet data and your television signal are carried on the same wire, but your Internet use doesn't affect your ability to watch television since the signal is a video signal and not data. The broadband connection is capable of keeping the Internet data, television video signal and if needed, a voice phone call all separate and independent. That's the power of broadband.

What about cellular compared to broadband?

Broadband typically refers to physical wired connections, with fiber optic and coaxial being the most widely used broadband technologies. Wireless networks provided by cellular companies are always increasing their speed for a wireless phone connection and with a fast enough wireless signal it's possible to watch videos from Netflix or YouTube and download or play music from a variety of music services.

If you have a fast enough wireless connection, you could use that for your home Internet service, but it tends to be priced not by speed but by usage, whereas broadband Internet connections to your home (or business) are priced based on the maximum speed you purchase and don't charge you for how much data you use. That's why people usually have broadband at home since there aren't any usage charges, and the services are billed at a flat monthly rate.

To my way of thinking

Broadband is a great service for a home or business with fast Internet speeds, television broadcasts and telephone service all available from one cable connection. It's possible to mix and match and use different providers for different services, and it pays to compare prices and features every so often to see if you're getting the best price possible. Most people no longer have the older "dial-up" type of Internet connection that used the old twisted-pair telephone wires and if you install almost any type of telephone service today, chances are it will run over a broadband connection to your home.

Certain locations are simply not receiving broadband service if they are too far away from a cable or telephone facility and people located in these areas may be limited to the lower speed DSL types of connections or a satellite Internet connection.

Keep in mind that you can mix and match services from different providers and use options from your cellular company, to your internet or television company. In fact, many people don't have a home "land-line" telephone or dial up Internet and rely exclusively on their cellular phone. Explore these options and pricing to see if bundles and discounts are available for switching or signing up for a contract term and evaluate your pricing options every year to see if you can receive more features, options, or lower pricing, especially if your needs for phone, Internet and television service change.

Browser Cache

Browser Cache refers to the files from a webpage that are stored locally on a computer or other device. Cache is a term that refers to an area of memory that makes information available for quick access by a computer or software program. Just like the squirrels in the pine tree outside my house store a "cache" of pine cone seeds for easy access when they can't get fresh ones, your browser software stores a "cache" of website information so the browser can display the website faster.

How browsers display webpage files

Browsers are software programs that display webpages and webpages are at their basic just a different kind of computer file. You're probably more familiar with document and spreadsheet computer files, but any information on a computer is stored in a file. Some webpages include files for the format of the webpage along with the text.

Photos, images, videos, and other information are usually contained in additional files, so when a single webpage downloads from the Internet and is displayed in your browser, you may have one or more files that were downloaded from the Internet that together, make up a complete webpage.

A single webpage may be simple, or it can be quite complex, consisting of many images and other files that require a download for the webpage to work. The browser cache speeds up this process by keeping many of these files on your local drive, thus not requiring them to be retrieved again when you visit the site in the future.

Why does browser cache exist?

Your browser uses some memory on your computer or device and stores downloaded webpage files in a space called the browser "cache." Normally you wouldn't see these folders listed in your file folders since they are only used by your browser software.

Computers and devices keep files that are used only by a specific application in a separate location so as not to confuse you about seeing files that you didn't create yourself.

With a copy of text, images, and other files downloaded from a webpage stored locally on your computer or device, your browser can use these local files to display information in a webpage without needed to request these files from the Internet unless there is new updated information, or unless the information is no longer stored in the browser cache area.

The cache can make it much faster to display a webpage if your computer or device can pull the information from it's memory and as a result webpages display much faster, and faster performance is usually pretty important for people who use technology.

Another benefit of browser cache is that your computer or device can display a webpage without an Internet connection, as long as the webpage and all of it's files are kept in the browser cache. Once you download a webpage, as long as it's stored in the browser cache, you don't need an Internet connection to view it on your computer or device.

How browser cache works in practice

Imagine you've moved into a new home and you're stocking your kitchen for the first time. You write a shopping list to ensure that you return with everything you need. The first trip, it may take some time since you'll need everything on the list that any well-stocked kitchen requires. However, once you have the basics, any additional trips are for new grocery items or to replace any items that may have been used. Your basics are your "cache" and may last a while so you only have to bring home items that are for new recipes or to replace any used items.

Your first visit to a website is like a shopping trip with an empty pantry. Just as you must buy many staples to make whatever you're having for dinner, the browser needs to download many files and images so the webpage displays properly. However, once everything is downloaded, future visits to the same site only need to fetch what has changed. Just as with grocery trips when the pantry is full, these additional visits are quick and easy.

Management of browser cache

Browser cache can cause issues. Just as staples can go stale, so can downloaded items in the cache. Fortunately, all up-to-date browsers are smart enough to check for old content and ask for updates, but sometimes this fails to happen. Also, sometimes the cache fills up and uses up lots of disk space. Again, browsers are usually smart enough to detect and fix this, but when they aren't, clearing the cache is a lot easier than emptying a full pantry.

From a privacy perspective, webpages that you've visited may be stored in your browser cache, along with any files contained in a webpage. Up-to-date browsers will automatically remove old information to make room for more so you won't run out of memory on your computer or device, but there is a history of webpage files stored on your device.

Deleting the cache will remove these files from your computer memory if you want, but it's not necessary to do it unless you want your browsing history deleted from the computer. Each browser and device works a little different, so it's hard to give you one explanation for every possible software or device. You'll typically find the ability to do this located in settings for the browser on mobile devices or on the desktop menu for your browser history.

To my way of thinking

Thanks to the browser cache, the websites we visit most display much more quickly and as the software for browsers has become better and smarter, we see updates to web pages automatically. Since web browsing is often the most frequent use of a computer, smartphone, or tablet, a good browser that uses its cache is a hidden helper. As websites can be large, and grow more complicated every day, it is because of the browser cache's tireless, invisible effort that we may not even notice.

BYOD

BYOD is an abbreviation for "bring your own device," which occurs when employees use their personal smartphones, tablets, or computers as their workplace devices. Since many employees own their smartphones and prefer to use them for both personal and work use, the term BYOD was coined to refer to employee-provided technology in the workplace.

Traditionally, organizations would provide employees with the tools they needed to do their work, including computers, but with smartphones in particular, many organizations found that their employees want to use their personal portable devices, particularly smartphones, to connect to workplace applications such as email.

Why employees BYOD

Since many individuals already own and use a smartphone, they are more familiar with their particular model and brand. Employees can use their smartphone to connect to company email, telephone directories, and web applications and use the portable device they're most comfortable and familiar with using. If a smartphone is a job requirement, BYOD lets the employee get the benefit of carrying only one smartphone instead of one for work and one for personal use.

In addition to using a familiar device, the employee has the convenience of a smartphone with their personal email, calendar, contacts, and applications in their hand. At first glance, allowing employees to have a personal device with them instead of an employer owned device might seem risky, since the employee could do personal tasks on the device. But in reality, BYOD has resulted in employees taking their work with them almost anywhere, even on weekends and vacations. Employees can end up being "too" connected and have trouble ignoring a work email when it appears on their personal smartphone, even if they are on vacation.

Advantages of BYOD for the organization

For the employer, BYOD can result in the cost savings from avoiding the need to purchase equipment that the employee is providing. If the employer wants employees to have smartphones for work, it could be very expensive to equip their workforce with hardware and repair service.

With a personal, versus a company provided smartphone, the employee is responsible if the device breaks down or needs repair. The repair costs are the employee responsibility and expense.

Most organizations with a large network of computers pay technical support staff to maintain the technology that employees use on the job. In a BYOD business office, the maintenance is up to the owner. While the support staff proves help for the employee to connect their smartphone to the employer network and applications, the actual support and repair of the device itself is up to an employee, not the employer.

Disadvantages of BYOD

BYOD can potentially create one big problem for an employer, the security of the organization's information technology systems. With employee provided equipment connecting to the employer network, the employer needs to have information security policies and technology that protects organization data from access by a lost or stolen device. As a result, BYOD policies often require that employer can wipe all data from any employee device if it is reported stolen or lost. Depending on the necessary security, the technical support costs can make BYOD more expensive that employer provided equipment.

For the employee, as mentioned earlier, using one device for both personal and work use creates a new problem of managing time. When an email message is just a tap away, it's often easy to switch from personal use to work use when using a smartphone. You might know someone who is always connected to their work because they can't wait until the morning to answer a work email. A good practice that many employees have put in place is to have a discussion with their manager about expectations around work related email and messages while not "at" work.

To my way of thinking

BYOD isn't going away. It can save equipment costs for the employer and employees often prefer using their personal technology while at work. However, many organizations have sensitive data and will decide that employer-owned technology is the best way to control who can connect to the organization's data.

Other organizations will decide that allowing BYOD is a way to increase productivity from employees mixing work and personal use of their own portable devices.

If you are self-employed, you're already using BYOD if you use a smartphone or portable device for personal and work use, you just might not have known that's what it's called and didn't realize it.

C

CAPTCHA

CAPTCHA is an acronym for the phrase "Completely Automated Public Turing test to tell Computers and Humans Apart." If you've ever filled out a form on a website you've probably seen a place where you're required to enter some letters or numbers that appear in a picture. That's CAPTCHA, since only a human can read the characters.

Why is CAPTCHA used?

Websites and online businesses need to verify a form is being completed by a real human being. One of the main reasons CAPTCHA is used is to prevent hackers, spammers, and others from creating fraudulent user accounts

Webpages are only data and can be both copied and interpreted by computer programs. So it's possible to write a computer program that will read one web page after another and evaluate what it finds on those pages. The software program would automatically be able to create new user accounts on the website.

Such a program could come across a web sign up form and "know" that it is a document that accepts input from end users. Then the computer program would enter the user account data and create a fictitious user account. These types of user accounts are often the cause of hacking and spamming on the Internet.

Using CAPTCHA helps a website minimize the creation of fraudulent accounts by preventing computer programs from being able to complete the sign-up process. The Turing Test of requiring characters that can only be read by a person to be entered prevents a software program from completing the steps.

What is a Turing Test?

A Turing test, in the form of these odd looking characters, separates the humans from the non-humans. Without going into the details of what a Turing Test is, suffice to say a CAPTCHA presents the end user with a test that currently, only a human being can pass. The test takes advantage of the use of computer graphic characters and often an audio playback of the characters. By embedding the characters, often distorted, as a graphic image instead of plain text, a software program or digital camera can't be used to read the characters.

History of CAPTCHA

The term CAPTCHA was coined in 2000 by three scientists at Carnegie-Mellon University. The use of the original CAPTCHA software was made available for any website to use as open source software known as reCAPTCHA. Now used millions of times every day, the reCAPTCHA software is now available as a free service from Google.

Google uses reCAPTCHA to improve the accuracy of the Google Map data by presenting a test made from the text that appears in a street view image. By asking people to verify the text, Google receives feedback on their map images and helps stop malicious software.

reCAPTHA is also being used to digitize books that cannot be digitized by computers. These often include manuscripts of cursive characters that are difficult for computers to read. Written text is taken from a book and displayed as a CAPTCHA. Whenever a person enters the text into a reCAPTCHA form, the solution is used by Google to add to the digitized text. This type of test usually uses two words, the word that couldn't be read by the computer software, and another word to verify that a human filled out the CAPTCHA form.

Other forms of CAPTCHA software are available as open-source software and from companies that create and manage CAPTCHA tools.

Websites:

http://www.cs.cmu.edu/~biglou/reCAPTCHA_Science.pdf

http://www.google.com/recaptcha/intro/index.html

Where else is CAPTCHA used?

Testing to make sure a real person is on a website is used in many places besides website registration. Other common uses for CAPTCHA include preventing comment spam in blogs, protecting email addresses from being captured, online polls to verify the user, and other uses. Anywhere where there is a need to prevent automated programs from completing a form or entering information is an opportunity to use CAPTCHA.

To my way of thinking

Using the web and online accounts has become a necessary part of daily life. As new websites are created that provide useful benefits for people, there will be those that take advantage of these new opportunities. CAPTCHA is simply one way to keep the web a safer, more secure place. So while it may seem annoying, the use of CAPTCHA is a sign that the website you're using takes security seriously.

Catfisher

A catfisher is an individual who uses the Internet, and in particular, online dating websites to lure people into a scam romance. The general goal of a catfisher is financial gain by developing an online relationship with another person and ultimately asking for money. Besides financial gain, catfishes are sometimes people who prey on others and gain pleasure from online communications and manipulation. You also might hear the terms catfish or catfishing. Catfishing targets both men and women

Why do catfishers exist?

When you find large numbers of people in a location or doing an activity, you'll inevitably find others who see an opportunity to take advantage of them. With over 40 million persons in the United States actively using online dating, the online dating sites are an area where people are putting themselves on the Internet specifically for the purpose of meeting others. So there's no telling who might contact you and what you might know about them. However, with a little knowledge and common sense, it's possible to spot the scams and catfishers.

How do catfishers work?

Catfishers take advantage of human needs and social behavior. People are meant to be social, to develop connections. Most human beings, regardless of culture, seek out some form of relationship with other individuals. The way humans connect with each other includes so many it's impossible to count but think of marriage, partnerships, families, religious organizations, social clubs, and others as just some of the ways people connect. Then there are online ways to connect.

With the Internet, people could connect with other people using email, messaging apps, social networks, and dating sites. Online dating sites are specifically designed so people can find and contact others for the purpose of dating and often to develop a longer lasting relationship. The goal of finding a partner, particularly a romantic one, makes people more vulnerable to scams and fraud. A catfisher attempts to target and start communications with individuals that are emotionally vulnerable and naive and develop a relationship online. Catfishers rely on the nature of online profiles and discussions to practice their "craft".

Catfishers will never meet anyone face-to-face, which is one reason online dating date recommendations all encourage a face-to-face meeting within a reasonable time-frame. The catfisher will approach an individual through an online dating site with a fake profile. The online websites try their best to take fake profiles down, but it's so easy to set a profile up that it's a constant battle that never ends.

A catfisher usually lives too far away for any practical way to arrange a meeting; that's one sign that they are a potentially fraudulent account. Then an approach email starts, written fairly well, and good enough so that a back-and-forth dialog is started. That's when the catfisher knows they've got a potential target. Catfishers rely on telling people (both men and women) what they want to hear to keep the communication going. Often, the catfishers are physically located outside of the United States but use a false location for their profile.

Initially, email messages can use a template, a cut and paste approach that catfishers know will get a response if they send out enough emails. One way to challenge a catfisher is to ask direct questions and see if the answers come back with writing indicative of the education level of the profile. Often the catfisher doesn't speak English well, and you'll find grammatical errors. If you see this type of communications, it's time to start using common sense and report the account or block communications, since the person clearly isn't who they led you to believe based on their profile.

Catfishers prey on human needs to feel connected and provide people using online dating sites with a "relationship" that begins to form through online communications. Once the relationship builds up enough trust, the catfisher will start describing some situations that may require money. Never send money to anyone you've only communicated with through the online dating site. But it happens enough that catfishers keep setting up fake profiles and sending out "canned" emails approaching people since enough people are naive enough or emotionally vulnerable enough that they will become a victim.

Other types of catfishers

Besides the catfishers whose primary goal is financial gain, other types of catfishers are mean and manipulative. Their goal in communication is to build a relationship online that they can use to be vindictive, cruel, or to see if they can control another person and affect their emotional state through an online relationship. These are sometimes more dangerous than the fraudulent catfishers since the scammers only want money. The ones who do catfishing as a hoax for emotional reasons are unsavory people. But when you put yourself out there, you;ll be approached by all types.

Ten tips for identifying catfishers:

1. They are presently out of the country or state though their profile says they are local. Usually, the profile says they are from a big city like Los Angeles. They often say that they will be returning in a month.

2. They quickly ask you to communicate off site and give you an email address, phone number or ask you to set up a Yahoo! Messenger account.

3. They ask for this change of communications format for a variety of reasons, the most common being that they are closing their account or that their account could be closed by the online service if they're reported.

4. They ask for information that's already in your profile. Even honest people ask for information that might already be in your profile, so it's not a deciding factor, but it does show that the person isn't paying close attention.

5. They don't answer direct questions.

6. Their comments don't make sense or are out of context (a sign of non-English language skills)

7. Their use of language; grammar, spelling, capitalization, and phraseology is incorrect or odd. With a scammer, the writing is not consistent. When they are writing about their emotions or what they are seeking, then the language is good. When, and if, they answer direct questions, the language is notably worse.

8. They will often claim to be orphans and that they have no close family.

9. They primarily write about their emotions and what they are looking for in a partner, but not about where they are. They write, often at length, about their feelings, how they want you to feel and all the great activities you'll do together when they finally get to see you. But they never give you specifics about their work, where they are, or daily life. The communications are always about emotion, desire, and romance.

10. They come on strong, ridiculously strong. It may be flattering at first, but how much can a pen pal care about you who you've never met and who won't answer your questions?

To my way of thinking:

Dealing with people online requires the same common sense we use offline. When you first contact someone you don't know anything about them and their profile could be fake. After all, most people using online dating sites use a fake name to protect their identity. While email communication can sometimes last a while and still be honest, at some point

eHarmony recently introduced a profile verification tool for people so they can present themselves as a "real" person. I expect we'll see other online dating sites trying this out as well.

CD's and DVD's

A CD, or compact disc, is an optical (meaning light) disc that is used to store sound recordings, music, photographs, videos, text files, and other types of information. DVD's are similar in size and shape, but use a higher capacity way to record and can store more information.

Both CD's and DVD's were made possible with the invention of the laser, which creates a focused beam of light. Computers and other devices can play CD's and DVD's if they have a "reader." The CD or DVD reader, also referred to as CD/DVD when it plays both types of discs, has a laser beam that can read the data from the disc. Computers and other devices with CD or DVD recorders are able to write data to the disc with a laser beam. Most DVD players can play CD's and most DVD recorders can record CD"s so there's not usually a need for separate devices.

Let's discuss CD's first.

What are the uses for a CD and where did they come from?

The top of a CD will usually have a label identifying what it contains, or what it is used for; the bottom of the disc will be shiny and reflective.

CDs can be used to listen to music, watch videos, keep a digital photo album, and even store important text files. When most people hear the term CD, they think of the music CDs of recording artists or bands that are commonly sold in stores; in fact, some people even refer to them as the modernized version of vinyl records! They were created by Sony and Philips which made the CD specifications available for other companies to use, resulting in the CD becoming a standard. Initially, they were only used only for music; however, they were gradually able to be used for many other types of digital information, or data such as software, and file storage.

What are the benefits of using a CD?

Unlike cassette tapes and records, CDs are not worn out during the process of playing them. For this reason, CDs last a lot longer than their predecessors if they are cared for. Compared to tapes and vinyl records, CDs are smaller, and the audio quality is more consistent over time since the CD doesn't have anything touching it when it playback the sound. A small laser disc shines on the CD to "read" the disc.

Computer programs and digital files can be contained on CDs allowing you to take files with you wherever you go and keep a backup copy stored in a different location from your computer. CDs can make life in the digital world safer by keeping your important files safe in the event that your computer breaks. You can copy your important files to a disc to keep a backup copy in case your computer breaks or to share a copy with friends and family.

What is a DVD?

A DVD, or Digital Versatile Disc, is a format that was created to store movies and other video files, but can be used to store other files. DVD's are read and used by DVD players, found in computers, personal gaming systems, and dedicated DVD players connected to televisions and home theaters. DVD's look almost identical to CDs with a label on the top identifying its contents and a shiny, reflective bottom, and the same size dimensions.

What are the uses for a DVD and where did they come from?

DVDs were originally created in the 1990s after film companies realized how successful the music industry was using CDs to sell music. Philips, Sony, Toshiba, and Panasonic worked together to create the DVD industry standard. Because DVD's cost less to manufacture and are smaller, they have replaced videotapes for recorded movies. The film industry officially adopted the DVD as the industry standard in November of 1995. DVDs can also be used to store digital data just like CDs, and they offer a larger storage capacity because of their capacity. You can't see any additional capacity just by looking at a DVD compared to a CD, but your computer will know the difference. Fortunately for us, the industry standard requires that the CD or DVD logo be used on any disc so you can tell the difference at a glance.

What are the benefits of using a DVD?

DVDs offer superior audio and video quality compared to their predecessors, VHS tapes. In addition to storing movies, they can also hold alternative film endings, audio and/or subtitles in different languages, deleted scenes and other extras, biography of cast members, footage on how the films were created, and some even allow users to choose between the square television screen size or widescreen that is similar to the movie theater screen; this allows consumers to have a bigger and better experience.

Because they can hold a lot more data than a CD, some people use them to store their important digital files; this allows them to place a lot more information on a single disc instead of several. As long as they are taken care of, DVDs can last a long time and their small size allows for easy storage.

Check-in on Facebook

A Check In allows you to share your physical location with your friends on Facebook by using the Facebook app.

It's always fun to connect with friends in different ways, and that is exactly what the Check In feature allows you to do. From your smartphone, you can alert your friends and family as to where you are by tapping the "Check In" button in the Facebook mobile app. Using Check In allows people to see what you are doing as you venture throughout your day.

A Check In is a special type of status update that uses existing information on Facebook to locate businesses, places, and locations using your smartphone location features. Since your smartphone has the hardware to know your current location, Facebook can use that location to identify places that are nearby you. When you tap the Check In button, a list of places appears, and you simply select the one you want to use.

In addition to the location being listed in the Status Update box when you tap the Check In button, you can add text to expand your message and add photos just as you would with any other Status Update on Facebook.

How does Facebook get the list of places?

The locations that Facebook knows about are the result of people, businesses, schools, governments, and other organizations who create a Page on Facebook. Pages are what you can Like on Facebook, and they aren't just for businesses. If the Page has a physical address that the Page creator provided when they created the Facebook Page, that Page listing appears when you use the Check In option since Facebook has the address and location information.

Using Check In

Using Check In may seem a bit unusual at first, since you probably aren't in the habit of letting people know your location. But Check In has some useful aspects. You're letting any friends who happen to be close by know where you are. If you are out and about on your own, you may be able to find a friend nearby for lunch, coffee, or to say hi.

Check In is also a great feature that allows you to stay in touch with your friends and family. Instead of typing out a text message on your phone, making a phone call, or sending an email, you can alert everyone who needs to know where you are, whether you are shopping, picking up food, or just running late.

It's also fun to use the Check In feature to promote your favorite businesses and locations. When you patronize a business, it's often because you like it's products or services. When you Check In, the business location is shared with your Facebook network, and you've provided a form of endorsement to that business. Endorsements are especially helpful for small businesses who rely on word of mouth for reaching new customers.

A Check In is also a way to help any local business you patronize obtain more visibility on Facebook. The Check In update is sent to your friends and appears in the News Feed of your friends and connections. The business receives an update on it's Page with a new Check In added to its total.

While many businesses have their locations listed on Facebook for Check In, there are other types of locations as well. Some of these include schools, museums, parks, tourist attractions, monuments, theaters, and buildings.

Check In Privacy - It's Not

Keep in mind that when you Check In, the Check In is a Public update which can be viewed not only by your friends, but by anyone one Facebook. Because a Check In is a type of status update in connection with a Page, and since all Page activity is Public, your Check In is Public. To just let someone know where you are right now, and keep it private, it's better to use texting, email, or that old fashioned form of communications, a phone call.

To my way of thinking

Though checking in has many advantages, perhaps one of the best ones is that it allows us to connect more concretely with the people we care about. A lot of people have talked about how social networking brings us closer together. Even if you cannot be with someone that you care about, you can at a glance see where they went to lunch, where they shopped for shoes and where they went after class or work. When you cannot join someone that you care about for their day, this is perhaps the next best thing.

It's also very useful in the event of an emergency since it can assist emergency responders and loved ones to find you if necessary.

The next time you are out and about, why not try checking in? You never know who is nearby, and it is a great way to share your day with your connections and help a local business!

Chromebook

Chromebook is a personal computer that runs using Google's operating system, known as Chrome OS. It's available pre-installed on computers from many manufacturers including Asus, Samsung, HP and others. It's an alternative to the traditional Windows laptop, and one of the main benefits is that the operating system, Chrome OS, uses all of the applications available from Google and third-parties.

Chromebooks are also inexpensive. With prices starting at below $200, Chromebooks are economical alternatives to traditional laptop computers running Windows software.

Web-based software on a computer.

Chromebooks are designed to use web-based apps and programs, which means two things; one, a Chromebook requires an Internet connection to realize its full potential, and two, a Chromebook updates the operating system and software through the web. While it might seem as though this might be a limitation, your data (documents, spreadsheets, presentations, and files) can be stored both online and locally. The advantage of a Chromebook is that it automatically updates its software, much like a mobile smartphone or tablet.

How are Chromebooks selling?

For most of the people who take my classes, I don't recommend taking a chance on new technology. People want to buy technology that's supported and has options available on the marketplace. So is the Chromebook a dead-end product or something that's a new option to Windows and Macs?

While Windows is still the top selling PC operating system overall, as of 2016 Chromebooks have now become the largest selling computer in the K-12 education market, surpassing both Windows and Apple OS X personal computers. The combination of low-cost devices along with an easy to maintain operating system has made Chromebooks popular to use.

Overall, with Chromebook sales increasing steadily and with more companies including Toshiba, Lenovo, and Dell announcing Chromebook products, there's a commitment to this product. But is it for you?

What Chromebooks are like to use.

If you're searching to transition from another laptop, the Chromebook runs very intuitively. Based on the Chrome web browser, a Chromebook's programs are designed to look and operate similarly as they do on Windows and Macs. All you really need to get started is a Google account. Google is dedicated to improving the Chrome user experience, ensuring that their machines run up-to-date and won't interrupt your browsing with constant requests to upgrade. Chromebooks are also noted for how fast they startup and how much faster they run compared to traditional laptops, because Chromebooks use an efficient operating system with excess programs removed.

The Software

Most computer users spend almost all of their time doing two things, using websites and email. Think about your computer use, you use websites for finding directions, banking, shopping, social networking, and maybe even watching video. If you have one, your mobile device, such as a smartphone or tablet, can also do all of these things. So if you take a look at the time you spend on a computer, it might not be as much as it was before mobile devices entered your life. Even if you do use a computer, the web and email are what you probably the functions you use day in and day out.

But what about word processing and spreadsheets? Chromebooks have you covered here, and include Google's word-processing, spreadsheet, and presentation applications, all of which can import and export from Microsoft Office application files. These productivity applications, in addition to email, are designed for you to use with or without an Internet connection so you stay productive. All of the software from Google is updated automatically, without requiring you to purchase updates for new versions.

In addition to Google's applications, third-party software applications that work with the Chrome browser can be used on Chromebooks.

Using Chromebooks with Android mobile devices

Another convenient feature is the connection from Chromebooks to Android mobile devices. Since Google makes both, it only seems natural for Google to provide some benefit and integration, and they do. One example is the ability to access your Google Drive from your Android device, another is the ability to edit photos taken with an Android phone on your Chromebook. Using your Google account, your photos will sync automatically. So if you're an Android user, a Chromebook can help you get more out of your mobile smartphone or tablet.

The hardware.

A typical Chromebook looks a lot like a traditional laptop, with a keyboard, screen, trackpad, built-in WiFi, and a small amount of local storage. The local storage capacity of Chromebooks is smaller than a traditional laptop computer since most of your work is stored in the cloud on Google Drive, which provides 100 Gigabytes of space for two years as part of your purchase. You simply don't need to store everything locally on your Chromebook (nor do you on a laptop, but that's how we've been working for a long time.) New models are now available that are for use as a desktop computer, with you supplying the monitor, keyboard, and mouse.

When is a Chromebook not for you?

Chromebooks are an excellent addition to any household and are probably one of the most trouble-free computers on the market. However, it may not be for everyone. If you require the use of an application that is only available for Windows or Mac, then you need to buy that type of computer to use those applications, since Chromebooks only run programs designed for Chrome OS.

If you don't have access to the Internet and need to work "offline" frequently, then a Chromebook may not be a good solution either, since Chromebooks need to access the Internet in order to update the software and access your Google Drive storage.

Should you change your computing?

Professionals in the computer industry usually take a look at what someone needs to do with a computer, then recommend the computer based on a person's needs. When the only choice was a Windows computer, the recommendation was pretty simple. With Chromebooks, there are new choices, since Apple has the Mac. Since more is being done on the web and "cloud," you may not need or use a software application that requires a Windows operating system on a computer. If so, then consider a Chromebook as an alternative to a computer, or even to a tablet. If you're considering a Mac as an alternative to a Windows computer, here's some advice on when to consider Apple.

Apple includes productivity software (word processing, spreadsheet, and presentation) for free, along with free operating system upgrades, and while they are a premium priced product, Apple support is regarded as the best in the industry with their network of stores and support plans, and Apple makes software applications that only work on Apple computers. The premium price also gives you a single place to go for support and help, and maybe that's what you need.

What's ahead

Google announced in May 2016 that Android apps will be available to Chromebooks. This availability will increase the available number of apps for Chromebooks and allow Android users the ability to install and use the apps they like.

Clickbait

Clickbait is a derogatory term that describes low-quality content on websites that exists for the purpose of getting attention and enticing people to "click" with their mouse to view the content. Think of clickbait as misleading headlines of a sensational or curiosity providing nature that are designed to encourage people to click and read more, but the article or content isn't high-quality information.

Clickbait works a little bit like the news teasers on television when a news broadcast promotes a sensational or high-profile story during prime-time hours to encourage you to watch the eleven o'clock news. Another example is the tabloids you see in supermarket checkout lines where the headlines are written to attract your attention.

Clickbait on social networks

Clickbait became so prevalent on the Internet in recent years that a backlash developed, and social networking sites such as Facebook and others created technical measures to minimize the amount of clickbait displayed. In fact, clickbait has often been used to encourage sharing of the headline to spread it as widely as possible.

Some clickbait encourages people to share articles, funny images or other material with friends and family over social networks. Other forms of clickbait simply want to encourage people to visit a certain site to be able to increase revenue from advertisers.

How the term originated

Clickbait is a coined term formed from "click", the action of pressing on the principle button on a computer mouse, which often emits a clicking sound when depressed, and "bait", from the hunting term for food or other attractive treats designed to lure game animals. While no one knows the exact date of when the term originated, it became a popular term used as the internet became increasingly ubiquitous in daily life.

How and why it works

Clickbait works by taking advantage of a psychological characteristic in the human brain called the "curiosity gap". Headlines create a curiosity gap by leaving out a key piece of information. The reader, if curious, to click to read more. To fill in the "gap," a reader has to click to read more, hence the term curiosity-gap.

While the title may promise an amazing story, the material that follows clicking on a clickbait is usually sub-standard, and may not even be relevant at all to the original headline. Powerful social networks such as Facebook have announced measures to try to weed out clickbait from their systems.

Clickbait has become such a well-known phenomenon lately that a parody site entitled 'ClickHole' now exists, making fun of prominent clickbait websites around the internet. Whereas the term clickbait was once used just by industry insiders, it has become a household term in the past few years.

Journalism quality and clickbait

While all quality journalism articles use certain stylistic hooks to increase reader interest with a good headline, it is considered uncouth to promise scandalous or gossipy information in a headline and then deliver only unsubstantiated rumors or rehashed news articles from years ago.

Clickbait works by sounding so interesting and enticing that the reader feels compelled to click through and consume the promised content. Since clickbait is a derogatory term, it most often refers to enticing headlines that promise sensationalist information but then reveal themselves simply to be marketing gimmicks designed to drive up ad revenue. Savvy internet users are increasingly staying away from clickbait websites and spending more time on quality sites with authentic stories instead of inflated, sensationalist gossip about celebrities and politicians.

To my way of thinking

Organizations and marketers are always looking for ways to attract attention on the Internet and clickbait has worked but may be falling in usage. Internet users learn quickly and have become savvy enough to start to recognize sensational headlines that promise more than they deliver.

Web sites like Facebook want their users to have a high-quality experience when using the site and seeing information worth sharing. As a result, these websites have worked hard recently to create filters to minimize clickbait types of content.

Attracting attention on the Internet is important so there will always be attempts by marketers and others with creative methods to encourage people to click.

Cloud

The Cloud is a term used with more and more frequency to refer to services (both hardware and software) that exist on a network. The most common cloud-based services are accessed via the Internet, but a business can also have its own cloud-based services within a private network as well. The term Cloud itself refers to the cloud-shaped symbol used to depict this service in network topology diagrams.

What Does the Cloud Do?

The most common implementation of the Cloud is through online storage of files. The files are typically accessed through a web browser or by a small program designed to access these files. This means that a user in New York can modify a file that can instantly be accessed by another user in California. That same user can then view the file on any device at any time. Similar to other secure transactions on the Internet such as online banking, the Cloud uses encryption to keep data safe from malicious users.

Benefits of Using the Cloud

Cloud computing is making its way into every facet of both business and personal computing. The benefits to using the Cloud are many. Personal cloud services such as Google Drive and iCloud are allowing users to access data (documents, files, pictures) from anywhere using a smartphone, PC, or tablet. Businesses have begun adapting cloud services as well. Since important files are no longer stored locally on an individual's hard drive, the risk of losing important data due to equipment failure or natural disaster is substantially mitigated. Group collaboration even across international lines is easy to accomplish thanks to the Cloud. Many large software companies have started offering cloud-based services to small and large businesses alike. This drives the cost of doing business down drastically and can provide a more seamless experience.

Although the term may seem ambiguous at first glance, the Cloud is taking technology in a new direction. The benefits of using the Cloud increase daily as companies begin to leverage this technology to keep costs low and work more efficiently. Gone are the days of forgetting an important document at home or at the office. With just a few mouse clicks, that file is available anywhere.

Cookie

There was a time when a cookie was nothing more than a sweet, round, and flat baked treat you dip in a glass of cold milk. But in the digital age, the word "cookie" has come to mean a whole new thing.

In technology, a cookie is to a small bit of information that is sent from a website you're visiting, then stored in the browser you're using. When you visit that particular website again, it fetches the data saved in the cookie so that the website would know about your past activity. It consists of a set of letters and numbers that identify a specific computer when it accesses the Web. A Web browser, in case you haven't been a subscriber, is the software application on your device that is used to browse and display Web sites. The most common ones are Microsoft's Internet Explorer, Apple's Safari, Mozilla Firefox, and Google Chrome. They are all good, and they all accept and store cookies.

Why Are Cookies Important?

Why is this important? Think about some of the websites you need to log on to, like Facebook, Twitter, or even mine, bobology. It would be inconvenient to have to log in every time you visit -- even if your visits are within the same hour. Wouldn't it be great if these Web sites remember your email address and password? Thanks to cookies, you can make a website store these important bits of data, and get them when needed.

Cookies and Privacy

However, not all cookies are believed to be helpful. Some cookies store what and how you search online, so that third-party advertising companies, social networks, and other Web sites can know exactly what kind of ads will interest you. Many people think this is a major violation to their privacy. But unfortunately it's the price we pay for many of the free services we receive on the Internet. Facebook, Twitter, Google, Bing, and many other Web sites provide services and resources for us for free, but in exchange, when we accepted the terms and conditions for setting up our accounts, we agreed to allow the Web site to track our behavior, and sometimes use our information for targeting ads.

Using Shared Computers and Devices

Other than privacy issues, there's one other side to cookies that can be harmful. If you use a public computer, or share a computer with someone else, a cookie on that computer may think it's you when you visit a shopping cart or commerce site and allow you to login. Other people may end up getting access to your email, social media profiles, etc. if they use the same computer after you're done with it. This is because information pertaining to you is still stored in the cookies. This applies not only to computers, but to smartphones and tablets, since the cookie is stored in the browser application, and all devices use browser software to display Web pages.

Why You Need Cookies

You can't get rid of cookies altogether because many websites don't work properly if you disable them. What you can do is clear your cookies after you finish surfing the Internet. Even if you're sharing your computer with other people, they will not have access to your personal online accounts. Remember, you will probably need to login with your user account and password if any Web site you used stored that information for you, since they probably used a cookie.

Deleting Cookies

Here are links to the support site of each browser with their instructions for deleting cookies, and instructions for iOS and Android devices.

Microsoft Internet Explorer

http://windows.microsoft.com/en-us/internet-explorer/delete-manage-cookies#ie=ie-10

Google Chrome

https://support.google.com/chrome/answer/95647?hl=en

Mozilla Firefox

https://support.mozilla.org/en-US/kb/delete-cookies-remove-info-websites-stored

Apple Safari on a Mac

https://support.apple.com/kb/PH21411?viewlocale=en_US&locale=en_US

Delete Cookies in Apple Safari on iPhones and iPads

Tap Settings, then tap Safari, then tap Clear Cookies and Data

Delete Cookies in Chrome for Android

Tap Menu, then tap Settings, then tap Privacy, then tap Clear Browsing Data

Crash

A crash occurs when a computer stops working as a result of any software or hardware failure. A crash makes the computer unusable, either because it is "frozen" (still powered on, but not responsive) or has the computer has turned off completely and will not operate.

When a computer crash occurs, any work not saved before the crash may be lost, such as a document you are writing in an application, so knowing what causes a crash will help you get back up and running faster.

Any computing device, such as a smartphone, tablet, game console, or even an automobile has the potential to crash since they all have both hardware and software that are required to keep them functioning. As a quick refresher, software includes your operating system and programs (or apps) installed on your computer, while hardware includes the physical parts of your computer, such as the processor, memory, hard drive, etc..

Since a crash results from a major malfunction within the computer, it helps to understand better what can go wrong with either software and hardware and the differences. A little understanding of what caused the crash can sometimes help you diagnose and solve the problem.

Diagnosing computer problems is a little bit like a medical diagnosis. For example, when you have an upset stomach. Your stomach might be upset from smoothing you ate or as a result of a virus. If you know what caused the upset stomach, you'll have a better chance of understanding how to provide relief.

All computers are vulnerable to crashing, and it isn't possible to completely prevent it from happening. Chances are if you've used any computing device you may have experienced a crash.

There are a number of different types of computer crashes, each with separate causes so let's take a look the different types of crashes.

Program, App, and Software Crashes

A program crash happens when a fatal error has occurred within the application software. This type of crash might result in one specific application not being usable, or it could result in the entire computer not being usable. It's possible for one application to cause a complete computer crash. While operating systems try to isolate the problems to a specific application, so the computer doesn't crash, it can sometimes happen.

Program crashes happen for a number of reasons, and it's often not advised to go on using the program in question until the error is corrected. Most operating systems for desktops, laptops and smartphones have a means by which you can shut down and stop a particular program or app. If the operating system is still functioning, then it's usually possible to shut down the specific program and restart it to continue using the program.

Operating System Crashes

An operating system crash is a more complex type of failure. In this type of crash, the operating system such as Windows 10, Mac OS and iOS (for Apple mobile devices) or Android has failed in some way. With an operating system crash, none of the applications work and the computer has stopped working, even though the power and hardware are functioning.

With an operating system crash, your computer or device may be completely unresponsive to anything, such as the mouse click, keyboard stroke or screen tap. In this case, a power shutdown and power on restart is necessary and often solves the problem since a power shut down and restart results in a reboot of the operating system and enables the computer to function properly.

Hardware Crashes

A hardware crash happens when a physical device inside or attached to the computer fails, causing the entire computer to crash. For example, if the hard disk drive (the device responsible for containing all of your computer's data) fails, the computer will become mostly unusable.

To fix a hardware crashes it's necessary to replace the component that failed. If the failed part is the hard drive on a desktop or laptop, your data could be lost if you didn't have any backup. Hard drives are replaceable and the operating system and application programs can be reinstalled (as long as you have the license for the software), but personal data can never be replaced, so backups are always important.

To my way of thinking

It's common for a computer technician to ask about the version of a software program or operating system when trying to solve any problem. The version information tells the technician if the latest software update is in use on your computer or device. You can usually find version information yourself from the support website of the software or hardware manufacturer, and often there are instructions for checking the version, and if necessary, how to update your software.

One important reason for software updates is that the update often fixes a problem that might have caused a crash. An update to the latest version of the software might fix the problem in the software that caused the crash.

Cord Cutting

Cord-cutting is the act of doing away with expensive cable subscriptions and changing to a low or no-cost TV channel subscription through the use of an antenna or Internet service.

Cable subscriptions can be expensive, but many people are learning how to replace their viewing entertainment with over-the-air free broadcasting through an antenna or over-the-top low-cost broadcasting through an internet service. In fact, the number of people subscribing to cable TV is declining and is a trend the industry is watching closely.

Using an antenna to receive free television is one of the easiest ways to implement cord cutting. All TV manufactured after 2007 have a digital tuner. Digital tuners are necessary since all TV broadcasts are digital, not analog. With a digital tuner, you can receive many channels without being connected to a traditional cable service. These tuners are also built into 36" or larger TVs that were manufactured after 2005, and 25" or larger TVs that were manufactured after 2006.

If your TV has a built in digital tuner, then you can use an antenna and plug the antenna's coaxial cable directly into your TV. If it is not equipped with a built in digital tuner, you can purchase a digital converter box, VCR, DVD player, or DVR equipped with a digital tuner. However, with TV prices being pretty low, it's probably better just to replace your TV.

To install an antenna, you won't need to crawl on a roof. TV broadcasts are now digital, and you can purchase a high-quality antenna like the Mohu Leaf Paper-Thin Indoor HDTV Antenna for less than $50. This antenna is about the size of a wall calendar, and I just hung it on a wall next to a window.

Once connected to an antenna, you can start watching free broadcast TV by scanning for free broadcast channels. The scan is done through the "menu" on the television, and automatically scans for channels that are picked up by the digital tuner. Once the scan is complete, you won't need to scan again unless the tuner gets disconnected. This was great when Time-Warner was blocking CBS broadcasts.

Internet service is a staple in any home that utilizes a computer or other tech devices, and can easily be used to watch a multitude of television shows and movies. There are a few mainstream ways to make viewing possible. First, users can purchase a separate receiver box such as Roku or Apple TV. These devices make it possible for users to watch television available through Internet services.

Options include a subscription to Netflix, Hulu or Amazon, the most popular services which contain thousands of movies and television shows that can be watched instantly. These services include the ability to pause and rewind on demand, search, and setup a watch list. When watching a TV series, Netflix and Hulu allow you to watch one episode after another, all without commercial breaks. This has given rise to the popular term "binge watching."

The other option is using a smart TV with the built-in capability to access application channels like Netflix and Hulu, eliminating the need for a separate receiver. Most BluRay and DVD players offer the option to access these channels, and the latest console game player devices usually include Netflix and Hulu now.

Though Netflix and Hulu are two of the most popular application channels, they do require a low-cost subscription. Many application channels, such as Crackle, PBS, HuffPost, PBS Kids, and various news stations are available for free if the user has an appropriate receiver. Using your Internet connection and these services, you can view many popular television shows, movies, and newscasts. This can save the user about a hundred dollars each month depending on the cable plan to which they currently subscribe. An extra benefit these application channels provide is the lack of commercials.

Amazon's Prime is a service that works using Amazon Kindle Fire devices and plays TV shows and movies on certain portable Kindle devices. Amazon, Apple, and Google also have content stores where you can purchase individual TV shows, series, and movies and download this content to your computer.

The latest entry into cord-cutting is Google with their Chromecast accessory. For about $35, this accessory plugs into a USB connector on your TV set and then connects to your home WiFi network. Using the Google Chrome browser, you can send your content to the Chromecast device and play it on your TV set.

Cord-cutting is becoming easier, offers more flexible options, and makes in-home entertainment available for a fraction of the cost than a monthly cable bill.

CPU

A CPU, or Central Processing Unit, is the brain of a computer and does all the calculations that perform the work of a computer. Sometimes just referred to as a microprocessor, or a processor, a CPU/Processor is a vital component found within laptops, desktop computers, cellphones, smartphones, game consoles, and almost any electronic device.

These small, incredibly powerful computers, no bigger than a silver dollar, have put technology everywhere, so it's worth learning a little more about CPU's. Every day you benefit from at least one, if not dozens, or even hundreds, of CPU's working their brains out for you.

Once made of up of vacuum tubes and taking up several cubic feet, CPUs now are made on a small chip of silicon, with an average size less than an inch square and less than a quarter of an inch thick. A CPU "chip" puts a lot of computing power in a small space, with very little weight.

Where CPU's are Built

Inside the CPU are transistors, which is a type of electronic circuit, that can be used to perform calculations like addition and subtraction. Millions of these tiny transistors no more than a few centimeters wide are packed into the CPU with specialized manufacturing done at factories called foundries. Unlike a traditional steel foundry, a CPU foundry is a very quiet place, and all the work takes place on a microscopic level, often in dust and dirt free clean rooms to prevent the smallest spec of material from landing on a chip while it's being manufactured. In fact, much of the process is automated. Foundries are pretty expensive to build, well over $1 Billion each, and take big investments.

More means Faster

Since transistors do the calculating, more transistors in a CPU results in a faster CPU, and therefore, a faster computer. Putting more transistors in a CPU chip means making the transistors smaller, which is what advances in CPU manufacturing have made possible. As CPU manufacturers such as Intel and AMD are able to produce smaller and smaller transistors, they are able to create faster CPUs containing more transistors packed into each chip.

Faster

CPU's have a tiny built-in clock circuit that determines how many cycles the CPU can perform in one second. One cycle performs one set of calculations, so more cycles per second means faster calculating, and the term for measuring one clock cycle per second is called a Hertz. The processing speed of a CPU is measured in hertz (Hz) and relates directly to how fast a processor can complete a clock cycle.

A one Hertz CPU can perform one cycle per second, a 100 Hertz CPU performs 100 cycles per second, and so on. Rather than saying "one million Hertz," the more common term "Megahertz" is used to describe one million cycles, and for one billion cycles per second, that's called a Gigahertz. So a one Gigahertz CPU is running one billion calculations per second. More Hertz means a faster CPU, so CPU manufacturers work to make their processors as fast as possible.

One danger with all this calculating is that the tiny electrons moving around inside the tiny CPU chip generates heat from friction. This heat places a practical limit on how fast a CPU can perform. Faster CPU's need fans and a way to cool off, which is why computers have fans or other ways to move the heat away from the CPU.

Mobile devices like smartphones, which are completely sealed and don't have fans, use chips that run cooler along with materials that can handle the heat from the CPU.

Cores

In addition to more transistors on a chip and faster clock speeds, CPU makers have figured out ways to put more than one CPU on a single chip. By doing this, they can connect CPU's in pairs and split the computing work between two or more processors. These multiple CPU's on a chip are called "multi-core" and each single CPU is a core. A dual-core CPU has two CPU's on a single chip, a quad-core has four CPU's, and so on.

By putting more than one CPU on a chip, two, four, or more CPU's can be manufactured at the same time, lowering manufacturing costs, so a multicore CPU can be less expensive than building two separate CPU's and connecting them together in the computer. Multi-core CPU's are extremely common and are common in most computers, but also on most smartphones and tablets. As a general rule, if you have a choice, buy a computer with a multi-core CPU rather than one with a single core, since it's almost always faster.

Putting it Together

From a practical standpoint, there are many factors that affect how fast any computer performs work in addition to the CPU. Two cars with the same horsepower engine might perform differently on a race track, but the race would be close. In a race between two cars with vastly different engines, odds are the car with the more powerful engine will win.

That's true of computers also, and two computers with exactly the same CPU might perform differently. But one with a more powerful CPU, the one with a faster clock speed and more cores, will usually outperform one with a slower clock speed and fewer cores. What's helpful to the average user of CPU's is that manufacturers keep working to make faster CPU's less expensive, so they become more common everywhere.

Crawler

A web crawler is a software program that automatically discovers and scans websites by following one web page to another. Search sites like Google, Yahoo! and Bing use crawlers to discover web pages and the content on those web pages to create an index of information which is stored by the search site and used to produce search results when people enter search terms.

Web crawlers are also called "bots" which is short for robot. Another term for web crawlers is also "spider," but that term has been falling out of popular usage and Google, which is the most popular search engine, has it's own crawler called the Goolebot. Microsoft has a crawler called the Bing bot and is also used by Yahoo! since Yahoo! sold their search service to Bing. In fact, there are over 300 different crawlers are listed son the website Robotstxt.org. So what do all these crawlers do on the Internet when they creep around?

What a crawler does

A web crawler needs a list of website addresses to start its work. The crawler then visits the website, much like a person would when typing in a website address, but the crawler is a little more detailed. The crawler will identify all of the links to other webpages, adds them to at the list of webpages to visit, and then visits all of those webpages. Think of it as an automated link clicking program that clicks on every single webpage link that it can find. But that's not all a crawler does while it's working.

In addition to visiting webpages and collecting link information, some web crawlers collect information from the webpages they visit and send it back to a database. This function, called archiving, is how Google and other search engine crawlers create a database of information on the Internet and learn what information is on each and every webpage they crawl. Once the information about a webpage is in a database, the search site can use the database to identify useful webpages and websites for people who use the search site.

What to crawlers collect?

Not all crawlers collect all of the information available on a webpage, but crawlers do have the option to collect any information that is publicly available on the webpages they visit. Since webpages are visible to anyone, a crawler can scan all of the visible information on a webpage and return this information to a database. However, there's more information on a webpage than just what appears to you when you see it on your computer or smartphone.

In addition to the visible information, webpages contain a wealth of hidden information that a crawler can scan and send back to its database. Text information such as file names and descriptions are contained in the web page's structure for items on the web page like pictures and graphic images, but don't appear on the visible webpage. This structure, or format, of a web page, is managed by a web standard formatting language called HyperText Markup Language (HTML for short), and you might already be familiar with the term.

Crawlers have priorities too

A 2009 study presented by A. Signorini and A. Gulli at the Association for Computing Machinery estimated that the Internet at that time had over 11.5 billion individual webpages. The study went on to determine that even the largest search engine crawlers probably identify and crawl no more than 40-70% of all webpages on the Internet, and other studies have set the number of webpages crawled at less than 20%.

Even the best and fastest software crawling programs have limits on how many webpages and websites they can reach, and how much information they can send back to their databases. As a result, crawlers have some rules their masters (the programmers who wrote the crawling programs) created to prioritize how they crawl the Internet.

Since we use the work done by search engine crawlers (Googlebot, etc..) I'll focus on how these types of crawlers decide what to do when they crawl the Internet. These crawlers prioritize their effort based on these factors:

What websites and what webpages to crawl

With the billions of web pages on the Internet, even the best crawlers can't get to every web page. Search Engine crawlers (like Googlebot) focus on crawling websites and the webpages that are most relevant to their users. Frequently visited websites, websites that update information often, websites that include many web pages and websites with links to other webpages are common ways search engine crawlers prioritize which websites to crawl.

How often to revisit a webpage or website

A crawler will keep track of how often a website updates with "fresh" information and how frequently those updates occur. The crawler then creates a schedule for how often to revisit the website. Crawlers have to balance the need to visit different websites with the need to visit a website that makes frequent updates. For the database of a Search Engine to be useful, it has to have the most current and up-to-date information about a website. For example, a news site like CNN.com needs to be crawled almost continuously to stay current, while a single webpage type of website might only need to be crawled once a month or even less.

Not overloading any website from crawling

When a crawler visits a website, the website considers the crawler a visitor just like a person visiting the website. Since the crawler "clicks" on links like a person, the website has to respond, which requires some computing effort on the part of the website and the computer that runs the website. Crawlers try to be "polite" not overburden the website and detract from functioning for people who use the website.

Synchronizes data collected from multiple crawlers

To crawl all the billions of webpages on the Internet search sites have multiple bots out working and sending back information. There's a chance that two bots might crawl the same website or webpages, so the crawler has to understand if the same website was visited by multiple bots and make sure to remove duplicate data.

If you have a website

For website owners, it's important to submit any new website address to Google and other search engines. While the Googlebot might find your website, if you submit your site address to Google, Google will know about it. The other two popular search sites on the Internet are Bin (Microsoft's) and Yahoo!. Yahoo! uses the Bing search site, so you only need to submit your website address to Bing, and you'll have taken care of both Bing and Yahoo!

Websites

Here are the addresses for both Google and Bing submission pages:

https://www.google.com/webmasters/tools/submit-url

http://www.bing.com/toolbox/submit-site-url

Keep in mind that if you have a website, the crawler will try to follow ALL of the links on your website, so if you have any confidential or private information on your website, work with your website developer or manager to make sure it's blocked from any crawling.

To my way of thinking

Web crawlers are a necessary tool for search engine sites to function and to help people find information on the billions of webpages that exist on the Internet. While crawlers can't crawl and identify all of the webpages that exist on the Internet since there are just too many of them, the work they do to find relevant and useful websites and create the search site databases is helping make the World Wide Web more useful for us every day.

Cross Platform Software

Cross-platform software is a type of software application that which works on multiple operating systems or devices, which are often referred to as platforms. A platform means an operating system such as Windows, Mac OS X, Android or iOS. When a software application works on more than one platform, the user can utilize the software on a wider choice of devices and computers.

The benefit of cross-platform software

The benefit of a cross-platform software app or program is that you can use the same program whether you're on a Windows PC or whether you're logging in from your laptop or smartphone. The Microsoft Office suite of applications, which includes Word, Excel, and PowerPoint, are available on Windows 10, Mac OS X, iOS (iPhone/iPad) and Android. While there are differences based on how the platforms work, you'll have a similar experience within the application between all of your devices.

Having a similar experience across any platform means there's a much smaller learning curve, if one even exists at all, so you'll be more productive and be able to use a software product you're familiar with regardless of the operating system or device you choose. In addition, your files can be moved much more easily between your devices so you can use the software with whatever device you have with you at the time. And there's a way to keep all of your work in sync across all of your devices, by using the cloud.

Syncing of files with cloud storage

Cross-platform software doesn't require the use of cloud storage, but cloud storage is often integrated into the software to make it easier to keep your documents and files in sync across all of your devices. Microsoft's Office 365 will automatically save your office files to a cloud drive, and Apple and Google also offer cloud storage for their cross-platform applications.

For example, if you own an Android smartphone, an iPad, and a Windows PC, you have three different platforms, all with different operating systems. A popular note taking app, Evernote, works on all of these platforms, as well as on Mac OS X. Evernote allows you to create a note on your phone and makes an identical copy available on any other device you use with the Evernote software.

Larger organizations like cross-platform hardware

Cross-platform software applications also allow large organizations like businesses and government agencies to keep the software running independently of the hardware platform and operating system. Often the investment in a software application for a large organization is much larger than the investment in hardware, so cross-platform software allows an organization to make hardware decisions independent of the software application.

Cross-platform software background

Cross-platform software didn't always exist. When a computer manufacturer such as IBM or Hewlett-Packard built a computer, they also typically created the operating system for their hardware. In the early days of computing, large organizations such as governments and businesses were the only type of customer that could afford computer systems, and software applications were created by their staff. When an application was built, it was created on a specific brand of hardware/operating system, and it only worked on that one type of platform.

Eventually, hardware manufacturers started offering their application software, and it was designed to help them sell hardware. In order to use the software application, the customer was required to purchase a specific type of hardware. There are still some of these types of applications for both large organizations and consumers. An example is Apple's GarageBand audio editing software, made by Apple and only available on Apple hardware products.

Software companies who want to sell more software choose to make their application available on many platforms, so it's possible for more customers to use their product. If the software application is available on both Windows 10 and Mac OS X, there are more potential customers.

Cross-platform software became more common with the rise of computer platforms such as Linux or Mac OS X. The advent and rise of smartphones have also led to increasing cross-platform compatibility. Many app developers create apps for both Android and iOS (Apple) devices. Making the app available on both of these popular platforms enables them to make the most money when selling their apps or through advertising revenue. Some apps, including social networks, work best when there is a larger user base. The software developer can then reach more users if the software is available across many platforms.

To my way of thinking

While Apple would prefer you buy all Apple products, and Microsoft all Windows products, people and organizations often have a mixed set of computing devices. While there are usually benefits to using a single platform solution, there are many reasons people and organizations own and use different platforms, and that's not likely to change.

Increasingly, even single-platform software is being adapted to the web, where it's often possible to use an application on almost any device that can access the Internet, giving you more freedom and choices that come from the availability of cross-platform software.

Crowdsourcing

Crowdsourcing is a way to obtain something that uses the cumulative work of any group of people. Instead of hiring or asking an organization to do a job that requires the efforts of many people, whoever needs the work done goes directly to individuals who perform the tasks.

Crowdsourcing usually uses a website to outsource work to an online community of people. The community can be open to the public or restricted to a group of invited members. Depending on the organization doing the crowdsourcing, they are called a crowdsource or crowdsourcer.

Crowdsourcing is used to outsource tasks, obtain feedback from customers or clients, and perform research. The work is distributed across many individuals. taking advantage of the power of the "crowd."

While some crowdsourcing is done to distribute tasks so many people can perform them, sometimes work is crowdsourced to obtain better results. A crowd of people who work collectively, whether in a virtual or physical setting, tend to produce better ideas and higher value than when they work independently.

Examples of crowdsourcing.

Wikipedia, the free Internet encyclopedia, is an example of how crowdsourcing can be successful. Wikipedia is the collaborative work of volunteer researchers, writers and editors around the world. The founders of Wikipedia did not hire employees or independent contractors to create and develop the content on the Wikipedia website. Instead, they crowdsourced that work to the public. The result? One of the most exhaustive encyclopedias ever created.

Companies run crowdsourcing websites to obtain suggestions for new product ideas. Using a crowdsourcing website, anyone can make a suggestion for new product features. The suggestion is made public and other website viewers can vote if they like a suggested product feature. The company can utilize what are essentially free ideas for product features and also see what ideas are most popular based on the votes from the crowd.

Crowdsourcing in Action

Instead of hiring an ad agency to think of ideas, Ford Motor Company invited people to film a stunt demo of the 2013 Focus ST and submit their videos. Ford used bits of footage from 20 submissions to produce a 30-second TV commercial for the new car. On a larger scale but similar note, an electrical parts manufacturer wanted to expand their customer base. Instead of hiring R&D employees or contractors, the company appealed to the masses by creating a website where anyone could submit new product ideas.

Crowdsourcing can lower costs

For any organization, crowdsourcing opens up an enormous source of labor. Some crowdsourcing sites are specifically designed to manage tasks. By distributing work across many people using the Internet, work can be done globally. Current technology allows a growing crowd of non-technical people to deliver their ideas and perform complicated and creative tasks at little to no cost to the crowdsourcer.

Amazon runs a large crowdsourcing site called Mechanical Turk. Amazon created this site first as an internal resource, then made it available for others to use for crowdsourcing. People and organizations who need work performed apply for an account, which is free. Then the work is described and posted for individuals to perform.

An example of a task might be to sort out and label a large photo library of automobiles by car model so it can be used in a database. Photos by themselves have no way for software to know what's in the photo, so this task is useful for any organization trying to manage a photo library. If you have photos on your computer, you have some idea of what this is like. Unless you created a label for every photo, you might have difficulty finding the proverbial needle in a haystack.

One way to do this work is to hire employees, another is to hire a contractor. By using Mechanical Turk, you can create a list of car models and provide a reference guide so anyone doing the work can identify a car and see how you want the photo labeled. Mechanical Turk lets you create a "task" for assigning a label to the photo. Then you would post your photo library and guide for workers to do the work. Once the job is up on the site, people who have applied to do work through the Mechanical Turk website can see the job requirements, what your pay rate is, and do the work.

Crowdsourcing isn't for all types of work

Certain types of tasks are better suited to crowdsourcing. Obviously, if work has to be done in a certain physical location it's not going to work to invite people over the Internet. If work has to be performed at a specific time or supervision is required, it's also not likely that it would be possible to crowdsource the work.

However, many types of work can be crowdsourced and often have these characteristics:

• The work can be performed remotely.

• An individual can accomplish the task.

• Instructions are easy to create and understand.

• Individual work can be combined into a larger result.

While organizations and businesses pay for crowdsourced work, there are many people who participate for free. They contribute to sites like Wikipedia and other non-paying crowdsourcing activities content with receiving personal recognition or participating in a community.

Crowdsourcing is Efficient

A business with a clear set of objectives can find a crowd of talented people, particularly from an online community, who are willing to work towards achieving those objectives. Crowdsourcing helps a business receive the best options because the crowd will offer its best ideas and skills. The business can choose from more than one best option as opposed to receiving one best option from one provider. From designing marketing campaigns to brainstorming new products to solving research and development problems, crowdsourcing can produce good quality results much quicker than traditional business methods.

Cyberloafing

Cyberloafing is a term that describes using the Internet while at work, to do anything that is not work related. Such activities include: sending personal emails, interacting on social media sites like Facebook or Twitter, watching movies or even searching for a home repairman. Cyberloafing is a slang term that came into being in the 1990s during the advent of the technological revolution. The prefix "cyber" refers to anything having to do with computers or the internet. Cyberloafing denotes wasting time instead of working.

Who's cyberloafing?

As computer related jobs have increased, so has the percentage of employees who engage in cyberloafing. According to a 2013 study by the Joseph Ugrin, an assistant professor of accounting at KSU, and John Pearson, an associate professor of management at Southern Illinois University, it's estimated that almost 80% of American employees are guilty of cyberloafing. That is up from 23% to 25% in the 1990s.

Many employers see cyberloafing as not only a threat to productivity but as a risk of increased liability if an employee breaks the law while online. To mitigate these concerns, many companies use special software to monitor their employees' online activities. Some companies use proxy servers to block access to questionable sites. Other companies try to find a balance between keeping employees happy and productive. -- update statistics

Many younger employees who were raised using computers see nothing wrong with browsing the Internet for personal reasons. To them, the Web has replaced the office water cooler, and email has replaced the telephone. The question, however, remains: Does cyberloafing result in decreased productivity?

Is cyberloafing good or bad for productivity?

Some studies by researchers indicate that cyberloafing increases productivity. Researchers theorize that cyberloafing provides a mental break needed to recover from work-related stress. Another study concluded that cyberloafing increased employee productivity by 16% over traditional work breaks away from the computer. However, both studies emphasized that there was a difference in results depending on the specific activity the employee is doing while cyberloafing. Emailing seemed to be counterproductive, while surfing the Web resulted in increased productivity.

Another interesting find by researchers concerned gender differences. Researchers discovered that men were more prone than women to cyberloaf. Men viewed cyberloafing as a necessary break from work. Women, on the other hand, had a more negative view of cyberloafing and preferred more traditional work breaks.

Do employees have any privacy at work?

For the most part, the answer is no. Employers generally have the legal right to monitor the performance of their employees in the workplace, and almost always include some language in their employee policies about monitoring electronic communications. Even if an employee uses a personal email account, if it's done while using a computer, smartphone, or Internet connection provided by the employer, the employer has the right to monitor an employee's activities. While an employer can monitor your workplace activity, it does not mean they are doing it all the time. But, if cyberloafing affects an employee's productivity, the employer may start taking a closer look at what the employee is doing.

To cyberloaf or not to cyberloaf?

Whether cyberloafing is stealing valuable time from an employer, or whether it is a necessary form of relaxation for over-taxed employees, the issue of cyberloafing is a dilemma faced by modern companies conducting business in the technological age. To my way of thinking, we all need to consider forms of relaxation other than cyberloafing. I've even heard that a very good way to relax and energize is getting up from your computer and taking a walk.

D

Datacenter

A data center is a facility filled with computing equipment that stores and allows easy access to digital information. It's like a library that houses books in a central location that is easy to access, only all the information is electronic.

If you've ever used a cloud service or a social media website such as Facebook, and wondered where all of that information "goes," the answer is that it gets stored in a data center.

Without data centers, the cloud and much of our use of the Internet would not be possible. You probably have a few questions now like, who runs them, what does a data center look like, how do they run, and why should you care about this?

Who runs data centers

Companies such as social media websites like Facebook, device makers like Apple, software companies like Microsoft, or communications companies run data centers to store enormous amounts of information, customer account information, phone messages, emails and other services that require storing vast amounts of data.

Governments and their agencies (think three letters) that monitor global communications also require large spaces in which to store information for analysis at a later date. Data centers are the most efficient way to store these enormous quantities of information, almost indefinitely.

Some data centers like a storage facility, where a smaller organization and individuals can rent space and equipment for their computing and storage. Even more amazing is that some data centers operate as computing utilities, where everyone rents computing resources. In fact, one of Amazon's largest lines of business is a service that rents computing and storage capacity on-demand, much like a utility provides electricity or water on an as-needed basis. Many cloud services and websites use Amazon's network of data centers and just write a check every month rather than own their own equipment and space.

What do data centers look like?

Data centers can come in any variety of sizes, from as small as a room to the size of a modern shopping mall. It's not the size that makes a facility a data center; it's the fact that it was built to hold computer equipment.

Computers and computing equipment use power and generate heat. You may have noticed that any room in your home that has a computer seems a little warmer than other rooms, and this is because of the heat generated by your computing equipment.

Most home and office computers have a "standby" mode which reduces power consumption and heat when you're not using them, but in a data center, the computers run all the time. Put a few dozen, a few hundred, or thousands of computers in one room, and you get the idea.

The computers and electronics in data centers mount in racks and take up much less space than our home equipment. Looks and appearance on a desk don't matter, it's size and space utilization that counts so many of the pieces of equipment are about the size of large coffee table sized books. The sides of these "books" have brackets for mounting in a rack so many of them can be stacked in a small amount of floor space.

Power, cooling, and locations for data centers

Large mall-size data centers require a great deal of electricity in order to support the machinery, as well as needing a way to keep it cool. The largest data centers use as much energy as a small town so finding reliable, low-cost electricity is important, as well as a locale with a cooler temperature that needs less air-conditioning.

As a result, data centers are built around the world and often companies locate their data centers near each other since they all need reliable, low-cost power and a cooler climate. In the United States, the Portland area is a popular location for data-centers on the west coast. It's close to the Columbia River dams that generate reliable power for much of Oregon, and it's not a hot-weather area.

Another requirement for data centers is a fast Internet connection so that all of the computers and data can be accessed through the Internet from outside of the data center. After all, having it all in one place doesn't make sense unless you can get to the computers and data fast. With improvements in network technology and equipment, Internet and network connections of all types have become faster, which has allowed organizations to centralize computers in a location.

In a way, we're moving back to an older style of computing that used mainframes and dumb terminals where people used a desktop device to access information and software that was centrally managed by an information technology staff.

One is not enough

Organizations like to use data centers in different locations to create redundancy and have a back-up in case a disaster affects one data center. If one data center cannot operate, another data center can take over the computing and use a back-up copy of the data. The backup process is usually automatic, but the software and expertise required to manage it requires a lot of technical preparation. Providing customers virtually non-stop access their accounts, data, and information requires computer experts and a well-designed data center operation with lots of planning for any contingency.

The ability to keep the computers and equipment running is a priority for any data center operation, and backup for power outages is an important issue. Most data centers come with a backup power supply if they ever lose access to their primary source, such as when they experience a blackout during a storm. Systems such as gas generators or batteries keep the data center running during a power outage.

Environment and security

The environmental impact of a large data center is significant, usually because of the power consumption. As a result, companies are looking into ways in which to provide environmentally friendly data centers which use less power. Some data centers that don't need to be near population centers are being moved to arctic locations, like Norway as the outside air temperature helps to cool the data center machinery.

Because information is a valuable commodity, data centers often use sophisticated security devices to prevent unauthorized entry to the facility both physically and electronically.

To my way of thinking

Moving that picture to the cloud, sending an email, accessing an online bank account, booking a trip, or posting on a social media site use the resources of a data center, which is pretty amazing and has changed all of our lives immensely.

Devices

A device is a computer that simply isn't a personal computer. It includes a CPU, memory, and a way for a person to use the device. A device can do many, if not all, of the things a personal computer can do because it is a computer by any other name. It's called a device because it just doesn't have the traditional case, monitor, keyboard, and mouse we often associate with a personal computer. In a way, devices are to computers like breeds are to dogs.

Your already probably familiar with what a dog it, so let me draw a little comparison between computers and dogs. Dogs are four legged mammals with fur that are all descendants of a type of wolf. Humans, through breeding, have created all kinds of breeds of dogs in an amazing assortment of sizes, shapes, colors, and temperaments. But chances are you can recognize a dog when you see one, regardless of what breed it is. Devices are like the different breeds of dogs, only they are different breeds of computers, and we haven't stopped making up new ones.

Common Devices

The most common devices are tablets and smartphones, but devices can also come in other forms. Let's take on tablets, smartphones and look at some other "devices." Tablets Apple is credited with making the tablet popular with its iPad product, and now there are other manufacturers of tablet devices since they have become a popular form of computer. Tablets are a computer, with a CPU, storage, and a screen. The screen uses a technology called a "touchscreen" (explained later in the mobile section) and a person uses the tablet by touching the screen. The touch causes the device to respond.

What's happened is that your fingers have become the mouse and your taps are the equivalent of mouse clicks. The keyboard is part of the display, and when it appears your fingers can make contact with the display to enter text. So tablets have all the major parts of a personal computer, which include a CPU, memory, storage, along with a display, keyboard, and "mouse" which is your finger contact. If this sounds a lot like a personal computer, you've got the right idea since a tablet is at it's most basic definition another physical form of a computer.

Smartphones

Smartphones (explained in more detail later in the mobile section) are phones that do more than just make phone calls. The popular definition of a smartphone is a device with a CPU, storage, a touchscreen, and includes it's own phone number for making and receiving phone calls. It's actually just another type of computer. These are smaller than a tablet (so you can hold it up to your ear to make a phone call), and include a built-in phone. Think of a smartphone as a portable computer with a phone function built-in and you've got the right idea. So maybe you know about tablets and smartphones and are willing to accept that they are "devices" that are really just a different size and shape. But there are more devices out there.

Other Devices

There are other types of devices besides smartphones and tablets which are computers. They don't fit the traditional definition of a personal computer, and they aren't a tablet, or a smartphone, but they have the basics of a computer. Often these are computers dedicated to a specific function or a type of activity. Game consoles, which are pretty common, are one type of device you might know about, and these are computers designed specifically to play games. The Sony Playstation, Microsoft XBox, and the Nintendo Wii are common Game Consoles. They have a CPU, memory, use game controllers instead of a keyboard/mouse, and typically use a television as a display.

As the power of computing hardware improves, devices sometimes cross over into other functions. And this is blurring the lines of computing. Devices can include forms of computers that might already exist such as a game console, but you might be hearing about "wearable" computers. Google already has produced a set of glasses with a computer built-in, and several hardware manufacturers have announced plans for a "watch" device.

To my way of thinking

I visited a dog show and was amazed at the number of breeds of dogs. All of these sizes, shapes, colors, and temperaments are dogs, and you can probably recognize a dog when you see one. Computers are a lot like dog breeds. Remember, as long as it has a CPU, memory, and it does calculations of some sort, it's a computer by any other name.

Digital Native

Digital Natives and Digital Immigrants are terms used to describe where people fall on the technology timeline based on when they were born, before or after 1980. The term has nothing to do with how tech literate people are, just has to do with when they were born. The concept was created by Mark Prensky in a 2001 article, "Digital Natives, Digital Immigrants."

I heard this term recently when I was preparing for a class and an English instructor was still in the room packing up. During our discussion, he mentioned that he was a High School English teacher and that what it's not safe to assume that a Digital Native always knows how to use technology. He described a situation where he had to show one of High School students how to print the page using a computer in the school's computer lab. Being a certain age doesn't mean a person is or isn't "tech savvy."

When I heard him mention the term Digital Native, I thought explaining it would offer an possible explanation of how the relationship between age and technical expertise has come about.

Who are Digital Natives?

Digital Natives are defined as those born after 1980 following the introduction of digital technology. In other words, they are "born into it." In many parts of the world, Digital Natives are surrounded by technology, often from their early childhood, and their daily activities include learning and using digital technology. Digital Natives are savvy to smartphones, iPads, xBox, Facebook and other technology. Whether or not they embrace it, they can't remember a time when technology as it is today did not exist.

Who are Digital Immigrants

Digital Immigrants are those born prior to 1980. According to the definition by Mark Prensky, these are the people who grew up reading newspapers, playing board games and cards, know what a record is, and watched the news and weather on television. A large portion of Digital Immigrants still do so and are quite content with their lives, often mixing "older" ways of doing things with newer digital technologies. It's just that Digital Immigrants didn't grow up in with today's "always-on" technology.

The funny thing about Digital Immigrants is that it contains the very people who often created the technology in the first place. Many Digital Immigrants also love new technology and can't wait to get their hands on the newest gadget. And, just to be clear, not all Digital Immigrants are technologically impaired, just as not all Digital Natives are digital geniuses, nor do they all want to be.

Who knows more about technology?

As I mentioned earlier, which one you are does not dictate how much you know about technology. A teenager born in an Amish community in 1998 that has never touched a cell phone or video game controller, much less a laptop is considered a Digital Native while Bill Gates is a Digital Immigrant. The concept is falling out of favor, however, because it doesn't apply to vast groups of people, such as third world or impoverished cultures and societies like the Amish. It's a bit difficult to group people based on something that doesn't exist in their culture. It really only applies to industrialized nations, such as here in the U.S., who have technology just about everywhere.

Domain Name

"Domain" is a term that is widely used in Internet speak. It refers to a space on the Web that's reserved for a website. Just like you have a home, a website also needs a home, and it's referred to as a domain. To visit a web page, you must provide a Web address that is unique to it.

How Do Domains Work?

The system of domains on the Web operates in kind of the same way as the U.S. postal system works for snail mail. Every house, apartment, store, and location has its unique address, and when you send a letter to a particular place, its address will take it to that location.

In the same way, a website needs to have a domain name to be found. Just as a street address has two parts, the number and the street name, each Web site on the Internet has two parts: the text on the left side of the dot or period; and the text to the right of the dot or period. All domain names must carry both of these parts. The text on the right side of the dot must come from a list which is managed exclusively by an international organization called ICANN.

Common examples of these used in the United States might include .com, .net, .org, .info, .edu, or .gov or .me. Many additional ones are used internationally, and many countries have their individual ones that are assigned by ICANN.

Using a Domain Name for a Web Site

Choosing an effective domain name calls for creativity, but before you secure that name, you must perform a search to ensure that the domain name you want is available ~ that is, it isn't already being used. This search is done through companies that perform domain-name registration. When you request a domain name from one of these providers, they will search the Internet to ensure that the name is not being used. Yahoo!, GoDaddy, Network Solutions, and many others, as well as companies that host Web sites can do this.

Domain Names, Hosting and Email

Many people assume that it's necessary to have your website with the same service that registers your domain name. You can use two different services, one for domain name registration and another for your site location. The domain name system on the Internet uses information to point to where your website is located, so it's feasible to use one company for your domain name and another one for your site.

The services that provide domain name registration usually include a free domain email address. A domain email puts your domain name in your email address, so it reads "john@mydomainname.com" or "marcy@thedomainnameIuse.com." Using an email address that contains your domain name puts it in front of every person you send an email to and will help people remember how to find you on the Internet.

Domain Names are Borrowed

When you register a domain name with a service, you are reserving the use of that domain name for the period you pay your registration fee, usually an annual amount ranging from $10-15 per year. If you don't pay, you lose the rights to the domain, and anyone else can claim it for their use. Domain registration services include the ability to auto-renew as well as multi-year registrations, so you don't have to worry about remembering to renew the registration.

Domain names and Social Media accounts

Obtaining the domain name of your choice can often be difficult since so many of them are already in use. Now, with Social Media sites, using the same name for your Social Media services can be challenging.

Let's say your domain name is samsseafood.com, and you want to use samsseafood for your Facebook Page name. You might find that someone is already using the address facebook.com/samsseafood, in which case you aren't able to use it. Twitter, LinkedIn, Instagram, YouTube and other sites give you a user account which appears after their domain name, so your account will always be after the backslash in the Social Media site domain name.

A useful service recommended by one of my students that helps identify where a name is used on the Internet is called NameChk.com. A free service, NameChk lets you see if the domain name you want to use is already registered, and if the name is in use on Social Media sites. Using NameChk can help you make a decision on choosing a domain name that can be used for your website and for Social Media accounts to maintain consistency.

To my way of thinking

Domain names make it easier for people to find websites they want to locate since the Internet can fetch a web page as long as you know the domain name and enter it in your browser.

For people or organizations using a domain name, it gives them a way to create a brand identity on the Internet.

Download(s)

A download is a file you can acquire from a computer on a network and save to your local computer or device. Moving a file is called downloading, which refers to the process of moving a file from a networked computer to your local device.

Downloading takes a file, usually from the Internet, and copies it to your computer's memory so you can access it when you're not connected to the Internet (I'll use the word computer to refer to any device with local memory, which can include smartphones and tablets). A download is the opposite of an upload, which is when you send a file from your computer 'up' to the Internet.

Why download?

There are many reasons why you might want to use downloaded files. You might want a local copy of a document to make changes, a copy of a song to play, or the owners manual for an appliance stored locally on your computer. Download files can be made up of anything that can be stored in a computer file, which is a wide range of information. What's in the download file isn't relevant to downloading, since downloading just has to do with moving the file from one place to another.

When do downloads occur?

Downloading occurs fairly often in day-to-day computing activity. It happens any time you save an attached file from an email, anytime you update a software program, and anytime you visit a webpage and "download" the images and text from a webpage to your computer. In case you didn't know it, when you visit any website, you are downloading a webpage file from the Internet to your computer, and the browser software program installed on your computer displays the file (called an htm or html file).

To download a file is simply to 'load' something 'down' from the internet to your computer. It's similar to making a photocopy of a document or a page from a book that you can only find in a library. By copying a page, you are creating a second copy that you can hold on to and use when you leave the library. You have "downloaded" a physical copy of the information, and your copy is available for you to take with you and use.

Paid downloads

Not all downloads are free. Some websites (like the Apple App Store, Amazon, and Google Play Store) sell software or electronic documents which they sell for a fee. These types of downloads are products, they just don't exist physically, but you buy access to the document, song, video, or program just the same, and move a copy to your computer.

Risks with downloads

Some downloads are hazardous and include malware, which is often included in spam email attachments. A good virus protection software will help, but don't open the downloaded file if you don't know the source. Even with malware and antivirus protection, it's best to only download files from sites you trust or official websites from trustworthy companies.

Making the most of downloads

Downloading is one of the primary, most useful functions of the Internet. It has made the Internet the best source for many things that we used to have to go to the store and purchase. There are many forms a download can take, and many reasons you may want to download those files.

Some downloads enable you to install new apps and programs; other downloads can take the form of pictures or music files. For example, you might go to your library's website to download music or electronic books. You might visit the public radio website to download the radio show to your computer or phone for listening later. If someone you know posts a good picture of you, your friends or family on the internet, you might download it so that you can print copies. If you want a new program to write or paint with, you would go to that program's web page to download it. You can even download games.

With billions of computers, smartphones and tablets, along with faster Internet speeds for home, office, WiFi and cellular, downloading has become one of our most common daily activities. The fact that downloading happens so often and so easily has given people access to a new world of information and content.

Dropbox

Dropbox was originally referred to as an online data and information backup service. Now that the term cloud storage has become better known Dropbox promotes itself as a personal cloud storage service. As with other cloud data storage services, Dropbox makes file sharing and collaboration much easier than before the cloud and other such storage services were available. Dropbox works with Operating systems for computers running desktop operating systems for Windows, Macintosh and Linux. There are also apps for smart phones Android, iPhone, RIM-Blackberry and for iPad devices.

The Dropbox service provides less free storage than the other cloud data storage systems, with only 2 gigabytes allowed on a free plan. There are another 100 gigabytes that can be obtained from one of the Dropbox for-fee plans. For companies or organizations that have a lot of collaboration taking place, there is a special Dropbox for Teams plan, providing 350 gigabytes of storage. Dropbox uses a third party storage location, which is the Amazon Simple Storage Service and encrypted in several ways.

Dropbox provides an application that places a special folder on the user's desktop. This folder works like all other folders but is meant for files and documents the user plans to share or have access to from anywhere else or on any other machine. As with other services, logging into the Dropbox service allows access and the ability to download, share and upload files. If the Dropbox user wants to share a file with others, they may generate a unique URL. Anyone with that URL and an Internet connection may view the document online, restricted only by authority to use and/or modify the file. All versions of files are saved in case errors are made.

An interesting side note is that Dropbox is named for video film vendors, libraries, post offices and banks where people can drop off items securely after hours.

E

Ebook

An ebook is just the digital form of a regular book. Instead of having an inch-thick novel in your hands, you have a file sitting in your computer, tablet, smartphone, or ebook reader.

You can read ebooks on your desktop or laptop, but if you want them to feel like the real thing, you can read them using your tablet instead. Tablets with a screen size of 7-inches are about the same size as a trade paperback, so you can at least pretend that you have a printed book in your hands.

Advantages of Ebooks

The great thing about ebooks is that you can have thousands of them in your ebook reader or tablet. You can switch between ebooks anytime you like. This surely beats standing up from your bed and reaching for a new book from the shelf. Also, think of the convenience when you travel! You don't have to lug around books in your hand-carry anymore.

If some printed books seem to have really tiny text that makes them hard to read, you can say goodbye to that problem. Another great thing about ebooks is that you can change the font size to suit your vision. You don't have to squint anymore to make out the words. Conversely, you can make the font smaller if you want to take in as much as you can in a single page.

When you want to buy ebooks, you don't have to go to the bookstore and look for the titles you like. Just log on to online stores and buy as many ebooks as you want from the comfort of your own home. And guess what? Ebooks are less expensive than printed books because they don't use paper to be mass-produced. Thus, you can sustain your bookworm lifestyle without hurting your budget.

Amazon started pushing ebooks when they started shipping their ebook reader, the Kindle. With a low cost, and with a screen that uses e-ink, it made ebooks popular. Amazon just happened to be a very large online bookstore, and along with the Kindle device, Amazon has made sure that customers can access an extremely large collection of ebooks online. Amazon makes a free Kindle app available for Android and Apple devices, in addition to their own readers. Their approach to buying ebooks is "purchase once, read everywhere." So if you have an Apple or Android smartphone or tablet, you can read your Amazon books using the Kindle app.

Ebook Readers and Apps

In addition to Kindle devices, iPads, iPhones, Android tablets, and personal computers, there are a few other ways to purchase and read ebooks. Barnes & Noble offers ebooks through their Nook reader device, and the free Nook app is available for Apple and Android devices. Apple offers books through their iBooks app, and Google has books available from their Google Play store. Google even makes a reader app called Google Reader that works on Apple devices.

Public libraries offer ebook borrowing and have apps that usually work with Kindle, Apple, and Android mobile devices. Your local library can tell you what app they use and how to borrow ebooks from their collection.

Ebook Stores

Something to be aware of when buying an ebook from one store is that it you will likely need the app or device from that store to read your book. In order to keep you as a customer, some of the ebook stores don't let you read your ebook in another app or device. For example, any ebook you purchase on Amazon requires a Kindle reader or Kindle app, and your Amazon ebook can't be accessed by the iBook of Nook app.

Since Amazon, Google, and Nook are all available apps for Apple and Android devices, you just need to install the app on your tablet or device to read the book. A nook reader, however, won't be able to access your Amazon books. As a result, the iPad is the most versatile device since the iBook app is only available on Apple devices, and as a result, Apple devices have the widest selection of ebook reader apps.

However, since Amazon is such a large ebook store, Amazon still has the edge over all the other ebook stores in selection and availability of ebooks. As a result, many people have both a Kindle reader and a tablet. The Kindle is less expensive than a tablet and with the latest technology from Amazon, called Paperwhite, it almost looks like a printed page.

Earlier Kindles didn't have any built-in lighting, but newer models do, and make an excellent dedicated ebook reader which I still consider the best ebook reader on the market.

Printed Books Are Still OK

The printed book is still an excellent way to read. It's lightweight, portable, and many people still prefer the fresh smell of the pages of a new book. But you've got to admit that ebooks have their own uses and charm.

Emoji and Emoticons

Emojis are images used in text-based communication that express an idea or concept, and emoticons are characters or images that express an emotion. You've probably seen the smiley face emoticon ☺ used in messages. They are often used in similar situations and the terms are often used interchangeable, but they each have a slightly different history and meaning.

Why they are popular

Using these graphics and symbols, you can express feelings such as; happiness or anger, as well as communicate concepts such as; surprise, and adding more meaning to the message. Instead of providing an entire line of text to tell someone you're unhappy, a simple graphic of a frowning face tells the recipient how you feel.

Email and text messages have become a standard way to communicate. However, typing a message removes the interpersonal connection that can show moods or further communicate ideas. People are "wired" genetically to interpret facial expressions and voices. Take away the face-to-face built-in capabilities we have to understand a shout, laugh, smile, or frown, and our ability to communicate a message depends on words alone, and the experience of the writer. To be honest, while more of us use text methods of communication, not all of us are skilled at communicating emotions and context in our text. So, as a result, emoji and emoticons can be our helpers.

History of the terms.

Emoticons have been around for quite some time. The term itself is a shortened combination of "Emotion Icons." They are used to portray your emotions or moods while you are sending a message, email, in social media posts, or in any text message. Since a text-based communication doesn't provide a way to observe someone's facial expression or tone of voice, messages can be misinterpreted without this human feedback, hence, the usefulness of inserting an emoticon. A smile can change the interpretation of the message, and help the reader understand your context.

For example, a simple joke can be taken out of context unless you add a ":)" within the message, the symbolic smiley face emoticon, which helps clarify the meaning of the information. There are many ways that emoticons can be inserted from smiling to expressing tears of happiness, or even horror and disgust.

Text emoticons and images

Today, emoticons are often replaced by actual images and many text-based applications will automatically convert the symbol from text to the image. Try it sometime in an email or on your smartphone by typing a colon and right parentheses characters (with no space between them) and you might see it automatically converted to a smiley face image. While not all moods have been incorporated into these systems, the most popular emotional expressions are present. For a list, here's a link to the Wikipedia link http://en.wikipedia.org/wiki/List_of_emoticons of emoticon text symbols.

Differences between emoji and emoticons

Emojis are different from emoticons. While an emoticon denotes your emotional state, an emoji can have a complete meaning and thought behind the picture. For example, you could use the image of a clock, bus, and school building to send a three character message stating that it's "time to go to school."

Emojis center more around ideas rather than the emotions of the person composing the message. The use of emoji's originated in Japan, and the word emoji means "picture character." The range of emoji is broader than emoticons and includes pictures of animals, transportation, business icons, and others.

However, there are a lot of emoticons integrated into the list of emoji simply because of how incredibly popular the system for emotions had become for digital communication. Smiling, crying, laughing and angry faces can express emotions inside a group of emoji. For example, placing a smiling face before the clock in the example above to tell your reader that you are happy it's time to go to school.

Where can I use emoji and emoticons?

An international organization called Unicode (www.unicode.org) helps to maintain industry standards for characters used in text messages, websites, and mobile devices. Most major technology companies use this standard for their hardware and software, and the Unicode standard includes symbols for emoticons and emoji, which has helped to make the use of the terms interchangeable. As a result of this standard, most computers, mobile devices, websites, and software applications can use and display emoji and emoticon symbols, as long as the symbol is included in the industry standard.

For computer users, inserting and using emoticons is done using the keyboard characters for the symbols, which will usually result to the symbol appearing automatically after the space key is pressed after the last character. Another way is to use the menu option called Insert, then select Symbol. Selecting this will display the emoticon and emoji symbols you can insert with a click.

Adding emoji and emoticon symbols to a mobile device.

For mobile devices, you can usually add a set of emoji and emoticons as an additional keyboard.

For iPhone and iPad users, go to Settings, then General, then select Keyboards. Select Add New Keyboard, then look in the list for Emoji and tap it. When you use your keyboard, look to the left of the space bar for a globe symbol, tap this and you can switch between your standard keyboard and the emoji symbol keyboard.

For Android devices, the emoji keyboard is built-in in the latest version, called KitKat, which allows you to press and hold the enter or search key to access the emoji keyboard. Older Android versions will require an Emoji keyboard app for installation (there are dozens), and applications sometimes include their own emoji symbols since it hasn't been included in Android until recently.

If you get right down to it.

Emoticons and emoji are simple methods anyone can use in order to deliver a message. Whether you are trying to express a joke through text or want to send an ultra quick pictographic sentence about your plans for after work, these images can deliver almost any message you want to write, add more expression to your communication, and can be fun to use. Who knows, you might impress your friends and family with your newfound skills!

Encryption

Before there were smartphones and computers, encryption was used to create coded messages in a way that allowed only authorized people to read them. Encryption describes any method to create a coded message and computers use software programs to accomplish this. An encrypted message requires a "key" generated by the software to open the message, which "decrypts" the message. Without the correct key, the message is unreadable, so encryption is like a lock on a door of a house, only it's a lock on a data or file such as an email message, a credit card number, or other private information.

History of Encryption

The term encryption comes from cryptography, the field of creating and decoding secret messages. Cryptography has been used for thousands of years to communicate with words that can't be understood if they are intercepted. The word cryptography is derived from the Greek word kryptos, which means hidden. Encryption of messages is commonly used by military organizations so communications can take place secretly, and there are some stories about encryption.

You might have heard of the Enigma machine, which was Germany's cryptographic technique used during World War II. It was the subject of the recent movie "The Imitation Game" starring Benedict Cumberbatch as Alan Turing, the mathematician who broke the code. An encrypted the British were able to use to intercept messages, but the coded messages were impossible to understand until the system was broken and the decryption key was discovered.

The effort to decrypt the Enigma messages used work that Polish intelligence started on as early as 1932 when they broke the original Enigma machine. Improvements and changes by the Germans required the British five and a half months, even using the prior work shared with them by Polish intelligence. Alan Turing created a computer to decrypt the messages from the Enigma machine, but a new encryption code created by the Germans every day required the description process to being every day and sometimes it wasn't finished in time to decode the messages. Turing's work reverse engineering the Enigma machine resulted in many principles of modern computer science.

There's another type of secrecy related to cryptography called steganography, which is the technique of concealing a message. The term comes from the Greek words steganos (to cover), and graphein (to write) and is an ancient method of concealment. With cryptography, the message can't be understood but can be intercepted; with steganography the message is concealed, so it's hidden. The need to protect information before there were computers produced some creative methods using steganography.

In ancient Greece and Persia, messages were sent using a steganographic technique that shaved the hair off a messenger's head. The text was written on the scalp of the messenger, and when his hair grew back, he was sent to deliver the message. If captured, the only way the enemy would know about the message was if they shaved the messenger's head. Of course, once the enemy learned about the technique, the messages could be intercepted, and a new system was required. The weakness of steganography is that once someone learns how the information was hidden, they can read every future message.

Encryption on computers and smartphones

Encryption on electronic devices and smartphones use software programs that scramble the file and create a unique code to lock and unlock the file or message. An unencrypted email message can be read by anyone who can open it. The process of encryption takes all of the information in the email message and scrambles it into meaningless combinations of characters and assigns a piece of data, the key, that is required to unlock and unscramble the characters back into readable information.

Here's an example of how you could encrypt a message with a simple encryption method called substitution. Let's say you want to send a coded message to someone that said: "I walked my dog." By substituting the next letter of the alphabet in the words, you could create a coded message that reads "j xbmlfe nz eph." Someone would have to figure out what method you used, to create your message to unlock or decrypt it. Your method for coding the message requires that the reader understands the key to unlocking the message. In this example is a simple process of letter substitution, but it still conceals the original message.

Now imagine that you had a powerful calculator that could create much more complex scrambling of characters, numbers, symbols and spaces and you have an idea of the power of encryption with computers.

With the calculating ability of today's chips, it has become possible to create software keys that can make a device or program tamper-proof. Software companies, websites, and device makers are sensitive to the privacy concerns of their customers and include encryption tools for users. You might not have realized you were using an encryption method when using the Internet, buy here are some examples you might have used without knowing it.

Encryption is necessary for computer security when using the Internet since it's a public network The Internet is a public network, and as a result, any message or file can be intercepted, so encryption offers a way for people to use the Internet and keep information secure and safe. While usernames and passcode provide a level of security to make it harder for someone to access any accounts you use, encryption creates an additional layer of secrecy for information which requires anyone to use the right decryption key to unlock the message.

The https prefix

Secure websites use the "https" prefix with the added "s" to note that the website is secure. With a secure site, the information sent between your computer and the website is encrypted and can't be understood or read by anyone except you or the website. Online banking websites and shopping carts use this method of web encryption for secure online transactions. The encryption on https website is extremely strong and decrypting an https message would be virtually impossible, so this type of data is very secure.

Another method is to encrypt the code used to unlock an entire device, like a smartphone.

The passcode lock on iPhones, other iOS devices, and Android devices is an encrypted code that is required to unlock and use the device. Since the device owner is the only person who knows the passcode, the device is useless to anyone else since Apple requires the device to be unlocked before any apps or data can be accessed. If too many attempts are made to unlock the device with an incorrect passcode, the device is permanently locked.

iOS devices give you ten attempts to enter your passcode while Android devices give you three attempts before you're locked out permanently. The hardware can be reset to factory settings, but this destroys all of the data on the device.

How good is encryption?

It took the British team led by Alan Turing about five and half months to decrypt the Enigma machine, which was a mechanical device. Modern computers and software programs have significantly more calculating power and can create encryption keys that are almost impossible to break. It's not to say that any encrypted file or message can't be accessed; it's that the effort to do so may be available to only people (like governments) with the computing power and resources to do so. Even then, success isn't guaranteed, and the encryption may be so effective that it could be impossible to read the data.

To my way of thinking

Keeping information private is possible using methods like encryption. Technology makes it possible to encrypt messages, information, devices and files that might require a massive effort to decrypt. Who should have access to someone's private secrets and when is something that you'll have to determine, but knowing what encryption is and how it works can help you understand the technology better.

For some additional reading on the history of cryptography, check out this article at Fordham University by Jacob Mathai

http://www.dsm.fordham.edu/~mathai/crypto.html

Ethernet

Ethernet is the most widely used technology for wired (as opposed to wireless) network connections and is an industry standard managed by the International Electronics and Engineering Association (IEEE). Wireless technologies such as WiFi or Bluetooth have their specifications and standards. While a network may have a combination of wired and wireless connections (such as a wired computer and a wireless laptop), the wired part of the network refers to Ethernet.

Invention of Ethernet

Ethernet was developed by Bob Metcalfe at Xerox PARC in the mid-1970s, and made an IEEE (802.3) standard in 1983. Ethernet technology eventually replaced the use of many vendors-specific networking protocols by the mid-1980s because it used less expensive twisted-pair cable wiring and was an industry, rather than a company standard.

Ethernet technology is more than just a cabling specification. Any technology such as a wire, connector, computer, or network device that uses the term "Ethernet" must meet and comply with the specifications for Ethernet technology. Having an industry standard gives any product maker the ability to design their products using the standard and provides consumers and businesses with product choices.

What Ethernet includes.

The Ethernet standard of 802.3 is now part of a larger set of standards that cover both wired and wireless network technologies referred to by the IEEE as the 802 standards. The original Ethernet specifications for networks described specifications for what are called "layers." Each layer described the technical specifications for a particular part of how Ethernet and network communications between two connected devices would work.

The concept of layers for Ethernet works a little like a house. At the bottom you have a foundation, then a frame, walls, a roof and other hardware such as plumbing and wiring. The furnishings can change depending on who moves in and what the occupants bring with them.

Layers

Ethernet includes a number of layers, but to keep it simple I'll describe the two most important ones, the physical and data link layers. The physical layer is the actual physical cable, connector, or adapter that is used to carry information across wires that meet the Ethernet standard. When you plug an Ethernet cable from your computer into your home based router, you're using the physical layer of the Ethernet specification. The cable and connectors, along with the network circuits of the devices are physical components and by using the Ethernet 802.3 standard, they all work with each other.

The other important layer is the data link layer, and this is the layer you don't see. The data link layer is the part of the specification that describes how the bits of data are "packaged" in order to send them from one device to another. The data link layer makes sure our email messages are sent and received, and pictures from websites appear on our screens. All of the information consists of digital data (zeros and ones) and the link part of the data link layer makes sure sending and receiving information (email, pictures, etc.) from one Ethernet-connected device arrives accurately and safely.

Sending data from one device to another is something we take for granted since it happens so easily but in the 1970's connecting multiple computers together on a network was a challenge. Imagine when only a few hundred people owned automobiles. There simply wasn't a need for traffic signs or rules of the road. Put a few million cars on the road and the rules become very important. As computer users wanted to connect more computers to each other, rules were needed to make sure data didn't collide or get lost and the Ethernet specification is a set of rules for how a piece of data travels over the network.

Collisions and errors

Two important parts of the Ethernet specification describe how a physical device like a computer or router is detected by the network and what happens with lost or damaged data. The specification spells out what happens when data collides over the network and how the data is retransmitted so the correct data is sent and received.

To solve the need to send lots of data, Ethernet carries multiple bits of data in a larger package called a "frame." A whole piece of information like an email or picture uses many individual frames, so Ethernet describes how the data (like the picture or email) is broken down into frames. So if the data is broken into pieces like frames, you might be asking how the frames get reassembled on the receiving end so we can read the email or see the picture?

Each frame contains a special piece of information about previous and next frame in the sequence for the whole package of data, like the email or picture. Each piece of network hardware can verify that each piece of data is correct on the network and see if any frame is missing in the whole sequence. If one is, or if a frame is damaged or incomplete, the hardware can ask the source for any missing or incomplete frames.

Other things Ethernet describes

Each Ethernet network has a layout called a topology - a set of rules for what devices physically connect to what parts of the network. For very small networks, like typical home uses, that topology looks like a hub and spokes. The central hub is a router, and each computer connected to the router has to have a network adapter installed on it. Larger networks use larger, more specialized equipment, called "hubs" and "switches." Many times a home or small office Ethernet network is referred to as a Local Area Network, while larger Ethernet networks are referred to as Metropolitan Area Networks.

Ethernet also comes in different speeds described in the 802.3 specification. The hardware, cabling, and adapters are all rated to operate at a specific network speed. The most common types used in home and small business networks are Category 5 and Category 3 cables, connectors, and adapters. The cables and connectors have speed ratings, such as a Category 5 (Cat5) which can operate at 100 Megabits per second. However, the physical components, the cable, connectors and computer adapter ports all need to be Cat5 in order for the maximum speed to be available. If you use a component with a slower speed rating, your whole network is slower.

As new technology is introduced, Gigabit speeds have become available on Ethernet, which can transfer a full-length movie over a network in less than a second. You might have a computer with a Gigabit Ethernet connector but if your wiring or router only operate at 10 Megabits per second, you'll only be able to send and receive 10 Megabits per second over the network connection.

Cable length is also part of the specification. The Category 3 and Category 5 cables are limited to a maximum of 100 meters while other cable types have longer distance ratings. It's possible to create longer distance networks using a network device such as router or hub to extend the network.

To my way of thinking

Since it was invented, Ethernet has gone through many improvements and will continue to improve as new technologies emerge, changing the standard along with it to accommodate new and improved technologies.

But it's worth knowing that the technology is being managed by the IEEE and as a result of being an industry standard, allows consumers and business to make network cable connections easily and quickly using components from many different manufacturers.

F

Facebook

If you were someone who was trying to engage with friends and family online, then you want to be on social media. Facebook (facebook.com) is a social media site where users network online. The site gives you connection to other online users who you choose to interact. Engagements on Facebook include updates about peoples lives or day to day activities. It can also be used for entertainment purposes, keeping in touch with others, as well as engaging with family and friends.

How do you use Facebook?

Facebook has a way for people to sign-up on their site online at Facebook.com. Once you register to use the site, you can create a user profile. After you make a profile with your information, you can change your personal settings to your choice. This will enable how much of your profile you want to be seen by those you later add.

Adding users

Adding someone is quick and easy. You can either type the name of the person into the search section on the top of the website. Or, users can request to add you using your name or email. Additionally, users can join groups such as work related, school, or other various categories. You may also add users to different friends lists such as "Close Friends", "Family", "Restricted", and "People From Work".

Messaging users

Apart from adding other users as "friends," you can send and receive messages, post updates, upload photos, share videos, and add links to your status. You can receive notifications about other users as well.

To my way of thinking

Facebook can be used by individuals, to promote businesses, fan pages, like pages, community groups, etc. Facebook helps you to network on a more personal level, as well as on a larger scale. You can tailor your profile to be open to the public, which allows for more communication among other users. Depending on your use for Facebook, there are several ways in which this social media site can be useful for you! Whether you are someone looking to stay in contact with friends and family, or a business looking to promote their new product or service, or a band trying to create content to send to their fans, Facebook can be useful for anyone looking to connect with others.

Facebook Groups

A Facebook Group is a community of Facebook users who share a common interest. Just like groups of any kind, Facebook Groups are organized around families, activities, schools, religious organizations, work, projects, specific events or any other common interests such as fan clubs and political ideologies. Groups are an excellent way to create a community of people who share a common interest, but instead of meeting in person, the group meets and communicates using Facebook, instead of face-to-face.

Who creates and manages a group?

Any person who uses Facebook can create or join a group on Facebook. The person who creates the group is called the group "administrator." Groups typically have rules for who can join, and Facebook allows the group administrator to manage the rules for the group. The person creating the group decides whether to make the group open to the public, require administrator approval to join, or make it a private group with membership by invitation only. The group settings for privacy determine who sees updates and posts made in the group on Facebook.

How group updates are shared.

If you're not familiar with using Facebook, one of the most common activities of people using Facebook is to post updates about their activities and share these posts. An update can be a sentence, photo, video, or a link to another website. Groups allow people to post updates in the group, and the posts are visible to any other member of the group. Unless the group is public, posts made by members are available to and seen by only other members of the group.

Any member of the group can comment on any update posted in the group. When a user posts a comment, anyone in the group can see the comment in addition to the original post. One benefit of groups is to keep in touch with the other members of the group. To help group members keep up to date on group activity, Facebook displays group updates with updates from friends.

Group Example

An example of an actual Facebook Group is: "We Grew Up in Corpus Christi." Members are people who grew up in Corpus Christi, Texas. Membership is by administrator approval and is subject to certain requirements. The person who created the group set up the rules so that approval is required before anyone can become a member of the group.

People who want to become members request to join the group on the Facebook Group Page, and then the administrator receives the request and approves or denies a person's membership. The group administrator also has rules about what types of updates are acceptable, rules about promoting a business by members, and rules about appropriate language usage. Failure to adhere to the group rules can result in expulsion from the group since the group administrator can remove any group member.

Where do you find Facebook Groups?

Fortunately, Facebook includes a search function on virtually every screen, for both the website and mobile app. Simply enter a topic in the search area and add the word group to your search term. Facebook displays a list of groups along with the numbers of members in each group.

How are Groups and Pages different?

Unlike your own personal Facebook Profile or Facebook Group, a Facebook Brand Page, on the other hand, is public by default. Its purpose is to create a space on Facebook where individuals, public figures, businesses, organizations and other entities can make known their beliefs, ideas or products.

Anyone on Facebook can follow a Facebook Page by clicking the "Like" button at the top of the page. The button will change to "Liked," letting you know that you are now following that page. After that, you will receive status updates from the page.

Some Facebook Pages allow followers to post comments; others do not. It is up to the page administrator to make that decision. In any case, any comment posted on the Page is public, so anyone can view it. Privacy in Brand Pages on Facebook is different from groups since only the posts in public groups are public. Any post or update by a member in a private or closed group is only visible to other group members.

Many businesses, organizations, and individuals have discovered that having a Facebook Page is a great marketing tool. It can be used to create brand awareness and generate interest in a person, topic or product. Usually, there is a link back to a website at the top of the page where the creator offers more information on the page's subject.

To my way of thinking

Here are some guidelines for when to use a group versus a brand page:

- If you want to have some member privacy, use a group instead of a page.

- If you want to control who can join or participate in your community, choose a group.

- If you want to advertise on Facebook, use a page.

While Facebook doesn't say what the limit is for the number of members in a group, a page can have an unlimited number of likes. Although I've seen groups with over 15,000 members.

Whether it's in the real world, or in the world of Facebook, connecting with people who share your interests can lead to new experiences, new friends, and new insights, all of which are worthwhile pursuits.

Facebook Status Updates

A status update, also known as a Post, is information that you create and publish on Facebook. In almost every web page you see while using Facebook, a blank box appears. As this book is being written, the box has the message "What's on your mind?" in it, but this message changes from time to time so you might see something different. If you place your cursor inside the box and click, the box expands and some additional options appear around the box. A tap on a mobile device does the same thing.

Only after you click on the Post button is your update posted on your Timeline and shared on Facebook with your connections.

Text

With your cursor in the Status Update box you can type in any text you'd like to share as a Status Update. Posts can be short and quick, or long. It's up to you. Facebook has increased the length of text in a post to over 60,000 characters (63,206 to be exact). To put this in perspective, the average novel is 500,000 characters in length. Prior to this change, Facebook status updates were limited to 420 characters.

Other than the limit on length, what you post is completely up to you.

Photos and Videos

Most photos on Facebook are shared using the Status Update box and the Photo/Video button on the box. In fact, you can start a post with a photo, then add text later. You can even add more than one photo at a time. Both the desktop and mobile app support photos.

Since many users of smartphones use the built-in camera, the Facebook mobile app makes it easy to upload a photo from your smartphone photo album and even take one with your camera from within the Facebook app. On your Facebook app, just tap the Photo button and you'll see the options for selecting a photo and the camera icon to take a photo.

Adding a video in a post works the same way.

After uploading your photo or video, you can add any text to the update before posting.

Links

Web pages all have addresses, called links. A link is the term used to describe text that, when clicked, links to a web page on the Internet. You can enter a link in any Status Update. Sometimes Facebook will go to the website you link to and see if it can pull a photo from the site which can be used as a thumbnail in your update. This doesn't always happen and depends a lot on the way Facebook scans the web page in the link so if you want to be sure and have a photo appear in a Status Update, it's best to add it as a photo.

Post Privacy Settings

Near the Post button is the privacy button. The privacy setting last used by you for posting an update is the one that appears. To change who can view the update, click on the privacy button, then make your selection. Only the people you choose will be able to view and comment on the update.

Keep in mind however, that nothing on the Internet is really private. Once information is available to anyone, they could copy it and share it with anyone.

Places and Location

The Status Update on Facebook gives you the option to include your location for the post. Sometimes your location will be visible next to a map pin by the Status Update box. If you want to indicate your location at a Place page (a type of brand page on Facebook for public locations), you can click on the Place button.

Most web browsers and websites have the means to identify you're location based on the network you're using, or if you entered some location information in your profile. Mobile devices are even more accurate with cellular towers and GPS chips built-in.

Scheduling Posts

The clock icon allows you to schedule when your post goes "live" and is shared with your connections and is visible on your Timeline. Click on the icon and enter the year, month, date, and hour for your post.

Using the scheduling feature, you can back-date posts. For example, if you take a vacation but want to post pictures with the real date the photos were taken, you can use the schedule icon to mark the post with the accurate date and time.

File Extension

A File Extension is a short group of letters, occurring after the period in a file name, which indicates the format, function and identity of a given file of information.

The actual file name is the text used to the left of the period while the text to the right is the file extension. For example, if I wanted to save a file on my computer and call it "letter" I would be using the name "letter" as the name of my file. Let's take a look at how these two parts are used, then take a closer look at file extensions.

Why Do Computers Need File Extensions?

Even though I now have a file named "letter," there's something missing. Nothing in the name of the file tells my computer what type of information is in the file, or what type of software I would need to open, view, and use the file. If I add the extension ".doc" to the name of the file and call it "letter.doc" it has more meaning. The .doc extension is used to describe files that are created and used in word processing software. Now we know I have a document file. To open and edit the file I would need some type of word processing software on my computer.

So a very important role for file extensions is to help you, and your computer determine which programs can interact with different files. Your computer associates every type of file extension with a software application that can use that file extension. For instance, a file name with an extension of .xls would tell you the file is a spreadsheet that can be opened and edited with a spreadsheet program.

File Extensions and Specific Software Applications

You may have noticed that I didn't refer specifically to Microsoft Word when discussing a .doc file extension and instead referred to "word processing software." This is because there are several software applications capable of using the .doc file extension. For example, you can open a .doc file using Apple's Pages application or the Google Docs application. So how is this possible?

Software applications often include tools to convert files from one file extension format to another. By converting the file, the software makes it possible to open and work with files created in a different application. If this wasn't available, it would be difficult to share files between people with different types of computers or different versions of software applications. Software companies usually make a point of letting you know in their description what types of files their software will work with, and this is a major selling point of them.

When opening a file, your computer looks at the file extension and then starts the software for opening files with that extension. Most software applications let your computer know what file extensions they are capable of working with. Your Web browser software (commonly Internet Explorer, Safari, Firefox, Chrome) is used to open Web pages with the .htm or .html file extension. You don't have to tell your computer what software to use with the .htm or .html extension since your Web browser software did that for you.

But in some cases, software might not have told your computer to use it for a specific file extension or you may not have the software needed to open a specific file extension. In this case you might see a message appear on your screen asking you to choose an application from a list. If you know what type of information is in the file by knowing a little about file extensions, you can them tell your computer what software it should use to open a specific file extension.

File Extensions are Used as Nouns

File extensions are often used as a noun, separate from any specific file name, to describe the type of information in a file. Written in the form of an abbreviation or acronym, the file extension is used as a format such as .doc, .xls, or .pdf, which are some common file extensions you may have already seen and used. It's also correct to use the file extension without the period. In this case the files are just referred to by the text used for the file extension, such as doc, xls, or pdf, and you might even see the extension used in all capital letters such as PDF. Regardless of the way they are used, the file extension refers to the type of information contained in the file and software required to open and use the file.

Knowing About File Extensions Can Help You

Even though there are thousands of different file extensions, it 's not necessary to learn them all. Usually your computer knows what software to use for specific file extensions. But if you can familiarize yourself with the most common file extensions, you can quickly learn how different files interact with different programs.

First, knowing the meaning of common file extensions can help you easily identify the type of information in a file. For instance, if you are searching for a group of images or pictures, you can search for image file extensions. Examples of common extensions associated with images are JPEG, GIF, and PNG. Additionally, if you are looking for an audio or song file, you can limit your search to files ending with WAV, MP3, FLAC, OGG and AIFF extensions.

As you become more familiar with different file extensions, you can learn which programs are compatible with different file types. Knowing that a video file might have a file extension such as .mp4 would make it easier to recognize that the file is a video. If you were looking for a video that's great, but if you were looking for files that were images you would know to skip over the video .mp4 files.

Knowing that a file contains a spreadsheet, such as a file with the XLS extension, can help you locate information quicker and save you time. You won't have to open the files to see what's inside if you understand the file extension when you see it.

The best way to learn about a file extension you don't recognize is to do an Internet search for the file extension name. This will usually reveal an explanation of the file extension and software that uses that extension.

Flash Drive

When you use a computer, there are certain devices you will probably become familiar with. One of these is a flash drive. A flash drive is a small device that contains a USB connection on one end so that it can be attached to a desktop or laptop computer. It is small enough to stick in your pocket or purse so that you can carry it around. Some flash drives even have rings on the end so that you can attach them to your key ring.

In a nutshell, a flash drive is used to store content from your computer that you want to have in a separate drive. It is similar to an external hard drive, except that it is much smaller and has considerably less storage space. A flash drive can be available in storage amounts of 4GB, 8GB, 16GB, 32GB, 64GB and, most recently 256 GB. You can buy them at any electronics store.

Who Uses a Flash Drive?

A flash drive is most often used by someone who needs to keep certain documents with him no matter where he goes. For instance, if you are a student who needs to present a homework assignment on a computer at school, or if you work in an office and need to take work home with you, a flash drive can be your best friend. Many people use flash drives as a backup for saving documents, images and other data in a place separate from or in addition to their computer's internal drive or standard external hard drive. A flash drive also allows you to share whatever you have saved on it with another person on her or his computer.

How do You Use a Flash Drive?

To use a flash drive on a PC, you merely need to plug it into any USB port on the computer. When the computer recognizes it, a new small window will appear with the words "Removable Disk" at the top. The "Open Folder to View Files" option will appear at the very bottom of the page. To view your files, click on that line. You can also add, remove or modify content that is saved to your flash drive. If you wish to remove your flash drive, go to your computer's Start menu, click on "Computer" and a new window will appear. Right-click on the drive containing your flash drive and select "Eject."

For use on a Mac, plug the flash drive into a USB port, then open up Finder. Your drive appears in a list under the heading called "Devices." Simply click on the flash drive (could appear under any of a number of names ~ if it isn't clear, then check around a bit) and it will take you to the files on the drive. To remove the flash drive from a Mac, click on the "Eject" icon next to the flash drive in Finder.

Be aware that flash drives should never be simply yanked out of your computer when the power is on. Always follow the above directions.

Freemium

Freemium describes a pricing approach for software applications and mobile apps that are free to use and offer paid upgrades for additional options and features. Software companies offer freemium software as a way to encourage people to use and try their software and apps, and make money from anyone who chooses to pay for the optional features.

Freemium versus Free Trials

The freemium business model provides a fully functional program for free, but you can opt to pay for additional upgrades. Unlike free trials, which have time limit for how long you can use the software. you eventually have to upgrade or you can no longer use the software. With a freemium software or app, you get many basic features of the program. The free version may be more than adequate for your needs and you may never need to pay for any optional features. Freemium software allows you and other users to choose if they want premium features with what are called in-app purchases.

For example, many mobile apps qualify as freemium. You can download them for free from the app store, but you must pay for in-app upgrades. In the case of Facebook games, you can get more lives and items if you pay. Often, those payments are less than $1 per upgrade, but this money quickly adds up. It's how companies such as Zynga, which created FarmVille, have become successful despite not charging for their software.

What are some of the upgrade options?

While you don't have to spend any money, upgrades often allow you to achieve an objective -- message more people, add more storage, turn off ads or finish a level in a game. In freemium games, for example, you might be able to purchase clothing and accessories for your characters that aren't available for free or that could take you a long time to earn. Sometimes additional game play options are available with an in-app purchase. The freemium model can also apply to cloud services that save your documents and data.

A freemium office program may allow a certain amount of space on the server, and you'll have to pay to upgrade from that base amount. Music apps that only allow users to skip a certain number of songs in a specified time period qualify as freemium, too.

Freemium caution is advised

Freemium provides a good balance for users, because only people who want or need the paid features need to buy them. But it can cause some problems. In-app purchases can quickly add up, which is why companies such as Apple and Google have made it more difficult for children to make in-app purchases. Children often don't understand that those purchases cost real money, no matter how little the purchases appear to be.

With any freemium purchases, it's important to keep track of what you spend, unless, of course, money is no object. While 99 cents for additional paintbrushes or to move up a game level doesn't seem like much at the time, it's still just a penny short of one dollar, so keep track of your spending to stay within your budget.

To my way of thinking

Most mobile freemium apps are listed as free, so there's absolutely no risk in installing and trying one. Whether you use an Apple or Android device, or are looking at desktop applications, it will be clear when you have to make a payment to unlock or obtain some additional features. If you use Apple, your purchase is charged to the credit card you have on file with your Apple account. For Android, you can use either a Google Play account or the Amazon App Store to make a purchase, and your checkout is either with Google or Amazon.

Many of the mobile apps listed in the Top Grossing charts in the app stores are freemium apps, so it's a business approach that's seems popular with both consumers and app developers and offers you a way to try an app before spending any money.

G

Game Console

A game console is an electronic device used with a display and controls to play video games.

Game consoles are actually very similar to computers, but they are designed specifically to be part of an entertainment system, which means they're easy to connect to your TV and stereo. Even though game consoles can seem to be more basic than computers, they use the best possible hardware components for playing games. Compared to a computer, game consoles are simpler to set up and operate.

Basics of Game Consoles

Usually a game console is plugged into an outlet for power, and then plugged into the TV to display the gaming images. A controller is then used to play a game. Different buttons have different commands; for instance, the "A" button may make your on-screen character jump and the "B" button may make your on-screen character punch. The controller will have a joystick and/or directional pad for making your on-screen character move forward, backward, left, or right. Some controllers even have trigger type buttons for more command options.

Certain games will require a special controller, like a steering wheel for driving games, a dancing pad for dance games, or a gun for hunting games. Game controllers, with specialized buttons and handsets, can make playing a game easier and a better experience than using a keyboard or mouse on a computer. Some models use wireless controls and sensors to follow body motions and allow players to control the game with their motions.

Newer games come on compact discs or can be downloaded via an internet connection directly to the console, and some older games come on cartridges. All games are sold to work with a specific brand or model of game console, and popular games are often available in different versions for playing on different brands of game consoles. Game console makers try to make exclusive deals with game designers, so any user wanting to play the game needs to own their specific brand of game console.

History of game consoles

Game consoles first gained popularity in the early 1970's with the game console Atari and its iconic first game, Pong. The popularity of in-home game consoles continued, and in the 1980's Nintendo Entertainment System released their successful game console, which was a worldwide success with games like Excitebike and Super Mario Brothers. The creation of Playstation (made by Sony) and Xbox (made by Microsoft) game consoles followed. As game console development has grown, graphics have improved and the games have become more complex, allowing for a greater level of user interaction. Nintendo, Playstation, and Xbox are still the three major game consoles available on the market today.

Why do people buy them?

Game console users find playing video games to be a fun and relaxing way to experience different worlds and storylines created by video game designers. Many of today's game storylines even rival the stories and character depth of Hollywood movies. There are a multitude of games available, including dance and fitness games that can help improve the health of users by encouraging exercise. Whatever a person's reasons for playing video games, they are a great addition to any home entertainment system and can provide fun experiences for users of all ages.

The future of game consoles

As new models are released, game console makers are adding features that offer more types of entertainment activity. It's all about the competition for what you connect to your television set in your living room. Since game consoles are usually connected to a television set, entertainment features such as a DVD player for playing movies and online services like Netflix are now available.

Games are sold for specific models and versions of a game console. As a result, a game console owner could make a significant financial investment in games over time, so switching from one brand of game console to another can be expensive. Game console makers usually try to make new models that will play games for current models of their game console. Owners can then upgrade the game console and use their existing games, which keeps a game console owner from switching to another brand. The owner can use their existing games and purchase new games that take advantage of the new hardware to expand their game collection.

What's ahead?

The biggest change for the future is the popularity of gaming on mobile devices like smartphones. While games on smartphones may seem limited, smartphone makers always come up with new models and pack more features in with each new model. However, like any computing device, it's the software that will determine if people want the hardware. And for game consoles, the software is the game. If a game plays faster, with better controls, and with higher quality graphics on a game console than on any other device, the people who play games will buy the game console over any other hardware.

Geocaching

Geocaching is an outdoor recreational treasure-hunting game that uses the Global Positioning System (GPS) to identify locations where containers are hidden for the game players (anyone can play) to find. Volunteers of all ages and backgrounds hide the geocache containers of various shapes and sizes all over the world and post the GPS coordinates online on one or more geocache websites.

The goal is to use the GPS coordinates to search for the geocache. Volunteers of any background can create a geocache or search for one, and the whole activity of geocaching is essentially non-commercial. If you're familiar with a scavenger hunt, just think of geocaching as the modern high-tech version on a global scale.

What's the goal?

As a recreational activity, the goal of geocaching is to have fun and enjoy the challenge of searching for these geocaches. The containers might be in a local park, a parking lot, in popular tourist destinations or even under water, as long as the property owner has given permission to place the cache. Each cache contains a logbook for you to sign once you find it, and the containers often contain small items such as keychains, coins, and other trinkets. You can take an item from the geocache if you leave something of equal or greater value.

Types of geocaches.

There are many different types of geocaches. Some are simply hidden containers at the given coordinates. Others involve a puzzle that you must first solve to find the coordinates. Multi-cache geocaches send searchers to two or more locations before they arrive at the final location of the final cache.

Guidelines for creating a cache include some common sense and helpful aids for the players. First and foremost, anyone placing a cache should obtain permission from the landowner, including public land. The U.S. National Park Service and U.S. Fish and Wildlife Service prohibit geocaching. Choose a location that doesn't set off alarms and avoiding a treacherous area that could be dangerous to any player.

The person who places a cache takes responsibility for maintenance and upkeep with regular visits. The geocaching community requires that the cache container be waterproof and include a logbook. After placing the cache in position, the person placing it enters the cache GPS coordinates on one or more of the geocache websites (listed below).

Some listings require that the cache be visited by another player before being listed for public access. This verification of the cache by the player community is the way the community makes sure the cache follows community guidelines before being available for play. Once the cache is listed, the person who placed it checks up on periodically to make sure it is in good condition.

More advanced geocaching

Sometimes the geocaches include items called "trackable" that have unique codes that allow their movement to be tracked as it travels around the world. Some items called "travel bugs" are items that are trying to get to a specific location; the goal is to help the travel bugs get closer to their goal.

Some caches don't have a physical container and are called virtual caches. Community guidelines say that if a physical cache can be used, it should be, so a virtual cache is only used in locations where a physical cache can't be placed but still must abide by the rules and laws of placement just as though it was a physical cache.

How did it start?

Geocaching began in May 2000 when the U.S. Government removed military restrictions for public use of more accurate GPS locations. With the removal of these restrictions, commercial GPS receivers could be accurate within 4 meters. That's how accurate our smartphones and car navigation systems can be in identifying a location.

The first geocache - a black bucket placed in the woods near Portland, Oregon - was placed by Dave Ulmer with the goal of testing the improved technology. He put several items in the bucket - videos, books, software and a slingshot - in the bucket and posted the

GPS coordinates online. Within three days, two individuals saw the coordinates online and used their GPS devices to find the container. Over the next several days, others starting hiding their containers, and the concept of geocaching took off.

Merriam-Webster added "Geocaching" to its dictionary as a new official word in 2012 and "Geocache" was added to the official Scrabble dictionary in 2014.

How popular is geocaching?

Both the Boy Scouts and Girl Scouts of America have geocaching merit badges. As of 2015, The website geocaching.com has over ten million people registered users that participate in the activity searching for over 2.6

million geocaches around the world with over 1 million in the United States.

There are several websites and a mobile app for smartphones where you can register so you can find geocache locations and keep a log of your activity. The websites have additional information on how to create and place your geocache along with community guidelines for participating in the activity. These are the two most popular if you're interested in learning more:

geocaching.com - free membership with optional paid upgrade for features such as custom searches, member only caches and a trip planner

opencaching.com - free and no membership fees

To my way of thinking

Geocaching is a personal quest, one that you can enjoy as an individual, family, or group use it to make your exploration of the world a little more fun.

Google Alerts

If receiving an email alert for something you'd like to be watching on the Internet sounds like a convenient tool you'd like to use, then Google Alerts is something you can use. Google Alerts is a free service from Google that sends you an email when Google finds new results on any topic that interests you.

Using Google search in your Web browser to find new and useful information is convenient, but it requires that you conduct a search every time you're interested in a subject or term. Google Alerts use the same power of Google Search to find websites about a topic on the Internet but sends you an email whenever the word or phrase appears on a Web page. It's like an automated search on Google.

Creating an alert

Creating a Google Alert is very easy, and you don't need to know anything special about how Google searches, just the words you're looking for on the Web. Here's how to create one:

1. Go to the website for Google Alerts - https://www.google.com/alerts

2. In the box called "Create an alert about" enter the words, you want to monitor. A list of websites appears next so you can preview the results and refine the topic if necessary.

3. Click on Show Options to set up the frequency of the emails you receive for that alert, the types of results you want, and other options such as the sources, language, geographic region, and only the best results (filtered by Google) or all results

4. Then click on Create Alert

Emails will arrive in your inbox with links and snippets of websites that include your alert topic.

Google account and non-Google account

When you visit Google alerts, you may be asked to sign in with your Google account or set up a Google account. The account is free, but it's still possible to use Google alerts without a Google account. If you choose the latter method and don't use a Google account, you'll need open a confirmation email that's sent to you and click the link in the email to complete the verification.

Alert suggestions

When you visit the Google alerts web page to set up your alert, you'll see a list of alert suggestions about topics. Some of these are suggestions based on popular topics for Google alerts, and some are suggestions based on your personal search history. Favorite topics may include companies, automobiles, fashion finance, and sports. Some of these are listed because they are popular Google alert topics used by others. But some of the suggestions are tailored to you.

For Google account users, Google uses tracking to learn what you search for when using Google search and will make suggestions in Google alerts based on your search history. Once you enter a topic in the box 'Create and alert about..'' the suggestions page is replaced by the preview page.

Improving alert results

Similar to using modifiers for Google search terms, you can also use modifiers to narrow your results. Some common ways to limit results are to use quotation marks to set the alert to a phrase or set of words in a particular order. For example, an alert for online dating might produce results for online and for dating, but putting the topic in quotations like this: "online dating" will limit the results to websites that refer to the phrase online dating. You can do this with any group of words.

Another common way to narrow your results is to use a minus sign in front of a word. For example, when using an alert for a city name such as Glendale, using a minus sign in front of Arizona (Glendale -Arizona) will prevent results for Glendale, Arizona from appearing. For more advanced users, all of the Google search operators for limiting searches that work in Google search will also work in a Google alert.

To my way of thinking

The Web has a lot of information available if you know how and where to find it. If there's a topic or an area of interest and you want to receive an email message when Google finds the topic or term on the Internet, a Google alert is an automated way to keep up-to-date.

Google Analytics

Website owners that want to understand who visits their site and what visitors click can use tools like Google Analytics. Google Analytics is a service offered by Google that allows website owners to collect and analyze data about how viewers find, view, and interact with their website. This information gives the site owner the ability to understand how to optimize their website for search results and determine what visitors like most about the site, and what don't find useful. This data helps website owners to make changes that can increase traffic, sales, and the usefulness of the site to visitors.

How does Google Analytics work?

Anyone with a website can signup for a Google Analytics account on Google's website. The standard account is free. Once enrolled in the service, you or your website manager will need to insert a special code in your website that allows Google to collect data. After installing the tracking tool (you may need help from a developer), data is collected and available for logging in to your Google Analytics account. Google keeps all the reports and information in your account for as long as your account is active so you can easily compare historical information.

What data is collected?

Almost every website software can collect information on the number of visits. Google Analytics goes into greater depth. When a visitor clicks on a page, a "session" is started and tracked. For the entire time that user is on your website information about what they do is being collected.

Here are just some of the useful statistics collected:

• How many users visited by day, week, month or year

• How many total pages were viewed

• Percentage of users who were new and returning

- Number of pages did the average user visit

- Average time each user spent on your website

- Number of users by country, state and city

- What browser application was used

- What operating system was used by desktop and mobile user

- How many users found your website through search

- What search keywords were used when someone visits your site

- How many users found your site by typing or clicking on a link

- What sites refer traffic to your site

- Referrals from social networking sites

- What pages on your website do people visit when they visit and when they leave

How is it useful?

If your website is for business or professional use, collecting and analyzing this information can help you understand not only how many people visit, but what they do when they visit. It's like watching someone who enters a grocery store and collecting information on what aisles they visit, what items they look at and how long they spend in any one location of the store, whether they make a purchase or not. This type of information is useful to any business that's trying to understand what it's customers find most appealing, and that's how you can use it to help improve your website value to your visitors.

For example, the most frequently visited page that new visitors land on when they visit is the article "6 Things to Know about Emoji and Emoticons." This page was responsible for almost 40% of all the visits. The second most visited page is "What's the Difference Between 3G or 4G and WiFi." This type of data tells me that my site visitors are interested in technology about mobile smartphones. In fact, the top five web pages visited on my website from search engine clicks are on mobile technology topics. So for me to drive more traffic to my site, a strategy would include more articles related to this subject.

With this information in hour hand, you can improve your website value by focusing on content that your visitors like best, add content that can help you appear in search results, and understand if there are problems with any of the website by looking at the path people view before they leave.

Free and paid service levels

The paid service level called Premium, includes the assignment of a dedicated account manager from Google, training from Google experts, and a variety of 24x7 support capabilities. The pricing as of May 2016, is $150,000 per year, and is aimed at high volume websites rather than small businesses and entrepreneurs. But the Standard free plan is more than enough and far better than the simple site visitor data collected by most website management software and will help you understand your website traffic.

To my way of thinking

For marketers, this is invaluable information and those website owners that use Google Analytics, or any other analytic tool, can improve the performance of their website and their business goals.

Website

http://www.google.com/analytics/standard/

Gorilla Glass

Gorilla Glass is a trademarked brand name of a very durable type of glass created by the Corning company. If you or someone you know owns a smartphone, you have probably heard of Gorilla Glass, since it's used in almost every smartphone as part of the display that makes up the touchscreen.

Gorilla Glass is very popular for almost any device that uses a touchscreen, and it's used not only in smartphones, but also in a variety of other electronic devices such as computers and TV sets for the top surface of the display.

However, there is so much more to it than that that makes this specific type of glass considerably different than other types of glass.

Gorilla Glass is introduced

Gorilla Glass was introduced to the world in June 2007 when Apple announced the first iPhone. As a device, the iPhone changed everything about mobile phones, and the use of Gorilla Glass is one of the technologies that made the introduction of this revolutionary (at the time) portable device possible.

Characteristics of Gorilla Glass

Gorilla Glass has special characteristics as a material that makes it an essential part of smartphones and other devices using a touchscreen. It is not only durable but very thin and extremely scratch resistant. These characteristics make it ideal for use on a portable device like a smartphone that's in use every day. There's one other property of Gorilla Glass that makes it ideal for a touchscreen device, which is the ability to apply layers of other materials to the Gorilla Glass.

You might not realize it, but the touchscreen of your smartphone (or any touchscreen device) is made out of several layers of materials. In addition to the glass layer of the screen, there's a layer for the Liquid Crystals that display the visual images, and also a layer of material that can sense when your finger makes contact with the screen. This explanation is a bit simplified, and there are usually several more layers of materials, but that's another topic.

The important thing to know about Gorilla Glass is that is doesn't affect how these other layers function, and forms a lightweight solid base material so the other layers can be applied in very thin coatings during the manufacturing of the touchscreen. This property makes it possible to manufacture reliable, lightweight, and scratch-resistant touch-screens, which are an essential part of our smartphone, tablet, and touchscreen devices.

History of Gorilla Glass

As mentioned earlier, the first generation was introduced with the iPhone announcement in 2007. Subsequent generations of Gorilla Glass have resulted in improvements in scratch resistance and cracking when a smartphone or tablet is dropped.

Cracked Screens

While Gorilla Glass is a pretty durable material, like all glass, it can crack. You may have had a cracked screen on one of your devices, and if so, the only repair possible is to replace the screen and the glass layer, and potentially the display layer as well.

Most manufacturers of smartphones and tablets conduct a "drop test" that drops the device from a certain height to see if the device works and the screen doesn't crack. And in fact, dropping a device is the most likely way to crack the screen. The case used in the manufacturing helps protect the device and the screen, and you no doubt have seen, or even own, an after-market case that provides additional drop protection.

Apple and other repair centers offer a repair service for replacing a cracked screen, but I always recommend that you check the cost of repair against the cost of replacing the device, since screen repairs can cost over $200 sometimes. And it's important to know that even with a cracked screen, services such as gazelle.com and technollo.com will offer a trade-in value for a smartphone that's otherwise in good working order. So you may be able to trade-in your smartphone with a cracked screen and upgrade to a newer model.

Screen Protectors

Screen protectors were once more common on the earlier generations of Gorilla Glass, which did tend to show scratches and were less durable. Even the 2nd generation was a major improvement over the first and reduced the need for an after-market screen protector.

If you use your smartphone or tablet in a hostile environment with a lot of dust or sand, like the beach, a baggie with a zipper-type top makes an excellent inexpensive solution. It may not look elegant, but it works and is dust, sand, moisture-proof and inexpensive.

If you need a durable case that can help your smartphone or tablet survive rough handling, there's an accessory for that. Lifeproof, Otterbox, Ballistic, Speck, and Incipio, who are some of the largest makers of cases, all make models that are waterproof, snow-proof, dirt-proof, shock-proof and have built-in screen protectors.

What's else is coming?

Apple is preparing to introduce a sapphire glass screen material, rumored to be introduced in their upcoming Fall iPhone announcements. Apple is already using sapphire glass in the iPhone 5 as a protective surface for the camera lens, and for the fingerprint sensor in the iPhone 5S.

Sapphire glass isn't really glass, it's a crystal that's grown. Its major advantage over Gorilla Glass is that it's a lot tougher and stronger, so less likely to crack and break. Apple has even set up its own factory in Arizona to make sapphire crystals for it's devices. Since Apple is known for premium products, the currently higher cost of a sapphire screen, compared to a Gorilla Glass screen isn't much of an issue for their top-of-the-line newest model iPhone. As costs come down over time, expect other manufacturers to introduce sapphire glass in their products and for the sapphire glass screen to appear in tablets.

What goes into Gorilla Glass?

In general, you cannot tell the difference between Gorilla Glass and other types of glass when you look at them. Most forms of commercial glass are simply made using ingredients of sand or silicon dioxide, limestone and sodium carbonate which are then melted together at a high temperature. Corning utilizes these substances but combines them with additional chemicals before melting them down into a solid glass material called aluminosilicate. This type of glass is made up of aluminum, silicon and oxygen. Sodium ions are added to complete the glass-making process.

Before making the aluminosilicate into Gorilla Glass, Corning performs a process called "ion exchange." The glass is dipped into a vat of potassium ions and then bathed at around 752 degrees Fahrenheit. This dipping creates a highly durable protective layer on top of the glass that makes it perfect for use on smartphones, computers, tablets and TVs.

Website

http://www.corninggorillaglass.com/en/home

GPS

GPS stands for global positioning system. The system is composed of 24 satellites that are constantly orbiting the earth from 1200 miles above it. Originally launched in 1978 by the U.S. Department of Defense, the satellite system was opened up for civilian use in the 1980s. The satellites constantly transmit information and run on solar energy.

Although the government does not charge for use of the system, you must purchase a receiver in order to access the system. The receiver is the GPS device that is sold and that you need to use in your car, boat or other vehicle. Many cellular phones, for example, iPhones and Android models, have built-in GPS receivers. The GPS receiver accesses the data transmitted from the satellites and interprets it in order to identify your location.

How a GPS receiver works.

It may seem like magic, but the GPS receiver is really a computer with software that calculates the data it receives from the satellites into information you can use. It needs to receive data from three satellites in order to identify your exact location.

You then enter your destination address. GPS software includes a map database that converts your location provided by the satellites, and the destination address you have entered, into a map that shows you the most direct route to your destination. It also includes the distance and travel time. Some other examples of GPS map databases are golf course GPS devices, which have golf course maps stored in their database, and hiking GPS devices, which contain a hiking trail database.

Some GPS receivers have an additional capability and can connect to the Internet. Usually this is through a cell phone network like Verizon, AT&T, or Sprint. Smartphones like the iPhone and Android models include this capability, and other GPS receivers are available with the ability to connect to the Internet. Using their Internet connection, these devices can access information that's available on Internet databases, such as real-time traffic information, and show it on their display screen.

Why some receivers are more expensive.

The cost of the receiver depends on the software included. You can add software that can locate and map specific locations. For example, you can get directions to the nearest Starbucks or gas station. You can buy one without a screen that tells you what to do by audio, or one with a screen so you can follow your progress on the map. The cost depends on the software you want included and the size of the screen.

The receiver needs a good antenna in order to receive the data from the satellites. Because the transmissions from the satellites travel by line of sight, the receiver does not work in caves, buildings, underwater or in tunnels.

Benefits of a GPS receiver.

The system works in all types of weather and works 24 hours a day. It will tell you exactly how to get to your destination from your current location, how long it will take you to there and how many miles away it is. If you use a GPS receiver, you may never get lost again.

Graphics Processing Unit

A graphics processing unit, usually referred to as a GPU, is a single chip computer processor that is used to boost the performance of video and graphics on a computer or mobile device. Graphics processing units are used to improve performance for graphics, which can improve the speed that graphics is displayed for both games and videos.

How Does a GPU Help?

Most computers use the CPU, or processor, to do the calculations necessary to draw information on the screen of the computer or device. For many applications, the screen doesn't change very much. For example, in a document when you type, most of the computer screen stays the same, only the characters you type create a need to display new information on the screen. Some types of applications, such as a video game or video files require constant updating of the display. These are considered to be "graphics-intensive" applications.

The computer's processor, if it's powerful enough, can perform all the calculations for any application, but some of the graphic-intensive applications may be too much work for it to do by itself, which means it may not have enough capability to run intensive graphics.

Think of it like driving your car up a steep hill. With only you in the car, your car might be able to reach a certain speed going up the hill. Put a few additional passengers in the car, and it won't be able to get up the hill as fast.

When your computer or mobile device is running an application or communicating with the Internet, it takes some processing power to do these tasks. Add on another passenger load, like we did with your car, and the additional graphics work may cause your computer to slow down and could affect how fast the display is updated. Hence, the need for a graphics processor, which acts as a booster for the added graphics necessary to keep the display snappy and quick.

Here's a common situation with a computer, playing high definition videos and modern games. These are two tasks that the computer's processor, if it's not fast enough, will struggle to handle. It may be able to perform these tasks, but the display will be slow, sluggish, and unimpressive in appearance.

By using a dedicated graphics processing unit, your computer, laptop or mobile device will handle more demanding graphics applications, making your display refresh fast and playing videos smoothly.

Built-in and Upgrade

Mobile devices often use a processor where the graphics capabilities are designed into the main CPU, so it already includes a built-in graphics processing unit as part of its design. Desktops and laptops, and even some tablets and smartphones use a graphics processing unit, which can often result in visible improvements in performance.

For desktop computers with a case that opens, an add-on graphics circuit can be installed. The add-on graphics processing unit circuit results in improved graphics performance.

The additional graphics processing unit is a separate circuit card that plugs into a slot in the computer's main chassis. The addition of a GPU adds a second computer to the chassis, which requires additional power and cooling. More powerful graphics processing is often the reason one model of computer is more expensive than another, since it requires a larger power supply, more fans for cooling, and if it's a laptop or smartphone, more expensive materials for the internal components since the device runs at a higher temperature.

History of the GPU:

The first graphics processing unit came out in 1999. There was only a small demand for a GPU in its first few years of existence, but the increase in high quality computer games led to rapid improvements in GPU technology. With users playing games, editing video files, and watching a lot of TV or movies on their computer, it was necessary to develop sleek, high performance and high efficiency graphics processing units.

Do you need a graphics processing unit?

There are many desktops and laptops that do not come with a graphics processing unit, and their users may not care. If you use your computer for basic tasks such as surfing the internet, listening to music, writing Word or Excel documents, and watching YouTube videos, you may not need a GPU. Most recent computers and smartphones all have processors that are capable of playing high-definition videos smoothly.

If you are going to create graphics, edit photos or videos, or play recently released games where a graphic processor unit is recommended, then you should buy a computer with a graphics processing unit.

Graphic User Interface (GUI)

A graphical user interface is visual the way a computer (or any computing device) communicates with a person. It consists of the layout and design on the screen of a computing device to give a person (the user) a way to use the computing device. Let's discuss why it's called a user interface.

The User and the Interface

The visual layout can include any combination of text, numbers, symbols, or other graphics to help guide the user while they use the computer. In this case, a computer can be any computing device with some visual display. It's what appears on the screen that's makes up a user interface, and the type of computing device doesn't matter.

Computers include connections both inside and outside which allow the computer hardware to connect to other types of electronics. A common example is when you use a cable with a connector to connect a computer, tablet or smartphone to something else. The connection is sometimes referred to as an "interface" which is a computer term that describes a connection between two different things. The term "user interface" describes a way for a computer or computing device to connect to a person, which is something different from a computer.

If you drive a car, you're familiar with another type of user interface, the driver controls. The gas pedal, speedometer, and brake are all part of a car's user interface since they are used by the driver to control the car. The user interface of a car is pretty common, and when the speedometer dial starts to move, you probably know you're going faster.

To control your speed you use the gas pedal and brake, and the dial on the speedometer gives you feedback on your action. The dial is a pretty good user interface since it's simple, and you can probably recognize a gas pedal, brake, and speedometer on almost any car you might drive.

GUI Design

Computer monitors and touchscreen displays can display almost anything that our eyes can see and can change what appears on the display. The ability to change the display with a program makes the display very flexible and allows a computer to perform many different functions. But someone had to figure out what to put on the screen for you to use the computer.

People that design computers and devices have at their disposal what is essentially a blank sheet of paper when they create a user interface. Whether it's the text on a web page, the design of a button on a touchscreen or a symbol on a desktop computer, someone created the design and layout of what appears on the screen. All of these design decisions create a visual display that you can use to perform tasks on your device. GUI designers have a lot of options available to create what you see on the display and these are very important decisions.

While people can read text, symbols or icons make it easier to understand navigation aids. We like signs and directions that are easy to follow. As a result, GUI's often include visual symbols, called icons, that provide a symbolic way for a person to perform a function or use a feature. They're like the traffic sign symbols for the world of computers. A driving test often includes a question or two that displays a traffic sign and a multiple choice answer. Hopefully, not too many people get the stop sign wrong.

In GUI's, icons and symbols can help make it easier to recognize common functions. For example, in Windows it's common for a user to click on the "X" in a window to close a program. Touchscreen users tap on an app icon to start an app, and Mac OSX users are familiar with the red, yellow and green buttons that are used to manage a window on the desktop.

Good GUI and Bad GUI

The user interface is an important part of the design of any software program and application because how easy it is to understand can have a major impact on the success of the program. In fact, you're a GUI expert. If a GUI is easy to use, it's good if it's hard to use; it's bad. GUI's are supposed to do one thing, help the user. Good GUI's do this by being simple and consistent.

Simple means using a symbol or word that is easy to understand by the user. Being consistent makes it easy to find that word or symbol when it's used the same way and in the same location on almost any screen. We don't like our GUI's to change since it can be disorienting when familiar things are moved.

When GUI's Change

As people get used to using one user interface for a computer, program, or application they become comfortable with knowing where things are located on the screen and what they mean. Anyone who switched from the menu's in Microsoft's Word 2003 to the Ribbon GUI in Word 2007 or later knows that it takes time to learn a new GUI. Another example of this is switching from an older version of Microsoft's Windows operating system to the new Windows 10.

The user interface for Windows 8 uses objects on the screen called tiles that are square and rectangular. Windows 8 is also designed to be used with a touchscreen more than with a mouse. As a result, some people find the change to Windows 8 to be a challenge. It's because they have to learn a new GUI.

I had a friend who posted on Facebook about their frustration with a new Apple Mac laptop computer. Their previous computer was a Windows 7 laptop. While all their friends told her that Mac's were easy to use, my friend is a little frustrated while she learns the new GUI on a the Mac since some common symbols and icons on Windows 7 are different in location and appearance on a Mac.

New Technology Means New GUI's

Since computers have new features and functions that may not be commonplace in other forms of technology, you are likely to see new symbols, words, and graphics that may not always make sense. If there isn't anything that's commonly used to represent a task or function, then the GUI designer has to come up with something that will work for the users. They do test them out, really!

It's like learning a new language, with symbols that represent words or phrases. Only the symbols represent functions and features that may be just as new to you as the symbol itself.

Don't worry though, if you can learn a few things at a time you can become familiar with any GUI and learn how to use them. One thing I see in my classes is that people forget that any new technology is new, and it might take some practice to learn how to use it. Think about when you learned to drive a car. Was learning how the gas pedal and brake worked something that you were able to do the first time you got in the driver's seat? Maybe not, so give yourself a break on how much you can learn in a day with technology.

Gyroscope (Smartphone)

A smartphone gyroscope is an electronic circuit contained within smartphones that provides information about the orientation of the smartphone in three-dimensional space. Apps use the data to perform functions on the smartphone such as rotating the screen and apply gesture commands like the shake gesture (used to undo typing).

Gyroscope basics

A common gyroscope is a spinning wheel or disk mounted in a frame which can rotate in three dimensions. When the disk spins, it's orientation is unaffected by the tilting or ration of the frame. A simple example of a gyroscope would be a spinning top, and if you played with tops as a child you were using a simple gyroscope, you just might not have been aware of the physical principal.

When the top spins fast enough, it remains in an upright position and resists any attempt at falling over. The physics behind this is that the spinning motion generates an outward force that can counter other forces. One force is gravity, which wants to pull the top down, and if the top starts to spin too slowly, gravity will become stronger than the force generated by the spin. Since the outward force of the spinning disk pulls equally in all directions, the top stays balanced.

Think of a line going through the center of the while it's spinning. This line is called an axis, and in this case, the vertical axis. The flat surface the top is spinning on is the horizontal axis. And the third dimension is any angle that the top takes on as it spins around. These three dimensions make up what's called orientation, which can be measured.

If the three axes had pressure sensors, the sensors would detect when each axis was being moved out of alignment. For example, if straight up and down is vertical, and tilt or wobble is off the vertical axis. Think about when you lay your smartphone on a flat surface and then pick it up to hold it to your ear to make or answer a phone call. The smartphone changes orientation from the flat surface to something different, depending on how you hold it in your hand.

Our bodies have sensors that provide orientation information to our brains. The inner ear has a fluid filled sensor that can detect orientation, so we can walk without falling. Our brains also use our eyesight to provide orientation information and combines these sensors to calculate if we are right-side up, lying down or standing at an angle. All pretty useful information for us to have handy. And smartphones can also use this type of information on their orientation.

Smartphone gyroscope circuits

Orientation information for a smartphone uses a circuit that can tell where the smartphone is in the three dimensions. So a circuit had to be invented that would measure this information and made small enough to fit into a smartphone.

Electronic engineers knew that when certain materials have electrical current passing through them, they'll vibrate. If the material is in the shape of spokes projecting from a point, then the spokes create a line along an axis. Pressure sensors along the spokes can detect any movement and send that information to a circuit that collects all the information from all the spokes in the sensor to create a three-dimensional view of the sensor, and therefore the smartphone.

Unlike a mechanical rotating gyroscope, this a vibrating spoke gyroscope lends itself nicely to miniaturization for micro-electro-mechanical systems or MEMS. These circuits include both electronic and mechanical components, this the electromechanical term, and are miniaturized, which is why they are micro-electro-mechanical circuits. These solid state components give smartphones and other devices the ability to sense any rotational changes to themselves. The smartphone gyroscope allows the smartphone to rotate the screen to match the user's perspective or to imitate gravity in video games as you turn and rotate your smartphone.

To my way of thinking

Smartphone gyroscopes make the smartphone a better sensing device since it can tell its position in three-dimensional space to match our human position. As a result the smartphone becomes a better hand-held device and more useful since it "understands" it's position and how we are holding it.

H

Hackathon

A Hackathon is an event where computer programmers gather together and develop software programs collaboratively in a short period. Hackathons are also called Hack Days, Hackfests or Codefests and can last a day or up to a week in duration.

Why do Hackathons exist

Hackathons allow programmers to break through problems and obstacles in software development in a short period. The goal of a specific objective for a software program, dedicated team effort and commitment to complete a project by a deadline all help create the necessary conditions conducive to achieving results.

Like a sporting event where a team is working to win the game, a team of programmers can be focused on a specific goal and the teamwork, along with a time deadline, can bring out better achievement than programmers working independently.

Many large companies such as Facebook, Google and LinkedIn organize Hackathons regularly in order to incorporate new ideas that benefit their users. Hackathons are commonly used to both build and create new apps that can help further the community or solve a particular problem.

Hackathon groups are usually less than five people that work together over a couple of days. The most common goal of a Hackathon is to create a working prototype of a software program by the end of the Hackathon. There are no limitations to what can be created through these gatherings. With the combined knowledge of the programmers, creative solutions and ideas can be brought to life.

History and types of Hackathons

One of the first documented Hackathons was in Calgary in 1999 and consisted of ten developers who wanted to develop software in Canada that was not possible to export from the United States. This was followed quickly in another company by a challenge to write a specific Java program that used infrared hardware technology. From there, the use of Hackathons multiplied since it was a novel and creative way to produce collaboration by programmers.

Some Hackathons began simply from a late night and spontaneous gathering of programmers while others were premeditated and set up by companies for a specific purpose. Many innovative projects are created by Hackathons. Competitive Hackathons pit teams of programmers against each other with a prize or reward going to winning programming team. Sometimes Hackathons are used for company recruiting events where programmers are evaluated for job openings.

Hackathons almost always involve an abundance of food and beverage (not usually alcoholic) and often there are people who function as a support staff to help fetch any necessary refreshments. All of this is to give the programmers the physical energy they need in order to come up with optimum solutions and ideas.

Benefits of Hackathons

From developing software to solving complex problems, Hackathons have a wide range of benefits. One programmer may be able to solve a problem over time, but when you bring together multiple people with extensive knowledge, the teamwork and collaboration can get things moving quickly.

To my way of thinking

Programming is thought of as something done by an individual, and this is often the case where the actual writing of software code, like almost any type of writing, is usually done by one person while working at a computer. There are many situations where writing a program as an individual is the best approach for creating software programs.

Teams, however, can sometimes produce better results than any one individual, and when a deadline exists, a team of people can often create better results than any one individual. This technique is applied in sports, the military, and in business. Hackathons add some fun, teamwork, and excitement to an otherwise individualist occupation.

Hard Drive

A hard drive (also known as a hard disk drive or HDD) is a type of disk drive that is used for storing software and data on a computer. A hard drive consists of a single piece of hardware that encloses one or more magnetic platters and the components necessary for the hard drive to function.

Hard drives are used because every computer needs a storage device to store data. Hard drives also store large amounts of data at a low cost compared to other types of storage.

Physical Construction

A hard drive is sealed to protect the internal working parts. The drive has both electronic and mechanical pieces inside the case, with some moving parts. One moving part is the platter, and the other is a magnet called the read/write head. The platter looks a like a record or CD, only with a magnetic layer coated on it. The read/write head is a little magnet that moves in and out from the center on an arm. The read/write head is held just above the platter.

The hard drive is connected to the computer with a cable that sends and receives data when the computer is operating. While powered off, nothing happens inside, and any data stored on the hard drive is saved. All hard drives start out blank until data is stored or "written" on the drive using the read/write head. One characteristic of a hard drive, compared to Random Access Memory (RAM), is that data is stored without the need for power.

What goes on inside

In operation, the hard drive uses a motor that continuously rotates the magnetic platter, just like a phonograph turns a record. When the hard drive receives instructions from the computer to read or write data, the read/write head moves in or out from the center of the drive to the edge.

Magnetic disks have "tracks" that form rings on the disk

If you think of growth rings on a tree trunk you'll have the idea, only hard disk tracks are all the same width. If you look at the hard drive platter, you won't see any physical rings. The "tracks" are managed by the electronics on the drive, which positions the head a precise distance from the center. Each incremental distance of the head from the center to the edge is a track.

In addition to the tracks being invisible, each track is broken up into areas for storing data called regions. If you took a pie and sliced it up into really small pieces, you'd have a good picture of what a region looks like. The regions on a track are the spaces where the data is stored. Since magnets have two polarities, a region can store a one or a zero depending on the polarity of the region. Since zero's and ones are used by computers, the hard drive is capable of storing, reading and writing data.

What your hard drive does for your computer.

When you power on your computer, your hard drive starts spinning and is ready to read and write data. The computer them installs the operating system by reading it from the hard drive. In fact, all of your software and data are stored on your hard drive, then moved from the hard drive into your RAM when you use your computer, any application, or any data or file.

Your hard drive spins continuously whenever it's on and is ready for commands from your computer to read or write data.

When you save a file to your hard drive, it uses the magnetic head to write the data on the magnetic material on the platters. To read data, it uses the magnetic head and positions it where the data is stored so it can read the data for your computer. Without a hard drive, you wouldn't be able to store any information when you turned your computer off.

Performance of hard drives

Since hard drives use moving parts, their performance is affected by how fast things can move. The most significant difference is in the rotation speed of the hard drive, which is measured in revolutions per minute (RPM). Most current hard drives have a rotation speed of either 5400 or 7200 RPM. A 7200 RPM hard drive is faster at reading and writing data than a 5400 RPM drive since it can move the region of data to the magnetic head faster.

Reading and writing data from the hard drive can affect a computer's performance significantly. A 7200 RPM drive is literally about 30% faster than a 5400 RPM drive. Since computers are reading and writing data to a hard drive, any performance difference would be noticeable. For people working with larger files, like photos, movies, or large documents, it's worth it to use the fastest hard drive available. It also will improve the time it takes to startup a computer.

Laptop makers often use 5400 RPM hard drives since they use less power and can help the laptop run longer on a single charge. So when you consider a new computer it might be worth it to look at a faster hard drive if you work with larger files.

Solid State Drives.

While not technically a hard drive, a solid state drive is an alternative to the traditional hard drive for storage. Using electronic "flash" memory, a solid state drive has no moving parts and serves the same function as a hard drive. The drawback to a solid state drive is it's cost, they are simply more expensive that hard drives for the same amount of storage capacity. Solid state drives use the same internal electronics as a flash memory USB stick. They are larger and can connect up to the same internal connectors as a hard drive on your computer.

The advantage of a solid state drive is really fast startup times for a computer. Since there is no waiting for a platter or head to move, data is moved faster. A solid state drive can often be a bigger performance improvement than a faster processor. If you like the faster almost "instant on" you see with a smartphone or tablet, a solid state drive will help you get there.

A new alternative called a hybrid drive is being used by Apple, as well as other computer manufacturers, and hard drive replacement makers. A hybrid drive is a combination of a hard drive with a platter for low cost storage along with a small solid state drive for performance. The computer keeps the most commonly used data on the solid state drive, while storing other data files on the hard drive.

Data is priceless

Your hard drive is a workhorse component of your computer, and like any component, it can break down and fail. When it fails you lose data. That's why backups are important and why every computer expert recommends a backup. You can replace hardware and applications, but your data, files, photos, and anything else you created are unique.

Most office supply stores and online retailers sell backup hard drives for under $100. These are separate hard drives that connect to a USB connector on your computer and include a backup program that will automatically scan and create a second copy of your data on the backup drive.

While some students tell me that they use a flash drive or make a CD copy for their backup, human beings can forget to make copies. If you use your computer every day you create new data daily, and daily backups are something people aren't good at remembering to do. That's the hazard of a manual backup.

A backup software program is meant to run automatically so whenever you add a new photo, create a new document, or make changes to any of your data, the updates are automatically added to the backup. Any office supply store or major electronics retailer will carry popular backup solutions and all of them are pretty good.

Hashtag

What some people know as the pound symbol "#" is also referred to as a hashtag. When the pound symbol used before a word or phrase in a post (called a Tweet) on Twitter, the symbol and the phrase it's used with are referred to as a hashtag. There are no spaces between the hashtag and the phrase, so it appears like this "#smallbiz" in a Tweet (without the quotes).

Hashtags, because they create a clickable link within a Tweet, are used to organize and categorize Tweets. Here's how this works on Twitter. The pound sign symbol tells Twitter that the phrase is a hashtag, Twitter finds all the Tweets using that hashtag phrase, then Twitter makes the Tweets that include that hashtag into links that connect to each other. Clicking on a hashtag link in a Tweet results in your screen showing only those Tweets that contain the hashtag. Tweets are displayed in chronological order, with the most recent Tweet at the top of your list, making it easier to find the most current Tweets about specific topics and to hold conversations.

Community Conversations

Click on a hashtag that appears in a Tweet and your screen displays all the Tweets that contain the hashtag. Unlike your normal Home page which displays Tweets from the users you follow, you're now following a hashtag topic on Twitter and only see Tweets that contain that hashtag. This feature is important because of something that Twitter does for you automatically.

At this point, with the hashtag topic open in your display, when you post a Tweet on your own, Twitter automatically inserts the hashtag in your Tweet, so anyone else following the topic will see your Tweet in their display.

By including hashtags in Tweets, it's easier for one of your Tweets to be found if you use a hashtag in the Tweet. You can find Tweets about a specific topic by clicking on a hashtag or using it to search Twitter.

Searching for Hashtags

Twitter has a search function which searches all Tweets on Twitter and you can use searching to help find hashtags even if you don't know one already. The magnifying glass icon opens the search screen, then you enter a topic, person, word, or phrase. The search results that are displayed show user accounts and Tweets that contain the search term you entered. If the phrase you searched for is commonly used in a hashtag, you'll see it in one of the Tweets that appears in your search results.

During a major live event such as an election, the World Series, or the Olympics, people like to follow Tweets about the event as they are posted. By searching for one of these terms, for example, Olympics, you'll see the hashtags #olympics and #olympics2016. Each of these is a live link on Twitter, so clicking one of them will display all of the Tweets that include the hashtag and you can keep up to date or join the conversation.

Using either search or hashtags makes Twitter a great way to keep up-to-date on any live event or activity. You can find others that are posting updates about any topic, even if you're not connected to them as a follower on Twitter. If a hashtag is popular, Twitter features it in their "trending" topics list on everyone's Twitter account Home page.

Hashtags on other Social Networks

Since hashtags are so popular on Twitter and Facebook, other Social Networks started using them also. You might see a hashtag included in a Facebook update, with an Instagram photo, or on a Google+ post, and they work the same way as they do on Twitter, creating a clickable link that allows you to see all the updates that include the hashtag.

Creating Hashtags and Hashtag Etiquette

Hashtags can be created by anyone on Twitter by using the puns symbol in front of a word or phrase. However, there are many common ones already in use on Twitter. The Web site hashtags.org includes a list of commonly used hashtags and a search feature to search for hashtags.

Twitter offers a help page on creating hashtags with recommendations for how to use them at this link http://support.twitter.com/articles/49309-using-hashtags-on-twitter.

Like any Social Networking activity, the impulse to reach people easily and broadcast a useful message can be interpreted as spam by someone else. As a result, Twitter recommends only using a hashtag if the Tweet is related to the topic, and using at most two hashtags per Tweet.

Twitter Usefulness

Hashtags are one of the features that make Twitter such a useful Social Network, but many people don't know what they are, so they don't give them a try. Think of it like trying out a new restaurant that opened up nearby. Give Twitter a try if you aren't using it and see if using hashtags make it more useful for you.'

Websites

www.hashtags.org

http://support.twitter.com/articles/49309-using-hashtags-on-twitter

HDMI

HDMI (High-Definition Multimedia Interface) is a standard for connecting video and audio signals using a single cable from one electronic device. Using a single HDMI cable, a video, and audio signal can be sent from one device, such as a DVD player, to another device using HDMI like a television set. Since HDMI is an industry standard, consumers can purchase any device with HDMI and connect it to another device that uses the HDMI connection.

Created in 2002, the standard for HDMI developed by Hitachi, Panasonic, Phillips Electronics, Silicon Image, Sony, Technicolor, and Toshiba. The standard includes specifications for the connectors, cables, and electronic video and audio signals and it currently managed by HDMI Licensing, LLC. HDMI Licensing is an industry organization that licenses the HDMI technology to over 1600 manufacturers of electronic equipment who use HDMI. With billions of HDMI devices shipped, HDMI is supported by major motion picture studios.

HDMI cables and connectors

The unique shape and size of the standard HDMI connector is how many people recognized an HDMI connection. With the standardized size and shape, one end of an HDMI cable can only fit one way into an HDMI connector. There are several different sizes of HDMI connectors, however since the standard was adapted to make smaller connector sizes possible for smaller d vices. For example, some video cameras and smartphones use the mini-HDMI size connector and a cable which has a mini-HDMI connector on one end can have a standard size connector on the other. The smaller size makes it possible to connect a video camera directly to a television set or monitor with an HDMI connector even though they have different size connectors.

Cables for HDMI can be different lengths as well, and the standard allows for cable lengths as long as ten meters. A longer connection is even possible with an electronic repeater but is usually not necessary since most HDMI devices are located near each other, like a cable box and a television display.

There are currently five different types of HDMI cable types. One type is strictly for automotive use in automobile video systems and is designed specifically for automobile manufacturer-installed and after-market video systems. You usually won't even see the HDMI cables in a car since they are concealed and hidden from view.

Two other types of HDMI cables are for standard HDMI or High-Speed HDMI. Standard HDMI is the most commonly used HDMI cable for home audio and video. The High-Speed HDMI cable standard is for 3D video, Blue-ray disk players, and the newer 4K (for 4,000 lines of resolution) video. You won't need the High-Speed HDMI cable types unless you use one of these types of devices. Both the standard and the High-Speed HDMI cable types have another variation, and that's the ability to carry Ethernet, so each type is available as anEthernet capable version or non-Ethernet capable version. You only need the Ethernet version if your equipment specifies that requirement.

History

HDMI was introduced when High-Definition television was introduced and required higher-quality video signals than existing video connectors could provide. In 2002, the television industry was going through a transition from standard-definition television to high-definition television.

Television creates a visual image by displaying an image made up of lines that light up the screen in some way. High-Definition television uses more lines than standard definition so the image is clearer and sharper and can be larger in height and width and still seem clear to the human eye. Standard - definition displays 352 lines on any display, regardless of how large the display is. With a small display, the human eye can't make out the lines and the image appears relatively clear. High-Definition displays use either 720 lines (called 720P), or 1080 lines (called 1080P) which is over twice as many lines on the display as standard definition video.

As a result of the higher number of lines of high-definition video compared to standard-definition video, images on the same screen appear sharper and clearer and screens can be larger without losing detail. In addition to the higher number of lines and sharper images, the High-Definition changed the ration of the image width to the height from 4:3 ration to a 16:9 ratio. The 16:0 ratio means every High-Definition display is wider than the older standard-definition display.

In addition to the screen being a different format, the higher number of lines for the image required more information to create each image on a screen. As a result, the industry started using a digital signal using digital data with zeros and ones. The electronics industry decided to make cabling easier for consumers and include both the video and audio signals on one cable.

HDMI Advantages

Before HDMI cables existed the video, and audio signals were sent from one device to another using separate cables, one for video, and one each for left and right stereo. Add surround sound and audio and video cables created a spaghetti-like mess to connect a home theater system together. Add to that separate components for the video and audio sources such as a CD player, DVD player, cable box, video game player and different cable types and connectors was getting in the way of consumers buying and easily attaching consumer electronic devices.

The invention of HDMI has replaced eleven separate types of cables previously used for audio and video connections. HDMI technology also provides a higher quality signal for higher resolution video, higher quality audio and now also includes the ability to carry an ethernet signal between devices. Using an HDMI switch, several separate devices can be connected to an HDMI hub, which can then be connected to an HDMI connector on a television set even if the television set has only one or two HDMI connectors, making it possible for you always to connect any additional home electronic HDMI compatible devices to your television set.

To my way of thinking

HDMI has simplified cabling for television and audio systems for the average consumer as well as made it easier to buy electronic devices from one manufacturer and use them with another, as long as both use the widely-used HDMI industry standard.

High Dynamic Range (HDR)

High Dynamic Range (HDR) is a photo editing technique for combining multiple photos of a scene into a new image with better image details. It's an option on many smartphone cameras that often confuses people who think HDR stands for High Definition Resolution.

High Dynamic Range isn't new to just digital photography or smartphone cameras. Photographers use a variety of techniques to improve or enhance their photos. High Dynamic Range is a technique often used to help the photographer obtain a photo that appears better than one a single image might provide. By combining several exposures together, the final photo can sometimes appear better to our eyes than any one single photo.

The key here is sometimes, since an HDR photo isn't always better than one of the original shots taken, and it helps to know how HDR works and when to use it for the best results.

What is Dynamic Range?

The term "dynamic range" refers to the degree of variation between light and shadow in a photograph. With the use of several exposures, the HDR imaging process can increase this range, resulting in an image with a "better" look. After all, with photography it's all in the eye of the beholder, and our eyes see things differently than someone else.

How does your smartphone camera take an HDR photo?

HDR starts by taking several photos of a subject with different camera exposure settings; typically three shots are used. One with standard lighting exposure, one with an underexposed setting, and one with an overexposed setting. These three photos are taken extremely quickly by your camera in the time you'd normally take one photo so you typically won't even notice that three shots were taken.

These three photos are then digitally combined into a new image using the software in your smartphone camera app. The new image contains enhanced definition and detail in both the darkest shadows and brightest highlights of a scene determined by the HDR image enhancement process in the software.

What do the results look like?

HDR images often have a surreal look. Here's why: The variation between the bright and dark areas in an HDR file exceeds that which a digital camera can capture. By combining multiple photos made with different exposure settings, HDR essentially extends a camera's capacity to record light. In fact, a raw HDR file contains much more digital information than any computer monitor can display.

In the final stage of the HDR enhancement process, called tone mapping, these broad variations of light and shadow are compressed back down into a single image by your smartphone camera app. An image generated by this process sometimes appears different from how the scene naturally appeared to the eye. Depending on how the tone mapping software is used, this effect can be quite extreme.

Photo storage

Because digital photography allows a camera to take several images quickly, and the software can combine the images, HDR is an option included in most smartphone cameras. Since it combines multiple images, your smartphone will keep the standard exposure original photo and the additional HDR image, using up twice the memory if you decide to keep both the original and the HDR.

The other two exposures are not stored in your camera and don't use up memory. There are usually options in the camera settings to choose if you want to keep the original exposure or only the HDR final image, which can help save memory and storage on your smartphone.

When and why should I use HDR?

Creating the distinctive images commonly associated with HDR is not the only application of the process. HDR can sometimes help a photographer gain more subtle control over photographic lighting. For example, when making a photo of a room interior that features a window with a spectacular view, it can be difficult to capture in a single shot both the dimly lit room and the sunlit view outside. Using HDR, the photographer may combine a properly exposed photo of the interior with a separate photo of the window, and still attain a very natural looking result.

Here are some recommendations on when and when not to use HDR:

Use HDR when:

- You're taking a picture of a landscape since the contract between the sky and land is difficult for your smartphone camera to deal with in one exposure. The multiple HDR exposures will often result in more detail in the final HDR photo.

- Portraits in sunlight can be improved with HDR since the bright reflections of the sun on hair, dark shadows, and glare can all be improved with HDR.

- Low-light and backlit scenes can be improved with HDR since a the multiple exposures can help bring out highlights that might be missed with the standard exposure for low-lighting.

Don't use HDR when:

- You have movement since it's harder to freeze movement when your camera is taking three photos instead of one.

- High-contrast lights and darks in one scene often add quality and vibrancy to a photo and HDR will subdue this effect, resulting in a less intense photo.

- Bright colors in a photo are also subdued when using HDR so if you have a scene with vivid colors, don't use HDR for that image.

Remember, your normal smartphone camera setting will save the standard original photo besides the HDR one, so if you do this you've got two choices for the photo depending on which you prefer.

To my way of thinking

HDR imaging is easy to learn, but can be difficult to master using manual camera settings, so smartphone apps and settings make it easier for anyone to achieve impressive results for the right photo.

For the more advanced photographer, taking multiple exposures with a digital camera and using photo editing software to enhance the images offers the most flexibility in creating distinctive images.

HTML

The acronym "HTML" stands for HyperText Markup Language, which is the programming language used for creating web pages on the World Wide Web.

HTML is used to tell Web browsers how to display information and content on a Web page. Compared to programming languages used to create software programs, HTML is considered relatively simple. That's because HTML's purpose is to mark up, text and images on a Web page. The formatting instructions, also known as "tags," are hidden so they don't appear on the Web page when it's viewed. So what are these instructions and "tags?"

167

HTML Formatting and Tags

Let's take a look at something you might know better, like a word processing application on your computer. If you use any type of word processing software, you are probably familiar with formatting options. Things like paragraphs, font sizes, and positioning photos in a document are all ways you can format your document's appearance and layout. Your word processor uses information that you don't see, called formatting tags, to control how your text and images appear. The result is that text and images that are displayed, in the style and layout you chose in the formatting.

Like a word processor, HTML includes it's own set of formatting tags to format text, images, and the layout of these items on a Web page. It's pretty similar in the way your word processor formatting works, it's just designed for Web pages, not sheets of paper.

Browsers Interpret HTML

Browsers such as Internet Explorer, Chrome, Firefox and Safari are software programs that are used to read and interpret HTML in a consistent and standardized way. As you may use the English language to communicate with someone in London, think of HTML as a way to speak to an Internet browser. Using HTML, Web site owners can be sure that their Web pages will be accessible to anyone with an Internet-ready computer. No matter what type of browser someone is using, the universality of HTML code causes the Web page to display the same across different computers, mobile devices, and operating systems.

HTML Standard

HTML is a standardized technology and it's not owned by any one company. It's also free to use. Much like the Associated Press governs the standards for journalistic writing and grammar, the World Wide Web Consortium, or the W3C, maintains the standards for HTML writing and coding. This standardization allows for the consistent interpretation of different elements within the HTML language.

HTML Language

To use the Web, you don't need to know anything about HTML. Your Browser and computer will take care of interpreting the HTML and display Web pages with the correct layout and formatting. But if you plan to use the Web for creating a Web site, blogging, ecommerce, or other activities, learning a little bit of HTML can help you expand your options.

Just as knowing some Swedish might help you on your trip to Sweden, it might also be a good idea to learn some HTML before exploring the nooks and crannies of the World Wide Web. In either case, learning a new language can open up new and unforeseen possibilities and allow you to communicate effectively with people anywhere in the world.

HotSpot

From coffee shops to train stations and airports, you may have noticed the increasing visibility of signs indicating that these places are hotspots. No, that doesn't mean there is volcanic activity brewing beneath your local coffee shop. A hotspot is simply an area with wireless Internet access. No one is sure just where the term hotspot started being used, but the best guess is that the Finnish cellular company, Nokia, may have been responsible for creating the term.

Hotspots can be thought of as a local area within which people can connect to the Internet wirelessly. A hotspot is created when a wireless router is connected to the broader Internet. The router generates a Wi-Fi (wireless Internet) signal, which creates an area where other devices can receive the hotspot signal. Any person with a computer or other Wi-Fi enabled device can then connect to the hotspot. In other words, hotspots are areas where you can connect to the Internet without having to use cables or other physical connections.

Benefits of Hotspots

Hotspots afford customers and clients an opportunity to access the Internet while doing everyday activities like studying for tests or fueling their cars. For instance, you may have noticed men and women working on their computers while drinking a cup of coffee; they are likely connected to the Internet within a hotspot. And this is the greatest benefit of hotspots: they provide individuals additional ability to multitask. Instead of having to choose work or play, you can do both, completing tasks while enjoying yourself in a non-office environment. Conversely, you can simply surf the web while doing a necessary chore. Common hotspot locations include restaurants, hotels, hospitals, airports, bookstores, grocery stores, libraries, and schools. Some cities have even gone wireless with public wireless networks!

An individual can use a device that contains a wireless connection, like a laptop or phone, in a hotspot. Smartphones and mobile hotspot devices sold by cellular companies can create what are known as "personal hotspots." Using the cellular networks that these smartphones and devices use to connect to the Internet using their cellular data capability, they can use their WiFi capability to create a personal hotspot to connect nearby devices to the Internet. Personal hotspots are especially useful for travelers and others who might want to connect multiple items to the Internet in an easy and affordable fashion. For example, if you had a laptop or tablet that only had

WiFi Internet capability, you couldn't connect to the Internet unless you could connect to a WiFi hotspot.

Use of Wi-Fi in a hotspot isn't always free. While establishments are increasingly offering Wi-Fi services free of charge, others only provide it at a price. You may have to enter credit card information as you log-on to wireless service, so be sure to confirm whether it's free or not if you want to avoid charges. Some hotspots aren't available to the public and may be locked, allowing only those individuals who have the password the ability to use the hotspot. If you have a wireless router in your home, your hotspot probably requires a password to use the Internet, which makes it a private hotspot.

To my way of thinking

Since hotspots are so widely available, using the Internet and working without a cable connection is easier all the time. So the next time you see a hotspot sign, take it as an invitation. Open up your tablet, phone, or laptop, and do more.

I

iCloud

Many computer users have heard of cloud computing, but when they hear the term iCloud they are confused. Is this something new or part of the cloud computing system they have already heard about. The iCloud is a service from Apple Computer. When you use this service you essentially have a storage device, similar to a hard drive, but not physical computer hardware located on your desk or in your laptop.

Apple currently lets you access the iCloud from an iPhone, Ipod Touch, iPad and all Macintosh computers. Utilizing the iCloud gives all of your Apple devices access to every type of data you use, keep or store with your Apple device. This means you have easy access to apps, contacts, photos, movies, music and any other personal data you consider worth storing in the iCloud. When you access data in the iCloud any changes or additions you make are automatically updated and ready for your use with any other Apple device. The term for having this ability to have access to constantly updated data is synchronization. Not only is the data kept updated in the iCloud, any data that are concurrently held on one of your Apple Computer devices is automatically updated.

The Apple iCloud is like other cloud services. While it may seem that your data is mysteriously out there somewhere, as if in a cloud, in fact, the data is stored somewhere on a physical storage device. For safety and security most cloud services, including the Apple iCloud service have multiple constantly updated copies of all data you load into your iCloud storage area.

By using the Apple iCloud service you benefit because you can store every type of data you need and use every day, without being tied to a specific location or piece of hardware to access your data. You may access your data quickly at any time and from anywhere. The iCloud service also makes a purchase of anything offered in the iTunes system very simple because iTunes purchases are automatically downloaded, or indexed, in your personal iCloud storage area.

The indexing of iTunes purchases means that music, apps, photos and books you obtain via iTunes or your personal Apple photo stream will not take up any space in your free 5GB of cloud storage. In the future, purchase and registration of any new Apple Computer device can automatically be downloaded into your new device.

ISP

ISP stands for Internet Service Provider. In short, an Internet Service Provider is a company in the business of connecting people to the Internet. You, as the computer user, pay a fee to the ISP and in return, they connect your computer (or computers) to the Internet. Phone companies, cable companies, cellular providers, and other telecommunications companies are usually the businesses that provide Internet connections. They may offer additional services, but we're talking about them being your ISP right now. Familiar ISPs are often your local cable company, phone company or satellite television company, and with names like AT&T, Verizon, Time-Warner, COX, Charter, etc. There are many independent ISP's also, and some common names are Earthlink and NetZero.

The Internet Utility

If you think of the Internet as a utility like water, electricity, or gas, there are many similarities between ISP's and these utilities. ISP's provide the Internet access by purchasing access to the Internet in large amounts of capacity, then break it down into smaller amounts for home and business use. Internet access is similar to the electricity, gas, and water that's used by a utility. The Internet comes to your home, business, or mobile devices in the data that's contained in Web pages, emails, and other files. ISP's, just like utilities, have to have ways to get the Internet data to and from their customers. This is the distribution system, and it's often referred to as the "pipes" of the Internet as a slang term by techies. Internet speeds are determined by the type and capacity of the connection to the ISP. So what are they?

Internet Capacity

Depending on the speed of your service and your ISP, you might connect with a dial up phone connection, a wireless connection, a satellite connection, a cable connection, or a fiber optic connection. Dial up is the slowest of these, while fiber is the fastest possible connection. Internet pipes can be slow if they can only handle moving a certain amount of data, just like a water or gas pipe is slow if it can only handle a certain amount of liquid or gas. Larger pipes, with larger capacity, can move water and gas faster, and so can larger pipes for the Internet. However, just like a water or gas pipe, you don't have to use all the capacity that's available. How much capacity you have to your home or business depends on how much capacity you purchase. So how does pricing affect what an ISP does?

Internet Pricing

Internet connections from ISP's are usually priced similar to each other. After all, the Internet isn't different from one ISP to another, it's access and capacity you're paying for with the ISP. One ISP can't offer you access to a different part of the Internet than another ISP, so pricing is very competitive. Each ISP will have a different cost structure based on your location in the country, the kind of connection you want to establish and how much you plan on accessing the Internet. So how do they vary in price?

ISP Differences and Services

ISP's offer different pricing based on the amount of data you want receive and send when using the Internet, and with a variety of additional services. For home connections, we usually want fast downloads since most of our home activity is receiving data from the Internet on our computers. This includes watching movies, playing music, and browsing the Web. As a result, most home ISP's offer a fast download, but a slower upload, since we don't really need to send much information to the Internet as home users. Business, academic, and professional users often need to both receive and send larger amounts of data than home users, and pricing is usually higher for faster upload and download speeds. So basically, the more capacity you use, the more you pay, just like more water, gas, or electricity on your utility bills.

Some ISP's offer different types of services and support and their prices vary. For example, if you wanted priority support 24 hours a day, you would probably have to pay for a more expensive service. If you wanted email accounts from your ISP, one might be free, but additional emails might cost more.

How to Choose?

The decision on which ISP to choose has a lot to do with your Internet habits and how quickly you need the Internet to respond. Unless you have many computers or wireless devices like tablets or smartphones in your home, the basic ISP services will likely be more than enough for what you need. If you have a family that uses the Internet for watching movies has a lot of devices, or you have a small business, you might want to look into upgraded services.

Testing Your Internet Speed

ISP's use speed testing tools and monitor your capacity and can often tell how much capacity you are using and need by contacting technical support. There is a Web site at www.speedtest.net and an app for smartphones called SpeedTest that can test your connection speed and show you what your download and upload speeds are. If your curious, check them out. With cellular phones, connection speeds can vary greatly based on your location, cellular provider, and phone capability, while home and business connections tend to be more consistent since they use wired connections to the ISP.

In the alphabet soup that is the tech industry, knowing what an ISP is and what it can do for you will give you a leg up in making decisions about how you interact and connect to the Internet.

Image Stabilization

Image Stabilization removes blurring from pictures caused by camera movement, for example, when a hand shakes while taking a picture. It is a feature found in most smartphones and digital cameras that result in sharper, clearer pictures by reducing the blurriness caused when taking a picture. It's why many professionals use a tripod to hold the camera steady.

History of Image Stabilization

Canon camera was the first photography company to create and implement a photo image stabilization software. This software was used for the first time in Canon's optically stabilized lenses in 1995. Since then, the capabilities of camera stabilization technology have been improved with each passing year. In fact, most smartphone users now take pictures regularly with little or no blurring as a result of image stabilization. Clear, non-blurred pictures are an incredible feature considering that most people's hands shake, even a little, when trying to take a picture with a smartphone. Images on social media and sharing sites include beautiful, clear pictures that were all taken by non-professional, smartphone-using individuals that have little or no blur and an incredible picture quality.

Why steadiness is important for clear pictures

In the past, a photography artist would have to take extreme measures to make sure that there was no blurring in his or her pictures. In fact, even the most professional of photographers would regularly struggle with blurring, which was a direct result of their camera being unstable in their hands. Sometimes, even bipod and tripod stands couldn't fully resolve the issue. Thankfully, image stabilization technology has been able to solve most of the blur issues that existed prior to image stabilization. A photographer no longer has to worry about issues of picture quality; rather, his or her job can focus on capturing the picture perfect moment.

Digital versus Optical Image Stabilization

Optical Image Stabilization, the best type, uses an electronic circuit in the camera (or smartphone with a camera) to sense movement, often called a gyroscope or gyro-sensor. As a child, you might remember using a top that you'd spin on a table or flat surface, and as long as the top was spinning, it stayed upright. Since the top keeps its balance, it acts as a basic gyroscope. There's an electronic version of a gyroscope inside most smartphones, and in many digital cameras that use image stabilization. Sensing the orientation of the gyroscope, a gyro-sensor inside the camera or smartphone can tell the angle and direction of any movement and compensate for the movement. Since electronic circuits are very fast, the adjustments are usually made faster than your hand can move.

Digital image stabilization uses software to compensate for any movement. There are two ways, and sometimes they are combined. The software used is usually included in the camera app or digital camera so there is nothing necessary to purchase or install.

The first method of digital image stabilization enhances the image in order to take the picture with a faster shutter speed. The shutter of the camera opens and allows light in to create the image, and the longer it stays open, the more chance there is of a blurred image. Think of when you take a picture of a fast-moving object like a car, if the car is moving too fast, the car appears blurry, but a faster shutter speed can stop the motion. The picture is crisp as a result of the higher shutter speed which stopped the motion. Since the original image is enhanced by software, it may be crisp, but it may not be as accurately exposed as an optically stabilized image.

The second method uses software to stick together multiple images recorded when taking the picture. The software compares the images to each other and locates blurry and unclear areas, then pulls portions from each of the images to stitch together a clear picture. Again, since software is doing the image stabilization, while it may be good enough for many people, the optically stabilized images will always be higher quality.

Often you'll find that more expensive models of smartphones and cameras by the same manufacturer include the higher quality optical image stabilization. However, digital image stabilization with the right smartphone and camera can still create great pictures and virtually eliminate hand-shake and camera movement. It all depends on the brand and model.

To my way of thinking

Everyone who owns a smartphone or digital camera now can take sharper, clearer pictures as a result of image stabilization, making it easier and more fun to take pictures with camera that we often have with us at all times, like the ones in our smartphones.

Instagram

Instagram is an online social networking service that allows users to take photos and videos, then apply filters and other effects, and share them on other popular social networking sites. It's a free service and a fun way to share photos.

Photo and video sharing via the internet has become a part of mainstream popular culture. Instagram is one the most popular application used to create sharable photos and video shorts of 15 seconds or less.

Users of Instagram typically use their smartphone, using the Instagram mobile app. The user takes a picture or video of their desired subject matter, then uses one of over 17 filters available in Instagram to change the picture, and then shares the photo on the Instagram social network.

The filters give any picture a "professional" look with the touch of a button. While it doesn't take the place of a professional photographer, Instagram helps make photos look better, which makes it really useful for most people.

What the filters do.

Each filter has been created with an optional border, and changes the look of the photo by either enhancing the colors or creating soft glows or vintage looks. Instagram effects are not limited to digital filters.

The tilt-shift feature allows the user to apply an adjustable bar or circular focus on the photo, creating the appearance of an altered depth of field. This effect is traditionally created by photographers by using specialty lenses, and it can turn a standard cell phone picture into an artistic and professional looking photograph.

There is a rotate button that can rotate a photo clockwise 90 degrees each time it's tapped, allowing users to change the orientation of their photo as needed. Finally, the Lux effect, represented by a sun icon, is an auto-enhance feature that creates rich colors and contrasts.

Captions, labels, and tags

Users can also add information to explain the photo, include a search term, and identify themselves or other Instagram users. A caption can be added below each photo to explain more about the photo to viewers. Labels can be added with a hashtag (text with a # sign in front of it) which allows other users to find and search for photos using that hashtag.

People can also be identified with by using an @ symbol before their Instagram username which creates a "tag." Once the user is finished applying filters and effects to their photograph, it is automatically shared online with Instagram. The user also has the option to share these photos on their social networking accounts. The photos can even be printed at photo centers, like Walgreens, and are shaped in an iconic 4"x4" square that is reminiscent of Polaroid photos.

History and use of Instagram

Instagram was launched in October of 2010 by San Francisco based Kevin Systrom and Mike Krieger, and less than a year after its creation, Instagram had over 10 million users and over 150 million photo uploads. Acquired by Facebook in 2012, Instagram now has over 150 million active users. An Instagram picture can be shared not only to a user's Instagram account, but also to a user's Facebook, Twitter, or Tumblr social media account.

Using their existing lists of friends and connections already created in these accounts allows a user to share the photos with their existing social network connections.

Enabling everyone to easily share quality photos, Instagram allows for a new dimension of connection between people over social networking sites. Creating artistic photos of food, animals, life events, parties, kids, and friends is no longer limited to the realm of professional photography.

Internet of Things

The Internet of Things, or IoT, describes what the Internet is when it's used to connect to anything besides a computer. The Internet has traditionally been used to connect computers and computing devices to each other so they can do things like sending emails, display web pages, or transfer files. Things are objects which are not computers themselves, but can be connected to the Internet if they are made "smart."

What's a Thing?

A "thing" is just something that hasn't been traditionally thought of as a computer, like a refrigerator, door lock, light switch, or thermostat. These kinds of "things" have been pretty dumb, but are getting smarter all the time. When they become smarter, it's usually because a computer has been added to them, but it's a specialized computer made just for the device's function.

For example, a thermostat could use mercury to tell the temperature, then when the mercury rises to reach a certain temperature, a switch is flipped that turns on a furnace. As digital sensors were made that could sense temperature, it became possible to build thermostats that didn't need mercury. Digital thermostats could communicate with digital computers, and as computers became inexpensive to build into a thermostat, the old mercury thermostat became a new digital programmable model.

Many "things" have become programmable, and usually they all work in different ways. Video cassette recorders are well known for cumbersome, challenging, and frustrating programming options, and programming a TV show recording still isn't as easy as many people think it should be.

Why would I want a "thing?"

The ability to build some intelligence into a thing that didn't have it, if it's done right, offers useful capabilities, so let's consider what's happened with our old mercury home thermostat. A recent product, the Nest thermostat has become a fairly popular "thing" and is a good example of what can be done if a product is designed the right way for the Internet of Things. The Nest is a programmable thermostat that can learn how you want the temperature in your home, and create a program based on what it learns.

While that in itself doesn't need an Internet connection, adding the Internet connection to the Nest allows you to control the temperature in your home using Internet connected devices, such as a computer or smartphone. This means that you can adjust your thermostat using your smartphone from anywhere in the house, or even better, while you're away from your home. In case you forgot to turn the heating or air conditioning off when you left the house, you can do it remotely from the Internet. You can even start to warm up your home before you return from work, making it cozy when you walk in the door.

As your settings and temperature changes are being recorded, the Nest thermostat can work with a software program to learn your preferences, adjusting the temperature up when you're in the house, or down when you leave for work, and create a customized program, so you don't have to learn how to program the device in the first place. In addition to creating the program, it can monitor energy use, and advise you about your usage, offering suggestions and changes for saving money.

Now imagine that in addition to your thermostat, your light switches, water heater, car, and even refrigerator become "smart" and are able connect. An electric car connected to the Internet allows my son to warm up the interior temperature with a smartphone app before he gets ready to walk out the door.

While the average person might not need to upgrade their thermostat or change their light switches, larger users of resources that spend more money on energy or other resources are connecting things to the Internet and at a faster pace than ever before.

Connecting objects to the Internet

The first use of the Internet of Things is attributed to Kevin Ashton. He explained his purpose for it in a 1999 article:

"If we had computers that knew everything there was to know about things - using data they gathered without any help from us - we would be able to track and count everything, and greatly reduce waste, loss and cost. We would know when things needed replacing, repairing or recalling, and whether they were fresh or past their best".

Things and objects that are independently connected to the internet can digitally represent themselves, which then changes the existence of the object itself. The physical world will take on what is known as "ambient intelligence" since physical objects will no longer only relate to the user, but will be connected to other objects and databases.

Change is coming with more Things on the way

The Internet of Things is changing the way much of the world does business. When objects can be connected to the Internet and are digitally represented, they can be controlled from anywhere, with increased efficiency and safety in industries like manufacturing and healthcare. With the ability to collect information from things, companies are looking at how the Internet of Things will improve operating processes, client and customer interaction, and products or services.

While many products, homes and cars equipped with this technology will not appear any different, their functions will be dramatically changed as these objects will be able to access data provided by other objects and databases of relevant information. Roadway sensors could alert cars to road hazards, and home appliances could alter their power usage based on pricing information received from a 'smart' power grid. This type of information sharing will change the way people interact with objects and their usage.

IP Address

An Internet Protocol Address, more commonly referred to as an IP address, is a unique number assigned to each device on the internet. Think of an IP address as a computer's home address.

Today there are literally billions of devices on the internet ranging from personal computers to smart phones and other connected devices. Together they form a complex network in which any device can communicate with any other device all thanks to their unique IP address.

Why Do Computers use IP Addresses?

Any computer or device connected to the Internet requires an IP address. The IP address is a unique number that allows other computers and devices to send information to any computer with an IP address.

Whenever a message (like an email) is sent from your computer, your computer's IP address is included in the message. You don't see this, and you don't need to worry about it. But any other computer or device on the Internet will know what IP address sent the message. So if it's necessary to send a reply back to your computer, any other computer will know to include your computer's IP address in the message so the Internet will deliver the message to your computer.

There are, however, many types of messages that are sent and received by computers when using the Internet. Often these include Web pages that are sent to your computer when you're browsing the Web, information you might use to fill out a form on a Web page, and files, like photos or documents, that you might download from a Web page or another computer on the Internet. Each of these actions uses the IP addresses of your computer and the other computer or device to make sure information is sent and received to the right location.

The easiest way to relate to something you are familiar with is how we use postal addresses to send physical mail and packages. When you prepare a label or address an envelope to be mailed, you're required to complete an address that tells the postal service where the item is to be delivered. The address is unique, meaning there is only one location that receives deliveries. While we use names, street numbers, cities, states, and postal codes, the Internet just replaces all of that with one number, the IP address.

When mailing an item, you also place your return address on the envelope or label. This is primarily used in case your item can't be delivered, and then the postal service returns it to the sender's address. Your computer's IP address is used for the same purpose. Just in case your message can't be delivered, the Internet will notify your computer that there was an error. If it's an email, you'll usually receive an email message telling you your email couldn't be delivered.

Why Don't We Need to Enter IP Addresses?

While computers are very good at numbers, people generally prefer a language, like English, Spanish, etc.. To make our lives easier, smart people that invented the Internet created a special software called Domain Name Servers, or DNS for short. Now you may have heard about DNS or something called a DNS server, but whether or not you have, here's what they do for you.

A DNS server is a computer that translates IP addresses to Domain Names and vice-versa. While Domain Names was the topic of a different tech term newsletter, you use them all the time when browsing the Web and using email. When you address an email to someone, what comes after the @ symbol is the domain name. Common email domains are @gmail.com, @yahoo.com, @outlook.com, and you may have your own domain name for your own email. Web sites use the domain names as well, only with the www before the domain.

Domain Name Servers translate the domain name into an IP address, so messages addressed to a domain are delivered to the right computer on the Internet. Without DNS, we'd have to remember every Web site or domain by it's IP address. Trust me, domain names are easier to remember than IP addresses, so thank you to the people that invented DNS.

Sources and Types of IP Addresses

IP addresses are assigned by a special group called the Internet Assigned Numbers Authority, or IANA for short (http://www.iana.org). IANA is part of the Internet Corporation for Assigned Names and Numbers (http://www.icann.org) which is an international non-profit. This way, all IP addresses work the same all over the world, and the IANA is the source for all IP addresses. So who can get an IP address from them?

Organizations that run Internet operations, which include Internet Service Providers, Web hosting services, large corporations, schools, and governments are eligible to apply for a set of assigned IP addresses. The IANA reviews their request, and if approved, assigns a specific set of IP addresses which the organization can use in their operations. However, IP addresses can be assigned to a computer for temporary use or for permanent use.

Temporary IP Addresses

While the organization that has the use of the IP addresses can assign them to computers and other devices connected to the Internet, an address can be assigned for temporary use or for permanent use on a computer or device.

Temporary IP addresses, also referred to as "Dynamic IP Addresses," are IP addresses that are not assigned permanently to a specific computer or device. The IP address is "loaned" out for the computer or device to use while it's connected.

For home users, your Internet Service (usually your cable or phone company, but there are others), has the use of a block of IP addresses. When you connect to their network, they assign your computer a temporary IP address for your use. Although temporary, it's unique to your computer or device, and any computer on the Internet will know your address.

This temporary address is yours to use as long as you're connected to the Internet. Power off your computer, or disconnect your network connection, and you could be assigned a new IP address the next time you connect. Your computer knows how to make this work, and it allows Internet Service

Providers a way to make much more efficient use of their block of assigned IP addresses.

Locations like coffee shops, hotels, libraries, and schools allow users to connect and assign a Dynamic IP Address since the computer or device is often connected for a short period of time.

In your home, your IP address may be assigned to each of your devices by the router provided by your Internet Service Provider. In this case, your router is assigned an IP address by your Internet Service when it connects to the Internet. This is a Dynamic IP Address assigned by your ISP. Then your router assigns IP addresses to your computers and devices internally.

Private and Public Addresses

Your router uses a special range of IP addresses that are set aside specifically for this type of use, called Private IP Addresses. These Private IP address cannot connect to the Internet directly since the are not unique, and no computer on the Internet will be able to direct traffic to them. The advantage of using Public IP Addresses is that these IP addresses can be used over and over for any private network, since no two private networks ever connect with each other directly.

Your router uses a range of Private IP addresses that are part of the factory settings and assigns them one at a time to any computer or device, like a printer that connects to your home or small office network. The router uses the Public IP address assigned by your Internet Service to connect to the Internet. Internet devices only know your router's IP address, and it's up to the router to keep track of your local, Private IP addresses. By using Private IP addresses, it's possible to reuse the same set of IP address numbers for any Private Network. This makes it easier to setup a home or small business network since unique assigned IP addresses are not required.

Permanent or "Static" IP Addresses

Some computers and devices have a static IP addresses that never change. A static IP address is often required for certain functions on the Internet. It's used by computers that host Web sites, email services, remote backup sites, routers, and other network and computing devices.

Static IP addresses are used when it's important for a computer to have a permanent location that other computers can locate. For example, the computer for the home page of Yahoo! would be hard to find if it relied on a Dynamic IP address. By assigning a Static IP address, all the thousands of Domain Name Servers can remember Yahoo!'s location and quickly translate the domain name to the correct IP address.

Will You Ever See an IP Address?

Understanding a little about IP addresses helps you appreciate how sophisticated the Internet is. So often we take it for granted that when we type in a Web page address or click on a link in an email we receive the correct information on our desktop or mobile device.

If you just use the Internet for casual use, you may never see an IP address. When you connect to a WiFi network and are able to use it, you'll know that some device assigned an IP address to your computer, laptop, tablet, or smartphone so it can communicate with the Internet.

Tips for Solving Common IP Address Problems

Our homes and offices becoming more connected and dependent on the Internet. So knowing a little about IP addresses might help you solve some common problems with a network. Often, if the cause of the problem is with the IP addresses used by your computers or devices, it can help to power off everything, then power up everything. It's the first step that Internet Services usually tell home and small office users to do to solve network problems.

When powering every computer and network device off on your home network, you're setting them up so they will ask for a new IP address when they are powered on again. The first device to power on is your access device. Sometimes this is the router, but often it's just a box from your Internet Service that connects to them and has a single network connection. Powering this device off, then on, makes a new request from the device to your Internet Service for a connection, including a new IP address (remember, these are Dynamic IP addresses your ISP assigns to you). You should wait a few minutes before powering up the next device on your network, your router.

Then you would power on your router. It takes about 3-4 minutes to "boot," since it's a computer, but one that's dedicated to being a router. Once your router is powered on, then you can power on your other computers, but do them one at a time. This way each one can request and receive it's IP address. It's a good idea to test each Internet connection as you power on the devices by seeing if you can open a Web page to view.

Network printers are sometimes powered off and powered on, and sometimes they change their IP address in the process. If the printer's IP address changed, your computer may not be able to find the printer again on the network. Sometimes just removing the printer from your computer's printer settings and adding it back in solves this problem. Newer printer models generally have features that make it easier to connect to a home or small office network.

While routers (which we covered in a previous newsletter) are reliable, sometimes replacing a router that's a few years old with a newer model can solve IP address and network problems. If your router is more than 3-4 years old, it might not have been designed for all the mobile and wireless devices available today. While your router may work for most devices, if you're having trouble connecting some devices to your home network, a $50-$75 dollar router replacement is often less expensive than hiring someone to come out and fix a problem, which might involve a router replacement anyway.

J

Javascript

Javascript is a computer programming language used by software developers to create applications. Javascript is called a "script" language because it can be used to write lists or "scripts" of instructions that don't need translation into another form before a computer can interpret the instructions. Non-script types of programming languages require that a software developer create the language in what in one form, and require a conversion into another form before the program can by used on a computer.

On some web pages, you might see Javascript in action if you happen to see a web page that displays a .js in the web address. However, just because you don't see anything with .js doesn't mean that a web page you're visiting isn't using Javascript because the program can work in the background while you're using a webpage.

Where is Javascript used?

Javascript is used primarily in web pages to make the web pages interactive. For example, some web pages only display text and images. A web page that uses Javascript could do things to change what appears or accept input from the web page user. For example, change and update stock prices, or allow visitors enter information from a form on a web page and deliver a result, such as an interest rate calculator.

How did Javascript come about?

In 1994, browser developers invented a computer programming language called Javascript. Today Javascript is one of the most widely used programming languages.

When the first web browsers were invented in the early 1990s, they were applications that translated simple instructions into readable text, images, and video. They weren't able to make decisions or do anything in response to user input other than retrieve another web page with the familiar blue text that signifies a link from one web page to another.

Links from one document to another were useful enough to cement the web into our daily lives. But the ability to do more complex tasks would make the browser that much more useful. "Imagine," said the early browser developers "if we could check to make sure people are entering a ZIP code instead of a city name before they send us their sign-up form?"

Today, Javascript is used by almost every website and web application developer. All major desktop web browsers and most mobile devices like iPhones, iPads, and Android smartphones and tablets support Javascript. Compared to other programming languages, Javascript is easier to learn and use.

What does Javascript do for web pages?

Javascript can be written into a web page directly; it just doesn't appear as information that's displayed on your screen when you view it. When a web browser sees a Javascript program, it runs the program as part of the web page.

Here's an example of how this might work. If a web page were written to display the names of all the states, a Javascript program on the page might allow you to click one of those state names to enter it in an e-mail form automatically without having to type it yourself.

This kind of interactive capability makes the Internet more useful than if web browsers just displayed text and images. After Javascript was invented and incorporated into early browsers like Netscape Navigator and Internet Explorer, web pages were able to do complex tasks because a program could be run by the web browser application. Those capabilities turned the web into a software development platform and made the Internet and the World Wide Web much more useful.

To my way of thinking

If you use the web regularly, you are likely encountering and using web pages that depend on Javascript. In fact, it's made web browsers one of the most powerful software applications we use, whether it's on a desktop, laptop or mobile device.

JPEG, GIF, PNG, and PDF

Have you ever seen a web page that asks "would you prefer to download you file as a jpeg, gif, or pdf file? If your next step is to pick one at random, read on and I'll try to explain some of these terms.

Photos, pictures, and other graphics can be used on computers, tablets, and smartphones because they are digital files. The information that is needed to display a photo or image on a screen is contained in the file, and converted into an image on your screen by software on your computer and device.

The jpeg, gif, and pdf terms tell both you and your Computing device how the image is stored and what software is necessary to Open and display the image file. The letters jpeg, gif, PDF, are all called file extensions and are used after the dot in a file name. computers read the file name and use the extension to decide what software should be used to open and disply the file.

For example, a file might be "image.jpeg" and your computer (or mobile device) will know it needs to use software that will open up and display a jpeg file on the screen.

If your computer has software to do that, it will display the image. Fortunately, computers and mobile devices have built-in software that will display the most common image file types.

Image files differ in whats called resolution, which is the amount of detail and data contained in the image file. Images used on web pages are meant for displaying on a display screen and don't need a great deal of resolution. They can be smaller and as a result, display faster when viewed on a web page. The jpeg and gif file are commonly used for images on web pages. You might also see a file called png which is becoming more common.

Your computer or mobile device uses its built in software to display these types of files. Jpeg, gif, and png files are compressed, meaning that not all of the data that was in the original image is contained in the compressed file. Graphic artists and web designers use software that compresses the original file, converting it to a jpeg, gif, or png file, making it smaller in size, and faster for displaying on the web.

K

Keyboard Shortcuts

Keyboard shortcuts are a practical method to enter instructions that might take multiple keystrokes or mouse clicks. A keyboard shortcut can also be used to replace a mouse command, which is useful when entering the shortcut is faster than moving your mouse arrow and clicking, as is often the case with laptop computers or when using a large screen display.

Knowing even a just a few keyboard shortcuts can make many everyday tasks easier and faster to perform when using your computer. You might already know some common ones, like typing and holding the Ctrl (short for Control) and C key, which is the command for Copy, or pressing the Ctrl and X key, which is the command for Cut. I should mention here that there's a slight difference in keyboard shortcuts between computers using Windows and Apple's Mac computers.

On computers running Windows, the keyboard includes a key in the lower left corner named Ctrl, while on Mac computers the cmd (short for Command) key, just to the left of the spacebar, is usually used with similar shortcuts. There are some other differences in the keyboards between Windows and Apple computers which result in some different keys being used to accomplish the same task. As I mentioned earlier, to Cut an item, like text you've selected with your mouse cursor, the Windows shortcut is Ctrl plus C. On a Mac, the shortcut uses the Command plus C combination.

The action and results are the same on Windows and Macs, but each one uses slightly different keys to perform the same thing. At the end of the article is a link to the web pages for Windows and Mac keyboard shortcuts so you can learn more of them for your computer. However, since there are some slight differences in the keys, you might have to learn a few of the differences if you use both types of computers or if you're moving from one to another.

Keyboards and Computers

The simple keyboard, often taken for granted, is a pretty sophisticated tool for people to communicate with their computer, and whenever you press any key on your keyboard, you're giving your computer instructions about what you want it to do for you. Keyboards are the most frequently used way for people to send information to their computer, and a keyboard is a human data entry device. So what happens when we enter data by pressing keys?

A physical keyboard uses buttons in an arrangement of letters, numbers, and special keys that have a switch and electrical contact for each button. When you press down on a key, you create an electrical connection that sends the character information to your computer. Keyboards on touchscreen devices, like smartphones and tablets, work similarly to physical buttons, but they respond to where you touch the screen when you tap a key.

The software on your computer interprets the information you sent it by pressing on a key, and then does something with it. If you're using a word processing application and are typing on your keyboard, your computer's displays the characters in a document as you type. Using a combination of keys is a way you can give more elaborate instructions to your computer., you can give your computer instructions to do something more sophisticated and complex. But the sequence that you use is critical. Otherwise, your computer won't understand what you meant.

Modifier Keys

A "modifier" key is the first key pressed to start the shortcut. If you've ever typed a capital letter you've used a modifier key, in this case, it's the Shift key. Pressing and holding the Shift key and a letter enters an upper case character instead of a lower case one. Modifier keys for shortcuts work the same way, by modifying the instruction for the next key you press. Pressing Ctrl and the C key changes what the C key does when it's pushed, just like the pressing, the Shift key altered what case the letter C appears in the document.

Modifiers are keys that aren't used to enter frequently used characters, numbers or symbols. Ones like the Ctrl key (Command on Mac, the Alt key (Option key on Mac), and the Windows Logo key are useful modifier keys.

Some shortcuts use a combination of three or more keys. In Windows, you can use the Ctrl + Shift + arrow key to select a block of text. On a Mac, pressing the Command + Shift + 3 key takes a screenshot of your desktop and pressing the Command + Option + Control + Power buttons will quit all apps and shut down your computer.

You may have noticed that the keyboard shortcut descriptions I've been including are written with the name of the key, a plus sign, and the name of a second key, third key, and so on. Written keyboard shortcuts usually this follow a format in help guides. The plus sign indicates you should press one key, then press and hold another, etc.. The Mac website uses a dash between the keys to describe the shortcut, but you should hold down on each key in the sequence for the command.

Special Keys

Some keys have a designated function. On a Windows computer, pressing the Windows key opens the Start screen, press it again to close the Start screen. The ESC (escape) key, located in the upper left of your keyboard, is used to cancel or undo your last action and is used for this function on both Mac and Windows computers. Function keys often have multiple uses.

On both Windows and Mac computers, the top row of keys are called Function keys and have a small F and number on them. They're referred to as F1, F2, F3, etc.. with instructions. Many of them have an icon on them that indicates the "function", like a small speaker symbol on one, and a larger speaker for volume down and volume up controls.

Other buttons on Mac and Windows include a home button (to move to the top of a document), along with the page down and page up buttons which make it easy to navigate around a document with a single press.

Where do I find keyboard shortcuts

The menus at the top of your screen are a good place to look for keyboard shortcuts that can save you time and effort. When you use your mouse or trackpad to move your cursor to a menu and scroll down to select a menu option, there's probably keyboard shortcut available for that menu item. In Mac's the keyboard shortcut for any menu item is shown to the right of that item and this is a common format used in Mac's for all applications. Windows has several ways to locate the shortcut, so there are several ways to look for them.

In Windows, look for an underlined letter in the menu item, a description of the shortcut next to a menu item, or move your mouse cursor over a command icon. Sometimes keyboard shortcuts aren't apparent.

In Microsoft Word, the icons above your document are used to access commands with your mouse and a click. If you hold your mouse over an icon, the function is displayed in a small pop-up window along with the keyboard shortcut for that command.

Custom shortcuts

Both Macs and Windows offer ways you can create custom keyboard shortcuts. I was reviewing a document recently and I wanted to accept or reject edits from my editor quickly as I went through the manuscript. I was using my mouse and after taking action on each edit, I had to move the mouse to the next edit and click. I was able to create a custom shortcut that would accept an edit, then move my cursor automatically to the next edit. I created another one to reject an edit, and a third one to pass on the edit for later review. Having quick shortcuts let me move through the document faster than using individual keystrokes or mouse clicks and saved me the time when reviewing. I've included links to the support websites for Microsoft and Apple which explain how to create custom shortcuts.

To my way of thinking

Using a mouse or trackpad to move a cursor on a computer screen and clicking seems easy enough, but when it's for a repetitive task it can become annoyingly tedious. If that's the case for you, then it's time to take advantage of the keyboard shortcuts available in the applications you use most frequently.

Using just a few of the simple editing shortcuts like Copy, Cut, and Paste will save you the effort of moving your hand away from your keyboard to your mouse and back again. When touch-typing was still taught in schools, it was common knowledge that keeping your hands in position over the keyboard was important to fast and accurate typing. Sometimes we forget the basics of technology and forget that something as simple as a few finger movements can make technology work so much better for us than we thought possible.

Here are the links to instructions for creating your own on a Mac and Windows PC

Mac

https://support.apple.com/kb/PH18418?locale=en_US

Windows

https://support.microsoft.com/en-us/kb/237179

Links to keyboard shortcuts for Windows and Mac

Mac keyboard shortcuts

https://support.apple.com/en-us/HT201236

Windows 10 keyboard shortcuts

http://windows.microsoft.com/en-us/windows-10/keyboard-shortcuts

Keywords

A keyword is a word or group of words used to search the Internet when using web search sites such as Google, Yahoo!, or Bing. Regardless if the search term uses a single word, a group of words or a complete sentence, the entire search phrase is called a keyword.

Users searching for information on the Internet enter the keyword, and the search site goes to work and then displays a list of websites that are the most closely related to the keyword. These results and the lists of websites provided in response to the keyword search make the Internet a useful tool for finding out about almost anything and makes

search sites like Google a popular destination for many Internet users. However, keywords and searching have many options and capabilities that you might not be aware of when you do a search on the Internet.

How keyword searches work

There are no rules on what keywords you can use for a search, and you can enter more than one keyword at a time. Search engine sites have software tools that scan web pages on the Internet and create a library of what every web page is about using the information that appears on the web page. After entering your keyword, the search engine evaluates the keyword(s) you entered, then performs a search on all the web pages in the library.

The search site uses its software programming to determine which web pages from its library should appear on the search results page you see on your computer or device. The programming on the search site makes decisions on its own to determine what web pages it thinks are most relevant to your keyword search. There's a different result depending on how specific you are in your keyword search.

A general search keyword like "flowers" will usually return a list of web pages where you can purchase flowers, while a keyword search for "types of flowers" will produce a different result with web pages that can help you identify and learn about types of flowers. The more specific the keywords you use, the more specific and useful the results will be.

Privacy and tracking

Search sites like Google track your search activity when you use your computer in order to determine the best results for you when you do a search. In case you didn't notice, Google does explain their privacy and tracking policy to you with a message on the Google home page at the bottom with a link called "terms."

When you use Google or any other search site to search the Internet, you're using a free service provided by the search site, and in return you typically allow them to track your search activity on the Internet. The search site uses this tracking information to choose what types of ads to display to you and tries to make the ads more relevant to your search activity.

Because of this tracking, two people could enter the same search term and often see a different set of websites listed in the results. Google and other search sites use your recent search activity to determine what you were searching for recently and often display ads and other search results related to your search history.

Advanced searches

The careful selection of keywords, in combination with using phrases called "operators," can greatly improve your search results. Many search engines support ways to specify, limit, or select search options using "Boolean" operators. Don't be afraid of the term Boolean, since Boolean operators include simple words such as AND, OR, and NOT that help give a search site more specific instructions to conduct a search.

Search sites are basically software programs that take the keyword you enter and produce a list of results. The clearer you can be in giving instructions to the search site, the more likely you'll get the results you want when you conduct a search.

These Boolean operators can be used along with keywords to refine further the search and help the search site understand your search better. There are some common Boolean operators and below are some examples of you can use them in a keyword search.

The operator AND means that all the keywords specified must appear in the resulting list of web addresses, returning a limited set of results. The keywords Chicago AND tours will return web pages about all tours available only in Chicago.

The operator OR means that at least one of the keywords specified must appear in the web addresses returned, returning a larger set of results. The keywords hockey OR Blackhawks will return web pages about hockey in general or the Blackhawks specifically.

The operator NOT means that at least one of the keywords specified must be excluded in the web addresses returned, eliminating certain results. The keywords hockey AND sticks, NOT players will return a more refined search about hockey sticks and not hockey in general.

Using phrases enclosed in quotes. Some search engines allow keywords to be entered as a phrase and will limit the search results to websites that are relevant to the specific words in the order they are used within the quotes.

The good news is if the desired results are not received, making a change in keywords can lead to a whole new set of results.

Advertising

While the use of search sites is free to users, these companies have to make money somehow, and it's usually by selling advertising. Since searching is such a common activity on the Internet, search sites have a lot of people using them. Anyone looking to sell something, from cars to vacations, can pay for web ads to appear on the results page when people search for a keyword related to their advertisement.

To my way of thinking

Search engines are an incredibly useful tool for finding information on the Internet, without them the Internet would be a real challenge to use for locating information. By understanding keywords and how using phrases, questions, and some simple words like AND, OR and NOT in your search, you can find the results you want even faster.

L

LCD

An LCD, or liquid-crystal display, is a type of electronic display used in computer monitors, flat screen televisions, and other consumer electronics. They're energy efficient, so they use less electricity than other types of displays (like the older tube types). They can range in size from just a few inches for wristwatches and smartphones up to 120 inches or larger for television sets.

Your LCD computer monitor is actually made up of lots of little squares called pixels, but because they're so tiny, they can trick your eye into thinking that you're looking at lines, curves, and any type of shape imaginable. These little squares work independently from one another, so one might display green while the one right beside it displays white. Your monitor can show incredibly detailed images by using millions of these little colored squares at a time. For example, the most common computer monitor today displays more than 2 million colored squares. Each character that you see on this page uses hundreds of these little squares, but all you see from a distance are letters.

The only problem with LCDs is that they don't generate any light on their own. Hold you hand up to your monitor, and you'll see light reflecting on it. Light has to pass through the LCD to reach your eyes. Early LCD models used fluorescent lighting, but these displays were bulky, used a fair amount of electricity, and generated a ton of heat. The LED monitors and televisions you see in stores today still use LCDs, but they use energy efficient lighting instead of fluorescent bulbs. Newer models are thinner, lighter, and cooler.

Scientists have actually known about liquid crystals since 1904, but it wasn't until the early '90s that display manufacturers took an interest. As you might remember from just a few years ago, early LCD TVs were incredibly expensive. A 40-inch TV might have cost $5,000 in 2000, but today's prices for a similar TV are significantly less. Manufacturers continue to improve LCD picture quality, and new models can even connect to the Internet just like a computer.

If you've been thinking about buying a new computer monitor or television, an LCD can work as both. Larger displays can make it easier to read articles or emails online and catch small details in TV shows, movies, and sports games. Many new LCDs are lightweight enough to mount on the wall, which can free up space in your living room, and they've been dropping in price for the last decade.

LED

Light Emitting Diodes, or LEDs, is a type of light source that produces light from a silicon wafer made up of two different materials. When an electrical voltage is applied to the LED, it emits light. In the past LED's were used primarily for small lighting uses, such as an indicator light on a display panel or a number or letter display. Advances in LED technology have resulted in their use as a light source for general home lighting, automotive, aviation, traffic signals, and advertising displays. So what makes an LED light source an LED?

LED's are semiconductor circuits

LEDs are a type of electrical component known as a diode. A diode is a one-way type of electrical component. Diodes resist electric current in one direction but do not resist current flow in the other direction. The use of the two different materials creates this one-way direction for the current. When a voltage is applied to a diode, electrons move from one side of the diode to other. When an electron moves to the other side, it loses some energy that in LED's is released as light in the form of a photon. LED"s are different from other types of diodes since the electrons generate light when they release energy while other types of diodes and circuits generate heat.

The color of the light, (or more properly the wavelength) depends on the materials used in the LED. When LED's were first invented, they were made with a type of material called gallium arsenide, which produced infrared and red LEDs. That's why when they first started appearing they were always red in color. Now, other materials are used in LED's to produce white light and other wavelengths.

As LEDs have become lower in cost and are designed to generate light that is similar to familiar incandescent light bulbs, LED light bulbs have become available in sizes and shapes for home and commercial uses.

Since individual LEDs are small in size and one LED can only generate a little bit of light, a 60-watt LED light bulb uses many individual small LEDs that together create the equivalent light output of a 60-watt light bulb. By putting multiple LED lights into a lamp, engineers can create LED lamps for almost any use. But one of the biggest reasons LEDs are being used so much is due to their energy efficiency compared to other types of lighting.

Efficiency

The efficiency rating of a light source is measured by how many lumens of light are emitted per watt of energy. A lumen is a consistent measure of the total amount of light emitted by a light source. You may see lumens used on light bulb packages, and it's actually a more accurate way to tell how much light a bulb produces since lumens are independent of wattage or the type of light source. A 100 lumen light source will be consistent regardless if the light is incandescent, fluorescent, or LED.

So when it comes to efficiency, the real way to judge a light source is by how many watts of electrical current it takes to create one lumen. Let's compare the percentages of three common lighting sources, incandescent, fluorescent, and LED.

A typical incandescent bulb has about a 10 percent watt to lumen output. So for a 100-watt incandescent bulb, only 10 watts are being used to produce light, the other 90 watts are producing heat, which is why lit-up incandescent light bulbs are hot when you touch them.

Common fluorescent light-bulbs (also known as Compact Fluorescent Lights or CFL's) are more efficient that incandescent lights and have been commonly used as incandescent replacements. A CFL light has an efficiency from 45 to 80 lumens per watt, so they are pretty efficient and much more than incandescent lights. The reason for the wide range of efficiency depends on the design and technology used in the lamp. CFL lights have been used as incandescent replacements since fluorescent technology is very common, and the cost of the bulbs was fast to come down in price. There are some trade-offs for fluorescent lights however since they don't mimic the warm lighting from incandescents that's preferred by many people, and they aren't as easy to dim.

Both incandescent and fluorescent light sources have another issue when it comes to efficiency and that's the fact they emit light in all directions. Light bulbs and lighting fixtures for incandescent and fluorescent lights are designed to focus the light in one direction (like a reflector) or diffuse it, like a lampshade.

So how efficient are LED's?

A typical LED bulb generates at a minimum 80 lumens of light per watt, and the lumens per watt generated is increasing with new LED technology. In fact, the US Department of Energy has established a target for commercially available LED's to produce over 200 lumens per watt by 2025. Cree and Philip have both demonstrated prototypes that achieve this level of efficiency. But LED's have other benefits besides energy efficiency.

LED's last far longer than incandescent or fluorescent lights, usually for tens of thousands of hours of continuous use. LED's. Because LEDs give off light on one direction, it's easier to create lamps and fixtures since the LED's inside the lamp can be shaped to create the direction of light output. LED's have more advantages as well.

LED's are also more accurate in the color of the light so creating a lighting effect based on warm or cool lighting, or duplicating sunlight, it easier with LEDs. And one of my favorites is that LED's that you can dim, just like incandescents, what was a drawback to fluorescent lighting. You might have to change your dimmer switch to one that works with LED's, but you'll have the same level of precise control when dimming an LED light as with an incandescent.

To my way of thinking

As LED's come down in cost and replace older, less efficient lighting, they will result in cost savings, less reliance on imported oil, and less waste since they last longer. The DOE also supports research for improved LED technologies since their benefits will help everyone.

Phillips has an LED light called the Philips Hue that changes color and can sync with the SyFy cable network using an app called SyFy Sync. When you connect the Phillips LED lamp to the app, the app adjusts the lighting in your home while you're watching shows like 12 Monkeys, Defiance, and others on TV for a complete "environmental" lighting effect.

Websites

http://apps1.eere.energy.gov/buildings/publications/pdfs/ssl/ssl_mypp2014_web.pdf

https://itunes.apple.com/us/app/syfy-sync/id450488282?mt=8

http://www.lighting.philips.com/main/education/led-lighting.html

LinkedIn

LinkedIn is a professional- and career-oriented Social Networking site. Its focus has always been on the user's experience in the workplace. Unlike Facebook, LinkedIn doesn't have much room in your profile for information on your personal life and relationships. As a result, it's become popular among people who want to connect with others but prefer to keep job/career/professional elements separate from other aspects of their lives.

With over 433 million users around the world, LinkedIn is a popular way for people to connect with business, career and professional contacts.

Features built into LinkedIn allow you to showcase your professional and career expertise, and include a job-listing service where you can search for open positions listed by companies who use LinkedIn for recruiting. Because it is such a widely-used career- and occupation-focused website, it is actively used by career counselors and job search companies.

Free and Paid Accounts

LinkedIn offers both free and paid accounts, along with a special Recruiter account for employers and recruiters.

The free account includes many useful professional networking features. These include:

- create a full profile
- store your contacts in a contact list
- connect with other LinkedIn users
- save searches
- create groups
- join groups
- search for people, companies, jobs, and groups
- receive alerts about your network of connections
- ask for introductions
- add third-party applications.

Making the Most of LinkedIn

The list above includes a lot of features, and the majority of people only create a profile listing and establishing a few connections. As a result, many people don't know what to do on LinkedIn.

One of the best ways to make better use of LinkedIn is to join groups. Groups are free for any LinkedIn member to join, and there are thousands of groups. As you might expect on a professional social networking service, all groups are professional in their theme. Examples of groups include professional associations, college alumni, workplace alumni, small business, and professional topics.

Groups on LinkedIn are created by other users, who set the theme of the group and decide whether the group is public or private. A private group requires the group manager's permission to join, and only members of the group can see and participate in the discussions.

People discuss topics in groups, and any member of a group can start a discussion topic. Some common examples of discussion topics are industry news, events, job openings, or questions. Any user on LinkedIn can join up to 40 groups

Paid Accounts

LinkedIn makes about half their income from advertising, but the other half comes from paid accounts and services. Any individual user can open a paid account, which start at about $30 per month. Many recruiters and individuals open paid accounts because of the additional capabilities for searching, viewing profiles of people that aren't connections, and sending direct messages to any user on LinkedIn using LinkedIn's internal mail system called InMail.

Paid accounts offer additional features that

- Allow you to send messages and introductions to people who aren't part of your network, using InMail, LinkedIn's internal email system
- Premium search with saved searches and access to special search features
- Use LinkedIn's Profile Organizer for organizing and making notes on contacts
- Priority customer support
- See hidden user profiles and full profile visibility

Your LinkedIn Profile

Since LinkedIn is designed for professional social networking, all the information in your profile is about your professional and work related expertise and experience. LinkedIn provides forms for you to complete in order to build your profile. In many ways, it's similar to a job search website like Monster or Career Builder and has size limits on the amount of information you can type in for each position and employer.

As you enter your positions, titles, and job descriptions, keep in mind that the information on LinkedIn is searchable by users with paid accounts. If your goal is to highlight specific experience, skills, or expertise, be specific and use the proper terminology. Prospective employers will search for you on social networks and compare this information to any resume you may have submitted to see if there are discrepancies, so be accurate about dates, jobs, employers, etc..

As you complete your profile, you'll see a progress bar on the screen showing you how much of your profile is completed. To make the best possible impression, be sure to complete every step in completing your profile. The steps include not only job descriptions, dates, employers, and titles, but also education, awards, certifications, professional memberships, and a profile photo.

Looking Your Best - Your Profile Photo

More than any other social network site, a professional looking photo is important on LinkedIn. After all, if you're using LinkedIn, you're using it for professional networking, and you should make the best impression. While you may have a "good" photo, going to a photo studio and paying a little money for a high quality, well-lit professional photo will make a tremendous difference. Think of making the same impression you would want to make if you saw any LinkedIn user at your workplace.

Location Tracking

Location tracking refers to technologies that physically locate and electronically record and track the movement of people or objects. Location tracking technology is in use every day with GPS navigation, locations located on digital pictures and searching for businesses nearby using common apps. While location tracking is often associated with smartphone use since smartphones have a GPS chip, there are other ways location tracking is done.

Advanced Tracking in Your Pocket

The Global Positioning System (GPS) is location tracking technology that uses data from 24 satellites orbiting the earth. A GPS satellite calculates location by timing how long it takes a radio signal traveling to reach either a fixed or mobile tracking device on earth such as a GPS navigation device built into your car or a smartphone with a GPS chip.

Location and Location Tracking

Using multiple satellites, a GPS device can identify it's longitude and latitude location and display the information to the person using the device or send the information to a software app or program. A common everyday example is a use of Internet and mobile map applications on smartphones that can calculate your current position using your GPS location and show where you're located on a map. Because your location coordinates are sent to a map application, your location is now known by the application, which is location tracking.

How is location tracking used?

Some GPS devices don't send your location anywhere, they just record your location and keep a record of where you are and where you've been. Car navigation systems are a commonly used location tracking systems that don't send your location to anyone, but do keep a record of your location history on the navigation system memory. Your "previous destinations" option is a list of locations you've traveled to that you used your navigation system for guidance. If you drove somewhere and didn't use the navigation system for directions, it likely doesn't have a record of your travel.

Here's where location tracking comes in and is different from jus knowing your current location. I recently received a letter from my auto insurance agency about a great offer to save money on my auto insurance. All I had to do was allow them to install a device that would track my driving. By using the device, the insurer could learn where I travel, how far I drive, how fast I travel, and at what times of day. Location tracking is taking place since the location information is used to "track" and not just tell me my current location.

With certain smartphones, users have to allow any app permission to use location information captured by the smartphone. Sometimes it's necessary to allow an app to use your location for the app to function. For example, if you want an app to tell you the weather in your current location, you have to give the app permission to obtain your location from your smartphone GPS circuit. If you do allow the app permission, the app can obtain your location when it wants to and send your location back to the app computers that record information. You might not have a username and account with a weather app, but some apps want to use your location and know who you are.

Facebook is a widely known app that uses your location when your check-in using the Facebook app on a smartphone. When you choose to check-in with Facebook, you are letting Facebook and any contacts you share the information with where you are located at that time. Facebook learned where you were as well as your social contacts. If you're OK with sharing your location, it's not an issue.

Some smartphones track your location using settings you may have never touched. Recently someone using an iPhone asked me how her phone knew how long it would take her to drive to home or work. In iPhones, you give the iOS operating system permission to use your location when you do the initial phone setup. You may or may not remember having done this. In the iPhone, the operating system tracks your frequently visited locations. It knows your location, and it knows how often you go to or from that location.

By tracking "frequently visited" locations, your iPhone can tell you how long it will take to travel from one frequently visited location like work, to another you frequently travel to such as your home. The iPhone will use the GPS location information and map to determine if an address is yours if you have your contact information in the iPhone. But it doesn't even need that since the phone assumes you drive from home to work most days and will try to determine based on what you do with your phone if a location is your home or your work location.

By the way, on iPhones you can turn this off by going to Settings>Privacy>Location Services>System Services (at the very bottom of the list)>Frequent Locations. In fact, after you access Location Services in Settings, you can see what apps use your location and if they use your location always, or only when you're using the app. To turn anyone off move the slider from the green ON position to the gray OFF position and that app will no longer be able to track your location. Of course, if you want an app like Yelp! to tell you what's nearby, you'll need to give the app permission to use your location.

Outdoors, Indoors, Everywhere

Besides GPS, there are some different technologies and techniques for associating digital information with a specific location such a cell tower location information.

Cell site location information is created with the measurement of the a smartphone in relation to two or more cell phone towers. Cell site data is becoming almost as precise as GPS. Radio frequency (RF) technologies are other means of identifying and locating people or products, usually inside a building or within the range of RF scanners and receivers. Infrared (IR) tracking uses frequencies of light rather than radio spectrum to measure and determine an object's location.

Also, WiFi hotspot locations are often known because of Google Streetview, which uses Google vehicles to drive around and record pictures of street locations and the WiFi hotspot locations. When you use Google to search on your desktop or laptop; Google seems to know where you are located. Even though you computer likely doesn't have a GPS chip like a smartphone, since you're connected to the Internet through a WiFI location or other device with a WiFi antenna, Google has likely determined the location of that WiFi hotspot.

Industrial and Personal Use

Location tracking has many beneficial uses. Commercial businesses track expensive machinery, fleets of vehicles, and product shipments, seeking to prevent equipment inventory loss. Hospitals track patients to improve efficiency in busy ERs and to safeguard infants in maternity wards and allow only the parents to carry the infants using location tracking devices.

Parents and other uses

Additional uses for location tracking include wearable gadgets and apps for parents to track their kids and for law enforcement tracks offenders. The cameras you see at red lights, the cell phone app in your pocket, and activity monitors all have some location tracking capability, which makes the tracking of people's locations and every move a debated privacy issue as well.

To my way of thinking

Using a device like a smartphone along with a map app to help you find directions, learn about nearby businesses and facilities, and help navigate are useful reasons to allow an app to know your location.

The real question about location tracking is what is being done with your location information and how is it being used by whatever app or service might be accessing it. If you're concerned, it's important to read the privacy statements that appear with the use of any app or smartphone to learn what is being done with your location information and who might be getting access to it.

Locked Phone

A locked phone is any phone that has software installed to prevent the phone owner from using the phone with any other carrier's network than the carrier that originally sold the phone. The terms "locked" and "unlocked" usually apply to cellular phones, not land lines, since cellular companies sell their phones with a contract for cellular service that often requires a multi-year commitment for payments.

While the phone itself isn't labeled on the box as locked or unlocked, it's helpful to know the differences between these terms when you buy any type of cellular phone, particularly smartphones such as iPhones or Android phones which are popular models. After all, you're signing a contract with financial commitments and smartphone phones and cellular plans are becoming a significant expense.

What is the difference between a locked and unlocked phone?

While there are many models of cellular phones, they all are either locked to the cellular provider's service or unlocked and can be used with other carriers. Unlocked phones can be used on any carrier's network at any time, provided the phone is compatible with the cellular carrier's communications technology.

For example, let's say that you own a brand new unlocked iPhone 6. AT&T and T-Mobile have similar cellular networks and both offer service for the iPhone 6. As a result, since your iPhone 6 is unlocked, you could take that phone to the other carrier and ask them to set you up with one of their service plans. In this manner, someone with an unlocked phone can pick and choose which phone provider they want based on price and quality of cellular service. Furthermore, if that user decides that he or she wants to switch providers, they don't have to buy an entirely new phone to do so.

On the other hand, locked phones prevent a user from using their phone on any other cellular network. So, if you were to buy a locked iPhone 6 from a company like Verizon, you couldn't take that phone to any other cellular carrier if you wanted to change service plans.

Often it's possible to have your carrier unlock your phone once you contract commitment is up, which is typically two years. So let's look at why there are locked phones in the first place.

Why are there locked phones?

In the United States, cellular phone companies have typically subsidized the cost of the cellular phone to keep the cost of the phone lower than what it would sell for at retail. The prices you see in cellular phone stores for popular iPhone and Android phones are often around $200 for the latest models. This price, however, is not the real retail price.

The retail price for these types of smartphones averages around $650, and the cellular company is absorbing some of the cost of the phone by requiring you to commit to a multi-year (usually two years) service plan for cellular service. The remaining cost of the phone is included in the two-year total cost of the plan. Newer plans from cellular companies are leasing smartphones to users and separate the cost of the service from the cost of the phone.

If you were able to take your subsidized phone and switch to another cellular carrier mid-contract, the full cost of the phone wouldn't be recovered by the cellular carrier. As a result, there are cancelation costs or early termination fees if you want to cancel your contract.

This multi-year commitment is one reason phone manufacturers work with the cellular carriers to provide locked phones. The other is to make it harder for you to move your phone service from one carrier to another.

Locked phones can be unlocked

However, the software that is on locked phones that locks them can be changed by entering a code into the phone. In some cases, the wireless provider who sold the locked phone may be willing to unlock it for free if the owner is current with bill payments and/or fully completed his or her contract. However, sometimes mobile phone network companies won't be willing to unlock a person's phone. Reasons for not unlocking someone's phone can be the result of the user not making payments, or it can be due to the network provider simply wanting to keep the user's business and a policy in the contract.

International use

Some carriers allow a user to purchase a locked phone, but unlock it for use when traveling internationally. An unlocked phone can be very helpful since international roaming service can be very expensive. With phone models that are capable of use on international carrier's networks, it's possible to purchase a data card (called a SIM card) with a phone number and service in the local country. Once the SIM card is changed, your phone will connect to the local country network with a local phone number.

You can purchase the card in the local country with a pre-paid amount of cellular service at a cellular store or retail merchant. Then simply change out your SIM card and activate your new local service on the phone. The cost of using a phone out of the country is much lower this way than using your roaming service. As a result, frequent international travelers are aware of phone models and carriers that allow the switch of SIM data cards.

Are locked phones going away?

For the time being, locked phones are the way we have to purchase phones in the United States. While cellular companies are allowed to lock any phone, they cannot prevent you from keeping your phone number. As a result, some cellular providers are offering competitive pricing to "buyout" the phone and provide you with one so you can switch services.

Since there are differences in models that can work on each carrier's communications technology, sometimes a phone has to be replaced in order to switch carriers even when it's possible to unlock the phone.

Even now some carriers are offering two-tier pricing on phones, a locked price with a two-year contract requirement and an unlocked price, where you pay separately for the phone and service. As a result, it's becoming more complicated and confusing to compare plans.

To my way of thinking

An unlocked phone offers you more flexibility than a locked phone will, and you will be able to change carriers since there is no long-term contract. Reasons to consider an unlocked phone include better pricing or service options through another carrier, or if you travel internationally and want to keep your international cellular costs lower.

Keep in mind that the highest cost of your phone will likely be the cellular service. That's the monthly cost of your phone, text, and data (Internet) service from the carrier. Be sure to add the numbers up and see which approach might work best. And don't be afraid to ask your cellular company to review your plan every once in a while. I save money periodically by doing this and have heard from many others that they've lowered their costs significantly just by asking for a review of their cellular plan.

LTE

LTE is the acronym for Long Term Evolution; the name used to describe a type of cellular technology. The term LTE is used by cellular network companies like AT&T, Verizon Wireless. Sprint, T-Mobile, etc. to describe a specific type of network capability that can provide speeds faster than older cellular network technologies such as 4G and 3G. Right now it's the fastest type of cellular network.

Although LTE is used alone to describe an LTE network, it's also commonly used as 4G LTE and means the same thing when used this way. By the way, the G in 4G and 3G stands for Generation, which describes the generation of technology used.

Faster speed on a cellular network results in a faster display of web pages and emails. When you use your smartphone. Files are quicker to download from any cloud services you might use for storage, and faster speeds help music and video streaming services, like Apple Music, Spotify, Pandora and YouTube to play smoother when you use your cellular network connection.

When the letters LTE appear on the top of your smartphone or tablet, you'll know you're using an LTE network. The letters will appear to the right of the name of your cellular network company. When you're connected to LTE, it's the fastest possible cellular data network possible.

Where did LTE come from?

The term "Long Term Evolution" and LTE is a trademark that is owned by the European Telecommunications Standards Institute (ETSI). It's a technology standard that is managed by the ETSI for the benefit of it's members, which includes over 800 members including cellular providers as well as governments and small companies.

The technology was first proposed by a Japanese telecommunications firm in 2004 and studies on the feasibility of the standard started in 2005. New technologies were making it possible to increase the data capacity of wireless cellular networks, more cellular communications were being used for Internet data, there was less need for voice capacity on cellular networks. As a result, the companies in the cellular technology business were preparing for the future.

What's not LTE

There are times when you'll see letters at the top of your smartphone like 4G, 3G, or even the letter E. When these letters appear, you're using a cellular connection that's either 4G, which stands for 4th Generation, 3G, which stands for 3rd Generation, or E, which stands for Enhanced Data rates for Global Evolution and is one of the oldest data cellular technologies. As cellular companies improved their networks, different names were used as the technology improved.

By the way, this question comes up from students, the letters have nothing to do with the model of phone you have, these terms are used to help you see what type of cellular network you're connected to when you use your device.

How much faster is 4G LTE

On average, a 4G LTE connection is about ten times faster than a 3G connection. While a 3G connection is usable for email and most web page browsing, to stream music and videos and download larger files it's 4G LTE speeds that make it possible. In fact, sometimes a 4G LTE Internet connection can be as fast or faster than a physical broadband or WiFi Internet connection is the signal is strong enough.

4G alone can be up to 3.5 times faster than 3G. Since you're using a wireless signal, the strength of the signal can make a difference in the speed of your connection. That's one reason your smartphone shows a display with the signal strength of the cellular signal in addition to the type of connection you're using.

What do you need to use 4G LTE

For you to be able to use 4G LTE, you need to be within the range of a cellular tower from your provider that uses 4G LTE technology. As of this article, Verizon, AT&T, T-Mobile, Sprint and most others have upgraded their national networks to support 4G LTE almost everywhere.

In addition to 4G LTE coverage from your cellular provider, you'll also need a phone that is capable of using the 4G LTE service, which means it was built with the antenna and circuitry to use 4G LTE since phones can't be upgraded from 3G to 4G or 4G LTE. Almost all smartphones sold in the past 2-3 years are capable of connecting using 4G LTE.

If you aren't within the range of a 4G LTE cellular tower signal, your smartphone will automatically switch down to 4G, and if that's not available, to 3G, and even to EDGE. Your phone will automatically switch over to using the fastest network speeds possible as you move around, and you don't have to do anything.

To my way of thinking

With smartphones becoming the primary computing device that people use every day, having access to a fast Internet connection as often as possible is not only a convenience but almost a necessity. Especially if you rely on your smartphone for common computing tasks. Fortunately, cellular companies have upgraded their networks to make fast Internet access convenient and available, with 4G LTE speeds available almost everywhere in populated areas.

Being aware of the speed of your Internet connection when using a cellular smartphone, tablet, or any other cellular device can help you determine why your device is responding faster or slower. It simply might be the speed of your cellular data connection that's affecting it.

M

Macro

A macro is a set of commands and instructions that grouped together and performed as a single command in a computer program. Macros are usually mentioned when they are used in Microsoft Office programs like Microsoft Word and Microsoft Excel. In these programs, it's possible to perform many functions with a keystroke such as speeding up editing and formatting or automating a series of complex tasks that would take many keystrokes to perform.

With a single click on a keyboard, you can automate a series of complex procedures, saving you time and effort. While Microsoft Office applications are a common use for macros, many other software applications allow users to create macros for keystroke commands or other instructions for the application.

Example uses for a macro

Some examples of a macro in Word include applying a company letterhead format to a document, which allows users to create a blank document, then apply the letterhead formatting with a single click, inserting a pre-designed table into a document to maintain a consistent look and design rather than formatting a table every time one is inserted, and creating a custom book format for a consistent layout with a design anytime a book or pamphlet is created using Word.

Website

http://www.pcworld.com/article/2952126/software-productivity/word-macros-three-examples-to-automate-your-documents.html

Some examples of Excel macros include applying a pre-designed format to a spreadsheet, formatting cells with specific types of formatting and applying mathematical operations that require multiple keystrokes.

It doesn't matter what you do when using the application, anytime you have a repetitive task that takes several keystrokes to perform, it's a potential candidate for creating and using a macro.

Built-in operations

Microsoft often includes automated features to perform tasks that might have required a macro in an older version in newer versions of Word and Excel as they are released. Each new version of Office includes new features that address the needs of users who want tasks that take many keystrokes automated with simpler and easier to use commands and menu options. Many of these features were once macros that were commonly used be people and are now built-in features of the application.

As a result, you can use features that:

- Use paragraph styles to save and reuse a collection of formatting and apply multiple formatting commands with one click.
- Format a group of slides in a presentation with a standard layout in one click.
- Use the Replace menu to find and replace formatting of text.
- Convert bullet lists in PowerPoint to a SmartArt diagram.

Microsoft has an extensive library of training resources on their website at the Office Training Center for Office 2016 and older versions. Just be sure to select the training for your version of Office product since menus and features are different from one version to the next.

Website

https://support.office.com/en-nz/article/Office-Training-Center-b8f02f81-ec85-4493-a39b-4c48e6bc4bfb?ui=en-US&rs=en-NZ&ad=NZ

Creating macros

Creating a macro can be done one of two ways, by recording the keystrokes you use to perform an operation or by writing a macro using Microsoft's Visual Basic programming tools. In fact, any macro you create is a "program" since a program is simply a set of instructions for a computer. By recording your keystrokes, you're creating a program of your own and it's not as hard as you might think at first.

Microsoft has a support page on their website with instructions on how to create a macro using the keystroke recording method, which is the easiest way to create a macro if you're not a programmer. I won't go into the details on the step-by-step instructions since the Microsoft webpage is the best resource, but here are the basics so you'll have an idea if you want to try out recording your macro.

All versions of Microsoft Office include the ability to record a set of keystrokes and assign the steps to a single key, making the steps a macro. The steps to record are accessed using the Microsoft Office button in the upper left of any Office application, then selecting the options to bring up the Record Macro function. Click on the Record Macro button, then type out your keystrokes and save the macro. These steps are a little bit of an oversimplification, but the steps aren't that hard to follow.

Before you try and record your macro, search Microsoft's website or use the Help function in your Office application to see if there are any built-in features for automating a task you repeat over and over again. You may find a new built-in feature that will help you save time and make a time-consuming task easier and faster to perform.

Apple macros

Apple Mac computers have a built-in tool called Automator. Automator allows Mac users to create macro-like programs that Apple calls an Action, and it's very similar to a macro in Microsoft Office but since it works with the operating system instead of just an application, Automator Actions can be created for repetitive tasks across applications. Resizing an image in one example of an Automator Action I use almost daily.

I often need to resize images I use in my newsletter and blog to a specific size. Using the Automator tool, I created an Action that allows me to drag a photo of any size on an icon on my desktop and resizes the photo to 105 pixels in width. This Action works on one photo or a group of photos and saves me many keystrokes and mouse clicks when I need to resize a batch of images. There are other common Actions that make the tool very useful. Some of these are:

• Extract text from a PDF document

• Turn text into an audio file

• Convert a text file to HTML

History of the term

The term "macro" is the opposite of "micro" in computer jargon. "Macro" means "large," while "micro" means "small." In computer programming, when a macro is used, it makes the code or interface larger. The term macro was originally used with computer assembler language and was used prior to the time when a more easily coded language became more popular and more commonly used. In computer assembler language, a macro definition essentially explains how a computer instruction or single language statement can be expanded into a sequence of instructions.

A macro is especially useful in programming when a series of instructions are used many times. Macros are often helpful when there are some computer programmers working on a specific project as they break down the instructions in a way in which they are easier to understand.

If you need a macro and don't want to create one yourself, you can even hire a programmer with experience in creating Microsoft Office macros to write one for you and help you install it in your Office applications.

Freelancing websites like upwork.com, freelancer.com and fiverr.com make it easy to hire freelancers to write custom macros.

To my way of thinking

If there are frequent operations or steps, you perform that include using multiple keystrokes in an application like Word, Excel or PowerPoint a macro can save you time and convenience.

Mbps and Bandwidth

Megabits per second is used to describe the speed at which digital data travels from one point to another. The capacity of a connection is referred to as it's bandwidth. Bandwidth is measured in bits per second and one Megabit per second is 1,000 bits per second. Mbps are commonly used to describe how fast a connection is from a computer, smartphone, tablet, or network to the Internet. The higher the Megabits per second, the faster data moves from one point to another.

A bit is a single unit of data used in digital computing. Moving bits from one point to another is important as more people use digital devices. Using email and the Web all involve moving data from one location to another, so the speed at which data can be moved is important.

The Digital Highway

You might have heard of the phrase "the digital highway," which is often used to describe the movement of data across the Internet. And in many ways, moving digital data is similar to how vehicles move on the road. If you think of freeways, there are different sizes, shapes, and capacities. How fast a single vehicle travels on the road depends on the capacity of the road (bandwidth) and how many other vehicles are using the same road. The bits that travel on the Internet are similar to our vehicle analogy.

The Internet is a shared highway, just like our roads and freeways. Some roads have more capacity than others, with more lanes, higher speed limits, and even express lanes. The more capacity the road has for traffic, the faster vehicles can move from one point to another.

Data moves across both wired and wireless "highways." Our smartphones use wireless cellular connections to reach a cell tower, then the tower uses a cable to transmit data over wired, or what are called "landline" connections. For your information, any connection that isn't wireless is sometimes called a landline. Since the Internet is a shared "highway," it's necessary to have on and off ramps, only these are data connections made with wires, cables, and antennas, not roads.

The paths that carry data communications connect to points where data can be sent in different directions, just like when two freeways intersect, at a stoplight, or a traffic circle. How fast data moves from one point to another is measured in bits per second, and connections are usually fast enough now that the million is added on, making it Megabits per second.

What Types of Physical Connections Are Used?

The speed of a data connection depends on both what it's made out of (the material used for the connection), and the speed allowed by the owner of the connection to the users. So let's talk about the types of materials that are used for connections.

I already mentioned wireless cellular connections, but in addition to the cellular networks there are microwave, laser, and satellite types of wireless connections. Often it's easier to install a wireless microwave or laser connection to connect two buildings to each other rather than running wire or cable. For areas with no cable or phone wires, satellites are often used for data connections. Another example is satellite TV which sends broadcasts to your home using a satellite network.

Wired networks are often copper wire or fiber-optic cable. Copper wire is used in Ethernet, telephone, and cable TV connections. Fiber-optic cable is often used in networks because it has the highest data transmission rate possible. Now, just because you have a cable or wireless connection that is capable of transmitting data really fast doesn't mean you always get fast data transmission. That part has to do with the way the owner of the path sells it.

How Mbps and Bandwidth are Sold

Someone paid for all these cell towers, satellites, microwaves, copper wire, and fiber optic cable installed, so somebody owns the paths. Ownership of a data path is more like a toll road than public highways. Somebody owns the road, either the government or a private company. And a toll is paid in order to drive on that path. Data paths are privately owned, usually by businesses, and they charge users to use the path, depending on how much data, and how fast a user wants to move their data.

Typically, a data path has more capacity than what just one customer might use. For example, a cable or wired connection from your home might be just yours to use. At some point several homes are connected to a single cable, sharing the capability of that path. That cable then connects with other groups of homes, until the connection reaches a central office. Even then, one very high-speed connection might carry all the data traffic for from one city to another.

Cell towers are another form of shared connection. One tower may support dozens of users all making phone calls, using email, and browsing the Web. The cell tower is capable of supporting more than just one user at a time. Cell towers and cables get congested just like vehicle traffic, and when that happens the network can slow down. But it depends on whether a user has a "committed" bandwidth or not. Any user that has a committed amount of speed will be given priority over a user that has no commitment.

For most of our residential, cellular, and small business connections, there is no Mbps commitment from the provider, regardless if it's a phone, cable, or satellite company. If you read the fine print closely, you'll see that your Internet connection can be "up to" certain Mbps. You may get that speed most of the time, but it's not a level of service that requires your provider to meet any minimum requirement.

The Internet provider allows enough speed (measured in Mbps) so the average customer doesn't notice when their connection might be slower. Customers who need more bandwidth, because they need to move more bits or have more devices on their Internet connection, may notice that their Internet speed slows down. When this happens, your provider can add more capacity, like adding lanes to a freeway, but more often the provider offers an upgrade to a faster service for an additional fee. An upgrade to your Internet Mbps bandwidth is the equivalent of the freeway express lane, which requires a paid fee to travel in the higher speed traffic lane.

How Much Speed is Used?

If you have one computer in your home or business, even a 3-4 Mbps speed will allow you to watch Netflix on your Internet connection. But if you have more users in your home, you may need a faster connection since more users are sharing the available bandwidth speed. So a little math can help you figure this out.

Remember, a Mbps is one million bits per second. That means a file size of one megabit will take one second to move from the Internet to your computer. Text files, like emails and documents, are small files, they aren't usually larger than one Megabit, so email can move pretty fast even at one Mbps. A photo is a larger file, and some photos are larger than one Megabit, so many photos can take a little longer to travel. Two files that are one megabit each will take two seconds to travel on a one Megabit per second path. If the path is two Megabits per second, the files can travel in one second, since the path is 2x faster.

The average iTunes song is about 4 Megabits, so with a one Megabit per second path, it would take 4 seconds to download. Or to download a single song in one second, you would want a 4 Megabit per second connection. So your choices are to wait a little longer, or use (and pay) for a faster connection. If you have 3 people using a shared Internet connection, they all share the available bandwidth. So the one Megabit per second path we're using an example here is shared by all three users.

People and their devices are only using the bandwidth when they are actually sending or receiving data. So for a Web page, once the Web page is received on a user's computer or smartphone, their use of the bandwidth stops, until they click on another link and request a new Web page. Someone may be reading email, but they aren't using the bandwidth until they send and receive new mail messages.

If everyone wants to send and receive data at the same time, the path gets "congested" and reaches it's capacity limit, and everyone's data bandwidth slows down. If this is happening to you and you want a faster connection, you'll have to upgrade with your service provider.

A Little Perspective

At one time bandwidth was measured in kilobits per second, or Kbps. A kilobit is 1,000 bits, and a megabit is 1,000 kilobits, so a Mbps is 1,000 times faster. And a gigabit is 1,000 megabits, so one Gbps is 1,000 times faster than a one Mbps connection.

Meetup

If you were looking for a way to find and arrange meetings with real live people instead of communicating online, then Meetup could be the solution you'd want. Meetup (meetup.com) is a website service that is the world's largest network of local groups. Using the service gives you access to local groups that meet locally for almost any interest imaginable. Meetup is used by more than 24 million members in over 180 countries around the world. If you're looking for a way to find groups of people with common or shared interests, over 9,000 meetups take place every day.

What kinds of groups

Local groups include interests on almost anything, from bike rides, singles, dancing, website developers, music, writing, investing, business networking, volleyball, skiing, and more. All the groups have one thing in common; they have to be a local group that has face-to-face meetings.

Who organizes the groups

Users who create a Meetup group are called organizers. Any member of Meetup can become an organizer by clicking the link to start a Meetup Group. The first step in starting a group is to set the group's location, which is usually the city of the organizer's location. It's possible to change the place of the group to a different city or move it at any time. The next step is to select the topic of the Meetup Group from a list that matches your group's activities.

The organizer then agrees to create a real face-to-face community, since Meetup is about groups that meet in person. The organizer is responsible for finding a location for the meeting and some Then the organizer adds a description for the Meetup Group and agrees to pay the subscription fee. Participants don't have to pay a fee to join meetup.com, but anyone organizing a Meetup Group pays a fee. The organizer fees start at about $10 a month to organize up to three Meetup groups. Larger groups and other plans are available for an additional cost. Organizers can charge members dues for membership in the group or collect payment for a particular Meetup event using a payment service provided on the Meetup.com website.

If you're considering creating a group, I recommend attending some Meetup activities to see what you like and don't like about how meetings. Everyone has their preferences but some common sense works here. Pick a good location, start and end the meeting on time, and provide a good experience for the members based on what you would like them to get out of the group. Successful Meetups build a community, and are open and accepting while keeping to the topic at-hand.

How do I use it?

To use Meetup, you create a free account using the meetup.com website or by downloading the mobile Meetup app for your smartphone. You create an account and identify your current city then add profile information which can include a photo and short description of yourself.

Once completed, you can search for Meetup Groups based on your location or by topics of interest. Meetup will suggest groups that would possibly interest you if you add interests to your profile and will even suggest new Meetup Groups as they are created based on your interests and location.

To join any Meetup Group, you use your Meetup Homepage and click on the Find a Meetup Group link to view groups in your local area that match your interests. A listing shows groups by their title and the number of members. Don't go just by size as many small Meetups are good at bringing people with common interests together. A calendar view is also available which displays Meetup groups nearby you by day and date.

If a particular group looks interesting to you, click on the group photo and you'll see the screen for the group with a description written by the organizer and a list of members, and the dates. times and locations of the meetings or events that the organizer plans. You join the group by clicking on the "Join us" button. After that, you'll receive a welcome to the group message and sometimes an option to create some additional profile information visible to the members of the group.

After joining a group, Meetup will send you email notices about upcoming meetings and events planned by the organizer(s) of the group. For every group meeting or event, you'll have the opportunity to RSVP that you're attending, and you can see what other members have RSVP'd on the group information page.

Some other useful features

Allowing Meetup to access your Facebook account gives you the ability to see if any of your friends are members of a group you're considering or have already joined.

You can import any Meetup event into your smartphone or desktop calendar, send messages to the group organizer, and send messages to individual members of your groups. Meetup also has a review and rating option for members to offer feedback about the groups and individual meetings.

To my way of thinking

Meetup fills a niche where you can use the Internet to find real meetings where you can meet people with similar interests. It's become a way for people to expand their professional and social contacts and offers individuals and organizations the opportunity to build a community based on people's location and interests.

Meme

A meme is an idea, behavior, or concept from a culture that passes from one person to another, often on the Internet. A meme can be considered to be the smallest piece of information about a specific culture, and while information is useful, it only becomes a meme when it is passed along through some means of communication. On the Internet, ideas passed along from one person to another by social media often are referred to as memes.

Where did memes come from?

Memes come from a popularization of a Richard Dawkins book on genetics, called "The Selfish Gene." In his book, Dawkins describes how biology uses genes to transmit and replicate biological properties, such as hair color or eye color from one generation to another. Certain genes have the capability to spread and become more widespread, which in a sense, makes them selfish. A gene is commonly considered the smallest unit of biology which can be passed along from one generation to another. So how does this apply to culture?

A meme is the cultural equivalent to the biological gene, and is, therefore, the smallest self-replicating unit of culture. Like the biological gene, a meme has to have some characteristic that makes it unique in some way from other memes, and it has to have the ability to spread from one person in a culture to another. Deciding what makes up the smallest unit of culture is a matter of some debate, and that's often what makes the term meme confusing, since there is no real agreement by anyone what a unit of culture is in the first place.

The academic study of self-replicating ideas is called "memetics." From 1997 to 2005, there was an online academic journal devoted to memetics, and the word in common use has outlived the academic research that founded it.

It goes without saying that the term meme is often misused, but it's a way many people refer to an idea or concept that goes "viral," since going viral means that something is passed along from one person to another.

Types of memes

Memes provide an interesting point of entry to a discussion about media, journalism, and the lack of gate-keepers, like editorial boards. Memes don't have to be factually correct to get spread. The false meme is one type that is very common.

Some of the most widely spread memes use cherry picked data or outright falsehoods. An example of this is a quote, ostensibly by George Washington, that says "It is impossible to rightly govern a nation without God and the Bible." - according to the Mt. Vernon Historical Society, this has never appeared in Washington's letters, writings or speeches.

Another kind of meme is the time-warp. These memes, relating to the death of a celebrity, resurface years after the fact, presenting the obituary as breaking news. Sometimes, for celebrities with the right level of fame, they seem to come back every two to three years. (For example, Bob Denver, the actor who played "Gilligan" on Gilligan's Island, died in 2005 - his obituary gets turned into a meme every two to three years.)

Sometimes a meme shows up as a popular or well known phrase used on a photo, often in a social media post. While these current memes use photographs with text, they're older than the Internet. These types of memes are similar to chain letters, which date back to the 17th Century, which often asked people to send a duplicate letter requesting money to 5 friends as a get-rich-quick scam. With the advent of email, chain emails dating to the early 1990s talk about Bill Gates giving $5,000 to anyone who forwards the message on.

Popular Memes

Some memes are simply fun ideas that people seem to like and feel the need to forward on to their connections. As the meme becomes popular, other people pick up on the idea and create variations, adding to the spread of the meme.

A graphic may find someone creating a song, video, or animation, which is what happened to the dancing hamsters in 1998. The homage to the dancing hamsters was an animation that in 1998 people felt the need to spread and is considered one of the top ten memes in Internet history. The website address is listed here but be warned, because you WILL see dancing hamsters!

http://www.hampsterdance.com/classics/originaldance.htm

To my way of thinking

In general, memes are harmless - most of them are ideas that capture the attention of people around an idea or news event. With social media, you may find some of your friends who simply can't resist sharing a meme or two with you.

And if a meme seems particularly outrageous or upsetting, you can always use Google to check out the truth behind the picture.

Milliamp Hour mAh

A milliamp-hour (mAh) is a measurement of how much electric current a battery can deliver over time. Our increasing use of mobile devices like smartphones, tablets, and laptops has made us all aware of how long a single battery charge will last. There are one thousand milliamps in one amp. Since electronic devices are designed to work using smaller amounts of electricity, the amount is measured in milliamps versus amps. If you use anything with a battery, you already have some understanding of the term milliamp-hour, but you may not have understood how it affects your mobile lifestyle.

A little about why this term is the term of the week

The term came up when I was talking to my brother-in-law recently. He uses his smartphone quite a bit, including days when he plays golf. Once he becomes familiar with a certain piece of technology, he doesn't like to change so he had an older smartphone model, and the battery wasn't holding a charge quite as long. He couldn't replace the battery since they aren't made for his phone model any longer. He was looking for a solution that would give him a longer battery charge.

My brother-in-law asked me if the small rechargeable battery packs he saw for sale worked and if it would be a way to keep his phone charged for a longer period. I told him yes; they do work, and then he asked me how many milliamp-hours of capacity he should buy for his battery pack. So I ended up adding the term to my list. To understand what a milliamp-hour is it helps to understand a little about basic electricity.

Basic electricity

An ampere, or amp for short, is a measure of how much electricity flows in an electrical circuit. If you add the time, such as a hour, an amp-hour is the amount of electricity that moves in one hour. You might be familiar with the terms watts and volts, and they're related to amps. Ohm's Law is a formula that is used to determine the relationship between amps, watts, and volts.

The Ohms Law Formula is written "Watts=Amps x Volts." if you remember any algebra you know you can move the terms around in the formula. If you know any two values, you can calculate the third one. Let's take a look at AA batteries, something you're probably familiar with, to help understand the milliamp-hour and then we'll move on to smartphones and mobile devices.

Many devices use AA batteries. In fact, AA batteries account for over 50% of all batteries sold today. Batteries are an important part of our electronic life, and the AA battery is the workhorse, used for things like remote controls, flashlights, toys, and more. Amp-hours describes the amount of time the battery can deliver electricity, but since the AA battery is small, it's measured in milliamp-hours. As long it has a charge it can deliver power, when the battery is "dead," it can't supply electricity any longer.

Here's an example with a flashlight that uses batteries. The battery's light-bulb has a certain power requirement in order to function and illuminate. When the flashlight lights up, it consumes or "draws" current from the batteries, when it's off, it doesn't use any current. If it uses one amp when it's on, then it would need a battery capable of supplying one amp-hour of current to run for one hour. Since

In order to extend the amount of time we can use the flashlight with one set of batteries, we could either increase the capacity of the battery   or use a lower power consuming light bulb. If we use a lower-power light bulb, we might end up with a dimmer flashlight, and if we want longer battery life, a larger battery will make our flashlight heavier. So how do we keep the weight and size of the flashlight the same? We use better battery materials or more efficient light bulbs, or a combination of both.

That's why you see brighter flashlights using either larger batteries or more efficient lamps, such as LED lights. The larger battery supplies more power while a more efficient lamp such as an LED consumes less power.

Increased time with better batteries

Batteries made with materials such as Alkaline and Lithium-Ion material last longer than ones made with zinc-iron. In fact, a zinc-iron AA battery has from 400-900 milliamp-hours of capacity. In comparison, an Alkaline AA battery has from 1800-2400 milliamp-hours of capacity, almost 3-4 times as much.

Alkaline batteries added capacity usually makes them a better value when compared to a zinc-carbon battery. As a result, almost all AA batteries sold are Alkaline. Another material, Lithium-Ion, results in AA batteries with as much as 3000 milliamp-hours of life, but Lithium-Ion batteries are more expensive than Alkaline ones. Lithium-Ion batteries can be manufactured for one-time use or as rechargeables, so their high-capacity and the rechargeable quality makes them suited for mobile devices such as smartphones, tablets, and laptops.

Increasing time with lower power requirements

The other option for extending the time a battery can power a device is to make the electrical current requirements as small as possible. Without modern integrated circuits and electronics, our mobile lifestyle would be impossible since these types of electronic circuits consume very small amounts of power.

So how does a mAh affect my life?

In order to understand how long a battery charge will last on any device, from a flashlight to a smartphone, it's necessary to know how many milliamps (or amps if it's a larger device) it consumes and how many milliamp-hours the internal battery can deliver. And, there are device specifications for all of this to help you out.

The capacity of a smartphone battery is measured in milliamp-hours (mAh). However, smartphones use power at different rates depending on what they are doing. For example, Apple's specifications say the iPhone 6 will run for 250 hours in standby, but only for 10 hours when browsing the web. The iPhone 6 plus, with its larger case has a battery rated at 2915 mAh, has a standby time of 384 hours and 12 hours for web browsing.

If two devices consume the same power, the one with the larger battery will operate longer on a single charge. The internal circuitry of the iPhone 6 and 6 Plus are very similar, but the iPhone 6 Plus has a larger screen that requires a little more power, so while it has a battery with more mAh, it also uses a little more power because of the power requirements of a larger screen.

In spite of the specs provided by any smartphone maker you may never have enough mAh of battery capacity to keep your devices going all day. That's because our mobile lifestyle often results in many apps working even while in standby, such as email retrieval. So a common solution is to use a car charger, or for truly mobile battery power, an external battery pack.

One more factor affects mAh on a mobile device, and that's how efficient the software and operating system are at managing power. That's one reason that updates to operating systems on mobile devices, particularly smartphones, are important since the operating system and how it works can affect your device's power consumption. A few mAh of power usage saved can add up during the day and give you minutes or more of usable battery.

To my way of thinking.

Your usage will affect how long the internal battery on your smartphone lasts. For some people, a full charge can last a whole day while for others a full charge just isn't enough. You may also be in situations where you might not be able to find a power outlet, such as a campground or while on vacation. In these cases, a portable battery pack can be a valuable addition.

Most mobile battery packs use the same type of batteries like the one in your smartphone or other mobile device, so it's the size and weight that determine the mAh capacity. Your charging cable can be used to connect the portable battery pack to your smartphone or tablet. Larger battery packs are made that come with power adapters for powering laptop computers, but be sure to buy one with the right adapter for your specific laptop.

If your smartphone has an internal battery with a capacity of about 2000 mAh, then a battery pack with 6000 mAh will provide three charges. Portable battery packs need to be also charged, but now that you know what a mAh means, you can buy one that is the right size and capacity for your mobile needs.

MMO and MMORPG

MMO stands for Massively Multiplayer Online, and it is a type of video game or social game that allows multiple players from anywhere in the world to meet and play together in a virtual environment in real time. MMORPG stands for Massively Multiplayer Online Role-Playing Game, and it is the most common form of MMO. When you see the term MMO, it usually includes MMORPG games and any other type of MMO, some of which are not role-playing types. One of the most popular MMO games is World of Warcraft.

Why are MMO's Popular?

MMO's became popular for a number of reasons. On the one hand, MMO's appeal to younger generations as a cool new way to interact with the web. On the other hand, certain individuals took to MMO's because they saw the games as a way to escape and to create a fantasy character. Users can join groups online and participate in game play both individually and as a member of a team.

Brief History of MMO

Massively Multiplayer Online's began to take off at the beginning of the 2000's. It was at this time that Internet capabilities had grown to a point where dedicated computers on the Internet (called servers) could handle large numbers of users at the same time.

How MMO's are played (basically)

In 2004, the MMORPG "World of Warcraft" was released, which was extremely popular amongst the ever-growing gaming community. For most MMORPG's, individuals are allowed to create a character that lives in a massive universe. By completing various tasks and achieving certain goals, an individual can move their character up to levels to obtain new abilities and armor/weapons.

Single-Player Role-Playing games have been around for a long time, but World of Warcraft revolutionized the gaming world by allowing players to become members of teams in order to cooperate on "quests" to achieve common goals. In this sense, World of Warcraft, as well as other MMORPG's, have served to foster a sense of community amongst various players that gamers across the world have come to love.

If you are an avid gamer, you would probably enjoy MMO's or MMORPG's. There are many different kinds out there, and there is a type of online multiplayer game on the web that appeals to each gamer's respective tastes. However, it is important to note that most MMO's and MMORPG's have a monthly subscription fee. In fact, MMO games are a huge multibillion dollar industry which include companies like Sony, Electronic Arts, and Microsoft.

Social aspects of MMO games

Just because someone is playing an MMO doesn't mean they aren't communicating with online friends and learning teamwork. Communication between characters and players is an important aspect of game play and is just as complex as any other type of team activity you might be familiar with in any sport or workplace. It's important to understand since parents often don't realize that when they cut off their kids from online game play, they are likely cutting off communication with online friends.

Many players become friends through MMO games and attend weddings, meet for dinner parties, and share information with their online team members or individual players. Players span all types of social and economic backgrounds. All that's needed is a computer and access to the game through the monthly fee.

To my way of thinking

Like anything else in life, if it's strange and unfamiliar to us we tend to avoid it and make assumptions, and that's true of people who have never played an MMO game. If you have the opportunity and know someone who plays, ask them to explain the game to you a little bit so you can improve your understanding. Most MMO players like to talk about their games, and you might find a conversation starter.

Be careful about playing one though, as the game play is very appealing and can draw you into a new world where you might end up spending a lot of time.

MMS

MMS stands for multimedia messaging service, a type of text messaging that allows cell phone users to send photos, videos, documents, or sound clips as attachments. The ability to send different types of media files is why the term multimedia is used.

MMS is most commonly used to send photos or videos from a camera equipped phone to another cell phone user or email address. SMS, the standard text messaging service available on cell phones, is only capable of sending text messages. When a user wants to send another cell phone user a message with a media attachment, MMS takes over, usually automatically, and uses the cellular company's service to forward the message and the media attachment.

Most of the cell phones in today's market are equipped with MMS capability; even some non-camera phones offer MMS service. These messages are similar to emails since the content is attached to the text message and sent along with it to the recipient. The ease of sending these files directly from the user's cell phone gives MMS messaging an advantage over email since the files don't need to be transferred to a computer or sent as an email.

MMS actually uses a different service on the cellular carrier than SMS, but the cellular carrier often just offers "messaging", so the user doesn't see any difference in how the message is sent. MMS uses a "store and forward" capability on the cell phone carrier's service. When an MMS message is sent, the message is stored on the cell phone company's computers, then forwarded to the recipient cell phone.

If a recipient doesn't have a phone capable of receiving or viewing an MMS message and it's attachment, they receive a web page link in the message and can view the content of the attachment using a web browser. Another advantage is the ability to share a photo with multiple people by sending only one message.

Developed in the early 2000's, multimedia messaging service became globally widespread by 2005, and most of today's smartphones are fully equipped for MMS usage, though some older models or very inexpensive models of cell phones don't support it. When shopping for a cell phone, you should consider the phone's MMS capability if they think they may want to utilize this service. MMS messaging charges are usually included in the cell service plan as a part of the text messaging package.

The ability to instantly share these pictures, or other files, is a convenient way for people to stay connected when they cannot be together. Messaging, since it's a direct communication, is private between the sender and the recipient. MMS is also be more reliable in areas of poor cell service and may be your only way to send a photo or file attachment if you have no Internet access. Using MMS makes a useful alternative to email to send a media attachment if you can't access your email account or the Internet.

Employers may utilize MMS messaging to send and receive photos of construction progress, job sites, or important documents. Parents are notorious for sharing photos of their kids with grandparents, uncles, aunts, and close family friends without having to consider the risk of posting these photos on a social networking site. I had a student in one of my classes recently who did carpet repair and did quotes for customers who sent him a photo of their carpet via text messaging.

Users can even use MMS messaging to get the advice of a friend on whether or not they should buy the red dress or the black dress by simply sending photos of both from the dressing room of a department store. It's takes text messaging to a whole new level of communication for cell phone users.

Motherboard

A motherboard is a circuit board with electronic components that allow it to connect all the hardware of a computer together. It is a critical piece of hardware upon which every computer is built.

It's called a motherboard because its the main chassis in any computer. All the electronic components and hardware that make up the computer connect in some way to the motherboard. Any other circuit boards necessary to build a complete computer are referred to as "daughter" boards. Most personal computers that are built today don't have daughter boards and only use a motherboard, so you don't see the term "daughterboard" used very often.

What a Motherboard Does

Think of a computer as if it were a human body. The motherboard would be the skeleton. It doesn't do much on its own, but without it the body cannot function. Other pieces of hardware perform specific functions -- the heart pumps blood, the lungs breathe and the brain regulates everything -- while the skeleton supports them all. This is how a motherboard functions in a computer. It supports and connects the rest of the hardware. Unlike the body, of course, the heart, lungs or brain of a computer could be swapped out with more powerful versions that still connect perfectly to the skeleton.

Every computer and computer-like device has a motherboard. A television is controlled by a motherboard that has all of its parts permanently connected. You can't open up your television and upgrade its ability to display images. Smartphones are the same, with every necessary piece fixed in place. Laptop computers have most of the parts built-in to the motherboard in order to save space. No one would buy a laptop the size of a desktop PC.

Built-in Components and Upgrades

A basic motherboard can consist of only the electronic wiring necessary to connect all the components of a computer together. Components, like a processor and RAM are then added to the motherboard to build the computer. To make computers less expensive, or to make them smaller, such as a mobile smartphone, motherboards can include some of the additional components as built-in pieces.

Personal computer motherboards often include built-in sound and graphics components, eliminating the need to add them as separate pieces. This lowers the cost and size of the computer. If a motherboard is custom-built for a manufacturer, such as a tablet or smartphone, capabilities such as GPS or WiFI might be added to the motherboard. It just depends on who makes the motherboard. Most desktop PC's use motherboards that do not include the processor, which is added separately by the manufacturer. These motherboards can also be purchased as separate parts if you want to build your own computer.

Desktop PCs have the advantage of upgrades. The motherboard in a desktop has special slots where accessory cards can be inserted. Using accessory cards that can be installed, additional capabilities can be added to the computer for special uses. Some common examples are audio cards, graphics cards, and cards for special connectors. When you use accessory cards, a desktop offers the most expandable motherboard. Laptops, smartphones, and tablets don't have the space for any additional circuit cards to be plugged in, so any additional accessories have to connect to external connectors.

Connections

Connectors are a part of every motherboard. This is how you might connect a printer to a USB connector, or an ethernet cable to an ethernet connector, a keyboard, monitor, mouse, and other devices. The motherboard holds the connectors and provides the electrical connection to the rest of the computer. You just usually see the external connector.

Without a motherboard, there is no computer. A PC, smartphone, tablet, or any computing device would be nothing more than a fancy metal and plastic box filled with useless parts. The motherboard is what connects all the pieces together.

Mouse Over or Mouse Hover

A mouse over (also known as a mouse hover) is an action that happens when the user stops or "hovers" the on-screen mouse pointer above a specific element on a computer screen. Holding, or "hovering" the mouse in one location reveals additional information on the screen. This information usually appears in a small text box and is made available through the website or application being used.

Common uses of the mouse over

The mouse over action commonly appears when using a web browser on a desktop computer and is created by the website developer when creating the website. In fact, there is an HTML command called "hover" which is used to produce the effect on a website. When the user "hovers" or pauses at the on-screen pointer over the hover enabled area of the web page, a small text box will pop up, indicating to the user what options are available when clicking the mouse button.

Images often use the mouse over function on websites. When the user "hovers," or pauses the mouse over an image, additional information about the image is revealed, such as; the name of the photo or copyright information. Not every photo or image will display information since the mouse over function depends on the information being available in the website or software program.

The mouse over effect is also to hide options on the web page but still makes these options available when a user points to a specific area on the screen. A website developer might not want to display a button in order to avoid a distraction, but the seemingly blank area of the web page reveals options to the user by holding the mouse in a specific location. A common example is with Facebook's web page.

When viewing the NewsFeed on Facebook, hovering over a person's name at the top of a Status Update will reveal the person's profile image and cover image from their Timeline, making it easier to recognize and view updates from friends without the need to visit their Facebook profile. Another hover action is available when holding the mouse pointer to the right of a comment, which displays the option to hide the comment on your Timeline. Facebook makes changes often, so these are current as of this article and the mouse over actions on Facebook's website may change at any time (sorry, out of my control).

Another use of mouse over is to list options or choices that can be made by the user if the mouse key is clicked, in order to show the user the options available. A mouse over shouldn't be confused with a "right-click" mouse command, which is also a common action that reveals actions available to the user. A mouse over only requires holding the mouse pointer in place while the right-click action requires a mouse click.

Mobile devices and touchscreens

Since mobile touchscreens don't use a mouse (your finger is equivalent), the hover action isn't available when viewing websites on touchscreen web browsers. In fact, the size of the screen makes a difference. Tablets typically will display mouse hover information as a drop-down list, but smaller phone touchscreens typically ignore the mouse over action completely.

Since mobile devices are becoming a popular device that people use to view websites, website designers are struggling with alternatives to the mouse over, which has widely been used for desktop and laptop devices equipped with a mouse or trackpad. The missing capability on mobile devices to include help information or additional feature options without the mouse over function has created a dilemma as website designers are adapting to the explosion of mobile devices.

As a result, many websites are being designed with two different versions, one for the mobile device user (without mouse over or hover actions) and one for the desktop or laptop user with a mouse or trackpad. The use of the mouse over action may decline as a result of mobile device usage increasing since many people are visiting websites more frequently from mobile devices instead of desktops.

While website developers are concerned with both desktop (or laptop) and mobile device users, software programs designed for desktops or laptops know that the computer user will be using a mouse or trackpad, so they can design the mouse over action into the software program.

Using the Mouse Over or Mouse Hover with software programs

Many popular software programs, including word processing and accounting programs, have complicated toolbars and extensive layouts of tiny icons on the screen. "Hovering" or pausing the on-screen indicator over an icon or symbol reveals the name and function of that particular option. This information often includes help for the specific button, action, or even the area of the screen where the mouse pointer is resting.

Software programs commonly use the mouse over action to display help information that is within "context," meaning that the information pertains to the specific button, action, or screen that the user is currently using. As an example, when hovering over a button, a help tip may appear for that specific button to explain it's function.

To my way of thinking

Think of the mouse over or mouse hover as a way to explore more about the websites and software programs you use. By "hovering" or pausing the on-screen indicator over certain key elements on the screen before you actually click on them, you can be more confident about what actions will occur when you do click the Mouse key.

Whenever you are using a new software program or visiting a website for the first time, slow down and carefully move the mouse around the screen, allowing it enough time to "hover" over areas on your screen. You may be surprised with the information that appears. But remember, when using a smartphone or tablet, the mouse over function will likely not be available.

MP3

MP3 is the popular term used to describe an audio file that uses the MP3 format for reducing the size of the audio file. An audio file in MP3 format doesn't contain all of the original audio signals but instead contains enough data so the human ear can listen to the audio file and not detect any missing sound.

Sound, Hearing and Music

Sounds such as voice dictation and music contain a substantial amount of information. When someone speaks or plays an instrument, a sound wave is created. The sound travels by creating pressure in the air, and the air transmits the pressure. That's why sounds are louder near their source and become lower in volume the further you are from the source. Air is a medium that can transmit vibrations and there are other mediums such as water or even steel, both of which are capable of transmitting sound waves. Eventually, the sound wave vibration might reach a human being.

When the vibration reaches our eardrums, we can hear the sound. Humans have listening devices, our ears, which convert the vibrations of sound waves into electrical signals that our brains can interpret. The eardrum is the part of the ear that converts these vibrations by moving as the vibrations in the air hit the eardrum. Stronger vibrations create louder sounds, and variations in the frequency of the vibration create what we know as pitch. One vibration per second is equal to one Hertz, the scientific term for frequency, Humans can generally hear sounds from 20 Hertz to 20,000 hertz in frequency. A person or instrument with a low pitch voice has a low frequency sound while a person with a high pitch voice has a high frequency sound.

The human ear is not an analog, not a digital device, meaning that it listens to sounds as a continuous wave, and the brain can interpret the information also. By the way, the brain's ability to interpret audio information is one reason people who have progressive hearing loss go so long without it being a problem or it being diagnosed. I learned this when I was fitted for my hearing aids (a result of natural aging and listening to way too much rock music when I was younger).

It's possible to record sounds as analog information using a microphone and a recording device such as a tape recorder or computer. When the audio information is in an analog format, it contains all of the recorded audio information and can be large for a computer file. Experts looked into ways to reduce the size of the file so the audio file would fit into less memory space and be smaller for transmitting over the Internet.

By making an audio file smaller, the file takes less time to travel over network connections like the Internet and takes up less space in memory on a computer or a portable device such as a smartphone. Some of the information in the file must be removed to make it smaller, and that's what "compression" is called.

Reducing the size of audio files

Audio information is a continuous wave and when it's recorded in an analog file the amplitude and frequency are recorded as a wave. To convert the file to a digital file, it;s necessary to take samples of the analog information and use a software program that codes the amplitude and frequency as zeros and ones. As part of the process of the conversion, samples of the audio wave are taken at specific intervals. It's a little bit like chopping up a tomato. By chopping the whole onion into pieces you still have the flavor of the onion in each piece, but each piece is separate and can be used individually or combined. The more slices, the more pieces there are to use.

Sampling an audio file is little bit like chopping up the onion. By chopping the audio file into pieces, each piece contains some of the audio information. When the pieces are combined together, the audio file sounds very much like the original. If you took out sample pieces of the onion, you'd have a portion of the onion to work with and you might have enough to create the flavor you were looking for. Use too much onion and you've got too much onion taste, use too little and you don't have enough flavor.

Audio sampling experts try to solve a similar problem. They try to take as little as possible to keep the file size small but use enough samples of the original audio file to preserve the sound. This is often referred to as the sampling rate, and here's were we get back around to MP3 instead of onions.

Audio coders

A compressed file has enough information to be usable but is smaller in size than the original file since it doesn't have ALL the information of the original. Analog audio files are compressed using a type of software program called a coder that samples the sound, keeps a portion of the audio information and removes what's not necessary to preserve the sound. An audio coder that takes out too much information would create a compressed file that might be very small, but it could also end up sounding different from the original audio sound if too much information was removed.

A good audio coder program will remove enough information to make the file small, but still contain enough information so that our ears will still hear the sound as it was intended. Programmers that create audio coder programs, also known as "codecs," use their knowledge of human hearing and computers to create programs that sample the analog audio information and create a digital version of the audio in a smaller file size.

MP3

The MP3 format is the most commonly used industry standard audio coder format. It was developed by the Moving Picture Experts Group, an industry standard organization that has a mission to create and manage technology standards for the coded representation of digital audio, video, and related data. This is the organization that created the MP3 standard audio coder format. Most of the standards created by the Moving Pictures Expert Group are named MPEG and the MP3 format is part of the MPEG-1 standard and has evolved as technology has improved.

MPEG-1 Layer 3 is an audio coding format that provides excellent compression of music signals. There are MPEG-1 Layer 1 and Layer 2 audio coders, and Layer 1 isn't using much, but Layer 2 is still used for video broadcasting. The Layer 3 audio coder made portable audio electronics popular and widely available.

The MPEG-1 Layer 3 audio coder can compress a high-quality audio CD by a factor of 12, meaning that an MP3 song can fit in 1/12 the file size as the same song on a music CD disc and maintain a high audio quality, so the human ear doesn't hear a significant difference between the original audio file and the compressed MP3 file.

MP3 reduces the size of the audio file where it's practical to store in portable devices with smaller amounts of storage and to transmit or "stream" audio files using the Internet for music applications such as Apple Music, Spotify, and Pandora.

Today almost all audio devices playback the MP3 file format so in addition to your desktop or laptop computer, your smartphone, tablet, DVD player and car stereo can playback MP3 audio files.

To my way of thinking

MP3 made portable audio devices and listening possible and allows us to take our music with us wherever we go and enjoy it. If you're not using your smartphone for music, Apple users can obtain music from the iTunes store and Android from the Google Play store. Amazon offers MP3 files for purchase and apps like Pandora and Spotify make music available as long as you have an Internet connection.

Websites:

Moving Picture Experts Group - http://mpeg.chiariglione.org/

iTunes http://www.apple.com/itunes/

Google Play Music https://play.google.com/

Amazon Music http://www.amazon.com/MP3

Spotify https://www.spotify.com

Pandora http://www.pandora.com

Multi-Core

A multicore processor is a single processor chip that has more than one processor on a single chip contained in a single package. A processor sometimes referred to as a "core," is a circuit that performs instructions or calculations. Since a multicore processor has more than one processing unit, it can perform calculations and run programs at faster speeds than a single processor chip. Multi-core processors are commonly used in many of the current computers, smartphones and tablet devices and make our devices run faster than they would with a single core processor chip.

A quick explanation of a processor

A processor is a physical, electronic circuit that runs, or "executes" instructions from software programs. Contained in a computer, smartphone, laptop or another device, the processor is the "brains" of the device and does the mathematical calculations necessary for the software programs to function and do their work. More processors on a chip allow device makers to put the greater computing power of multiple cores in the space that a single core processor would take up, and improve the performance of the electronic device, whether it's a computer, laptop, smartphone or tablet.

A brief history of multicore processors

When the first chip-based processors were manufactured, the companies making these chips could only fit one processor on a single chip. As the chip-making technology improved, it became possible for chip makers to make chips with more circuits, and eventually the manufacturing technology reached the point where chip makers could manufacture chips with more than one processor and created the multicore chip.

Kunle Olukotun, a Stanford Electrical Engineering professor, and his students designed the first multicore chip in 1998. Advanced Micro Devices (AMD) and Intel released commercially available multicore chips in 2005. Since then virtually every chip maker has started producing multicore chips.

What do more cores mean for you?

Manufacturers of processor chips often use the number of cores in the descriptive material and specifications, so customers have some idea of how capable the processors are inside the device. Multi-core processors are usually referred to by the number of cores contained on the circuit. A two core processor is called dual core, a three-core processor is called tri-core, a four core processor is called quad-core, etc.

In general, the more cores a processor has on it, the faster it will be at running programs. But there are some other factors that affect a multicore processor's ability to speed up running a program. One is the actual speed at which the processor does it's calculations, and the other is if the software programs can take advantage of the ability to run the software. Let's discuss the speed of the processor first.

Processors are electronic circuits that perform mathematical calculations. These calculations take place at a fraction of a second. The time it takes a processor to finish a calculation is a cycle. The more cycles per second, the faster the processor can do its calculations. Most processors today are measured in gigahertz or a billion cycles per second. A two gigahertz processor runs two billion cycles per second, and one that's two and a half gigahertz runs two and a half billion cycles per second.

A dual-core processor running at two gigahertz can run a total of four billion cycles, two billion for each processor. However, to take advantage of the two cores, the software program need tone able to split its work between the two processors so it can run on both cores at the same time. Each core would perform different program calculations so the rest would be a program that would run twice as fast.

When multicore processors first started appearing in the early 2000's, software programs simply weren't ready to take advantage of the faster multicore capabilities. However, now that multicore processors are a common type of processor used in many devices, most software programs, and operating systems have been updated to take advantage of the faster speed that a multicore processor provides.

Where are multicore processors used?

Most current models of smartphones, laptops, desktops, tablets and gaming systems use multicore processors. For example, the Apple iPhone 6s uses an Apple-designed processor called the A9. The A9 is dual-core and has a speed of 1.8 Gigahertz. Many laptops are using an Intel i5 Core (TM) processor. The i5 model is available as a dual-core and a quad-core, depending on the price. So why the two choices?

The two core choices available are an example of how the model of a processor doesn't tell the whole story about the performance. A quad-core i5 will perform substantially faster than a dual-core i5, and that performance will be reflected in the price of the computer. In the case of the i5 model, all of the current laptop models as of this article are dual-core, while all of the desktop models are quad-core. So an i5 in a laptop will be lower performance than an i5 in a desktop because the laptop models are only dual, and not quad-core. The dual-core model uses less power and is optimized for portable laptop devices that need longer battery life while a desktop doesn't have to worry about battery life and can use a processor that consumes more power, like the quad-core model.

To my way of thinking

Multi-core processors offer computer and technology users more powerful processors in smaller packing and lower cost. Their advantages have made the use of all types of technology devices ubiquitous in our daily lives. As manufacturing methods improve, we'll undoubtedly see more cores and faster computing devices, and in smaller sizes.

N

Nanotechnology

Nanotechnology is the materials science and engineering of the very small, with surface features or material components ranging in size from 1 to 100 nanometers in size. A nanometer is a billionth of a meter, and a sheet of paper is about 100,000 nanometers thick. In practice, you're reading this newsletter on a device that uses nanotechnology, as the circuits and transistors that make up your computer's CPU and graphics card are all under 100 nanometers in size.

Nanotechnology is the fuzzy boundary between physics (how atoms interact with each other) and chemistry (how chemical bonds are formed). While there has been plenty of speculation about the ways nanotechnology might change the world - ranging from "magic transmutation machines" to "nanotech weapons" that you see in movies, the reality of nanotechnology is much simpler and practical.

Outside of electronics, nanotechnology can be thought of as custom-built chemical compounds and surfacing agents. Nanotechnology is used literally everywhere. Your DVDs work because a laser made nano-scale holes in the substrate when the data was recorded, and another laser reads that pattern of nanoscale dots. Your scratch-resistant sunglasses are coated in a nanotech material that provides that surface. If you have "no iron" wrinkle-free clothing, the reason that they always look fresh pressed is due to nanotechnology coatings on the fibers used. Micro-fiber cleaning rags - used for eyeglass cleaning cloths and dusting products like the "Swiffer" both use nanotech patterns, base off of insect wings, to trap dust.

Since the mid 2000s, solar cells use nanotechnology to make little grooves, narrower than the thickness of a human hair, that act as mirrors to focus light on the parts of the cell that generate electricity. Nanotechnology is one of the areas where battery technology may gain significant improvements in charge rates and reliability.

Moving slightly farther afield, nanotechnology is a major part of drug research. To do their job, drugs have to fit little areas on cells called receptors. Receptors can be thought of as locks, and the drugs fit the locks like keys. With nanotechnology, those drugs can be designed to fit receptors exactly, which means they can target cells that meet a specific profile, like cancer cells or cells infected by a specific virus. This should make more effective drugs with fewer side effects.

Nanotechnology has quietly moved from science fiction to everyday life, and is ushering in a revolution in tailored medicine.

Near Field Communications (NFC)

NFC, the abbreviation for Near Field Communications, is a technology that allows you to transfer data wirelessly between two devices. Like WiFi and Bluetooth, it's one more type of wireless communication standard that allows communication between any two devices that are NFC capable.

If you own a smartphone or if you are somewhat familiar with smartphones, you have probably heard of the term NFC. NFC is in the news more because Apple started including NFC in the iPhone 6 models and will be using NFC in the Apple Pay feature, but Android and Windows Mobile phones often have NFC already built-in and have had NFC for several years.

NFC doesn't require a smartphone, it only requires that two NFC capable devices be able to touch in order to connect with each other. So NFC can be used in computers, card-access doors, and other ways besides a smartphone.

NFC basics

Like any technology, NFC solves problems and creates a way for people to invent new ways of doing things. Let's look at the basic capabilities of NFC, and then we'll see why it's popular for certain types of applications.

NFC is an industry standard managed by the NFC Forum (http://nfc-forum.org/). This industry group includes thousands of companies and organizations who set the standard for NFC, certify products, and educate industry professionals and consumers. A new logo called the N-Mark is being used to brand NFC technology and products that use the standard.

For any device to be NFC capable, the device requires an NFC chip or electronic circuit inside. That means that any product you buy needs NFC capability built-in or the ability to install NFC.

NFC only requires a touch of the devices for any two devices to connect and communicate with each other.

NFC has a maximum range of 4 centimeters, so the two devices that are communicating using NFC have to stay close to each other. Moving either device more than 4 cm away from an NFC connection will break the connection.

NFC is designed to store a small amount of information in memory, such as a business card, credit card, or a command to start a program on a computer or smartphone.

NFC can be used without power, meaning information in an NFC chip can be read by another NFC device when the two devices touch each other. These unpowered NFC devices are often called "NFC Tags."

Now let's look at some examples of how NFC is being used.

Payments

With Apple Pay and NFC capability shipping in iPhone 6 models, Apple is adding it's clout to the acceptance of NFC technology. Google Wallet was unveiled in 2011, and Android users have been able to make purchases as a few select stores that had begun accepting mobile payments. Unfortunately, Google Wallet wasn't widely adopted since it requires the setup and use of a Google Wallet account to make purchases. Apple's approach connects with credit card processors like MasterCard, Visa, AMEX, etc.

A purchase involves a touch and a confirmation. To make a purchase touch (a short tap is all that's needed) two NFC devices together, then enter an authorization. A charge card terminal with NFC capability reads the payment information (credit card number for Apple or Google Wallet) automatically from your smartphone when you touch an NFC smartphone to an NFC terminal.

To confirm and authorize the purchase, the smartphone user must enter an additional code or identification in order to verify the purchase and prevent fraud. Apple Pay uses the Touch ID fingerprint reader on the iPhone 6 to verify the purchase, making it as secure as your fingerprint.

This use of NFC for payments is a way to replace smart credit cards and is just as secure, and it's referred to as Card Emulation Mode.

Sharing information between two devices (Peer-to-Peer Mode)

Another thing possible thanks to NFC is that you can share data from your phone (or any NFC device) with another person's smartphone (or NFC device). NFC isn't the type of wireless communication that's meant to send and receive much data, or to do it for any length of time. It works for smaller pieces of information like a business card or small file, so two NFC users can share information with each other without the need to connect other than by touching their devices together.

NFC can be used to connect the device to another device by initiating and establishing another type of network connection, such as Bluetooth or WiFi. By using NFC to establish a Bluetooth or WiFi connection between two devices, NFC can be used to establish a faster connection so more data can be transferred. NFC establishes the link, then the other wireless network takes care of the transfer of files and data.

Reader/Writer Mode

Since NFC can work without power, it's possible to store information in an inexpensive NFC chip (the NFC tag I mentioned earlier). So users of NFC devices can "read" the information contained in the NFC tag. A poster or retail store label could have an NFC tag on it, allowing people to view information like a product description just with a tap of their NFC equipped smartphone.

NFC tags are being used for labels on items for inventory, marketing, and education, providing information to any NFC equipped device with a tap.

To my way of thinking

NFC is about proximity, which means nothing happens without a touch or further than 4 cm from any NFC device. This feature makes NFC much more secure than other wireless forms of communication. Payments were one of the original uses planned for NFC when it was being designed. I imagine that one day soon all vending machines will be equipped with NFC so we can tap to buy a snack or drink.

With Apple and Android both using NFC now, Apple Pay coming in the Apple Watch, and major retailers like Disney, Panera Bread, Target and others all starting to accept Apple Pay and equip their stores with NFC readers, NFC for payments is going to spread quickly.

Other uses for NFC will appear, and tech-savvy users are already leading the way, since NFC is in most recent mid and high-end Android devices (lower cost devices may not have NFC). These users are already using NFC to turn their computers on and off, start or stop apps on their smartphones, and set timers with a tap.

Apple currently restricts access to the NFC functions so the NFC capability currently will only work with Apple applications. This restriction is probably a security concern and they want to make sure that NFC is secure and safe for Apple Pay before letting other applications use the NFC capabilities in the device. So for now, if you want to use NFC with a smartphone for your applications, it's only possible with Android.

NFC makes things happen with a tap. Since people like things to be easier, I'm sure we'll see many creative uses and maybe you can come up with some of your own.

Net Neutrality

Net neutrality is a policy where all users of the Internet receive equal treatment when sending and receiving data on the Internet, and that no user will be given preferential treatment over any other user. While net neutrality usually refers to the speed and amount of data the user can send or receive over the Internet, the term also includes freedom of expression, support of user choice and preventing discrimination on the Internet. When all users are treated equally, the Internet is also referred to as an "open" Internet.

Who's an Internet user?

A user is a pretty broad term to describe someone who uses the Internet so let's take a closer look at what "user" means. A user can be a person, small business, local city, state or national government agency, or a large organization, such as the U.S. Government, AT&T, Google, Microsoft, or Facebook.

As you can see by this wide range of Internet users, an organization that makes laws, sets tariffs, owns portions of the cables that makeup the Internet, or has the money to buy faster speeds and pay for larger amounts of data could obtain an advantage over a smaller organization or user.

In addition to size, governments of certain countries restrict both who is allowed to use the Internet and what the users can do when using the Internet. Some countries have tightly controlled Internets within their borders, and Net Neutrality is sometimes used more broadly to include the freedom to send and receive data without government restrictions.

Why does is matter?

When conceived, the Internet was a limited system of networks whose inventors had no idea how large it would become. The Advanced Research Project Agency, (ARPA) created the Internet in the 1970's as a way for the government, academia, and companies to collaborate on government research projects. As it grew, virtually every university which did research joined this network, and the Internet was privatized in the mid-1980's when the government sold the non-military portion of the network to commercial operators. These commercial operators at the time are names that you'd recognize, like AT&T, Sprint, and Verizon and other communications companies.

As the Internet grew, it added more users until billions of devices across the world became connected. In a way, the Internet is like a giant water system, with large "pipes" that move data from one city to another, and smaller and smaller pipes that eventually reach our homes or offices. Instead of pipes moving water, think of the Internet as moving data through the pipes. Just like a water delivery system, the pipes, or in this case cables, cost money to install and maintain, and as more users started to access the Internet, certain connection points of these pipes started to become congested, or slower, with the increased use of the Internet. Here's an example of how congestion on the Internet can take place.

An example of high Internet use and how it affects Net Neutrality

An example is the use of a movie streaming service such as Netflix. When sending small text messages such as email, only a small amount of data needs to move over the Internet since the email is a small piece of data. A full-length motion picture in High-Definition is a dramatically larger piece of data, and it takes up a lot more of the pipe to get from one point to another. It's estimated that Netflix, during peak movie watching times such as Saturday night, accounts for as much as 1/3 of all the data moving on the Internet. If every user had to get to the same place on the Internet to start watching a Netflix show, the connections to Netflix would become congested, which in fact can happen.

In addition to Netflix, individual Internet users watch YouTube videos, search Google, download files, and listen to music streaming services such as Pandora and Spotify. A common way for individuals to connect to the Internet is to pay an Internet Service Provider (ISP) a fee for an Internet connection. An ISP provides access to everything on the Internet for you as a consumer. However, moving large things like movies and music is much more expensive and requires larger and faster Internet "pipes" than moving emails and simpler web pages and requires more expensive Internet "pipes." So who pays for the pipe that delivers the data to you has become one of the hot issues for Net Neutrality.

The issue of net neutrality for bandwidth gets down to some people having deep pockets and others not. Could someone pay the company that delivers the Internet to consumers a fee to get to people's homes faster, and if they could, should they have to pay, and if so, what happens to the Internet users (like small businesses, schools, or individual websites) who don't pay?

Carpool lanes on the Internet?

As you know if you've ever seen a carpool lane when driving on the freeway, one way to reduce congestion is with carpool lanes. By giving access to the carpool lane to users who pay a fee or to users who purchase certain types of vehicles, the carpool lane becomes a preferential lane on the freeway. Just like using a carpool lane to avoid the cost of constructing a new freeway, the idea of a carpool lane can be used on the Internet to move some traffic lanes faster than others by restricting who has access to those lanes. However, the carpool users would get from point A to point B faster than the rest of traffic.

As the increase in traffic on the Internet started to become an issue in the early 2000's, the concept of net neutrality appeared. Some proponents of the Internet suggested that rather than give any Internet preferential treatment, the available bandwidth of the Internet could be conserved so all users of the Internet would have equal access and speeds. Tim Wu, a

Columbia law professor first invented the term "net neutrality" in 2003 in response to these discussions.

Neutral or Not?

A closed Internet would function a little like a meritocracy, where those who were more deserving would receive a larger share of resources. Several factors would define this worthiness, including the ability to pay more or preferential treatment for companies over individual consumers. In a closed Internet, your Internet provider could limit your access to certain websites based solely on whether those websites were also subscribers of the company. More importantly, an ISP could require a website with large files being downloaded, such as Netflix or YouTube to pay a fee in order to have their website and content display on the consumer's screen and not be too slow to use. Opponents of a closed Internet maintain that communications companies are seeking to create a monopoly for themselves or are attempting to create artificial scarcity by limiting the use.

In contrast, opponents of this concept argue that allowing an open Internet would halt innovation. Rather than allowing all Internet users to receive the same speed for data transfer, at the same costs for use, and the same access to all areas of the Internet freely, Internet providers may restrict access with a graduated fee scale that would give preferential access to customers paying a premium price. This "closed Internet" approach would in theory conserve electronic resources such as bandwidth, allowing access to telecommunications companies who argue they need it more and allowing these telecommunications companies to decide which websites and services were faster to display on your screen.

To my way of thinking

The first country to enshrine net neutrality in legal terms was Chile, whose laws do not discriminate against Internet usage, although the law does make an exception in disallowing harmful content. Of course, in the United States we have laws that apply to the Internet, such as the 1st Amendment, the Civil Rights Act of 1964, and others.

There are few laws governing Internet access, and the issue of net neutrality about bandwidth and this topic is currently being reviewed by the Federal Communications Commission (FCC). In February of 2014, the FCC was granted the ability to give preferential Internet access, which is a little like saying that the freeway you use every day is going to get a carpool lane. Whether that carpool lane is carved out of an existing one or is a new one that gets built to add more capacity will affect your use of the Internet just like a carpool lane affects your use of the freeway.

Websites

The FCC has a website where you can review over 270,000 comments made by people and organizations on net neutrality and add your comment to the discussion while the comment period is still open at this link:

http://apps.fcc.gov/ecfs/comment_search/execute?proceeding=14-28.

For more on the history of the Internet read the history as written by the people who created it at the Internet Society.

http://www.internetsociety.org/internet/what-internet/history-internet/brief-history-internet

O

Office 365

Office 365 is a subscription based set of software and services from Microsoft. Like many Microsoft products, it comes in different plans and pricing for home users, small businesses, and large organizations. All Office 365 subscriptions include online access to the popular Microsoft Word, PowerPoint, and Excel applications, plus a cloud storage service for storing documents. A subscription service for software may be a new concept to you, so let's look at the difference between a subscription and a software purchase.

The primary difference between Office 365 and Microsoft Office is the way it is purchased and updated. Traditionally, a user would purchase a retail package with a CD or DVD with a copy of the software on it, along with a license, and install the software on their computer. The license and CD/DVD was for a particular version of the software, such as Office 2007.

Why Do I Want a Subscription?

Periodically, Microsoft would release a new version of Microsoft Office, such as Office 2013, and the latest, Office 2016. Upgrading to the latest version required purchasing an upgrade package that included a CD/DVD and the new upgrade license to install and access the new version of the software. Upgrades weren't mandatory, and many people would continue to use the version of the software they had originally purchased since it met their needs. Software companies don't like users who stay with older versions too long, so let me explain why.

Since many newer features that make Microsoft's product competitive are only available in the newest version of the software, any user with the older version is not seeing the latest features and benefits of what Microsoft can offer. It's like comparing a 5 or 6 year old car to a new one, the new ones always look shinier while the older one looks a little worn. So users of older versions of Microsoft Office are comparing it to the latest versions of competitor's products.

Microsoft wants you to continue to use Microsoft Office and stay with the product as it adds new features and benefits. If you don't upgrade, you don't ever see what improvements Microsoft have made. When you compare your older version of Microsoft Office to a competitor, you will likely see the latest version of a competitor's product, and you might never see the latest version of Microsoft's. So one reason Microsoft wants you to use subscription based software is to keep you with Microsoft products and not switch to a competitor. (all software companies have this challenge with an installed base of users, it's not just Microsoft). But there is another reason for a subscription service.

Supporting different versions of software is one of a software company's largest expenses. Each version has to have a team of people assigned to maintain the product. The more versions that are in use, the greater the number of people that have to maintain and update the software for security issues and bug fixes. With the Office 365 subscription based software, Microsoft can release updates anytime they are necessary since all users obtain the software online and can be updated automatically. In addition, new versions of the software cane updated automatically. Like it or not, subscription based software is going to be the way of the future. When you use your Web based email or map Web site, you're essentially using a free software product. And there is one more reason.

Services are increasingly included with software. People who create documents need storage, people who use email need email accounts, and people who use business productivity tools usually need a phone and conference services. Office 365 plans include these and other services depending on the specific plan. So in addition to Word, Excel, and PowerPoint being available to you online, you can also store your documents in Microsoft's cloud storage, use Microsoft's Exchange email service, and use Skype. Another benefit is that you can use Office 365 on any computing device with a Web browser since the software is a Web-based solution.

But What if I Want to Use Software Off-Line

The basic Office 365 subscription doesn't include desktop copies of Word, Excel, and PowerPoint. So this means you need to be connected to the Internet to use these applications. If you need the software so you can work offline, on a laptop, for example, you just need to purchase an Office 365 version with the local software versions and install them. Then, whenever you connect to the Internet, your documents are synced. Having the online only version might seem like a limitation if you're used to using the local copy of software.

If you do any work offline without an Internet connection, for example, if you travel frequently, you will probably need an Office 365 version with offline capability or purchase the desktop software. Small Business Premium is the version that includes both online and desktop software and is described below. If you usually use your computer at home where you have Internet access all the time, it's not necessary. Pricing for the desktop software has increased compared to older versions so if you can use the online version, you can save some money.

Remember, one of the biggest advantages of Office 365 is the ability to access your information anywhere you can use a Web browser and the Internet, on any device, on Mac's, tablets, and smartphones that aren't Microsoft products.

Home Premium Version

The Home Premium version of Office 365 includes any number of users in a household and use up to 5 devices per user (not total, that's per user). It includes Word, Excel, PowerPoint, OneNote, Outlook, Publisher, and Access. It also includes 20G of SkyDrive storage and 60 minutes of Skype call time. It's priced at $99.99 per year or $9.99 per month on Microsoft's Web site. http://office.microsoft.com/en-us/home-premium

One caveat, you can't use Office 365 on Windows XP or Vista, you need to have Windows 7 or later or a Mac with OS X 10.6 or later.

Business Versions

In businesses and large organizations, the Microsoft Office software usually includes the use of Outlook's mail and contact management with Microsoft's commercial solution, Exchange. Sometimes additional collaboration tools are used by organizations that have a server based product from Microsoft called Small Business Server. Office 365 can completely replace this server and eliminate the need for costly hardware and software licenses and support. It can also give one or two person businesses access to professionally managed information technology previously available only to organizations that could afford servers.

If you're a small business and already use Microsoft Office products, you should really look into Office 365 for your own use (I don't work for Microsoft). The benefits of having Outlook with Exchange are worth it for email, calendar, and contact management. And you can use your email on both iOS and Android and keep everything in sync.

Security, Backup. and Other Plans

For security issues, Office 365 is protected with the latest and continually updated, protection schemes against viruses, spam and malware of every type. Office 365 also has excellent disaster recovery ability because of the Microsoft policy for use of multiple data centers and failovers that are automatic. For this reason, Office 365 claims and delivers a 99.99% guarantee of uptime.

There is an Office 365 Enterprise Plan that allows users connection rights to SharePoint services using only SSL encrypted connections. Only enterprise plan users have this special cryptographic security system for protection of their document transmissions.

Is Office 365 Right for You?

If you are an experienced user of Microsoft's Office products, then Office 365 is an alternative to purchasing a retail product CD/DVD. Office 365 eliminates the need to purchase new versions of the software, since new versions are available as part of your subscription. If you need business grade email, the use of Exchange mail with the Small Business plans will give you large organization email capabilities for a fraction of the cost, along with full desktop versions of the software.

For home users, household access to Word, Excel, PowerPoint, and Outlook is a very attractive price point. And if necessary, you can purchase a desktop license for only those household members that need a copy.

Why is Microsoft doing this? Well, they aren't the first ones to offer online versions of software. Another company, Google, has been doing this for years with their Google Docs suite of online office software. Microsoft is changing with the technology just like everyone else, and if you can take advantage of this competition, you can save money. Watch in a few weeks as I cover Google

Docs and Apple's iWork solutions, all of which will work on a Windows PC, Mac, iOS, and Android.

Offline and Online

Online means that a computer, device, or a person is connected to a network, and usually this means the Internet. While off-line means the computer, device, or person is not connected to a network, cannot be reached, and cannot communicate with any other computer or device.

Online and Offline for computers and devices

As you can see from the explanation above, online and offline refers to both technical devices like computers and smartphones, and to people, who use these devices. So a device or a person can be referred to as being online or offline, but it means something a little different if we are talking about a device or person.

Online and Offline for people

For a person to be "online," the device they are using must be connected to a network and able to communicate over the network. Computers and smartphones use both wired and wireless communications to connect to networks, and you may be familiar with connecting to a network using an Ethernet cable or a WiFi connection. When a device is connected to a network, the device becomes "online," and when there is no network connection the device is "offline." So how does this apply to people, instead of devices?

A computer or device can be "online" and connected to a network, but the person using the computer can be inactive, away from their desk, or have blocked communications for some quiet time. In this case, the person is said to be "offline," because the person isn't able to communicate with any other person who may want to communicate with them. Let's look at an example when using Facebook, which allows you to see if any of your friends are online or offline so you can see who is available for chat.

If you're using your computer and have the Facebook webpage open on your desktop, the chat function (usually in the lower right-hand corner) shows a list of friends and some of them will have a green colored dot next to their name. The dot indicates that they are active on Facebook and will receive a message from you if you start a Chat session. Some names will display the words Mobile, Web, or time. So what do these mean?

If there is a green dot next to a person's name, they are online with Facebook and you can communicate with them, using the Facebook chat function (it's usually a right click on their name or tap on the mobile app). Mobile means that your friend is on a smartphone or tablet using the Facebook mobile app while Web means that your friend is using a desktop or laptop.

The time indicates when your friend was last logged in, or "online," with Facebook. Keep this issue in mind when making friends on Facebook, since your friends will be able to see if you are online or offline, but since their friends it's usually OK for them to know this, right?

If you see a little gear icon at the bottom of the chat list or anywhere on your mobile app, you can change the settings for a chat. Using the chat settings, you can turn off chat, and all of your friends will see that you are offline, and there won't be a green dot next to your name when they see you in their chat list. Now you're "offline" on Facebook, but you are still connected to the Internet and may or may not be at your computer or using your smartphone. To your friends on Facebook, you're offline as far as they're concerned and any message they send you will be sent to your email for reading later. Using online or offline with Facebook is an example of how you can be online or offline within a specific application or function on your computer or device.

What happens when you are online or offline?

When you are online, it means you are connected to a computer network, and for most personal users this network is the Internet. In addition, it can also mean that you are using your email or instant messaging program that allows you to communicate with another person.

While online, you can do anything on the Internet, from sending and receiving emails or instant messages, engage in a video call with someone, use social network tools, work and even play games that require an Internet connection to work.

You can browse while you are offline as well, but you only able to view local copies of webpages that you had open during your last time online. These copies are stored locally in your local storage and can often be viewed even without an Internet connection. If you are considered "offline" on a smartphone, you can still do regular phone things like engage in voice calls, text message with other people and play games that don't require an Internet connection.

You are unable to browse the Internet on your smartphone or tablet while offline. Likewise, you cannot play any game that requires you be online, and you cannot stream music or video from the Internet while offline, but you can play anything that's stored on your device, since it's stored in your device's local memory.

Some odds and ends for using online and offline

Online and offline applies to devices like printers and other devices which can connect to computers and networks. Printers usually use either a direct USB cable or WiFi to connect to computers. If the printer is using a WiFi connection, the printer becomes a device on your home network reachable by other devices (like computers) that also use your home network.

In the case of a printer, online and offline mean that a device such as a printer is either communicating with your computer (online) or not (offline). In other words, if the printer is "offline," it means that a user would not be able to print documents that they sent via a computer. It doesn't matter if the printer is connected by cable or WiFi, if it's offline, your computer can't communicate with it. So it is possible for a printer to be powered on, but offline, if, for example, you didn't have the cable connected from your printer to your computer.

To my way of thinking

While you may not use offline and online in your everyday conversation, understanding how other people use these terms will help you understand what they mean. And if you're at all tech savvy, you'll be able to use online and offline to help you understand how your computer and smartphone work, and what you can do locally compared to when you have an "online" connection to the Internet.

OLED

OLED is the abbreviation for Organic Light Emitting Diode, a light source that uses semi-conductor wafers made from "organic" (more about "organic" later) materials. When an electric current is applied to OLED material, it emits energy in the form of light. OLED lighting is used most frequently as a display screen for smartphones and TV sets.

OLED's came from LED's

OLED technology is similar to LED lighting technology. The term LED stands for "light emitting diode," a solid state semi-conductor that, like OLED's, generates light when an electric current is applied to the LED material. You've probably seen LED lights since they are becoming more commonplace as a replacement for standard light bulbs. LED's are energy efficient, don't generate much heat, and there's a lot of industry experience using them in many sizes and shapes.

The organic part of OLED comes from the fact that OLED's are made with materials that contain carbon and hydrogen. Organic chemical compounds contain Carbon and hydrogen elements, but there's nothing alive in the OLED material.

I suppose it sounds like everything should use OLED's from what we've learned so far, so what other benefits do they have?

The benefits of OLEDs.

OLED lights can be made smaller and thinner than LED's. In fact, it's possible to make OLED's to be made as small as a pixel for a display screen. When OLED's are used to make up a screen for a smartphone or a smart TV, every single pixel within the screen is an individual OLED light, and can be controlled individually.

In contrast, LED's can't be used as a display just by themselves. The smallest size LED is too large to make up a single pixel (the dot) on a display screen, so displays using LED's need another material. The display screens use a sheet of liquid crystal, that when lit by LED's, creates colors pixel by pixel. The LED's are really a form of backlighting for the liquid crystal display, and all liquid crystal displays need to be backlit. This combination of LCD backlit with LED lights makeup what are commonly called LCD displays.

Because OLED's use a single layer of material, the screen can be thinner, lighter, and even more flexible than the LCD display's we are using every day right now.

Whether in the screen of a smartphone or a TV, OLED tends to be superior overall. Blacks are deepest and the truest, especially when compared with an LCD screen in which they are not quite as dark. The deep black found on an OLED screen tends to provide even greater contrast to the screen and more vibrant colors as a result. In contrast, LCD screens occasionally provide colors that appear more washed out. The viewing angles on an OLED screen are also better and can be viewed from a variety of angles, even from the sides. OLED technology also provides less motion blur.

So why aren't all displays OLED?

One of the downsides of an OLED screen is that, over time, the blue color in them tends to have a shorter life span. Since a display needs to generate red, green, and blue light in order to create all colors, any one color that doesn't work right creates a discolored image. If you ever printed something in color and ran out of one color of ink, your printed image does not look right since a color is missing. The incorrect colors are what happens when the display doesn't create the right amount of any one color.

A shorter life span for blue OLED's means that eventually, the blues in the screen will degrade, leading to the other colors breaking down as well. This color break down can also result in burn-in, a problem commonly found in devices with OLED screens.

In addition to the annoying problem engineers are having with making blue OLED's last longer, OLED's are more expensive to manufacture right now than LCD displays, because OLED's can also be easily damaged by water and require more expensive sealing to keep them waterproof. As a result, large screens, like those used on computer monitors and televisions, are still much more expensive to manufacture than LCD displays.

Who uses OLED?

Since owners replace smartphones and tablets faster than a television screen or computer monitor, the blue color issue isn't a major issue, since the devices just aren't going to be in use that long compared to the average television. As a result, OLED's have found their way into smartphones and tablet devices. The biggest user of OLED displays in smartphones is Samsung, who just happens to be a large manufacturer of display screens. Since the Samsung Galaxy S3, Samsung has used OLED displays in their Galaxy models, with display improvements coming out as they have released new models of Galaxy devices. In addition to Samsung, Motorola, Sony, and LG have also used OLED displays in some of their smartphones and tablets.

A flexible future

The biggest thing going for OLED displays is the fact that manufacturers can make them as flexible panels that bend. The displays being made in labs today are bendable, and some makers of televisions have shown off curved screens at recent trade shows. While a curved TV screen might not make sense in your home, imagine a curved display wrapped around a column or curved surface in a public location such as retail display.

It goes without saying that once flexible displays are available at a low enough cost, electronic devices can be made that will bend and flex, opening up new types of devices we haven't even thought of yet.

Online Banking

Online Banking (OLB) is a service that provides an account holder access to all of his/her accounts over the Internet. Some common functions available through online banking include viewing your account balance, printing statements, transferring money between accounts, paying bills and making deposits. Almost every bank, credit union, stock brokerage, insurance agency or other financial institution support online banking through a website or a mobile app. Some banks function as online banks only and don't even have a physical facility.

History of online banking

Online banking started in the early 1980's when four large New York-based banks (Citibank, Chase Manhattan, Chemical, and Manufacturers) started offering home banking services using a videotext telephone handset. Remember, in the early 1980's the Internet wasn't commonly available, and the personal computer had just been invented. Phone companies invented a special telephone handset that allowed phone and data communications and provided a small text display.

You don't see many videotext terminals around except in technology museums, and they were an early attempt to move technology into the home that was replaced by personal computers and the Internet. Consumer models of personal computers and new web browser technology of the late 1990's ushered in the era of website-based online banking. Banks and other financial institutions quickly created websites for customers to use their personal computer to access their financial accounts from home or work.

Online banking security and safety

Users of online banking services are required to create an account with a username and password to access their financial information and conduct transactions. Banks and financial institutions usually have the highest security requirements for creating accounts and often require stronger user information for safety and security.

Most commonly, an online banking account will require a complex password that includes a minimum of eight characters and has to include upper and lower case character, numbers, and special symbols. While often frustrating to remember, these requirements make password theft more difficult and exist to protect you. There are other measures as well.

Account holders are often required to create password recovery information, usually in the form of answering one or more questions with personal information that a thief is unlikely to know. These types of questions can be the name of the street where you grew up, your favorite teacher in school, the name of your first pet, etc. These bits of personal information are for security.

Take the time to fill out these questions since they are used to "challenge" anyone who attempts to access your account with an incorrect password entry. In fact, if you make a mistake entering your password more that a few times, you might be required to answer one of more of these "challenge" questions. Don't worry, if you forget your password or can't login, your financial institution can help you with phone support. However, they will require some information from you over the phone to verify your identity.

Your bank or financial service will never send you an email asking you for information about your account. Any request for information about financial information that arrives in your inbox should be treated as fraudulent. I recommend being on the cautious side and if you're unsure, call or visit your bank or financial institution. For all the transactions that take place, online banking is pretty safe, especially for the commonly used services like bill payment.

Services available

You can do a couple of different financial tasks with online banking such as check your account balances, transferring funds in and out of accounts, pay bills, set account balance alerts for a withdrawal over a certain dollar amount and chat online real-time with a personal banker.

Online bill payment is one of the most commonly used services and most banks allow you to connect your online account with a utility or other credit card so you can pay bills electronically often as soon as the next day. When without an electronic connection, your online bill payment service through your bank will let you send a paper check to whomever you want to send money.

It's even possible to connect financial accounts from other banks and financial institutions (referred to as external accounts) to your online banking account, enabling you to transfer money from one bank to another bank. You should review your banks specific instructions for doing this to set it up since easy one is a little different. It's common for your bank to make a small deposit to the external account and require you to verify the amount of the deposit to complete the electronic connection and enable you to transfer money, but once it's done it doesn't need to be repeated.

Mobile online banking

Smartphones added the ability for people to access their online banking services through their mobile devices, and with cellular service almost everywhere, your bank account is available to you 24 hours a day wherever you can access the Internet. Smartphone technology resulted in banks creating apps for mobile phones, making it easy to access and use your account using a touchscreen device without a mouse and keyboard. And then they figured out how to use the camera on the smartphone.

Since smartphones have a camera, banks figured out how to use the phone camera to take a picture of a check, making online deposits possible from your smartphone. Most bank apps have this capability already, and you can access it by using the check deposit feature of the banking app. Using the check deposit feature will open up a new screen instructing you to take a picture of the front and back of a check, and then enter the amount and complete the deposit. The app usually has instructions for how to line up and position your check. Smartphone cameras are such high quality that the image of the check you send your bank via that app are often higher quality than the scanned image from the teller scanning machine.

The future of online banking

Online banking and the ability of people to use technology such as smartphones for financial transactions is changing the way banks and financial institutions operate, and other organizations as well, like the post office.

Online banking and email billing have resulted in huge reductions of first class mail because fewer bills and fewer checks are mailed. New organizations that allow electronic transactions via email, the web, and apps are becoming more common. PayPal is one of the most commonly known and has allowed people to send and receive money via email for some time. Another one you might see is Square.

Square started out as a way for businesses to accept credit cards but also has an app called Square Cash that allows you to send money to anyone using a mobile app and doesn't require a fee. Square Cash makes it easy to split dinner bills instantly and send money electronically regardless of time zone and location.

With the prevalence of mobile devices and online banking, electronic banking is now a mainstream Internet function and here to stay.

Online Dating

Online Dating (also known as Internet dating) is a way for people to find and contact each other through the Internet to arrange a date, usually with the goal of developing a personal and romantic relationship. According to Statistic Brain (www.statiscbrain.com), as of May 2016 almost 50 million Americans have tried online dating. Some online dating services are free to use but most charge a service fee to access all the available services.

Online dating basics

To use online dating, a person creates a user account on an online dating site, then creates a profile with photos, descriptive information and match preferences. The online dating service uses software to provide the user with matches based on mathematical formulas (algorithms) which match one user with another based on their profile information, preferences, and interests.

While the matching features of online dating services present a user with potential dates, it's also possible for a user to search for potential dates based on location, age, religion and other profile information. Users can then make contact with a potential date using messaging or email services provided within the online dating service.

Online dating services

There are dozens of online dating services available. Each one has a slightly different marketing approach designed to appeal to various segments of the dating population. There are broad-based dating sites, the most popular of which is match.com, which called itself the "leading" online dating site and according to statisticbrain.com, Match has over 23 million members. eHarmony, another popular online dating site, has over 16 million members and markets itself as the "#1 trusted dating site for like-minded singles."

Specialized dating sites exist that focus on bringing people together with specific interested and preferences. There are dating sites for specific age groups, religious backgrounds, hobbies, sports, and age ranges. By using one of these specialized sites, it's easier for a person to find a direct match with others that share something in common. Some examples of specialized sites are jdate.com (for Jewish singles), ourtime.com (for mature singles), singleparentmeet.com (for single parents), okcupid.com (free with premium options), and there are many others based on sexual preference.

Online dating services have followed people who use their smartphones with mobile apps, and almost every online dating service has an app for both Apple and Android smartphones. Some online dating services have been designed specifically to take advantage of features on smartphones and use the user's location and smartphone gestures. One of the most popular apps to use features on smartphones is Tinder, which was launched in 2012 and by 2014, had over one billion (yes that's right) "swipes" per day and that number continues to grow.

Tinder users see potential dates on their smartphone screen and then swipe one direction to choose someone they are interested in dating or swipe the other direction to skip the match and move on to the next match. The user can then contact the potential date using Tinder's messaging feature in the app. While Tinder gathered a reputation early on as "hook-up" app, it's swiping feature has made it popular and is available in over 30 languages. By the way, the company that owns match.com, IAC Interactive, owns a majority stake in Tinder.

Online dating safety

One of the biggest challenges with online dating (or online communications of any kind) is safety and security. The online dating services all monitor suspicious activity and will delete a user's account if it is compromised or if it is being used for fraud or harm, however, they can't catch everyone, and it's important to be safe when using online dating.

Some common advice across is given by all the online dating services concerning safety. These tips include:

- Don't use your real name in your profile
- Never send money or gifts
- Arrange any meeting in a public place
- Drive yourself to and from your first meeting

While safety and security are a concern, use the same common sense you'd use when you're dealing with people in any situation and don't let it get in the way of meeting people. Oh yes, it's also becoming more common for people to use online tools to check up on old relationships, so the online sites all have ways to block users similar to social media sites.

Does it work?

A lot of research has been done to see if online dating has been successful in getting people together in relationships. Most Americans know a couple who first met through an online dating site.

Opinions are changing concerning online dating as a potential way to meet people. The Pew Research Center surveyed Internet users who used online dating.The results showed that 80% of Americans who use online dating think it is a good way to meet people and that 61% agree that online dating is easier and more efficient than other ways of meeting people.

One benefit of online dating is that it's possible to find more people that you might meet during your daily activity. The same Pew study found that 53% said that online dating allows people to find a better match for themselves because they can get to know a lot more people.

Online dating doesn't happen by itself either. It's best if you spend a little time day using whatever online dating site you choose (and I recommend trying a few since they all have a different appeal) to look at your matches and communicate with potential dates. It won't take more than an hour a day after you set up your account and profile. While this may seem like a lot of time, if you're serious about meeting someone look at it as an investment, not a chore.

To my way of thinking

While the vast majority of people in a marriage or long-term relationship still say they met their partner offline, rather than online, the proportion of Americans who are finding partners online is increasing every year.

Online dating is one of many approaches to meeting people, but it's not the only one. If you're single and involved in social activities that give you the opportunity to meet people you're less likely to find a need for online dating to get a date, but online dating does expand the available options for you to be matched with a potential date so don't rule it out.

Open Source

I've done quite a few Blogging and PC Performance classes so far this summer and software is a topic that comes up often. When discussing software, I'll use the term "Open Source" in classes to describe a software product. Just what is Open Source and what does it mean?

Software Licenses

Let me explain a little more about open source. When you pay for the software, you are really purchasing a license to use the software product. You don't really own the right to the original software code, only the right to use the software on one or more computers, depending on how the license is sold. You may have a physical media, like a DVD or CD, but you don't own the software itself, only the right to use it according to the terms of your license. This is the way almost all commercial software is sold.

The license usually allows you to use the software for your own personal or business use, or on a certain number of computers. But a commercial license doesn't allow you to include the software in any other software product for sale. This requires a reseller or OEM (original equipment manufacturer) license from the software company. With a reseller or OEM license you may be able to purchase the right to include the software in your own product, depending on the license terms available from the software company. You would pay a different fee for using the software as part of another product. In fact, this is how Google licenses their Android operating system to smartphone manufacturers. They pay Google a fee for each device that uses Android.

This "license" is what Open Source is all about. Open Source software carries a license which usually prohibits the sale of the Open Source software and any products which are developed with the Open Source software as part of the product. Open Source software efforts developed as a result of programmers wanting to write software code and share that code with other programmers. These programmers are often referred to as the Open Source community, and

Open Source is definitely a community effort. The idea behind it that since a community contributes to the software, no company can claim ownership and control the software. While an Open Source product may seem risky as a result of an all volunteer effort, it can often result in higher quality, more flexible software products, with new features and capabilities added quickly. Examples include Word Press for blogging, Open Office, an alternative to popular word processing, spreadsheet, Mozilla Firefox, one of the most popular browsers, and the Linux operating system.

People and organizations make money with Open Source by providing services, support, and complete solutions, but any product with Open Source software usually includes a free license to use the software.

Opt-In

Opt-in means that you have chosen the option of being included in an email newsletter service. When you opt-in, you give the company, person, or organization permission to send you email, usually in the form of a regular newsletter.

The organization that sends emails has a list of people that, for the most part, want to receive the emails. Spam is email that you didn't agree to receive. Remember, if you chose to receive an email newsletter, knowingly or not, it's not considered spam.

The term "opt-in" can have a positive and negative meaning, and it often depends on your point of view. Let's look at what opt-in means for the recipient of an email newsletter first, then we'll look at what it means for the email list sender.

Opt-in for the Email Recipient

For readers of email, there is usually just too much email coming in every day. Some of these emails are probably a list that you are subscribed to receive. Chances are, at some point, you chose to "opt-in" to the email newsletter, whether you know it or not.

These "opt-in" email choices are sometimes visible, but can also hide in various places on Web sites, emails and order forms. For example, when ordering a product or service from a Web site, you may have glanced over a check-box asking you if you wanted to subscribe to their email list for updates, specials, and announcements.

Web sites have become quite savvy at getting customers to opt-in to their email newsletters. One way you often opt-in without even realizing you have is after you place on online order. At the bottom of the order, a company will often automatically check a box with text similar to "Yes, please send me emails with exciting information about your products."

Another way Web sites get you to opt-in is by requiring you to supply an email address and opt-in before you can access a free service or download a free ebook or software product. And of course, you may also have willingly opted-in to a newsletter before you have seen a copy and then decide you have no interest in receiving it.

Opting-Out

You can opt-out of these emails and take steps to limit automatic opt-ins. First, when placing orders or filling out online forms, be conscious of any boxes with check marks. Companies often automatically select the "Yes" box for you making it your responsibility to uncheck the box.

Many email opt-in subscriptions require that you click on a confirmation link before you actually receive the subscription. Your first email from the list will include a link to a Web page that, when clicked, is your confirmation that you want to receive the email. If you don't confirm, you won't receive the email. If the email newsletter is something you truly want to receive, be sure to look in your inbox and spam folder (if you have one) for this "confirmation" email and click on the link. This "confirmed opt-in" is what I use for my newsletter.

Secondly, seriously consider the tradeoff for supplying your personal email to a company in exchange for a free service. The service isn't actually free. Your personal information is the currency in this exchange.

Lastly, if you have unintentionally opted-in to email newsletters, you can unsubscribe. Open an email from the company and scroll down to the bottom of the page. The email will usually contain a link to unsubscribe from the newsletter.

There is one other kind of email subscription that is harder to unsubscribe from, and that's the kind that requires you login to a Web site and manage your "user preferences." To unsubscribe form these lists you have to login to a Web site where your subscription is managed, then select the option or options to unsubscribe from the email. If you've forgotten your password, look for a link that will recover a lost password, then you can login to manage the subscriptions.

When you see the word "opt," think option. It's your choice, and you can opt to take part or not.

The List Owner's Perspective

When a person opts-in and agrees to receive your email newsletter, you have one of the best ways to stay in touch with them. A subscriber who opts-in has chosen to receive your communications, which means they are already interested in what you have to say (provided you have something of use for them to read). Provide good email content to your readers and your subscriber list will grow, making it a valuable asset, whether you're an author, company, or non-profit.

Most reputable email subscription list owners provide an easy way for subscribers to "opt-out." If you send an email list, please provide a link on your email allowing recipients to easily opt-out because you actually only want subscribers who really want to receive your newsletters. Don't worry about people who unsubscribe, because they wouldn't read the email, and by providing an easy way to opt-out, you avoid complaints about your email being spam.

In case you're interested, the email service I use is aWeber. If you are looking for an email list service and you click on the affiliate link, aWeber will provide me with a small affiliate commission, which will support my training and education efforts.

P

Password Locker

A password locker is a software program or website that stores and remembers your passwords for you. You only need to remember one password to unlock the password locker, and you will have access to all your passwords for websites that you use.

Why use a password locker?

If you've been on the internet for any period, chances are you have accounts to a lot of different websites. All of these websites have usernames and passwords, and remembering them all can prove to be difficult, especially if you use different passwords on different websites.

Some people store all their passwords in a document on their computer or smartphone, write all their passwords down in a paper notebook, or even use the same password on every single website possible. While these approaches are commonly used, they are not the most secure way to store passwords as I'll explain.

Using an app on your device

If you use an app or document on your smartphone or computer to store passwords, anyone who can access your smartphone or computer can open the document and obtain your passwords.

Paper lists of passwords

Using a paper document or notebook removes the passwords from your computer or device, so even if someone had your computer or smartphone they still wouldn't have you passwords. However, most people use small notebooks or pieces of paper and carry these items with them, along with their smartphone or laptop. Anyone obtaining the notebook or paper from a wallet or purse will have access to your passwords. If you keep the passwords in a paper document but only keep the document at home, your password security is better, since someone would have to find the password list in your home, which is generally pretty secure.

Using the same password

Many people use the same password for as many websites as possible, which makes it easier to access all of the websites and accounts than using a different password for each website. But even using the same password is becoming difficult since many websites require different numbers of character, special symbols in the password such as a dollar sign or explanation point or have other requirements that make using the same password everywhere challenging.

A password locker app or program can solve them. With a password locker, you can not only have a safe place to store passwords, but it makes storing and remembering different passwords for each website easier and more secure.

How Do Password Lockers Work?

Password lockers work by storing all of your passwords securely either on a website or in an application on your computer or device. You remember one highly secure password (often called a master password) to open and use the password locker that then gives you access to all of your passwords.

Most password lockers can automatically fill-in your username and password for you when you go to a website, so you don't have to go through the effort of copying and pasting the username and password for each website you use.

Password locker applications provide add-ons or plug-ins for the commonly use web browsers and operating systems, so you only need to log-in to the password locker software or add-on once to enable the fill-in capability. However, if you close your web browser or your device goes to sleep, you might have to reenter the master password. In any case, this is far simpler than having to remember each password and the auto-fill feature makes logging into websites faster.

One locker, different passwords

One major advantage of a password locker is that your passwords are encrypted and stored only on your computer or devices. The master password unlocks the app or add-on. Password lockers also help guide you to create a very strong and difficult to crack password for your master password.

Once you add a password locker to your web browser, it will activate several very useful features. One is the ability to record any password you enter to access a website or service. Once you enter the password for the website, it's stored in the locker for you to review and edit anytime. The second feature is the ability to have the password locker app or add-on create a password for any website you use and store it in the locker.

A third benefit is the ability to access your passwords from any computer or device you use using a smartphone or mobile app in addition to the web browser add-on. Being able to use one service enables you to access any secure website you use from any device without the need to remember your password.

Where do I find a password locker app?

There are many online password lockers that also offer mobile apps and these are the best and also most popular. While password locker applications are often free for web browsers, the mobile app versions that enable you to use the app on a smartphone are often a paid app, but they are relatively inexpensive and often less than $20 a year for a subscription.

Some password lockers are paid, some are free, and some have free editions along with paid options so you can choose one that fits your needs and budget.

Lastpass is a great free online password locker that also has paid options that enable mobile and other capabilities. Lastpass has add-ons for major web browsers such as Google Chrome, Firefox, and Internet Explorer so you can access your password locker at the click of a button.

Several other highly rated password lockers include dashlane and 1password.

To my way of thinking

Just like a good lock on your home, it's important to have a lock on your computer and websites. If you need a better method to manage all of your online passwords securely, throw out the paper notebook, delete the document, and try an online or computer password locker.

Pay Per Click Advertising

Pay Per Click is an advertising program first developed by Google. When a visitor searches for information on Google, the search engine shows two kinds of results. One is from sites that match the keywords used in the search, and the other is from advertisers who have requested their ads appear for those same keywords. Pay Per Click is often abbreviated as "PPC."

Pay Per Click is successful is because it produces results for advertisers. If you are advertising car tires and there's a way to put your ad in front of people who are searching for information on car tires, you have a much better chance of making a sale. In advertising parlance, your "conversion rate" goes up.

But Google takes the proposition one step further. The rule for PPC advertising is you only get charged a fee if someone clicks on your ad. Now the advertising budget only applies to ads that are at least somewhat successful. Prior to PPC advertising, an advertiser would pay to run an ad in a magazine or newspaper and pay based on how many subscribers the publication reached. The advertiser had no way of knowing whether people took action when they saw the ad.

With the ability to track when a person clicks on an ad, this new feature was now available to advertisers. If you're running a commercial for your burger stand, you will know how many people saw your ad, but you have no way of knowing which viewers made a decision to respond to that ad. With PPC, you do.

Google has turned PPC advertising into a multi-billion dollar worldwide business. Most people think Google is a search engine company. While they run one of the most popular search engine, the majority of their revenue comes from charging advertisers a variable rate depending on what keywords they want to activate their ads.

They are also not the only company to use the PPC model. There are numerous other companies that have implemented Google's model to generate ad revenue. Yahoo!, Facebook, Twitter, LinkedIn, and other websites base their income on advertising. They have experienced varying levels of success, but by and large, the model is a successful one provided there is enough competition for the popular and lucrative keywords.

Google certainly couldn't have invented PPC advertising at a better time. As more time is spent using the Internet, there are more hours in the day to display PPC ads to people using Google for search. Since there are more ways people use the Internet besides search, such as Social Networking, Facebook has become the 2nd largest company in terms of revenue from PPC advertising with over 3 million advertisers using it.

Google is always looking to find ways to make Google search more useful and has expanded PPC ads into gmail, YouTube, and Google's social network, Google +. The PPC business model is a sound one. It's likely to be successful for some time to come.

To My Way of Thinking

While PPC ads may seem annoying and intrusive, the public receives a powerful search service for free, since the advertisers support the costs. For now, it seems as though people are willing to live with PPC ads in return for free services on the Internet.

Paywall

A paywall is a barrier on a website that prevents visitors from viewing web pages unless the visitor makes a payment. Think of it as the toll-road of websites. While some roads are free, some roads require a toll in order to use them.

Why do Paywalls Exist?

While you might think of the Internet as a free resource, someone has to write the articles, take pictures, and shoot the videos that we view on the Web. Those people have to be paid to create the content by the people or organization that owns the website. So how do these websites get the money for this? Usually through advertising.

News about Paywalls

A regional newspaper, the Orange County Register, was purchased by some investors with no experience in the newspaper business. The new owners promptly made the online edition of the newspaper a paywall website and invested in hiring over 350 staff members. Hiring new staff in 2013 is pretty rare in the newspaper business, but the new owners believe that people will pay for better content. Two other newspapers, the Wall Street Journal and the New York Times are also known for their paywall online editions.

Besides newspapers, there are many speciality websites that charge for their content. These websites typically have some unique or original content that people are willing to pay to access. In fact, my website, bobology.com, is a paywall, with some webpages visitors can access for free and others that require a payment.

Advertising and the Free Web

Many websites can be viewed for free because of advertising. Advertising is all over the Web and appears often on websites, usually as a few lines of text, as a picture, or an image that's an ad. Click on the ad with your mouse and a webpage appears that has information about the advertised product or service. Google makes most of it's money from Web advertising and many websites make money and support themselves with their ads.

Paywall Supported Websites

Some websites have a different approach to making money and charge visitors for viewing the website. When a website wants to restrict access to some or all of it's information, the website creates an electronic barrier called a paywall. Some of the webpages are free, and these are considered "in front" of the paywall.

Other webpages and content require payment in order to view them and are considered "behind" the paywall. It's up to the owner of the website what is free and what requires payment, and how much to charge. As a result, some websites with paywalls give visitors access to some webpages for free while other webpages are behind the paywall.

For example, if a website wanted to make some sample content available, the website may offer access to some articles so visitors can sample the website and try it before they buy it. Other free webpages could include a shopping cart, news, or contact information. It's up to each website owner to choose what is free and what webpages require a payment to view.

Different Ways Paywalls Work

It's not hard to recognize a paywall. When you access a paywall, a message usually appears on the webpage letting you know that access to the webpage is restricted and required payment. There are some common ways paywalls work, with membership sites, and individual articles being the most common.

Membership Sites

A membership site requires a visitor to pay a monthly or annual member fee in order to access the webpages behind the paywall. With a paid membership, the visitor becomes a member and obtains a user account with a username. When visiting the website, there is a form for entering the username and the user's password, which then unlocks the webpages behind the paywall so the member can view these webpages.

Some membership sites have more than one level of membership, with tiers at different prices. For example, one level might be $5 per month, while another might be $10 a month. Usually this means that there is access to additional sections of the website that are only available to the higher fee membership level. So while some of the webpages might be visible to one membership tier, others might require a more expensive membership. It's a matter of how much the site owner wants to charge and if the content is valuable enough for people to pay for it.

Individual Pages

The other common type of paywall is the individual article or page type. In this type of paywall, viewing a single webpage requires a one-time payment. Pay the fee for the article, and you can then read the article. Often the one-time fee includes the ability to download a copy of the article to your computer.

This type of paywall is common with newspapers and publications who sell back-issues and articles, and this type of paywall can also be used with a membership site. An example is a membership site where members can view the webpages or articles that are available for one-time purchase as part of their membership. If you were going to purchase a certain number of articles, it might be more economical to purchase a membership.

Will Paywalls Become More Common?

Specialty websites with unique information and content have been able to make money by charging and have been using paywalls for many years. If the information is good enough, there are people using the Internet who are willing to pay for it. Most often these sites have been focused on specific industries, occupations, or topics where interested people are willing to pay for the content.

Print magazines and newspapers haven't been the recipients of most of the advertising spending, it's been search websites. So the old idea of supporting a magazine or newspaper with advertising income isn't working for many traditional periodicals. If advertising can't support the business, the creators of content and information will find other ways to make money or go out of business.

Digital magazine subscriptions are available for popular devices like Kindles and iPads, and the subscriptions are usually at a higher subscription fee than a subscription to the print edition. While you will still be able to find a lot of information on the Internet for free, you're likely to see more paywall websites when you start looking for specialized information or content.

Peer-to-Peer

A peer-to-peer network is a network of computers on the Internet created by a software program that's installed on multiple computers. Each computer running the software program connects and communicates with other computers running the software, usually using the public Internet as a way to send and receive information.

Once a peer-to-peer network is created, the software program has access not to just one computer, but a whole network of computers. Computing tasks and data files can be distributed across the computers on the network.

Why would anyone want to use a peer-to-peer network?

Since more computers are available for running a software program, the computing can be distributed across multiple computers, with more computers, where the program can distribute pieces of work out to many computers, then assemble the results. Like any job where you can break the work into pieces, the more people doing the work, the faster the work is finished.

In addition to distributing the work and adding computers to your "workforce," a peer-to-peer network can use the network of computers to share information across the network and break up files of data into pieces, creating one vast storage network distributed across many computers. The software then keeps track of which computer on the network has what data.

The advantage of this is that copies of the data can be stored in multiple locations on the peer-to-peer network, so if one computer is unavailable or busy, the software can find the data in another location on another computer. Essentially the software creates a directory of where various pieces of information exist, then uses the network of computers to pull together information from many sources.

So how would this be used by anyone?

Napster - an example of a peer-to-peer network

An example of a peer to peer network is the music sharing site Napster, who popularized peer to peer networking in 1999. Users sign up and gain access to the music and other digitized files other users have stored on their hard drives.

How peer-to-peer networks are created

A software program is required to create a peer-to-peer network, and the same software program needs to be installed on every computer in a peer-to-peer network. Since most peer-to-peer networks use individual computers connected over the Internet, let's look at that example and see how it would work.

First, the computer owner would download and run a peer to peer network program on their personal computer. Most peer-to-peer network software automatically searches for and finds other computers running the same software, but sometimes the computer user has to identify their computer. The peer-to-peer software program then adds the computer to the list of known computers running the software.

Once connected to the peer-to-peer network, the software program can use the newly added computer to do some work or share some data. In the case of Napster, each user shared their music files with all the other users on the Napster network and could download a copy of music from anywhere on the Napster.

Security issues with peer-to-peer networks

Since the peer-to-peer software is a program that's installed on a computer, it has access to the resources and data on the computer once it's installed. This can create security risks if the computer owner doesn't know what files and data the peer-to-peer program will access. The types of files shared can include books, movies, music, saved documents, games and scanned documents.

When you use peer-to-peer networks you may be violating the copyright on data, since your computer could be distributing copyrighted material.

Distributed computing has advantages

While Napster popularized peer to peer networking in the late nineties, many companies and universities have been utilizing versions of peer to peer networking for over 30 years. Since many computers in an organization are idle for part of the day, a peer-to-peer network can give a large computing task access to many computers that might usually require a large investment.

And, I might add, some peer-to-peer networks are commercially sold software products, designed to help organizations make the most of distributed computing.

The lesson here is that a peer-to-peer network in itself is not a good or a bad thing, it just depends on what the software program is meant to do.

Phablet

A phablet is a smartphone that has a screen size that's larger than a typical smartphone but smaller than a tablet. Unlike tablets, all phablets have a phone function and a phone number, which makes them phone devices that have a very large screen compared to most common smartphones.

Phablets don't have any industry standard or specification, so the term is primarily a marketing term used by manufacturers to highlight their smartphones with large screens. Phablet is a term usually used by manufacturers of smartphones that run the Android operating system.

Who makes the phablets?

Android is a mobile operating system that is owned by Google and licensed for use to product manufacturers that sell devices with the Android operating system installed. Companies like Samsung, LG, HTC, Motorola and others manufacture smartphones and tablets that use the Android mobile operating system.

Manufacturers using the Android operating system can design any size smartphone of their choice. With many manufacturers of Android devices and the freedom to design different screen size smartphones, more choices of screen sizes are available for devices using the Android operating system.

Since Apple is the only manufacturer of Apple smartphones and tablets, the only choices in screen sizes are those that Apple chooses to design. Apple doesn't refer to any of it's smartphones as phablets in their literature or marketing descriptions, but Apple does make a smartphone with a larger screen, the iPhone 6 Plus, with a 5.5-inch diagonal screen.

History of smartphone screen sizes

Apple's iPhone was the first smartphone introduced in 2007. A phone with a touchscreen that functioned as a display and keyboard all in one. For several years, Apple was the only company that manufactured smartphones until Google started licensing the Android operating system to manufacturers. Apple typically releases a new iPhone model every year, usually just before the holiday shopping season. With Android devices available from multiple manufacturers, new Android devices can be released almost any time.

With the Apple iPhone 3 and iPhone 4 models, Apple uses a 3.5-inch diagonal screen size. While these models were available for sale, Android smartphones makers starting delivering smartphone models in a wider variation of screen sizes.

Tablets started selling with the iPad by Apple with a 9.7-inch diagonal screen size. For a while, it was clear that a smartphone was a small handheld device with a screen size under 3.5 inches and a tablet was a device with a large screen size. Tablets took two hands to hold, smartphones one. If you wanted a larger touchscreen portable device, you would choose a tablet.

Android device makers started experimenting with different screen sizes to see if consumers would prefer different size devices. Android tablets with smaller screens were introduced with screen sizes from under 7 inches to as small as 5 inches.

Samsung is largely credited with creating the first device commonly referred to as a phablet with the introduction of the Galaxy Note in 2011. The Galaxy Note was an extremely large smartphone screen size device for it's time, with a 5.3-inch diagonal screen. At the time, Apple was selling the iPhone 4 with a 3.5-inch diagonal screen. Android smartphone screen sizes started getting even larger with screen sizes growing to over four inches, then over five, and now with screen sizes from some manufacturers available as large as 8 inches. We'll talk about what's practical for a phone later, for now, we're just reviewing a bit of the history of screen sizes.

With its annual product introduction cycle, Apple took a little longer to get larger screen iPhones out to the marketplace. In Fall of 2014, Apple introduced the iPhone 6 with a 4.7-inch diagonal display and the iPhone 6 Plus with a 5.5-inch diagonal display. This 5.5-inch size was close to the iPad mini, which has a screen size of 7.9 inches. For years, Apple dismissed the demand for larger smartphone screen sizes as unnecessary but then responded to consumer demand with the iPhone 6 and iPhone 6 Plus.

Choices

As a consumer, it doesn't matter what the device is called, what's important is that it fits your needs. Whether you want a tablet, a phablet, a large smartphone, or a small smartphone is simply a matter of being aware that there are choices for almost anyone.

A larger screen is easier to read, but it's larger to carry around. However, if you've been using both a tablet and a smartphone, a larger screen smartphone might let you simplify your life by using one device instead of two.

Tablets, with their larger screens, offer larger keys on their keyboards, so they are a bit easier to type using the touchscreen keyboard. However, if you do a lot of typing, there's simply no substitute for a real keyboard.

If you want a small device that slips easily into a pocket, then a smartphone is probably for you. With the variations in screen sizes, even from Apple, who still makes the iPhone 5, you have a lot of options for a balance between portability, size, weight, and screen size.

To my way of thinking

The good news is that regardless of what type of device you choose, over a million apps are available to make the device useful to you for either Apple or Android.

Phishing

"Phishing" is when someone sends you an electronic message disguised as a trustworthy, legitimate enterprise, in order to trick you into giving them your personal information. It's very easy to fall for this kind of scam if you don't know about it, because phishing scams are often very convincing and sound very important. However, with a bit of know-how about how to recognize phishing and protect yourself from it, you can easily keep yourself and your personal information safe.

Phishing has been around almost as long as electronic communication itself. The term is a combination of "fishing" and the term "phreak", which is what a lot of electronic criminals called themselves when phishing was born. The idea was that if enough "bait" was sent out to people, at least some were going to "bite" and unintentionally give the scammers their personal information (like account passwords, ID numbers, credit card numbers, or anything else of value). Unfortunately, these scams work and are still common.

So, what does a phishing scam look like? Well, it's usually in the form of an electronic message disguised as a message from an important, trustworthy enterprise, such as your bank. The message will usually say things like, "There is a problem with your account," or, "You need to confirm your account information." It will then contain a link that takes you to the "company's" website (often a near-perfect copy of the real one), where you can input your personal information. In reality, it's a fake website setup by criminals, and any information you put into the website goes straight to them.

So how do you protect yourself from phishing? It's pretty simple. Never trust an unexpected or unusual message on face value, especially if it makes itself sound urgent. If you receive a sudden message that looks like it's from your bank, call your bank to confirm it's from them (with your number, not one in the email!). In addition, never click a link in a suspicious email; instead, manually type in the address of the company's website. This way, you'll always avoid fake links, and phishing as a result.

Pinterest

Pinterest is a social networking site on the internet. Pinterest can be used with any Web browser and also offers apps for smartphones and tablets.

What do you do on Pinterest?

Using Pinterest is a bit like using a bulletin board to save your favorite pictures from all of the magazines that you read. When you sign up for Pinterest, you receive a free account with online "inboards" on which you can "pin" pictures from webpages. Your account, as well as everyone else's, is a collection of images pinned on these electronic bulletin boards. You can view anyone's boards, and your boards can be viewed by anyone other user on Pinterest.

Your activity on Pinterest consists of "pinning" images on your boards and following other Pinterest accounts to see what they've pinned.

Pins and Boards

Using Pinterest, you can click Pin It on an image. This image can be on someone else's Pinterest pinboard, or it may be from the web. This moves it to your personal Pinterest site. When a pin is entered into the Pinterest system, it always links back to the webpage for the original image. This way, someone browsing a pinboard can always view the image and the webpage where it was originally published.

Within Pinterest, a user can create numerous collections by creating a board on a topic. Topics tend to center on home, fashion, style, crafts, children, cooking, books, and travel. So far the majority of users are women. One pinboard may be titled "favorite home projects", featuring pictures of interesting decor, furniture, wallpapers and accessories. Another may be 'Yard Ideas' featuring lawn and garden photos. Still another may be 'Favorite Crafts For Kids'. The title and its content are up to the user.

Connecting with other Pinterest users.

Like other social networks, users can connect with each other and keep up to date on activity. By following another user, you can receive updates when they pin new images, and likewise, others can follow you and receive updates when you pin new images. To make it easier to find images that you like, a heart icon is located on each image. Click on this icon to like that image, and it's added to your list of liked images in your account. Of course, you can also "repin" any image to one of your boards.

A user can search Pinterest for pinboards on a particular subject. For instance, an avid reader might look for a book recommendation board. The family cook may sign up for many different recipe pinboards. In this way, Pinterest makes it easy and safe to find exactly what a person seeks without running into very much clutter. People of similar tastes or similar hobbies can find each other and share content safely. They can also store content safely. Since the images you're pinning come from public webpages, there's not much to be concerned about regarding privacy of your pinned images.

Marketing with Pinterest.

Although most users are browsing for pictures, Pinterest pinboards are playing a role in commerce. Small online stores and artists of all kinds utilize this person-to-person system to get their products before the public. And large brand names use Pinterest to increase their social network visibility and encourage word-of-mouth marketing.

Why is it so popular?

Pictures and images are popular on the Web, and Pinterest makes it easy for anyone to create a free online collection of pictures and images. Pinterest has become a modern way to window-shop and browse collections of images created by both individuals and brands. Anyone can express their own interests by creating a board and pinning images. It's extremely easy to use and fun for a lot of people.

Pixel

The Pixel Dot

Pixels are tiny dots. No, we're not talking the candy kind. Pixels are those tiny dots that create what you see on computer displays (LCDs or flat screens) and tube monitors (CRT or desk top computers and digital TVs). Pixel means PICture ELement.

You can't see pixels because they're very small, which is good because you want to see the whole image and not those dots that make up the image (or pixilated images). Pixilated images are possible to see with your computer monitor screen set to a low resolution, such as 620x460, which means the product of width times height, for a total of 285,200 pixels, which may seem like a lot, but computer screens need more resolution to be clear and sharp.

Image Resolution

In a general sense, the more pixels used to represent an image equals a sharper image. Image resolution is measured by PPI, or pixels per inch. Resolution is also expressed in pairs of numbers such as 640 x 480 (width x length). A MacBook Pro 15-inch monitor, for example, has the PPI of 110 PPI and a 1440x900 resolution.

A basic digital camera has a resolution capacity of between 2 million pixels (MP) to 5 MP and the more pixels the better. A 4MP camera makes really sharp prints that are 4"x6" and pretty nice larger prints at 5"x7".

Pixel colors

Every single tiny pixel contains three color channels of red, green and blue. Each color in this scheme is represented by an 8-bit number, or a byte, with the color of each pixel defined by three color bytes. These three colors combine in over 16 million color combinations to form the many different hues and shades you see on your screen and camera.

For example, if an image contains the color depth of 8-bits, it will seem grainy or spotted. A 32-bit color image looks much more smooth and realistic.

Pixels Are Everywhere

It helps to know how pixels work because everything is digital these days, from your TV to your computer screen to your camera – even to the images you see displayed on your cell phone. You don't have to be a technological wizard to understand the basics so that you can get the best resolution for what you need and like.

Plug-ins and Extensions

A plug-in is a small computer application that works in cooperation with a larger application. While the term "plug-in" may be used with almost any software, it's most commonly seen by consumers when using a web browser. It's also referred to as an extension since it extends the capabilities of the web browser software. A plug-in's job is to add a function and additional capabilities to extend the usefulness of the larger application. An example is the Adobe Reader plug-in that is used by web browsers to read and display a document using the Adobe document format, commonly called a pdf.

Why plug-ins are needed

Any website can have different kinds of data. There are web pages, which consist primarily of text and images, there are audio and video files, and there are files used by a specific application. Web browsers are very capable applications in themselves, but sometimes an additional application is needed to display or use a file on a website.

Early in the development of web browsers, they were only able to read a web page and present it as text and images. If a web browser came across another kind of data, it would check to see if there were any way to present it as text or an image. If it couldn't, then it would create a message that would appear on the web page for the reader, letting the reader know additional software was needed to open the file, and that additional software was usually a plug-in.

Why plug-ins are useful

When audio and video became more popular on the Internet, it became necessary for web browsers to display these kinds of data in a more useful manner. Although users could always download an audio or video file and play it on their computer using a local application, being able to play the sound or video in the web browser was much more convenient.

Web browser developers created a way for other software developers to build add-ons or "plug-ins" for the web browser. Think of a plug-in as an accessory for your car like a child's car seat. While it's possible for a child to sit as a passenger in an automobile, a smaller child is more secure and safer in a car seat. The car seat isn't included with the car, but the seat belts in the car allow an owner to purchase a car seat and use it when needed. The car seat becomes a "plug-in" for the car, available for anyone who needs one to use it, but not necessary for everyone to have built-in to the car.

As an example, if you wanted to display a type of video file on a webpage that used the Flash video file type, you would have to install the Flash plug-in for your browser. Most web browsers don't include the capability to play Flash, so a plug-in is needed. Once the Flash player plug-in is installed, whenever the web browser finds a web page with a Flash movie on it, the plug-in would be automatically activated, and the Flash movie would play in the web browser.

By the way, Apple's iPhone and iPad don't support the Flash player and it's not available as a plug-in for Apple's mobile devices. Apple did this because they saw new web standards for video developing and wanted to encourage website developers to use those standards, which allow video to download and play faster. As a result, Flash is falling out of favor as a way to display video.

Plug-ins Allow Faster Web Browsing and Customization

Since most web browsers allow the use of plug-ins, it makes it possible for you to use only the capabilities necessary for the websites you visit. You don't have to use a web browser that comes loaded with extra options, and, as a result, your web browser can operate faster.

By only including the most essential capabilities in a web browser and allowing users to install their own plug-ins when they need them for a web page, web browsers can display web pages faster for most users, since only those users who need a specific feature would install the plug-in. Every additional software capability requires resources and can slow down your web browser. Sometimes, as a student mentioned in one of my classes, a message appears when you open a web browser asking you if you want to run the plug-ins you have installed. Since each plug-in is a small piece of software, each plug-in could slow down your web browsing experience, so some computers give you the option to disable the plug-ins.

Where can you find plug-ins?

Each web browser has a directory of plug-ins and extensions. Here are their websites:

Mozilla Firefox: https://addons.mozilla.org/en-US/firefox/

Microsoft Internet Explorer: http://download.cnet.com/windows/internet-explorer-add-ons-and-plugins/

Note - Microsoft doesn't keep a website for add-ons, but CNET's site is very secure and lists them by popularity.

Google Chrome: https://chrome.google.com/webstore/category/extensions

Apple Safari: https://extensions.apple.com

To my way of thinking

Web browsers are one of the most commonly used applications on any computer, smartphone, tablet, or device. Since all web browsers make it possible to get "add-ons" for browser, every user can install additional capabilities in one of their most useful applications, making the web browser even more powerful.

Podcast

A podcast is a radio program that is broadcast on the Internet. The term, which is short for iPod broadcast, originated in 2004. While the original podcasts were designed for Apple's iPod mobile music player, they work with a wide variety of devices. Imagine being able to listen to your favorite programs whenever and wherever you wish. You can download podcasts onto a computer or any other device capable of playing music and listen to them at your leisure.

Podcast and Radio Differences

Radio stations play song after song, but when you download a podcast, you're downloading a single prerecorded radio program. Podcasts encompass every type of radio program from talk shows and interviews to documentaries and dramas. Some podcasts are devoted entirely to delivering an hour or two of commercial-free music. Newer podcasts may also include accompanying videos, so subscribers can watch the host interview guests. Some radio stations like NPR include podcast versions of their radio programs on their websites.

Just like radio shows, most podcasts are episodes in a long-running series instead of standalone programs, and they're released daily, weekly, monthly, or on any other schedule. To help listeners download new episodes, most publishers update lists of all of their episodes when they release a new podcast. Many publishers also provide schedules so listeners can see which episodes are coming up in the next few weeks.

What makes podcasts so revolutionary?

Because they're prerecorded, listeners don't need to maintain an Internet connection. They can download the podcast and listen to it on the plane or in the car. Podcasts are distributed over the Internet instead of the radio, so listeners can usually download them from anywhere in the world without being in the same region. Listeners don't have to tune in whenever the program first airs, and they can pause, rewind, or skip ahead to listen to podcast segments again and again.

Literary writers are also experimenting with podcasts. Novels are hundreds of pages long, and they can require anywhere from 10 to 50 hours to read out loud. Novel podcasts break books up into manageable chunks. A writer can fit about 20 pages into an hour-long podcast, making the format perfect for a daily commute. Listeners can download shorter podcasts faster than longer ones, so they can spend a few minutes downloading a chapter from a novel podcast rather than a few hours for the entire book. With all of these options, podcast listeners will never want to listen to radio the old way again.

With millions of people connecting smartphones in their cars and looking for listening material during workouts, savvy marketers are using podcasts to reach new audiences. With the use of podcasts, brand names are able to reach people who might not have the time to read an article on the Web, but are happy to listen during a commute or workout.

Where do you find Podcasts?

The simplest and easiest way to find podcasts is by using an app on a smartphone or tablet. Apple has their own Podcast app for iPhones and iPads. Using the app you'll be able to search for podcasts available from the iTunes store, and all podcasts are free. Android users can access podcasts using one of the popular apps like the highly rated iPP Podcast Player. Most podcasts can also be played directly from the Web site of the podcast on a PC or Mac.

Podcasts are available on almost any topic and can be educational and entertaining. Download one of these apps and try out some popular ones and start exploring.

POP and IMAP email

The most common types of email services are POP (plain old post office), and IMAP, short for Internet Message Access Protocol. Depending on your email provider, you'll typically have one of these two types of email accounts.

Which type you use isn't much of an issue until you start using email with both a computer and a mobile device, like a smartphone or tablet. Starting to use that second computing device introduced a second location where your email needs to be stored, sent, and received. Having your emails in two locations is easier to use if it's identical, or in "sync" in both locations. The type of email service you use determines if you have this capability or not, not your computer or mobile device.

If you already have an IMAP type of email service, you probably don't need to change anything. This article will help IMAP users understand how POP and IMAP differ, and maybe give some friends some advice on email. If you have a POP email service, I recommend you read on and change to an IMAP email service, unless there's no chance you'll ever get a smartphone or tablet. So let's become email savvy and learn about POP and IMAP.

Your Email Service Provider

You might think your computer, smartphone, or tablet determines how your email works, but that's not true. It's your email service provider and the type of email service they use that controls how you send and receive email, manage your email folders, and keep emails identical on multiple computing devices.

Email accounts are provided to you by a company. Companies that do this include the company that provides your Internet connection at home or work such as AT&T, Verizon, Charter or your cable provider. One or more free email accounts are provided as part of your Internet service. Your email address would be something like yourname@att.com, or yourname@roadrunner.net. These types of email services are usually POP email accounts, but they can often be changed to an IMAP account if you call your email service provider.

Google, Yahoo!, Apple, AOL, and Microsoft offer free Web-based email accounts. In addition to using a Web site to access your email, you can use the email software on your computer and mobile device with these services, so you're not limited to just using the Web to use your email. These email services are IMAP types of accounts. These are the most common free Web based email services available, and all of them are excellent choices.

What's Different About POP and IMAP Email Services?

There's one big difference between POP and IMAP email accounts. IMAP type email accounts keep a copy of all of your email on a computer that the email service provider uses for running the email service. POP type email accounts don't, so the only copy of any email sent or received is on your computer. If you use only one computer, this is something you may never notice. But when start using a smartphone or tablet, the way your email works will start showing it's type.

With an IMAP type of email service, a master copy of all of your email and folders is stored on a computer system managed by your email service provider. With IMAP email, when you delete, send, move, or change anything in your email, the master copy on the service is updated as soon as you connect to the Internet with any of your computing devices.

All of your devices and computers "check-in" when they are on the Internet and update the master copy with their changes. The master copy also tells your computing device what's changed, so emails are updated on your device. This process keeps all of your mail in "sync" with all of your devices. Here are some examples of how it works, and if you can do this with your existing email account you've got an IMAP type of email service. Move an email from your inbox to a read folder, and it will happen on all of your computing devices with IMAP email. Delete an email and it will happen on all of your computing devices with IMAP email. Create a new folder, and it will happen on all of your devices with IMAP email.

POP email does not do this. With POP email service, your email service is only capable of sending a copy of your incoming email to your device, and cannot match up any folders or changes you make while using email. You'll get two copies of every inbound email, once on your device, and once on your computer. You cannot duplicate any email folders you've created on your computer on your mobile, not because of any shortcomings of your smartphone or tablet, but because your email service doesn't know how to keep them synchronized with each other.

What To Do if You Don't Have IMAP Type Email?

If you want to use a service that synchronizes email, you have several options, all of which will work with your desktop computer and mobile device. Contact your email service and see if they can upgrade your service from POP to IMAP service, which would allow you to continue to use your current email address. You'll have to change your settings for email on all of your computing devices to the new IMAP service. Your emails already on your computer won't be moved to their systems, but all new email you receive and send will be stored from that point forward.

Here are your options:

• Open a new email account with an IMAP service. The most popular (not in any order) are Google's gmail, Yahoo!, AOL, and Microsoft's Outlook.com. All are free and all provide Web access to your email in addition to working with almost any desktop and mobile device.

• Open a new account with Apple's iCloud.com service. iCloud email will work on the Web, with Android, with Microsoft Outlook software, and on all of Apple's computing and mobile devices.

• Open a new account with a Microsoft Hosted Exchange service. I recommend this if you're used to using Microsoft Outlook on your desktop. This is what I use for my work, and if you've ever used Outlook in a workplace, you'll appreciate this type of email account.

About Microsoft Exchange

One other type of email service worth mentioning is one that's uses Microsoft's commercial business software. Used on desktops and mobile devices in almost all businesses and organizations, Microsoft has an email service called Exchange. Individual users can purchase the service from Microsoft and other companies like GoDaddy. If your'e used to using Microsoft Office on your desktop, paying for an Exchange email service gives you business grade email service and support and usually includes a free version of Microsoft Outlook for your computer from the email service provider. Your Exchange service provider keeps a copy of your email on their computers so email functions like an IMAP account, but also includes other features of Microsoft Outlook such as Contacts, Calendar, Tasks, and Notes.

Programmer(s)

Programmers are problem solvers who use software languages to write instructions that computers use to perform tasks. Since computers work 24 hours a day and with smartphones are in the hands of billions of people around the world, people and organizations are looking for ways to improve work and life using technology.

All of this technology requires software programs to make it work, and programmers create the software programs that are in use every day around the world. Every time you start your car, use a microwave oven, read your email, visit a website or talk on your phone your using software that was created by a programmer.

Programmers and Software Developers

Some programmers are also known as software developers, a term that often is used when a programmer knows more than just writing code in a language. A software developer is usually a more versatile problem solver and might have a better perspective on choices to solving a problem. Software developers can be either an individual or an organization, sometimes with thousands of programmers. A programmer is anyone who creates software code, regardless of the language.

Programs and Software Applications

A software language is used to write the instructions used by the computer to "run" or "execute" the program. When you tap on an app icon on your smartphone, you're starting a software application, which is a specific program written and designed to run on your smartphone. Similarly, when you click on an application icon on your desktop or laptop, you "launch" a software application, which is a program designed to run on your computer.

Programmers Use Programming Languages

Programmers use software languages to create written programs. Like any language, a programming language has a vocabulary and grammar, it's just in terms that help give instructions to a computer to perform a task. Most programmers tend to specialize in one software language, but many learn several. Like any language, knowing the vocabulary and syntax is important in order to read and write in that language, and each software language uses specific words and phrases. As a result, programmers often pick a language that is useful for the type of programs they will write.

Software languages are different for many reasons, such as the hardware and operating systems. Specific devices, such as an iPhone, require writing programs in programming languages that the iPhone can understand, which are Objective-C and Swift and are provided by Apple to programmers who join software development programs.

Programmer Skills

Programmers also are aware of the limits of software and can help determine if a software program can solve a task or problem before writing a program. While many people are in occupations that solve problems, programmers are problem solvers who use software to create solutions. A skilled programmer is capable of detailed, logical thinking; it makes sense since providing instructions to a computer requires detailed logical thinking as well.

While it's not necessary to be a mathematician to be a programmer, an understanding of mathematical problem-solving methods and the ability to approach problems with mathematics are skills that programmers and mathematicians have in common. If the individual has the right skills, it's possible for them to learn programming, and programming is becoming part of many schools curriculums in order to prepare students for new workplace opportunities.

Teamwork and Communication

While the act of programming is often a solitary one, with a programmer writing software code on a computer, programmers that work in teams or with clients need communications and interpersonal skills. Many programmers are excellent in speaking in the software language of their choice, but programmers who have excellent teamwork and people-related skills are in high demand.

Large programming efforts can require teams of hundreds of programmers. With large programming efforts, a more experienced programmer will divide a the work into smaller chunks, enabling programmers to work on pieces of the program simultaneously. Dividing up the effort to write the program into smaller pieces can make the work very assembly-line in nature.

In other cases, smaller teams work on a single program with the team members collaborating as each member contributes something new to the program until it is complete.

To My Way of Thinking

With millions of websites, billions of smartphones and an ever-expanding use of automation in our workplace and daily lives, the need for good programmers will only increase. All of these devices and software applications require someone with the skills to analyze a problem that can be solved by a computer and create a solution with a program.

Q

QR Code

Otherwise known as Quick Response codes, a QR code is a graphic image that contains information in the form of black and white squares. Shaped like a square with a black and white digital pattern QR codes are images, when scanned, link to a display of information. They are commonly used in printed material for users to scan with a smartphone and open a web page or other application.

By scanning a QR code, a user with a smartphone can scan the code with an app and open a specific web page. Advertisers and marketers use QR codes to make it easier for people to open a web page without the need to type a specific web address, which can often lead to typographic errors.

History and common uses

Invented in the mid-1990's by the Japanese, were used to help track parts and cars in manufacturing applications as a way to label the parts and other items used in automated assembly lines. Since QR codes use an international standard for their format, shape and design, their use expanded beyond manufacturing to marketing applications like the ones mentioned above.

How QR Codes work

Each QR code has a unique digital pattern that, when scanned, provides instructions to the scanning app. The information contained in a QR code is most often a link to a website with specific information. You might be familiar with the UPC barcode that you see on everyday retail products, and UPC codes contain price and inventory information as numbers or letters. QR codes can contain more information than UPC codes due to their black and white square format.

Smartphones can scan QR codes with a scanning app. Smartphone don't usually come standard with a QR scanning app, so downloading an app is necessary. Once the QR code scanning app is installed on your phone, scanning is simple. All you have to do open the app, then view the QR code within the scanner's view on your screen by using your smartphone camera.

It's as easy as taking a picture using the camera app, only instead of getting a picture, you get information that is used to open web pages or other applications on your smartphone. Some other common uses include using QR codes to open up a Facebook Page or display contact information.

Smartphone App for Scanning

To scan any QR code, you'll need a smartphone and an app. A free app that I use is SCAN, available for iPhone and iPad, Android, and Windows devices. As long as your mobile device has a camera, you should be able to use the app. The QR code at the top of this page is a real one, and can be scanned from a computer display by a smartphone with the Scan app. It's one that will take you to my new Web site department for app recommendations, App Docent. Download the app and give it a try.

Creating a QR Code

Scan offers a free service for creating QR codes, and I created one that opens the app recommendation lists I include in the App Docent department of my Web site. Creating a QR code with SCAN is free, but requires registration on their Web site. Once registered you can create as many QR codes as you like. In addition to linking the QR code to a Web site URL, Scan offers additional options for an information page. Using these options you can link your QR code to information and destination pages for personal and business use. Scan hosts these destination pages for you and makes it easy to create with simple to complete forms for the information and photos.

The options include:

• Scan to display a business information page

• Scan to display a personal information page

• Social Media actions, such as scan to check-in, follow, or like

• Scan to view a Website URL

• Scan to display a note or message

• Scan to login to a WiFi network

In addition to creating QR codes and scan information options, the Scan app provides tracking data for each QR code with information on how often, when, and if available from the user, a location of the scan.

To my way of thinking

There's still a lot of education needed to help people understand what a QR code is and how to scan it. Many people often see the QR code in print but don't understand that it's necessary to scan the code using an app.

If you use one for yourself or your business, be sure to include a note to "scan" this QR code or include a recommended app. The scan includes this information in every QR code at the bottom.

R

Radio Frequency Radiation

Radiofrequency (RF) radiation is the transfer of energy by radio waves. Cell phones and WiFi networks create radio waves when mobile devices send and receive information. The radio signals create radiation, commonly called electromagnetic radiation since a radio signal is an electromagnetic type of signal.

Radio and other types of radiation

Radio frequencies are used for wireless signals since they are NOT a type of radiation that breaks chemical bonds and, as a result, are much safer than other types of radiation. The energy level that's created by radiofrequency radiation is simply too low to affect the bonds between chemicals. Also, the Federal Communications Commission and other safety organizations further regulate the amount of energy that can be used on consumer devices, keeping the energy level very low.

Your probably familiar with some other types of radiation. Microwave ovens use microwave radiation, which is capable of heating up molecules (for your food). X-rays use X-ray radiation that can be harmful if used too often or at too high an energy level. Too much ultraviolet radiation will give you a sunburn. Radio waves don't have any of these effects.

Radiation

The term radiation is related to the word 'radiate', and refers to an outward expansion in all directions. Wireless signals are transmissions of energy that radiate outwards from a transmitter (such as one in your cell phone) and are then received by an antenna (the cellular tower). The reason most people learn the term radiation is that some types of radiation (like x-ray and ultraviolet) impact the human body, leading to concerns about the effect of any radiation on health.

Radio waves travel in all directions from a source, usually some type of antenna on a mobile device. The signal starts out strongest at the source and becomes weaker the further it travels from the source. All radio waves have a range limit which is why you'll see five bars or dots on your cell phone the closer you are to a cellular tower and only one or two if you're further way. Move out of range of a cell tower and you will lose any signal.

Health concerns

Extensive studies have proven that extended exposure to extremely high Radio Frequency Radiation fields in industrial settings can increase body temperate about one degree. The Radio Frequency Radiation strength levels used in wireless networks are orders of magnitude weaker and are regarded as safe.

While all wireless networks emit Radio Frequency Radiation, it is classified as non-ionizing radiation because the energy levels are too low to have any impact on the human body. Many people wonder if exposure to radio waves can cause cancer. The The International Agency for Research on Cancer (IARC) is part of the World Health Organization and has evaluated all of the scientific studies and only found one (out of dozens) that showed a possible link between radio waves and cancer. As a result, the IARC states that radio frequency radiation from wireless networks has a "possible" carcinogenic effect on humans.

The WHO report concluded that ordinary FM radio and television signals emit as much as five times as much radio frequency radiation as a wireless (WiFi) network. Unfortunately, the average adult human is exactly the right height to serve as an effective antenna for FM radio and TV frequencies. Significant;y higher frequencies used by cellular and home WiFi networks and are not even absorbed as well as FM and television signals by the human body. The very fact that radio and television frequencies have been broadcast continuously for more than half a century without adverse effect is believed to be positive proof that wireless networks, with their lower energy transmissions, are also completely benign.

According to cancer.org, the official website of the American Cancer Society, says that all of the studies so far have limitations on how they were done, how people were evaluated, and how long people were studied since most have released on how people remember their use of cell phones. However, no scientific study done so far has conclusively linked cell phone use to cancer, but more studies are being done to evaluate the risk. As a result, cell phones, along with most radio frequency radiation, are considered "safe" for people to use.

To my way of thinking

Cell phones are not now officially classified as a health risk by any regulatory agency, and if you've been watching TV or listening to FM radio for a while you've probably been exposed to more radiofrequency radiation than you'd ever receive from your cell phone. If you're concerned, you can limit your exposure to RF radiation by limiting how often you hold your cell phone close to your body. Effectively this means not making many phone calls, which many people already don't do with their cell phones.

However, if you use your speakerphone or text, you won't be holding your cell phone close to you and can minimize and RF radiation even further. So another good reason to get proficient at texting if you aren't already!

Website

For more information from the American Cancer Society here's their webpage on cell phone use:

http://www.cancer.org/cancer/cancercauses/othercarcinogens/athome/cellular-phones

RAM

RAM, or "random access memory," is the temporary storage space used by a computer while it's performing tasks. It is smaller both physically and in capacity than more permanent forms of data storage, such as hard or disk drives, but it can store and retrieve data much more quickly.

Why RAM is Used in Computers

Think of RAM as open shelf space that can hold data close at hand for fast, immediate access while you are doing work on your computer. Your computer has large amounts of information, or data, stored permanently in files on its hard drive. When you open up an application (software) - for example, the word processor or email - your CPU (central processing unit) is going to need room to store the data while doing its work with the application. But space on the CPU is limited. This is where RAM comes in. RAM is designed to allow its data to be accessed quickly, at very high speeds more closely matching the processing speed of the CPU. However, this access speed is gained at the cost of stability and permanence, because data on RAM is available only as long as the computer is turned on; lose the power and the data is erased.

What More RAM Does for You

The more memory a computer has, the more tasks it can perform simultaneously. Like anything else, RAM has both advantages and disadvantages when it comes to storing information. To evaluate these in greater detail, it can help to compare RAM memory to other types of memory storage available for computers.

When you determine that your computer needs more storage room, also known as memory, for additional data and software, you will have to decide which kind of storage will work the best for your needs.

How are RAM and Disk Drives Different?

Disk drives are one storage source for software and data. These have the advantage of storing large amounts of data relatively inexpensively. But they move data at slower speeds than RAM or CPU memory.

RAM is the storage choice when speed and efficiency are the paramount considerations. RAM is one of the easiest parts of a computer to upgrade, and gives the most obvious and immediate benefits. It is available as cards of memory modules that insert directly into computer circuit boards and comes in various speeds, sizes, and designs to better match specific computer types. However, RAM requires power to store data, which means that, unlike long-term storage systems like hard-disk drives that retain data, you lose RAM data whenever you turn off your computer. It may be fast, but it's temporary.

Ransomware

Ransomware is a particularly dangerous form of malicious software which uses extortion that holds the user's computer hostage. The most common form of ransomware scramble files on a computer (also referred to as encryption) and demands payment (the ransom) in order to unscramble the files and regain access to them.

Computer techs tell me that when users have attempted to bypass or ignore the ransomware, the ransomware raises the cost to purchase the decryption key. I've heard that the price to purchase the decryption key and regain access to the files has been as much as $300 to $450.

Virus Basics

Most computer viruses find their way onto a computer when the user accidentally downloads an infected file. Ransomware acts very much like any other computer virus. It downloads itself to a computer, but once there, it has an entirely different method of operation.

How Ransomware First Appears

Most users only realize they have a computer infection when it refuses to run normally, and they receive a message on their screen asking for money in exchange for their computer functioning properly again. Like an anonymous ransom note from kidnappers, the message may take the form of a threat that states all the information on the computer will be erased by a certain date unless the ransom is paid on time.

Other "ransom" notes are even sneakier, mimicking a message from a software company such as Windows that states the user needs to renew the subscription in order to use basic software. While official in appearance, these messages are false and are solely meant to extort money from the user.

How Ransomware works

Once the ransomware downloads itself to a computer, it can perform in one of two ways. The first way, known as encrypting ransomware, takes control of files on the hard drive, such as pictures or documents. The virus denies access to these files and will erase them completely with a deadline if the ransom is not paid.

The second way, known as non-encrypting ransomware, renders the user's computer unable even to boot-up when turned on, because certain files necessary for start-up and proper functioning are made useless.

Most ransomware creators demand payment in untraceable formats such as text messages that charge a fee or a wire transfer of funds, whereupon they send a special code that the user can input to free their computer from the effects of the ransomware. Some ransomware scams have netted their designers millions of dollars, making it an attractive way for the unscrupulous to make money.

What you should do to protect yourself and your data.

Protecting a computer from ransomware entails installing a good virus protection program onto the computer and avoiding certain risky behaviors, such as opening a file sent by an unknown person via email. While the effects of ransomware can be unpleasant, they are easy to avoid by using anti-virus and anti-malware software and keeping it updated.

Windows 10 comes with built-in anti-virus software called Defender, a free option with updates by Microsoft. New Windows computers often include security trial-ware that's active, and either the trialware or the Microsoft Defender options are good choices. Older Windows systems also need current versions of security software, and since Microsoft stopped updating Windows XP, anyone using XP is open to a greater security risk and should upgrade their computer as soon as possible.

Apple Mac users don't need to install any additional security software, Apple provides security protection, but it's important to update to the current versions of the Mac OS operating system, which is free from Apple. If you're not sure if you're current, you can schedule a visit to an Apple store for a checkup.

I also recommend you keep a copy of any important data and files on a separate disk drive that you can remove from your computer or in a cloud storage service. That way if you can always reinstall your files on a virus-free computer. But don't try to connect the backup drive to the infected computer since the ransomware may infect the backup copies.

To my way of thinking

Keeping data safe is now everyone's responsibility, and it's important to realize that there are criminals who will exploit people's lack of knowledge and awareness. If you know someone who needs help with understanding more about their technology, please pass along some helpful hints.

Reddit

Reddit is a source of what's popular on the Internet. It's a website where registered users can submit text information or a link to a website and vote on any listing published by another Reddit user. Allowing users to vote and publish text and links on the website, Reddit has become popular and useful to keep up to date on almost any topic and to share information with others who share common interests.

Reddit calls itself the "frontpage of the internet." It has a lot of useful information for people of all ages, displaying top stories contributed by users and voted as popular by users of the website. Comments are welcome, encouraged and are a top priority for many users. Frequent commenters gain "Karma points", so that good comments are appreciated and "upvoted", and those comments that do not contribute much to the discussion or are inappropriate are "downvoted".

History of Reddit

Reddit was founded in 2005 at the University of Virginia by two college roommates, Steve Huffman and Alexis Ohanian. I was purchased in 2006 by Conde Nast Publications (the people who publish the New Yorker, Brides, Golf Digest, GQ, and some other popular publications.) It's operated independently but offers Conde Nast's publications a way to discover interesting topics and trends. Reddit also sells advertising and is one of the

Voting on Reddit

Reddit uses a voting system to determine which stories make the top of the list of articles when a user submits an article, video, or photo, etc. This voting system is one of the most important aspects of the website, since users can raise or decrease the visibility of any published item with their vote. More upvotes, which indicates an item is popular with eReddit users, moves the item higher in the list of all published items.

Since any user can upvote or downvote an item, the ranking of any item is subject to the opinions of Reddit users, which are typically technically savvy and younger. As a result, many journalists, marketers and researchers use Reddit to find what's trending and becoming popular.

What's on Reddit?

While Reddit has a frontpage for all of the items posted, there are subcategories for almost any topic imaginable. These subcategories, called subReddits, are organized with navigation links and include Reddit posts and links related to a specific topic. Users can browse the subReddits or even create their own subReddit.

There are some standard subReddits for topics such as news and items that are rising in upvotes. These are all visible as links on the Reddit website. Other subReddits can be made up of various material such as music, books, history, television, jokes, including controversial content, which may include adult material which is generally described and tagged as "not safe for work" or "NSFW". These may be comprised of some graphic material that is not suitable for minors or to be used during one's working hours on the internet.

Reddit is mostly comprised of users who submit original content or reposts of others' material such as news about things going on in the world or other interests. SubReddits can be comprised of just about anything from cooking to science, and there are lots of "subs" in between.

Anyone can make a subReddit based on just about anything. When a user creates a subReddit, the user can even moderate their own subReddit, using rules that are provided in the FAQ section of the main site. Essentially a subReddit is like a group of people interested in a particular topic, whatever that might be. And it does offer an opportunity for marketing as long as the posts and links are useful and not simply promotional.

Companies and organizations often use Reddit for marketing to allow users to participate in crowdsourcing ideas and communicating with the company or organization staff. For example, asking users for feedback on an idea for a product or service is a common use of organizations who use it well.

To my way of thinking

Reddit is another free, user-supported community on the Internet and like any community-based website it offers useful features that it's users find beneficial. While there are a lot of sources of information on the Internet, Reddit offers a glimpse into a more tech-savvy community that is often at the forefront of trends.

Router

A router is a piece of hardware that is used to route data from one computer network to another computer network. OK, that may seem a little confusing since you might not know that when computers are connected together, they create a network. So let's use something you might be familiar with, like a public transportation system.

Moving Data is Like Moving People

Public transit systems often include high speed transportation, such as bullet trains, local trolleys, and buses. High speed trains require special rails, so any high speed train can only run on those rails. Local trolleys use rails also, but a different kind and buses use roads. The high speed rails, trolly rails, and roads are different kinds of networks. Each type has a different speed, and they don't always connect together.

If we want to travel from point A to point B, we might start out walking on the sidewalk in our neighborhood (one network), take a bus (another network) to a trolly station (another network), and then transfer to a high speed train (yet another network). Our little trip has taken us on four different networks so far. Then when we exit the high speed train, we might take another bus route (another network) to get close to our destination, and then walk (using the sidewalk) to our location.

While we've used several networks to get from point A to point B, we transferred across several networks since Point A and point B aren't connected directly to each other. Since we recognize how to follow public transit (well, I grew up in Chicago, so I used it a lot) we can direct ourselves from one network to another at certain points where the networks connect. These are the train stations, bus stops, and intersections we use to move people, as well as vehicles that transport people.

Routers are what's used to connect data networks to each other so the data can transfer from one route to another, eventually making it's way to it's destination.

What Data do Routers Direct?

Data is simply any information in digital form, usually in the form of files. When your computer wants to send data to another computer on a network, it sends a file that includes information about where the data is located. Routers are the devices that read the destination information and send the request to the proper location where the computer is located. The computer that receives the request then packages up the data and sends it back to your computer using your location information. Let's take a look at a common example of how routing helps you browse the World Wide Web.

When you visit a Web page, your computer, smartphone, or tablet sends a request over the Internet that includes the address of the Web page. Something like yahoo.com, or google.com, which is the address of the Web page you want to view. To deliver your request from your computing device to the Web page location, routers use the address information of the Web page to direct your request to the right location on the Internet. The computer with the Web page then sends the Web page back to your computer's address, which was included in the request.

Types of Routers

While all routers have the ability to direct traffic, they differ in size and capacity. For example, routers used in homes and small businesses are designed to handle small networks of computers, printers, and wireless devices like tablets and smartphones, and connect all of them to a larger network, usually provided by the Internet Service Provider (last week's newsletter).

Other routers, used by large companies like Google, Apple, Facebook, and Microsoft, have high capacity routers for handling lots of data. In fact, the Internet often resembles a public transit system, with a combination of speeds and capacity that vary depending on the amount of data that needs to be moved, or routed.

Private and Public Routing

Some routers connect one network to another network to create an even larger network. An example is a chain restaurant with many locations. Each restaurant location usually has several computer terminals where food orders are recorded which make up a local network. Each restaurant also has a router which is connected to the corporate office. The router knows which computers are in the restaurant (local), and the path, or route, to the corporate office, so it can send and receive data from the corporate office computers.

By connecting all the restaurant locations together, a larger network is created for the entire restaurant chain. Since the routers know the computers on their local network, and they know how to send and receive information from the corporate office, the entire restaurant chain is connected in one large network. In most cases, restaurants are not connected to the Internet, and this creates what's called a private network.

Your home or small business network also has a router which probably connects you to your Internet Service Provider. The Internet is a public network and can be used by anyone that can connect to it. Don't worry though, all routers have a security feature called a firewall which stops unwanted traffic from the public network getting to your local computer network.

Wired and Wireless

One last piece about routers has to do with wired and wireless connections. Routers usually come with several Ethernet cable connection jacks. Using these, you can connect computers, printers, and other Ethernet devices to your router and create your own local network.

Most home and small business routers also include an antenna for wireless connections. These routers broadcast a signal which allows wireless devices to connect to the router. The wireless signal is called WiFi and creates a connection from a computer or device to the router wirelessly, instead of using an Ethernet cable. You can read more on Ethernet cables under the section labeled "Ethernet."

RSS

RSS, which stands for Real Simple Syndication, is a technology used on the Web, primarily by Blogs, to broadcast a Blog's updates to the Internet. For people who subscribe to an RSS feed, using an RSS "Reader" software will provide them with updates from the Blog or Web site when new content is posted or updated. The RSS feed does not contain all of the new content, usually just a headline or a short set of key words to help the subscriber determine if he wants to read more. If so, then clicking on the link for the article takes him to the Blog or Web page where the full article appears.

OK, I usually get some blank stares at this point in my classes when I start explaining RSS, so let's go into a little more explanation. I have a Blog (bobology.com) and I write articles and "post" updates to my Blog. You can see what I have written and visit the Blog to check if there are any new articles, but this requires that you enter the Web site URL (http://www.bobology.com) into your browser to visit my Blog.

Using an RSS reader application or app to subscribe to an RSS "feed" creates a simpler way to see when a website or blog is updated. To do this with a Blog you might see a "subscribe" link or an RSS Feed icon, which looks like this:

When you "subscribe" to the RSS feed, you don't get emails sent to you every time there is an update from the Blog you subscribed to, but you do get to see at a glance a list of articles by using your RSS "Reader."

RSS is like radio on the Internet

Think of RSS as the radio of the Internet. Like a radio you need to have a broadcasting station that creates a broadcast. To listen you need a radio receiver and the frequency for any station you want to hear so you can adjust the tuner to the right station. A radio also has an on and off switch.

When your radio is off, it's silent, when it's on, you can hear the broadcast for any station you've got set on your tuner.

RSS is similar in many ways to radio. Websites that broadcast RSS send out updates across the Internet when new content is published. To receive the RSS broadcast, commonly called an RSS "Feed," you need an RSS radio, which is an RSS reader software for your computer or mobile device. Then you need the frequency, which on the Internet is the Web site's RSS Feed link, usually shown with the RSS symbol on the Web site. When you open your RSS reader software or application, you can then view or "listen" to RSS feeds and view the latest updates from the Web sites.

Before the latest versions of Web browsers, you would have needed a separate application called an RSS Reader. Most Web browsers and email applications come with built-in RSS Readers so you don't need a separate application for your News reader. In addition, mobile apps such as Feedly and Feedler make it easy to scan your RSS subscriptions while on the go.

Using RSS lets you catch up with updates and Web site subscriptions from any computer or mobile device that uses RSS reader apps. By using RSS, it's possible to subscribe to many updates and view them when it's convenient for you. In addition, it doesn't clutter your email inbox with new email.

Because Social Networking sites use RSS for their status updates, Blogs have become the Website of choice for anyone trying to publicize anything, since all Blogs come with RSS capabilities. Using RSS subscriptions also allows you to keep up with the latest news and updates from some of the best sources on the Internet.

S

Search Engine

A search engine is a type of Web site that specializes in searching the Internet for information. Google, Bing, and Yahoo! are three of the most popular search engines, and they are used every day by millions of people searching the Internet for information.

Using a search engine is pretty easy, and most people using the Internet have done at least one search for something. You've probably done one yourself. In case you haven't, to use a search engine, you go to the main Web site of the search engine, such as google.com, then type in a word or phrase. Within seconds, the search engine returns the results of the search on a Web page, and these results are usually a pretty good selection of relevant websites.

Search engines don't actually go out and scan the Internet for you when you do your search since that would take a lot of time. Instead, search engines are always gathering information about all the Web sites on the Internet. Don't worry, this is all done with software, which never gets tired doing this job. The search engine takes all the information it collects and creates a catalog of its own. When you request a search, it's searching it's own catalog. This is why the search results display in a matter of a few seconds or less.

Many popular search engines of today such as Yahoo! and Google started out as simple listings without the ability to search. Instead of catering to each individual, they'd provide a standard list of popular websites on various topics. As computers got more powerful, web developers started cataloging information about as many websites as possible and creating modern search engines. At the current time, search engines collect information about text and numbers, and media such as photos, videos, and music are cataloged using any text that describes them on a Web site.

Search engines have become very sophisticated at understanding what people are searching for, and will try to deduce what you are looking for based on how you typed in your search. For example, if you type in a search for the word flowers, the search engine is going to think you want to buy flowers, and will display Web sites where you can buy flowers in the search results. It's actually possible to type in a complete question when you request a search, and the search engine will know that you are looking for an answer to that question. You'll then see results that it thinks are likely to answer your question. Go ahead and give this a try and see if it might help the next time you do one.

Top search engines process billions of searches a day from millions of users around the world on almost every topic imaginable. Many users have their favorite search engine set up, so it is the first thing they see when they go online.

If you ever browse the internet, you've no doubt used a search engine to help you find information, locate specific websites, or just stave off boredom. You can also use search engines to see how popular a website is, and help others find your website.

Selfie

A selfie is a self-portrait photo, typically taken with a mobile phone or computer camera.

The term "selfie" is a shortening of what's commonly known as a self portrait. Selfies are taken by turning the lens toward the photographer, instead of pointing the lens at a subject. Seflies that include multiple people in one photo are known as "group selfies". Selfies are usually posted to a social media site, like Facebook, Instagram or Twitter.

The use of selfies has become a phenomenon of pop culture in the second decade of the twenty-first century. Some of the most famous people known for taking and posting selfies are Kim Kardashian, Justin Bieber and Miley Cyrus. But even well-known people who don't involve themselves with social media on a regular basis have been known to take a selfie or two, including President Barack Obama. Other note-worthy selfies include the selfie astronaut Aki Hoshide took while in outer space, and one taken by National Geographic photographer Jimmy Chin as he was stuck on a ledge halfway up a 3,000 foot cliff in Oman after his rope was sliced in two by some sharp rocks.

Self-portraiture has existed for centuries, but thanks to the prevalence of smartphone ownership and the ability to post photos to social media, 2013 has been dubbed as "The Year of the Selfie" by Oxford English Dictionary. They've even officially added the term to the current English dictionary. It has been estimated that close to 1 trillion photographs will be taken in 2014, due in large part to the explosion of the selfie phenomenon.

The taking of self-portraits for social media purposes began with the 2005-2008 popularity of social media network MySpace and became known as the "MySpace Pic". In 2009, Facebook overtook MySpace in virtual traffic and encouraged more self-portraits thanks to its design that provided for a higher quality profile picture.

When Apple released the popular iPhone 4 in 2010, a new feature was the front-facing camera. Included in the iPhone 4 for video calls, this new camera could also be used to point the lens toward the user, without the need to turn the camera around. This allowed the user to custom frame their self-portrait, adding to the growth of the selfie in 2010. The following year, the exponential growth of Instagram popularity further encouraged social media users to take and post selfies, even adding photographic filters which allowed users to edit contrast, brightness, and color tones of their photos.

While the term selfie was first mentioned on the social media site Flickr in 2004, its notoriety began in late 2012, and the term quickly grew into a social media buzzword.

Semiconductor

A semiconductor is a material that conducts less electricity than a conductor, like copper, and more electricity than an insulator, like glass. Semiconductors are used in virtually every form of electronic device and make our technical lifestyle possible. Some common types of components that use semiconductors are transistors, solar-cells, light-emitting diodes (LED's), and integrated circuits. Semiconductors are the "raw material" that make up out electronic circuits.

Basics of electricity

You probably know that electricity needs a conductor to work. A power outlet in your home conducts electricity, and when you plug something into it, like a lamp, the electricity can travel over the wires to the light bulb. Smaller devices use smaller types of conductors in their electronics, it's just the size and the amount of electricity that flows in a conductor that's different. So what's an insulator?

Insulators keep electricity from moving. They're the stop sign for an electrical circuit. The plastic insulation around a power cord keeps you from being electrocuted when your hands come in contact with the wire. Since your hand only touches the insulator, not the conductor, it's safe to handle.

Whether a material is a conductor or insulator depends on the properties of the material. For example, our bodies conduct electricity, which is why you don't want to touch a live electrical circuit. Copper is a common conductor you're probably familiar with since it's used in almost all wires and cables. And we mentioned plastic as an insulator, but some other insulators are glass and rubber.

So is a semiconductor a conductor or an insulator?

What's the "semi" mean?

The semi in semiconductor means that the material is somewhere between a conductor and an insulator in the material's ability to handle electricity. It fits in between a conductor and an insulator, meaning some electricity can move through it, but not all electricity will. It's this property of being a "semi" conductor that makes materials useful for electronic devices. If you could make a material control how much electricity it conducts, you could make a lot of interesting things happen.

This is the basic principal behind electronic devices that are commonly called semiconductors. The raw material is often made out silicon, which is how Silicon Valley got it's name. Semiconductors made with silicon and other semiconductor materials can be altered when they are manufactured to change the semiconductor electrical properties. It's possible to customize how much a semiconductor is a conductor, and how much it's an insulator.

How baking and making semiconductors are similar

Think of it like baking cupcakes, and changing the recipe to make them thick or fluffy. By changing the ingredients and the recipe, you can change the characteristics of the cupcake, and the same applies to semiconductor material. If you like eating or baking cupcakes, you've probably had ones with sprinkles, nuts, berries, or frosting, and each added item changes the flavor. And it's a little like that with semiconductor material too. Most semiconductors used in electronic circuits are made up of a thin sheet of material that's cut up into wafers.

Semiconductor wafers can be layered together like a layer cake, so two different types of semiconductors can be right next to each other on the wafer. This gives manufacturers the ability to etch out one layer to reveal the bottom layer to create circuits. It's like scraping the secret coating off a scratcher card to reveal what's underneath. It's also possible to add material to the wafer to customize the circuit during the manufacturing of electronic circuits.

Sometimes when two types of semiconductor materials are next to each other, they interact in a way that produces some interesting results. In fact, this effect is what makes light-emitting diodes (LED's) product light. The way the electricity moves between the two types of semiconductor material used in LED's creates light.

Moore's Law

A "chip" is the term given to an electronic circuit made out of semiconductor material. It is, in fact, a small chip of semiconductor material with a circuit etched into it.

Gordon Moore, the co-founder of Intel with Robert Noyce, has a famous quote that became known as Moore's Law:

"The number of transistors incorporated in a chip will approximately double every 24 months."

Moore's Law become the business model for the semiconductor industry, which is constantly using new technology to put more transistors and other electronic circuits on a single piece of semiconductor material.

The semiconductor industry is one of the largest industries in the world, with an estimated $300 Billion in sales by the Semiconductor Industry Association (http://www.semiconductors.org). It's also a relatively new industry, created as a byproduct of space exploration which required a replacement of vacuum tube electronics in order to put low-power, compact electronics in spacecraft.

New semiconductor materials

While silicon is the best known semiconductor material, researchers are always looking for new materials that make electricity behave differently. As new materials are discovered, improvements in existing electronic devices will continue, and new, unknown uses will be discovered.

Server and Client

Computers that do work for other computers (performing services) are called servers. The computers that ask for the services are called clients. Whether a computer is a client or a server describes the role it plays when performing a computing task. With computers connected together on networks like the Internet, some computers on the network can perform services (servers) for other computers on the network (the clients).

You might not have thought about what happens when you connect to the Internet, but there are computers on the Internet doing work for you. Let's see how clients and servers work in a restaurant.

You're the Client, They're the Server

You've probably eaten a meal at a restaurant where you were seated at a table, and a waiter or waitress took your order, brought you your food, and refreshed your beverage. We sometimes use the term "server" to refer to a waiter or waitress, and they "serve" us our food and beverage.

The server comes out to our table to communicate with us and takes our order. After that, we don't see what they do with the order, but we can assume that it's taken to the kitchen, where food is prepared for our meal. When the food is ready, the server delivers it to us at our table. You're the "client" and the waiter or waitress is the "server." You order food, and it's brought to you ready to eat.

Here's the neat trick though, a server can serve more than one client. You know this because your server has additional customers (clients) at other tables. The resources of the restaurant allows one server to take care of multiple clients. If you understand this, it's easy to understand client-server computing, which works almost exactly the same way.

Computers and Other Types of Clients

A personal computer is a common type of computer client. A PC can work alone, or on a network, like the Internet or your home network. Other types of devices function like computers, only we don't always call them computers. Tablets and smartphones are computing devices that also function as clients. They work alone, or work connected to a network. All of these devices can be clients since being a client means asking a server for something.

A computer client (tablet, smartphone, PC) communicates with other computers using the network. Since computers don't literally "speak' to each other, they exchange data and information using networks. The "server" is a computer located somewhere on the network that prepares information and serves multiple clients, with more resources, just like a restaurant kitchen helps the server take care of multiple tables.

Specialized Servers and Multiple Clients

Now let's go a little further and see how one server can help many clients. Let's start at the restaurant first. If a restaurant is large, it may have a specific person who prepares salads, someone else who serves beverages, and another person for preparing main courses, etc..

We know what's involved in preparing food, so it's easier to understand that there could be more than one food preparer, and that each one may have a specific task. Our waiter or waitress is our server, but they're really working with many other individuals, each of whom are helping to serve our meal. Now let's see how this works when talking about computers.

The Internet and Client-Server Computing

When you use the Internet, you're using client-server computing. The Internet is made up of many computers, connected in a network called the World Wide Web. A computer on the Internet often has a specific function or application, like email, and that is it's only job. If it's job is to do email, it's called an email server. Another computer might be responsible for hosting a Web site, so it's called a Web server. It's just like the restaurant that has a dedicated beverage server, salad preparer, or table server. We don't really care who does the job, as long as our "meal" is delivered correctly.

When you click on a link to a Web page, your computing device is the client computer, and the computer that sends you the Web page is the server computer. As a client, we just want our services delivered to us. The work could be done on one computer or many. We really don't need to know, as long as it's delivered. If a server computer is doing it's job, we get our services (email, Web pages, etc.) delivered to us.

Advantages of Client-Server Computing

One advantage of client-server computing is that it allows a software application to work either on the client, or the server. The people that make the software can use more powerful server computers located in a computer room, and the people using the software only need small devices that can connect to the servers. If the hard work can be done by servers on the Internet, then the client device can be smaller, lighter, and less expensive.

If you've ever used a Web site for a map or directions, you're an experienced client-server computing user. You used your computer to go to the map Web site and then entered two pieces of data, the from address, and the to address. Not much data, just two simple lines of text. The next step is to click on a button that usually says route, or get directions. What you've done is sent two small pieces of data to a Map server on the Internet.

It's the Map server that calculates the directions, prepares the steps and a map, and then sends you a Web page that displays on your computer or mobile device. Your client doesn't need to store the map database in memory, nor have the computing power to prepare a route. The server did all that for you, usually in a few seconds. Your client waited patiently for the server to do it's work, then it received a Web page and displayed it on your computer or mobile device.

SIM Card

A SIM card, or Subscriber Identity Module, is a small plastic memory card that is used in GSM cell phones. GSM stands for "Global System for Mobile Communications" and refers to the type of technology that is used by AT&T and T-Mobile in the United States and in wireless carriers abroad. A SIM card is a necessary part in the operation of your cell phone. It fits inside a slot (usually along the phone's edge) of a mobile phone and contains personal information about the phone's owner. The card must be inserted into the cell phone's SIM slot in a specific position so that the data stored on it can be read by the phone.

There are now three different sizes of SIM cards available on the market. You can get a standard one that is often referred to as a mini-SIM. This is the largest type of SIM card that is used today. Many smartphones now use a micro-SIM, which is considerably smaller. The first phone known to take this type of SIM card was the iPhone 4, released by Apple in 2010. The newest type of SIM is the nano-SIM card, which is used in the iPhone 5, iPhone 6 and iPhone 6s. The three are not interchangeable; you use the SIM card that fits your cell phone.

All SIM cards have gold strips on their undersides that is most likely made from tin or copper. These strips are essentially where all of your personal information is contained - items such as your phone number, service provider name (SPN), contacts, text messages and various other data. All SIM cards are internationally identified by what is known as an integrated circuit card identifier (ICCID) and contain a specific serial number.

The SIM card can be extremely useful. For example, if you frequently travel internationally, you can use your own phone if it is carrier- or factory-unlocked during your travels. The only requirement is that you purchase a prepaid plan with a SIM card at your destination and pop that SIM into your phone. Then, when you return home, you can go back to your regular SIM card and use your device locally.

SIRI

Siri is a software program from Apple that responds to voice commands to perform a variety of tasks on an iPhone or iPad. Apple describes Siri as an "intelligent personal assistant." The most common way to use Siri is to ask questions and wait for Siri to respond with an answer.

How to activate Siri

Siri isn't an app but is a function built into iPhones and iPads. To activate Siri, press and hold down the Home button. After holding the Home button for a short time, a message will appear on the screen asking "What can I help you with?" After the message appears, Siri is ready to listen to your voice and respond. iPhones with iOS 9 or later will vibrate when Siri is ready to respond.

There are other ways to activate Siri. The first is when your iPhone or iPad is plugged in and charging, and you can say "Hey Siri" to activate Siri without pressing and holding the Home button.

A second way is to change the Settings for Siri in the Settings app and turn on the feature that allows you to use "Hey Siri" without plugging into power. You'll need to use the Settings app, select General, then Siri and

Allow "Hey Siri." You can also disable "Hey Siri" by turning your device face down to avoid it accidentally responding.

You can use Siri with a headset that has a remote, such as Apple's headsets supplied with iPhones and iPads. Press and hold down on the center button of the remote until you hear the chime, then you can talk to Siri. If you're in a vehicle that supports Apple's new CarPlay feature, which connects your car to your iPhone or iPad, you can activate Siri by holding down on the voice-command button on your steering wheel.

Siri is also available on the Apple Watch and is activated by using the "Hey Siri" voice command or by pressing on the Crown of the watch.

Internet

To use Siri, you'll need to have an active Internet connection since Siri uses a program located on Apple's computers on the Internet.

What can Siri do for you?

Siri can access and use all of the Apple-supplied apps on your iPhone or iPad. As a result, Siri is capable of preforming many tasks using apps such as searching the Web (Safari), creating an appointment (Calendar), sending an email (Email), or setting a reminder (Reminders). Siri also can use the location feature of your device to help you with tasks related to your current location.

Some examples of what Siri can do for you are easy to find by asking Siri what she can do for you. Try this if you've never done it by activating Siri and asking Siri "Siri, what can you do for me?" You'll see a list of ideas for things that Siri can do for you on your iPhone or iPad.

Some commonly used examples of what Siri can do include:

- Calling a contact by telling Siri to call a person
- Sending an email to a contact
- Finding places nearby your current location
- Asking Siri to search the Internet for information
- Opening an app
- Playing a song in your Music library
- Getting directions to a location or contact address

Your relationship with Siri

While Siri is intelligent, Siri can't do everything or recognize every type of command. I like to relate it to dog training. It's about training the owner how to issue the right commands as much as about training the dog. Siri can be frustrating when you issue a command and Siri doesn't interpret it clearly and does something else. Don't get frustrated, just try a different way of asking.

For example, if you asked Siri to locate the closest gas station to your current location, Siri would probably give you a list. If you wanted directions to the gas station closest to you, you'd have to ask Siri to get directions. In this case, state your first question as "Siri, get directions to the nearest gas station" and you'll save yourself a few steps.

Siri works best without long pauses between words since Siri will often think you've stopped talking and try to respond. So when you ask Siri to do something for you, speak clearly and don't pause during your question. In fact, speaking a little faster than normal is often OK, unless you have a fast talking voice, and then speak normally.

iPhone, iPad. iPod touch and Apple Watch models

To use Siri your Apple device needs to have the Siri feature capability in the hardware. Models of Apple devices that use Siri include:

- Apple iPhone 4s and newer
- iPad Pro
- iPad Air or newer
- iPad 3rd generation or newer
- iPad mini or newer
- iPod touch 5th generation or newer

To my way of thinking

Using voice commands offers a new way of using a computer, and can make it faster and easier to get things done. If you learn a little about how to use Siri, your investment in an Apple mobile device pays off for you in many ways you never thought possible.

Skype

Skype is an online service that you can use for video messaging, voice calls, or to chat with other Skype users around the world. It is a way to share experiences or use for work, no matter where you are. You can use Skype on your phone, computer, tablet or TV. It is free to use. However, there are different versions with more features you can buy as well.

How to use Skype

Go to your web browser or app store to download Skype (Skype.com) to your computer, smart TV, tablet or phone. Once you download Skype, double click on the Skype icon in your downloads and create an account. After filling out the profile information, including setting up the different options you would like to use Skype for, you are close to ready! Next, start using Skype to stay in touch with friends or colleagues through group video calls, everyday chat, or to share photos and files of any size. You will need to add other contacts to use Skype's services. You can be in touch with other Skype users from around the world, no matter where they are!

Find friends and Add contacts on Skype

First, log in to Skype with your username and password. The Skype homepage will pop up with your contacts if you have any. To add more contacts - click on the "search tab" at the top of the Skype homepage. Then, type in the username of the person you wish to add, and "search Skype". Lastly, click on the person you are searching for, and click "add to contacts" and send them a contact request. You can also accept a friend request.

Video calls and messaging

When you see someone appear online, there will be a green checkbox on the top right-hand corner of your friend's icon. You can put your cursor over the icon and send a video request or chat. You first have to wait for the other user to accept your request to connect with them. Another way you can reach someone from your contact list is by clicking on the "Contacts" tab to view other options such as group video calls, instant messaging, and file sharing.

To my way of thinking

If you are trying to connect with someone from around the world, Skype is definitely for you! Skype is a place where you can contact family, friends, and colleagues through video chats, instant messaging, and file sharing. Some additional services do have low rates attached to them, such as the phone service, and these services might be good for those traveling internationally. Skype is a way for people to stay connected to those long distant relationships, including their professional and social contacts. It offers individuals the opportunity to connect with, and keep engaged in peoples lives.

Smartphone

It seems almost everyone has a smartphone today. One of the more complex and often mind-boggling decisions the non-tech-savvy person is confronted with is understanding the differences and choosing among the many mobile phones on the market now. It seems as though everyone should want a Smartphone, but is the opposite of a Smartphone a dumb phone? Let's try to break this tech term down into something understandable.

First, of course, is the basic cell phone. It's the least expensive to buy and usually the simplest to operate. It also offers the fewest functions, and as a result costs the least to use. Its user can make and receive phone calls, and virtually all basic phones can send and receive text messages. For some people, this is all they need.

What is a Feature Phone?

A feature phone is more technologically advanced than a basic cell phone and shares some similar characteristics with a smartphone, although it doesn't have as many features. It may allow you to download music and basic games, but you will not have the same Internet capabilities because they often connect only to slower Internet networks (GPRS or General Packet Radio Service), which is the slower compared to the 3G, 4G and WiFi connections that Smartphones use. If you have only GPRS on your feature phone, often you will only have access to the specific features (which is where the name feature phone comes from) your wireless carrier allows, such as news and weather. The features that are available can vary considerably from one phone or manufacturer's product to the next, which means that if you're considering acquiring one of these, you'll probably want to carefully research and compare which phones offer what features.

What is a Smartphone?

A smartphone is the high end among cell phones on the market today, and is truly a computer in your hand. This phone will have many capabilities that regular cell phones and feature phones lack. It often includes a touchscreen, used for navigation and starting "apps," which are like applications on a computer, only made for using on a smartphone.

A touchscreen keyboard is common on most smartphones, but some smartphones may have a physical keyboard with buttons for the keys, so a touchscreen is not the only thing that makes a phone a smartphone. Most people think of Apple iPhones and Android phones as the only smartphones, since they make up almost 90% of all smartphones sold today. There are others though. The Blackberry is considered a smartphone, and there are new Windows smartphones on the market now as well. They are all made for using with the Internet.

Compared to any other type of phone, smartphones also have powerful Internet capabilities, which is limited in feature phones and not used in most basic phones. To use the Internet, smartphones connect to the wireless carrier at the fastest speeds possible, using 3G or 4G LTE, which allows you to download data like music, email, watch videos, and surf the web just as you would do on a computer.

A smartphone also includes the ability to download and install apps from a third-party or manufacturer's marketplace, which allows you to add apps to your smartphone beyond the apps that were included with it. Smartphones, because they are really computers with a phone app, have faster processors (also known as CPU's) and more memory for storing apps, data, documents, games, photos, and other information.

Poll source: Pew Internet

Smart TV

A Smart TV is a television with an Internet connection and a built-in computer that can run applications. These applications typically include a Web browser for viewing Web pages and applications for viewing videos such as Netflix.

What's the Advantage of a Smart TV?

A smart TV is able to do things that a normal or "dumb" TV can't, so let's discuss what a normal TV is capable of doing. Televisions have display screens for viewing images and speakers for playing sound, so we use them for watching television shows and movies, which are sent or "broadcast" to your television.

Broadcast Television

Broadcast television includes what we can pick up over-the-air on television stations, on cable channels, or with a satellite. A cable connects from an antenna or set-top box to the television. If you have cable or satellite service, you receive the channels they provide. Almost all television shows are recorded on videotape so they can be played back and rebroadcast on a schedule. Recorded shows are commonly called "videos."

Since the video is recorded, it's possible to make the video content available in other forms such as a videotape or CD. DVD's and videotape's are just a way that are used for storing the recorded video. So let's review how you can play recorded media on a television.

Recorded Media

In addition to your cable or antenna connection, your television has additional connections, or inputs. These are used by devices such as videotape and DVD players so they can be connected to television and you can play recorded videos. Why did this happen?

Older televisions just had one connection, for the antenna. As videotape players became popular, television makers added separate input connectors for videotape players, which can also be used by DVD players. Televisions now have a whole range of connections, so it's possible to connect many devices and sources of video to a single television.

Televisions and Internet

Since televisions can handle different inputs, someone got the bright idea of adding an Internet input to the television. It's possible to move video on the Internet, which is what YouTube does, so if your TV has an Internet connection it can play video that comes from the Internet. But wait, how does it get from the Internet on my TV?

Here's where the term Smart TV comes in. For a TV to play a video, the device or antenna sends the video to the television one way. For example, a DVD player sends a video signal to your TV, and your TV plays the video. All the controls for start, stop, pause, reverse, and eject are on the DVD player.

311

If the video comes to your TV from the Internet, an application has to control the video. Functions like start, stop, and play all need to be available for you to control the video. And applications need computers to run on in order to work. So if you add a computer to your TV so it can control the Internet connection, voila, you have a Smart TV.

Most Smart TV's have both an Ethernet cable connection jack and a built-in WiFi connection for connecting to your home network. They connect to your network just like any computer, device, or printer would connect. Ethernet cable connections are generally faster, but require that you get a cable to your TV location. A WiFi connection will usually require you to know your WiFi network password so if you don't have it, you'll need to get it from your Internet Service Provider.

Smart TV Computers

Since television makers control what goes inside their TV sets, they control the computer and applications that are available for their models. Since Smart TV's access the Internet, a Web browser is usually standard on all Smart TV's. This means you can access any Web page, but without a keyboard and mouse, most Smart TV's are being used for video watching applications.

Almost all of them have the popular applications from YouTube, Netflix and Hulu Plus. YouTube is free while Netflix and Hulu Plus are video libraries, and charge a fee to access their services. The television maker has to work with each application in order to make it available on their TV.

What does this mean for buying a Smart TV?

These applications are usually fixed by model and brand and aren't often upgradable. If you want a specific video service or application, be sure to check that the model of TV you are considering will run that application. If the application doesn't exist on the model you are considering, you may have to go up in price or look at a different brand.

What's the Advantage to a Smart TV?

A Smart TV will give you access to sources of video and content that are available over the Internet, without the need to buy any additional equipment or device. With an application like Netflix, YouTube, or Hulu Plus built-in to your TV, all you need is to connect your Smart TV to the Internet to access these services and their content, no additional hardware or software is required.

Will you use this or not?

Increasingly, cable and satellite companies are fighting with the owners of the content. It's estimated that everyone with cable or satellite will experience some outage of a channel or channels due to a dispute if they haven't already. Having a TV with Internet capability will give you the option to choose your sources of video if and when you want to make a change.

SMS

SMS stands for short message service and is used to send text messages between cell phones, also known as "texting."

While SMS is the official term, users often refer to these messages as texting, text messages or text messaging. SMS messages allow for a short number of characters to be sent from one phone to another. While the original use of SMS allowed for 160 characters in a single message, many newer phones have the capability to use 224 characters. If a newer phone sends a message that's longer than the older 160 character limit, the message is received in two parts.

Any letter, number, space or symbol counts as one character. Most phones come equipped with a full QWERTY keyboard that allows for faster texting as compared to older style push button phones where numbers must be pressed several times to achieve one of the three letters assigned to them; for instance, 1 would be pressed once for A, twice for B, or three times for C.

Due to the popularity of SMS, cell phone companies offer unlimited text packages that can be added on to standard cell service contracts for anywhere from $5-30 a month. Lower cost packages can be found that offer a certain number of SMS messages to be sent and received before overage charges apply, and other plans don't include text messaging at all. If SMS messaging is not included in the cell service plan, then they can cost about 10 to 15 cents per message. If you plan to take advantage of SMS messaging, it's usually best to choose an unlimited package.

SMS messaging is most commonly used to communicate between friends, family, and co-workers. However, subscription SMS services exist that can provide the user with regular news updates, weather, retail coupons, stock quotes and sports highlights. Users of SMS messaging find it convenient to send short messages that might be wasted on a call, such as "I'm on my way" or "I love you". Another advantage of SMS messaging is the ability to send one message to many people at once. For instance, users may choose to announce a change to a party time or a newly scheduled meeting by sending one text message to multiple contacts from their phone. This eliminates having to individually call or text each person.

One advantage of SMS is the ability to create a message when your phone is disconnected from cellular service, for example, when you're on an airplane or out hiking a long way away from a cell tower. Just create an SMS message, then, when you get back in range, and your phone connects to your cellular provider, the message will automatically be sent. If you're out of range or had your phone turned off when an SMS message was sent to you, the SMS message is saved for you to "pick-up" when you turn your phone on or get back in range of service.

Texting is also a great way to communicate if the users find themselves in a place where it is not polite or convenient to make an actual phone call, such as in libraries or while commuting on public transit. Thanks to its convenience, SMS messaging is utilized by cell phone users worldwide.

Snapchat

Snapchat is a smartphone application used to share messages between friends called "Snaps" that contain videos and photos with captions. The primary way of using Snapchat results in messages, images, and videos being deleted automatically after being viewed. The sender of an image or video decides how long the recipient can view the image, from one second to ten seconds.

Snapchat also has fun and useful image annotation tools that allows a user to make notes and draw on an image before sending it. Similar to the filters feature that made Instagram a popular service, Snapchat's image drawing and annotation features allow you to draw or write on a photo.

Snapchat compared to other social networks

Created by a group of Stanford students who wanted to build a multimedia sharing application that didn't save any of the shared content, the idea resulted in Snapchat. Other social networking sites like Facebook, Twitter and LinkedIn keep a user's photos, videos, updates and other shared content as part of the user's history of activity on the social networking site.

As a result, all of a person's activity on a traditional social network becomes a historical journal. Snapchat's appeal is the fact that anything that's shared typically destroyed, and there is no personal history for anyone to view.

Like other social networking applications, users establish connections with an invitation. The invited user has to accept the invitation in order for two people to share anything with each other. Once two people connect, they can send and receive Snapchat videos, photos, and text messages with each other.

The combination of using a way to share with both parties agreeing to connect along with the limited time that any shared content is available to view a more private and personal type of social network. Privacy and un-saved content why Snapchat has grown so rapidly.

However, as Snapchat has grown, it has added additional sharing options for it's users where the content is not deleted automatically after being viewed.

Other sharing options with Snapchat

Replay: The replay feature allows a user to replay a previously deleted Snap. In any 24-hour period, a user can only use Replay once.

Stories: In addition to an individual video or photo message, it's possible to share collections of images and videos with a group of friends. Called a "Story" these messages can be viewed an unlimited number of times for a 24-hour period before being automatically deleted.

Text: With the May 2014 update, users can text chat with other users, as well as start a video chat if both parties are available at the same time and press a button that says "Here" to let the other know they want to chat.

Our Stories (meaning Stories created by Snapchat or partners)

Another way Snapchat is used is to follow activities where users have set the privacy settings to allow public sharing of personal Stories. Certain events such as music concerts often have many Snapchat users in attendance. Snapchat uses the public Stories from all of the users and creates a Story from all of the user's shared content. A recent Star Wars convention in Anaheim was a Snapchat story, and viewers could see videos taken by Snapchat users who attended the event almost as soon as the videos were taken.

Snapchat has media partners that also create Stories about news and other content. These media outlets include CNN, National Geographic, and Cosmopolitan Magazine. Like a televisions channel, these outlets each add from three to ten stories to feature on Snapchat and are updated every 24 hours. So Snapchat is a way for people to keep up with current events.

Snapchat and pornography

Snapchat's early use had a reputation for inappropriate and illegal messages, often involving minors who used Snapchat to send nude photos. Snapchat has taken action to address these issues and keep the service safe and legal.

Snapchat advises users that Snapchat is about sharing moments and fun and spell out what's not allowed, which includes nudity, pornography, threats, harassment, impersonation, self-harm and other rules which could result in the removal of content and prohibiting someone from using Snapchat.

Snapchat's investors want it to be a safe app for people to use in order to attract advertisers as Snapchat opens up opportunities to display ads and give advertisers the ability to reach the user community.

To my way of thinking

Using Snapchat helps you to share quickly and communicate everyday life events with friends and family in a much more private way than other social media. While Snapchat offers some useful features that contribute to more private communications, remember that once an image, video, or message has been sent, it's no longer a secret and could be copied or shared by the recipient.

Like all social networking apps, who you know that's using it will likely determine whether it's an app that makes sense for you.

Social Network

A Social Network is any online community of people or organizations who join the community, connect with other users, and share content and updates with the community.

Most people know Social Networks by their names, which include Facebook, Twitter, and LinkedIn, and are the among the most popular Social Networks. After teaching classes since 2007 on Social Networking (also known as Social Media), I've determined that all of them have three characteristics in common.

The three common features of Social Networks are these: join, connect, and share. Let's take a look at what each of these means and how they create this type of community.

Join

All Social Networks require a person or organization to join them in order to access the features of the community. This means setting up an online account with the Social Network, usually through a Web site. You provide your email address, create a password, and maybe have to supply your name and one or two other pieces of personal information.

After completing this information, which involves filling in a form on the Social Network Web site or mobile application, you receive a confirmation email. This email confirmation is an important step and is used to verify that you can receive their email communications. By clicking on a link in the confirmation email, you verify your account. Now you have joined the Social Network and can use all the features available to users.

It's similar to joining many other membership organizations. In order to receive the benefits available to members, you need to join. A credit union is an example of a membership organization. It provides financial services to it's members, and in order to take advantage of the services available, for example, a checking account, you need to join the credit union and become a member. Credit unions have members, and members have access to member benefits.

Social Networks, since they are online communities, use the Web, email, messaging, and other forms of electronic communications to communicate with members. Once you join, you have access to the member benefits. These benefits typically include the ability to connect with other members of the community and share information with them.

Why Are They Free?

All the major Social Networks are free to join, no money is required. They are, however, profit making organizations, and they make money by selling advertising to organizations that want to reach the members of the Social Network.

The fine print in the terms and conditions you are required to accept when you join a Social Network usually gives the Social Network the ability to collect information about you. This includes your activity while using the Social Network, and also allows them to make money by selling advertising to you. Don't be too shocked though. We are generally willing to give up something for a good deal.

You might have a member card with your grocery store that provides a discounted price on your purchases. In return, the store can collect data on what you buy, when you buy it, and use that to make money by selling shopper information to companies that want to learn more about shopper's behavior. We accept free television shows in return for commercials, and almost everyone has a credit card or ATM card, which include terms which allow the card company to track our use and purchases.

Personal information about you is never shared by Social Networks, but your information is collected so if someone wants to reach men that play golf (like me) the community can give advertisers that option. Your personal information is only used to manage your account by the Social Network and is never shared.

OK, so if you want to join and use the Social Network, you setup your account using your email address, create a name you would use in the community (some require your real name, others don't), and then you can use the features of the community, which includes connecting with other users. So now let's move on to the second characteristic of a Social Network, which is connecting.

Connecting

Since these are, after all, Social Networks, they assume you joined to be social, and not anti-social. The whole point of a Social Network is to find and make connections with other users.

Other users might be family members, friends, work associates, or a business or organization. All of these can have user accounts on Social Network. Ever see or hear ad ad that asks you to "like" something on Facebook or "follow" them on Twitter? That's a brand asking you to connect with them. Some Social Network treat people and brands the same while others have different types of user accounts for a business compared to a person. Let's see how this might work.

People who are users can connect with other people who use the Social Network. You might know someone who is already a user on a Social Network like Facebook, Twitter, or LinkedIn. You probably have their email address already if they are someone you communicate with on a regular basis. The email address of a user is a key part of finding and connecting with other users.

If you know someone's email address, and they are a member of a Social Network you belong to, you can locate them by searching in the Social Network search tool using their email address. You might be able to find them by name, location, school, or work history as well, but the email address is the most efficient way and it avoids making mistakes and connecting with strangers. Every Social Network has a way to search for other people, and others can search for you as well.

Once you find someone you know, you can connect with them. This is where Social Networks are different from each other. A "connection" is different on each Social Network and the how it defines a connection gives the Social Network it's "personality."

Facebook, for example, has people connect to each other as Friends. For two people to become Friends, they both have to agree. So one person sends an invitation, and the other person has to accept it; otherwise they don't become Friends on Facebook. A friend is the same connection whether they are a close friend or a distant one. The term Friend means that Facebook will share information about you that is only visible to other Friends, and that you will be able to see information about your Friends that is only available to view because you are a Friend. I'll go into the information part when I discuss sharing, so please hold on.

Twitter uses the terms "followers" and "following" for connections on Twitter. Anyone can follow anyone else, with no permission required, so Twitter is a lot more public than other Social Networks. The users who follow you are your "followers." Followers receive updates from the users they are following when they view their account.

LinkedIn uses the term "connections" for connections, which allows a user to communicate and view more information about someone that if they were not a connection.

The Social Network you use creates a way for people and organizations to share information that isn't visible without a connection to that user. This way, people and organizations don't have to send every one of their connections information because the Social Network takes care of sending the information to all of the person's or organization's connections.

OK, so this might be hard to understand. Let's say you send out a holiday letter by postal mail to everyone on your holiday card list. Each letter has to be individually addressed, stamped, and delivered. If you have everyone over to your home, you can give them one copy that they can read and view. If you have a sign in front of your house, it's public, but if you have something inside your house that only people you invite in can see, it's more private.

The Social Network you use has rules and resources for what you share with your connections. Facebook requires that you be Friends, Twitter lets anyone follow anyone else, LinkedIn makes your profile mostly visible, but only allows you to send a direct message to another user if you are connected to another user. So now on to what you are sharing.

Sharing

You share two types of information on Social Networks, your profile and your updates. Each Social Network has a unique approach to how much you can include, and how the information for your profile and updates are shared. So let's look at a few common networks and how they share.

Profile Information

What you share is really up to you, but some Social Networks, particularly Facebook, want to collect more information about you, your interests, and your activities compared to other Social Networks. Facebook has a very robust way for you to create a profile about yourself. You can include where you live, where you work, your contact information, and your interests, along with your "Likes." Your Likes are the brands, companies, and organizations that you choose to Like on Facebook.

Twitter gives you 160 characters to describe yourself, so it simply doesn't have room for much information in your profile. LinkedIn is primarily a work related Social Network, so your profile is your work history, experience, and skills. So each site has a little different profile approach. But all of them have "updates."

Updates

An update is a piece of information you publish in your account that is automatically sent to your connections. The information can be some text, a photo, video, or a link to another Web page. You are essentially publishing information on a personal Web site that the Social Network gives you, and they take care of sending a message to your connections letting them know you've got some new information to share. What you share is up to you.

If you want to share information about a vacation, your work, what you eat, who you see, it's totally up to you. People will learn about you by what you share in your updates. So your updates are like a journal you share, but everyone has a personal style and preference for what they share and how often they share. Social Networks usually allow you to share photos, videos, and links to other Web pages in addition to plain text. You don't have to be a writer to share on Social Media. Using a smartphone app from the Social Network, you can share your location with your connections since smartphones have GPS chips.

People and Organizations

Depending on the Social Network, people and organizations may be different types of users, with a different type of connection. When you Like something on Facebook, you are choosing to receive updates from that organization similar to the way you receive updates from your Friends. They don't see any of your personal profile information, or your updates because they aren't your Friend. So Facebook has a way for organizations to create a user account, called Pages, and people can Like a Page. Other Social Networks are similar, but with some subtle differences.

Google+ is pretty similar to Facebook, and organizations can have their own user account, and users can receive updates by following them.

LinkedIn has something called a Corporate Page, that is for corporations and other organizations. People connect with other people, but on LinkedIn, people follow a Corporation. By following a corporation, they can send you a direct message, but you will receive their updates in your LinkedIn account.

On Twitter, all users are the same, whether they are a person or an organization. So organizations have the same space for their profile (160 characters), can have followers, and can follow other users just like a personal user.

Advertising

The Social Networks I've mentioned are businesses that sell advertising. Their goal is to collect as many users as possible by offering free, useful, and interesting services for their members. With many members, advertisers are willing to pay to reach the members. It's similar to a television show like the Super Bowl. If your an organization that wants to reach viewers of the Super Bowl on TV you have to purchase a TV ad from the network that broadcasts the Super Bowl.

Advertisers who want to reach as many users as possible on a Social Network are willing to pay to reach you and other users. This is how Social Networks make a profit and how they are able to offer users like us free services.

The benefits of being able to connect and share information with people who live far apart, in different time zones, or just don't see each other that often make Social Media appealing. Human beings are social, with our families, community organizations, towns, schools, and other activities that bring us together. Social Media is just another way, the electronic way that people can be social.

Software Driver

A software driver is a type of software program that controls a hardware device. On any computer, smartphone, tablet, different hardware components that are part of the computer and attached devices need to communicate with each other for a computer to function and work.

Internal components such as the processor, memory, hard drive, and peripherals as a printer, speakers, keyboard and mouse all need to send and receive information to each other for your computer to operate. The software driver exists for each component or peripheral in order and enables that piece of hardware to communicate with other components and peripherals.

Physical connections and software connections

While a physical connection exists for data to move from one device to another across a circuit board or wire, it's the software drivers that tell your computer what type of device is connected, what it can do, and how to communicate with it from other software on your computer, including the operating system.

Mobile devices like smartphones and tablets usually don't need to install any additional software drivers since almost all communications with any accessory is done with WiFi or Bluetooth communication, and there's no physical connection. The manufacturer of the accessory usually provides an app that manages the accessory.

Apple has a specific partner arrangement for hardware makers that want to attach accessories to iPhones or iPads, and the manufacturer is required to have the accessory review and approved. When the accessory maker follows this approach, Apple will include support for the accessory in the iOS operating system so it will be recognized.

Android mobile devices are a little different than Apple mobile devices since Android devices have a USB connection. It's possible for users to connect an Android smartphone or tablet to many USB devices. As long as the manufacturer has a software driver for Android, the accessory will usually work without any special software installation.

Software drivers and operating systems

For internal components such as the processor, data ports and screen that are supplied by the computer maker you typically won't see the software drivers or need to be aware that they even exist. Since it's possible to connect many different types and brands of peripherals and accessories to a computer, a software driver has to exist for each one.

Depending on the operating system you use, software drivers usually come already installed on your computer. The most current versions of Apple and Microsoft operating systems include most software drivers in a library as part of the operating system. When a new piece of hardware is connected or installed the software driver is automatically installed from the library. Manufacturers of peripherals submit their software drivers to the operating system maker, so the software driver is included in the library of software drivers on your computer.

However, some computers require a separate installation of the software which is typically obtained by going to a device's manufacturer's website.

For example, a hardware device such as a printer is started and controlled by the software driver for that specific model of printer. When you connect the printer cable to your computer, your computer will typically detect the new printer and start the installation of the software drive from the operating system library.

The advantage of allowing the operating system to install the driver is that any software driver updates are downloaded as part of any operating system update and not from the peripheral maker's website. Using this process of including software drivers in the operating system makes it almost effortless to update any software driver since the updates are included in the operating system updates.

Software drivers that are downloaded and installed from the peripheral or device maker's website require that you visit the website for any update to download and install it. Sometimes the hardware maker includes a small software program with the hardware that will check for any updates and notify you if one is available. Another way hardware makers notify you of software driver updates is with an email notification if you provide your email to them when you register your product for warranty support.

Why do software drivers exist?

In older operating systems, each software program had to have it's own instructions for communicating with accessories and peripherals. That meant that each software program needed to include instructions in the program that allowed it to communicate with specific accessories and it was up to the software program maker to include the necessary drivers in their application.

As personal computers proliferated, it was clear to the entire technology industry that continuing this path would make computers more difficult and complex, rather than simpler and easier. As a result, operating system makers created a way for any hardware accessory or component to be used by any software application. The computer user could now install the software driver for any hardware accessory or component they purchased.

With the ability to install the software driver in the operating system, the hardware accessory or component maker would provide the software driver for their product on a disk drive or CD. You might have installed a software driver for an accessory using the included CD media, and this approach was common for most computers.

Today, some accessory makers still provide CD or download versions of software drivers for very specialized hardware rather than submit their software driver to the operating system maker for inclusion in the operating system. In some other cases, the accessory maker might include some application features on their download or CD version of the software driver that offers additional, but usually non-critical features, in addition, the version included in the operating system.

Updates to software drivers

If the software driver for a component or accessory is available through the operating system, this is the best and most convenient way to install it. Updates to the software driver will be included with any operating system updates automatically.

Manufacturers websites usually have very good information about software drivers for any specific type or hardware, component or accessory. Often the easiest and simplest way to see if there is any update available is to use a web search. Just type in "software driver for brand model product" and the search engine will most likely return a link to the manufacturers website with help and advice on the current version of any software driver for your operating system.

Software Programs

A software program is the set of alphanumeric instructions that are given to computers and devices to perform calculations. Without software, our hardware wouldn't be able to do anything useful for us. Software is like a recipe for cooking. The recipe is a set of instructions for the cook, and includes steps for the cook to follow. Software is the recipe that computers need to work.

Software Basics

Software is written in alphanumeric characters with a format that uses specific characters to create instructions for the computer. When these instructions are complete enough for the computer to do something, the software becomes a program. Software Programs do work and perform calculations. Often software is also called "code" because the way the characters are used doesn't result in something that is written in English or any other common written or spoken language.

Code is the language of computers. Programmers are people who know how to read and write software programs written in computer languages. The English language is a code. If you put noun in front a verb, you can communicate a thought or idea to someone else who understands English. Combine letters in the right pattern and you create words, and words can describe things and actions.

Say "I ran" to another person who understands you, and they have an idea of what these characters mean. But say "X lggg" and you might not be able to communicate a thought or idea, unless someone knew your "code" and how you used the characters. Software, like spoken and written language, can be used to communicate. When software includes instructions that perform a task, the software becomes a program.

Applications

An application is a software program that includes instructions for doing tasks that a person might find useful. For example, a word processor application is a program. It includes many tasks and functions that cause the computer to respond when we use the program. People who understand how to write instructions using software are called programmers. We depend on them for a lot of applications.

While many applications are complex, applications can also be simple. For example, a calculator is a common application on computers and devices, and it does some mathematical functions. Applications are the software programs that make computers so useful to use. The software program is written in code, but as users of the application we don't need to see the code because the software gives us menus, icons, and other ways to use the software to perform our work. Part of using software is the ability to translate, or interpret, instructions.

For a computer to use a software program, it has to be able to find and follow the instructions. This is what memory is used for on computers. The memory holds the instructions for the CPU to use. As the CPU follow the instructions of the software, it is moving information in and out of memory to perform the calculations.

Mobile devices like smartphones and tablets use software programs that are usually called "apps." An app is still an application, but since the devices started out smaller than computers, the term app was used and it seems to have stuck.

Operating Systems

While some software programs are applications, others types of software programs are called operating systems. An operating system is a software program that manages other software programs when they want to use the hardware. It's like a traffic cop at a busy intersection with a broken signal.

As cars approach the intersection, they are traveling a certain speed. Without a traffic cop, every car would drive into the intersection at the same speed it was approaching, and there would be collisions. The traffic cop manages how the cars can enter and use the intersection and sets up rules the cars have to follow in order to proceed through the intersection on their journey. How long one line of cars waits to use the intersection, who gets to make a left or right turn. And how fast they travel is all managed by the traffic cop.

An operating system, at it's most basic level, does the task of managing how other software programs use the hardware. An example is printing a document. When you want to print a document, the operating system manages when the processor can take care of printing. The operating system has to see what else is happening in the computer, stop any software program that needs to stop in order to print, then give the print job the resources to print.

The most common operating systems that you probably are familiar with are Microsoft Windows and Apple Mac OS X. Mobile devices use operating systems also, and the two most popular mobile operating systems are Android and Apple's iOS. Operating systems make it easier for programmers to write software since they can write the software and not worry about the hardware. So as a result, software programs are said to be written for a specific operating system. The hardware, software programs (applications), and operating systems all work together.

It's common for computer companies to build everyday applications, like a web browser, into an operating system. As a result, you might not be aware of when you're using the operating system and when you're using an application. Many operating systems include applications, so the computer user is more likely to use the application already installed and included with the operating system, rather than adding and installing an independent programmer's version. As a result, many computer users assume that applications for common functions like email, photos, and web browsing are part of the operating system. But there's a balance that an operating system maker has to manage.

The line between an operating system and applications is sometimes blurry. Companies and organizations that make operating systems usually try to keep a balance between supplying applications for the convenience of their customers, but making it easy for application programmers to create and sell additional applications built to work with their operating system. This is important since people want to do things with their computers, and it's applications that make computers useful.

Software Programs and Operating Systems

One of the purposes of an operating system is to communicate and manage the hardware. A programmer's job is made easier by the operating system. Operating system software usually does common tasks, like printing a document or displaying graphics on a monitor. The operating system has programs that can talk to things like keyboards, printers, cameras, networks, and displays, so the programmer doesn't have to worry about writing "code" for their program to communicate with the hardware and do common tasks. And as hardware might be from different manufacturers or different models, having the operating system take care of the hardware offers more devices that can use the application.

An Apple iPhone, for example, uses Apple's iOS operating system. For any software program to work on an iPhone, it has to work with iOS since that's the only operating system on an iPhone. Apple uses the same operating system on all of it's iPhone models so a programmer can write an application that will work on different models of iPhones with one version of the software. The application is written to work with the operating system, and the operating system takes care of the differences in hardware.

Since software applications work with operating systems, it's important to know what operating systems a specific application with work with. A software program for Windows doesn't mean it will work on all versions of the Windows operating system. An application must state that it works with the version of Windows you have installed on your computer.

Companies like Apple, Microsoft, and Google (who makes Android) know that while hardware is important, it's the applications that are the reason people buy a particular computer. As a result, good operating systems are important to attract more programmers to write applications.

Software Updates and Upgrades

Two terms that float around the computer world, sound similar, but have totally different meanings are "software update" and "software upgrade." You may even hear professionals incorrectly using the terms interchangeably, but there are important differences between the two that you should know.

Software update

An update is offered to you, free of charge, by the manufacturer of your original software. Manufacturers constantly monitor and improve their software programs to manage security issues that may come up over time. An update may also repair a problem that was discovered in the program code. A repair update is sometimes called a "patch." A patch replaces parts of the program to repair flaws while maintaining the integrity of the original program itself.

An update may improve a specific feature of the software, but if the software is not installed on your computer, you cannot update it. You are encouraged to download the update as soon as the manufacturer tells you it is available. The manufacturer does not want you to be using a flawed program that may have security issues.

For example, if you have Adobe Reader, you have probably noticed that you are asked frequently to update your program and it only takes a few seconds. Adobe constantly monitors it's program for security breaches, fixes them and provides updates to the software. You can only update Adobe if you have it installed on your computer.

Software upgrade

As opposed to the free software update, a software upgrade will cost you money. It is an entirely new improved version that totally replaces the older one. It's features are not just to get out the flaws or improve security but to provide an entirely new version with new basic features. You will need to install the entire software program the same way you do any new program.

Purchasing an upgrade is entirely optional and depends on the desires of the user. For example, Windows 8 is an upgrade to Windows 7. You may be very happy with your Windows 7 and, after reviewing the new improved features of Windows 8, decide you do not want or need it, so you do not purchase the upgrade. On the other hand, you may want the features of Windows 8. You purchase it from Microsoft and install it over Windows 7. You now have only the features of Windows 8.

Solid State Drive

Solid State Drives, abbreviated "SSD," are storage devices for computers that are usually used to replace a traditional computer hard drive. SSD's offer faster speed and performance than traditional computer hard disk drives.

Traditional hard disk drives have a magnetic disk which rotates on a spindle, and a magnetic read/write sensor which changes the magnetic setting for writing data to the disk, or reads the setting when reading data. Information is stored by using the magnetism of a special magnetic surface on the disk. The magnetic read/write sensor moves in and out from the center of the hard drive, and the hard drive rotates, or spins. These two movements allow the magnetic sensor to access any location on the hard drive surface. Hard drives spin whenever they are working.

SSD's use electronic circuits to store data, and are essentially larger versions of USB flash drives that are commonly used for storing and moving data. SSD's, like USB drives, use a type of electronic circuit that remembers the data when there's no power to the device. In comparison, your computer's RAM, or Random Access Memory, doesn't store data when your computer is turned off. This electronic memory is often referred to as "flash" memory an is used not only for SSD's and USB drives, but is also used on mobile devices like smartphones and tablets, which don't have any hard drive storage at all.

Since there's no mechanical movement in an SSD, it can read and write data faster than a traditional hard drive, which has to rely on physical movement to access data. Without moving parts, SSD's are quieter (as in silent) and more reliable. However, they are more expensive, when compared to traditional magnetic hard drives.

Recommendations: Just upgrading a hard drive on a computer may not improve all the performance characteristics you want. Performance depends on many factors, and you will see an improvement in the start-up time for your computer, but application performance may or may not be improves. If you're purchasing a new laptop, it's definitely worth considering if you're budget can afford it. SSD's are usually available as an upgrade option on most laptop brands. One option is to use cloud storage like DropBox for storage. You might be able to live with a smaller hard-drive with a lower price.

Spoofing

Spoofing refers to the impersonation of a legitimate source of information by an imposter. Spoofing usually occurs for the purpose of fraudulent or illegal activity and appears most frequently as an email message that appears to be from a known source, but is actually from an imposter.

The message includes links to websites that are designed to capture information you might enter into a form and then used for crimes such as identity theft. There are other types of spoofing besides email messages that I'll discuss as well, but email is so common it will help to start with email spoofing so you can learn how to recognize a spoof when you see it.

Spoofing, by the way, is a word which once meant copying a work of art for satirical purposes,

Email spoofing

If you're like most people, you've probably received an email from a recognizable name of a friend or acquaintance, only to discover upon opening it, that it was from someone else entirely. This technique is popular with spammers because many people no longer open emails from people or addresses they don't recognize.

An email message can be a spoof if the name in the FROM text displays as a person or email address you might recognize. In fact, the mail message may be from an imposter. Email FROM spoofing is becoming harder with some newer technologies introduced in 2012 that are being used by many email services on the Internet. It's still possible for someone to create an email with a FROM name that may be an imposter, but is it dangerous to open the email message?

Reading a spoofed email isn't a problem, it's just that since you think the email is from someone you know, you're more likely to trust any links to web pages and file attachments with requests to open them that create problems. Don't click on the links if you have any doubts, just enter the website that's referred to in the email directly in your web browser and go to the page. Email spoofing is often combined with these fraudulent web links in a technique called phishing.

Emails all have a set of information included as part of the message called the "header." The header contains information about the email message that is not usually displayed by your email software and the information is used by the email software to identify your email account, the sender, and other technical information that's necessary for email to function properly.

Often, but not always the real sender of the email can be identified by looking at the header information but it's not a necessity to check every email to determine the true source. If you're interested, however, each email program is a little different so viewing the header of an email is difficult to explain here. I recommend doing a search to find instructions for "how to find the header..." and enter your specific email software application in the search, and you'll find some technical articles and recommendations.

If in doubt, send an email to your contact's email address and see if they sent the email to you or not. In some cases, their email account might have been compromised or hacked.

Other types of spoofing

Each communication technology has its forms of spoofing. For example, telephone communication spoofing utilizes caller ID to gain access using a false identity. In caller ID spoofing, the caller-ID is falsified and displays on your phone as another name. The FCC has strict rules about caller ID spoofing and violators can be fined up to $10,000 for each violation. They also require telemarketers to transmit or display their telephone numbers and provide a number people can call to request no further calls from them.

GPS spoofing utilizes counterfeit GPS signals that behave like normal ones or a technique of rebroadcasting genuine signals that were broadcast at a different time or in a different place. GPS spoofing can trick the GPS receiver into believing that the transmitted data came from a legitimate location.

Social media might seem like an area on the Internet where spoofing would be more prevalent, but the social media sites all have the ability to shut down a user's account very quickly. As a result, while spoofing occurs on social media, any reports of spoofing or fraud are quickly removed.

Internet spoofing has several varieties, including Internet Protocol address (the 198.1.1.1 types of numbers for IP addresses) in which someone forges the header with a different IP address, so it appears that the data was sent by a different entity. The goals of this kind of spoofing are often to flood sites with so much traffic that they crash or to bypass network security measures that rely on IP address authentication.

Legitimate spoofing

However, not all spoofing is done for nefarious purposes. There are cases in which it can used legitimately. Network management techniques use a form of spoofing to speed network traffic and reduce congestion. This type of spoofing usually is done on private networks by the information technology staff who manages the network. In this case, it's for the purpose of improving the network performance, not fraud.

To my way of thinking

Spoofing is never going away as long as there are potential opportunities for people to commit fraud. Instead of someone misrepresenting themselves in person for gain, it's just over the Internet now.

Here's the advice from the Internet Crime Center of the FBI on how to deal with a suspicious email:

- Be suspicious of any unsolicited email requesting personal information.
- Avoid filling out forms in email messages that ask for personal information.
- Always compare the link in the email to the link that you are directed to.
- Log on to the official website, instead of "linking" to it from an unsolicited email.
- Contact the actual business that supposedly sent the email to verify if the email is genuine.

Website

https://www.ic3.gov/preventiontips.aspx#item-13

Spyware

Spyware is any software technology that collects information about the owner of that device without the owners knowledge or to otherwise gain control over the device.

Spyware has been in existence for nearly as long as personal computers have existed. Various computer hacking groups and individuals create spyware who seek to gain information concerning the user's computer habits, financials, or other important personal information.

Why is spyware used

Personal information such as account usernames, passwords, addresses, and credit card numbers all are bought and sold by cybercriminals all others looking to perform fraudulent activities.

How spyware attacks

The most common way spyware gains access to a computer or device is through internet downloads. Spyware programs can be attached and hidden in an online file, such as a web download. Photos, documents, and sometimes plug-ins for using the website may contain spyware. Computer hackers will often connect spyware to necessary or highly wanted internet-based downloads because they know that many people will attempt to obtain said downloads.

In fact, some downloads are specifically designed to deliver spyware. Creating a website or service with an appealing free offer enticed more people into downloading a file containing the spyware.

Spyware is more prevalent on Internet Explorer than on any other web browser since it is a standard browser on all Microsoft operating systems. Regular updates to Internet Explorer are provided for free by Microsoft (and other browser makers as well) to block any malicious software from exploiting the browser. Virtually all anti-virus software programs include spyware protection, it's just important to keep them up-to-date on a daily basis to install the most current protection.

What happens when Spyware appears

Sometimes spyware is so well written that a computer user doesn't notice any difference in the way their computer behaves. It runs quietly in the background, collecting whatever information the spyware maker wanted to collect. Typically though, when spyware makes its way onto a person's computer, the computer user may begin to notice that their computer behaves differently, usually with slower speed or longer times to load websites.

Spyware isn't always just one program, and a group of different spyware programs may be downloaded in a single file. The spyware maker uses this approach in an attempt to see if at least one of them might be able to get by any security measures. When your computer is infected, it is often highly infected, which can lead to more significant changes in the way the computer operates.

Dealing with Spyware

It's important to remove any spyware from any computer. While a spyware infection can steal valuable personal information, spyware can also make your computer's performance noticeably slower.

Most malware protection softwares on the market today do an effective job of cleaning up any Spyware present on one's computer.

If the spyware can get past your computer's security software, then a spyware removal program or calling a computer technician will be required to remove it. One of the most commonly used spyware removal programs is Malwarebytes, which can scan and remove many types of spyware. However, you might end up needing a service call to clean up your computer. As long as you can connect to the Internet, you can receive help remotely from several services.

Microsoft runs an on-line support service called Answer Desk with a one-year support plan, virus removal, one-to-one support, and an Automated PC Tune-up. When you use this service, you're receiving support directly from Microsoft employees at competitive rates. Some areas also have Microsoft Stores where you can bring in any brand of Windows computer for help with Microsoft Windows or any add-on Microsoft software.

Apple Mac users with Apple Care can receive help on the phone or in Apple Stores for any issue, but Macs seem to have fewer issues with spyware and other malicious software than Microsoft Windows. Since 90% of all computers are Windows-based, spyware makers go after the largest potential targets to attack.

Mobile phone and tablets aren't as vulnerable to spyware since installing any software requires that the software be downloaded from the Apple or Android application stores. Since these stores are run and managed by Apple and Google, the companies review any app that might contain malicious spyware before it is made available on the stores.

Websites

https://www.malwarebytes.org

http://www.microsoftstore.com/store/msusa/en_US/cat/Answer-Desk/categoryID.63433500

SSL and Heartbleed

SSL is the abbreviation for Secure Socket Layers. SSL is a security function used on websites to encrypt sensitive information. Encryption is a way of scrambling a set of number and letters with a unique "key" that prevents them from being read by anyone without the key. Encryption of data prevent eavesdropping and tampering of the data, which is necessary for many functions on the Internet.

Who uses SSL?

SSL is used by about 2/3 of all websites to encrypt credit card numbers, passwords, usernames, and other information. Other types of information such as email, electronic faxes, instant messaging, attachments, and voicemail are sent and received over the Internet in addition to communications with websites, and it's possible for these types of communications to be encrypted using SSL in order to prevent tampering.

What does SSL include?

While SSL stands for Secure Socket Layers, the SSL software used today also includes an additional security function called TLS, which stands for Transport Layer Security. When people use the term "SSL" today, they mean the SSL software that includes both SSL and TLS. SSL and TLS are combined in the software. SSL, with the TLS security features, have made secure transactions a daily part of using the Internet. SSL is available for most versions of computers that run websites, and it's up to the website owner to provide SSL security as part of their website, not a computer user.

How do you know SSL is being used?

You can tell it's being used when you visit a website and the "http" in the top of the address of the website changes to "https." The addition of the s indicates that you are viewing and using an SSL equipped website. You may also see a small lock icon in your web browser, indicating that the website you're currently viewing uses SSL security. If you happen to receive email using SSL, you'll know it because you'll have to use an included encryption tool in order to unlock the email.

In fact, you may wonder why physicians, hospitals, and other healthcare organizations don't use email to communicate with you regarding medical information. It's because email is usually unencrypted. In order to preserve patient confidentiality and privacy, medical information should only be sent using an encrypted email, or more often, the message is posted on a website requiring a username and password.

Why is it used?

SSL is used to protect sensitive and confidential information when it's sent from your computer, tablet, or smartphone, to a website. The SSL function takes the numbers and letters you enter and before sending them over the Internet, scrambles them with a unique one-time use encryption key. Locking the data from being read by anyone else. The only other location that knows the key to unlocking the data and unscramble it is the website that is receiving the data. When a website receives the data over the Internet, it unscrambles the information and then uses it to charge your credit card or log you in.

The Heartbleed Bug

On April 7th it was announced that versions of SSL using the open source SSL license (about 2/3 of all websites in the world) had a security flaw that was exploited by the Heartbleed bug. The bug was called Heartbleed because there is a part of the SSL security software that is referred to as the TLS Heartbeat Extension. A heartbeat on a computer software is kind of like a human heartbeat, which is where the name originated. So why do computers need heartbeats?

Heartbeats on computers are used to communicate with each other. A regular heartbeat signal sent from one computer and received by another lets the computers know they are each "OK." If the heartbeat isn't received by a computer that's expecting it, the other computer assumes the first one has "failed," and initiates steps to complete the operation.

Clearly there were some sophisticated people who worked on this bug, and the payoff, since SSL is used for credit cards, username, and passwords, is a big one. By using the SSL information on the website, Heartbleed can hijack a website's information such as usernames, passwords, and credit card information.

Yahoo! reported that their Tumblr service had been compromised by Heartbleed in the past, so the bug has been affecting many websites around the world.

Wait, is there any additional security besides SSL?

Yes, and that's the good news. Many websites that collect private and confidential information use additional layers of security to protect your information. These additional layers do not use the OpenSSL software that is compromised and are still protected. In addition, many websites do not use the OpenSSL software that was affected, and have not been compromised. My website, bobology.com, uses a different version of SSL and is not affected by the Heartbleed bug.

What should you do?

Here's a really easy way to check if a website you use is vulnerable. First, does the website address include an "S" after the http, so it reads "https" in the beginning. Only websites using https in their address might be vulnerable.

Second, I use a password storage locker tool from LastPass which stores all of my website passwords in a highly secure site. LastPass has provided a website where you can enter the address of the website in question, and they will tell you if it was affected by the Heartbleed bug.

Website

You can visit it at https://lastpass.com/heartbleed

To my way of thinking

By the way, I recommend you consider using a password locker like LastPass. By using one highly secure password, LastPass allows you to use a different password for all of your websites and will log you in automatically. So if you use the same password on any website now, you're website security is at risk even without the Heartbleed bug. These password locker tools will store and even create custom passwords, they work in all web browsers, and they have mobile apps. There are free versions, but the paid versions are less than $10 a year.

STEM

STEM Education is an educational initiative that focuses on the integration of science, technology, engineering and math (STEM) in education. The STEM education program uses these disciplines to teach students how to use and communicate critical thinking skills in integrated ways.

STEM isn't only about the subjects, it's an approach to education that addresses a need to make science, technology, engineering, and math a more focused part of our education programs with a goal to prepare students for life and job skills.

The STEM education program includes curriculums for 1st grade through high-school and is being promoted by state departments of education, the National Education Association, and individual school districts and schools. The STEM program was started by Judith A. Ramaley, former director of the NSF's Education and Human Resources division.

How does STEM differ?

Science and Math have always been part of educational curriculums but the rapid introduction of technology into our daily lives along with the need to address engineering and technology as subjects have prompted educators to look at better approaches for integrating these four critical disciplines.

Each of the disciplines has a focus that ties it to the other disciplines, much as science, technology, engineering, and math are connected in the real world. Here's how the different disciplines connect to each other and some of their differences:

Science students use Physical, Life, Earth and Space science skills to understand how the natural world works.

Technology students can use complex computer applications and simulations to manipulate natural resources to meet human needs.

Engineering students understand how engineering design processes are used to develop technologies. They understand how to use math and science applications to help in creating them.

Mathematics students use the language of mathematics to communicate in the other three situations.

Examples of STEM approach

While traditional approaches teach subjects separately with the assumption that students will figure out how to merge and apply what they know of each one to real life situations, STEM attempts to teach students how to pull together what they learn in each discipline and apply the knowledge in an integrated approach using all the knowledge from each discipline. The integrated approach is what makes STEM education different to teaching and learning subjects in isolation.

In a Robotics STEM program, students learn basic science and engineering concepts with a marine theme using an inexpensive kit to build an underwater remotely operated vehicle. Fire protection engineers use computer modeling and highly specialized laboratories to study fire behavior and design innovative approaches to managing fire, building safer structures and fire safety systems and creating effective fire prevention products and best practices.

Two Closely Related Acronyms

In STEAM, the A stands for art, which gives learners a pleasant way to draw connections between and apply math and science through art projects. A variation of STEAM focuses on applied mathematics instead of art. The R in STREAM stands for the additional field of religion added to the STEAM model.

Using a STEM Approach

STEM programs foster the kind of thinking and collaboration necessary to compete in global business, finance, health, and other fields. They help students of any age adopt more integrated perspectives and approaches to solve problems and create future innovations.

Websites

http://www.stemcertificate.org/

http://www.education.com/reference/article/what-stem-education-science-technology/

http://www.delta-education.com/stem/

Stock Photos

A stock photo is a photo purchased from a photo library for use in a graphic design, publication, website or other publication or reproduction. The photo library is usually an online service that maintains a searchable inventory of photos on a variety of topics and subjects. Stock photos save time and cost compared to a custom photo, so they are widely used by web designers, graphic artists, and even individual consumers.

Why use stock photos?

Stock photos fill the need for a photograph in a document or on a website when you can't take your photo. Even though smartphone cameras make taking photos quick and easy, you might need a photo for something and not have one in your personal library. Let's look at an example.

You've got a birthday party coming up, and you want to create an announcement flyer with pictures of a cake. If you happen to have a decorated birthday cake handy, you could take your photo and use that. That seems like a lot of work, unless you enjoy baking and were planning on making a cake anyway. So where do you find a photo of a cake, preferably with the words "Happy Birthday" written on it? The use of a stock photo can help.

Visit any stock photo website (a few that I use are listed at the end of the article) you can search the photo library for a birthday cake. After browsing the available photos of birthday cakes, you select the photo you want to use and purchase it. The photo is then available for you to download to your computer and use in your birthday invitation, whether it's a flyer, email or website.

How does purchasing a stock photo work?

Purchasing a photo on a stock photo website is a lot like using any online shopping cart website. You typically create an account using your email address, enter a credit card and complete your transaction. What you're purchasing is a little different than a product that's shipped to your door.

When you purchase a physical product like shoes or a DVD, you're receiving a physical item, and you own that specific item. When you purchase a stock photo, you are paying for the right to use the stock photo in a particular manner, for example, on a website or in an announcement flyer. You have the right to use the photo for any purpose allowed by the stock photo service, which typically include using the photo on a website or in a printed item like a flyer. You usually have the right to edit and modify the photo and use portions of it for these types of uses.

Using a stock photo gives you the legal right to use the photo according to the terms and conditions of the rights you purchase. Because most purchases include the right to use a stock photo on a website or publication, they are commonly used instead of custom photos. However, unless you purchase the exclusive use of that photo, other customers can purchase the rights to use the same photo. The advantage of a stock photo is that your cost is lower than if you purchased exclusive rights, and your may not need have the exclusive use of that photo.

In my classes students often ask if they can use a photo they see on the Internet on their website and the answer is usually no. Any photo that appears on a web page is part of that website's content and almost always the website owner places a copyright notice on the website which means nothing on the website be duplicated or used anywhere else without permission of the website owner.

Unlike using a photo you might see on a web page or in the results of a web search, a stock photo purchase gives you the right to use that photo.

Other types of purchase options

If you use stock photos often, it's worth looking at the packages and subscriptions that provide discounts since these can lower the cost of each photo you use. You also may have options for what size and quality you purchase.

Some stock photo websites sell photos at one price, with a high-resolution photo that you can edit or modify for whatever use you need. Other stock photo websites make photos available for purchase in different sizes and image detail. It's a better practice to use a photo at the original or reduced size to keep the image quality as high as possible. Stock photo libraries that offer size options give you more flexibility to purchase the maximum size you need to use and not pay more for a larger image.

While using a photo on a website or flyer might be fairly common, some stock photo libraries give customers additional purchasing options to the rights for that photo. An example might be purchasing the photo for exclusive use, which would mean that you purchase all the rights to that photo, and no one else can purchase or use it.

Who supplies these photos?

Typically photos are purchased from freelance photographers who receive a percentage of the fee collected when their photo purchased. Stock photo libraries continually update and purchase fresh photos since customers want to use photos that are unlikely to appear in use elsewhere.

Other stock media

In addition to photos, other types of "stock" media are available for purchase from stock photo and other stock media sites. It's possible to purchase illustrations, videos, and audio. These stock media options can provide you with access to a range of high-quality media that might normally be out of your budget.

To my way of thinking

Stock photos and media give you the ability to access extensive libraries of photos, illustrations, videos and audio media. However, don't rule out custom images or media just because stock images are available.

Websites like Fiverr, Upwork, formerly eLance or Freelancer, offer you the ability to put your image or media requirements out for bid, and you may find some unique media or content available within your budget.

Stock Photo Services:

- iStockphoto
- Fotolia
- Big Stock Photo

Streaming

First of all, let me say that streaming is, basically, broadcasting over the Internet. But as with anything technical, there's always more to it than a simple, one-line definition.

Streaming describes a specific way that video, music, or other media files are delivered to you over the Internet. When "streamed," the video you watch or the music you listen to is sent to you to see or hear while you're connected to the Internet. Without an Internet connection, you cannot view the video or listen to the music. Streaming uses the Internet much like radio or TV uses the airwaves to bring you their content.

So How is Streaming Different from TV or Radio?

To understand the differences, let's look more closely at both of them. When you watch a TV show, the TV is your "player," that is, it plays the television broadcast. The TV also needs a way to receive the broadcast, which would be done through the use of an antenna, cable service, or satellite dish. Radio broadcasts work the same way, using radio waves to transmit the music or audio to your radio. Both television and radio broadcasts come to you by way of transmission over the airwaves, cable, or satellite signal. On the other hand, streaming. to emphasize what we said at the outset, is broadcasting through the Internet.

What Makes Streaming Possible?

The recent development that has brought us this new capability is the introduction of high-speed Internet connections capable of broadcasting media like video and music. Video, music, and other similar information consume enormous portions of Internet capacity because they are larger types of files than things like email or photos. But fast cable, fiber, and other connections have become readily available to nearly everyone, and now that new cellular speeds are so much faster, it's finally possible to broadcast these types of content easily over the Internet.

What You Get, and Don't Get, with Streaming

Simply watching a show on TV or listening to a song on the radio at the time it's broadcast does not result in a tangible copy of it being available to you to watch or listen to later. You experience it in the moment, then it's gone. Streaming, since it's another form of broadcasting, also doesn't result in a copy of the TV show, movie, podcast or song being available to you.

In contrast, downloading creates a copy of the movie, TV show, podcast, music, or audio file on your computer or mobile device. Once you have the content on your device, you can watch or listen to it without the need for an Internet connection, as often as you want, wherever you want. For example, buying a song on iTunes results in a copy of the song being downloaded, by way of the Internet, to your iPhone or iPad; then you can subsequently listen whenever you want without having to connect to the Internet.

How do You Do Streaming?

Streaming is done by going to a streaming Web site on your computer, or by using a mobile streaming app. When streaming on a computer, you'll usually be able to access the content by using the same Web browser you currently use for accessing the Internet, for example, Internet Explorer, Safari, Chrome, or Firefox. Go to the Web site for the streaming service, and you'll have access to the streaming service's content.

Since mobile tablets and smartphones are able to access the Internet, most streaming applications also have mobile apps. Using a mobile app for this service makes it easy to use on common mobile devices like (iPhones, iPads, Kindle Fires, Android smartphones, Android Tablets, and Windows phones.

Free or Paid?

There are both free and paid streaming applications available to you. In most cases, the paid version of a streaming application requires a monthly or yearly subscription fee. There are some streaming applications that offer a free version, sometimes with the possibility of an upgrade to a paid version. Others may be free, but offer to sell you a copy of a song or other media in the app, which you can download to keep for your own use.

A few streaming applications only offer a paid version, and no free content is available. Some types of content, like movies, are a higher price type of content, and expensive to transmit because they are large files, so it's rare to find a free streaming service for them. Music is a little more competitive than movies, so it's more common to find free or free trial services for music streaming. TV shows are kind of a middle ground, and whether you can find a TV show available on streaming for free or paid often depends on the popularity of a particular show or series. Lastly, since the owner of the content controls how it's distributed, certain movies, TV shows, and music may not be available on any streaming service anywhere.

Some Examples of Streaming Services

Music streaming can give you access to a large music library, without the need to purchase individual songs or albums. For example, Pandora, a popular music application for streaming music, plays music from its extensive library of music when you open the app on your computer or smartphone. Remember, you need an Internet connection to play music. Pandora is an example of a streaming application that has both a free and a paid version. The free version is advertising-supported, much like broadcast radio and TV, while the paid version includes more options and is ad-free.

Netflix has both a DVD rental service and a streaming application. Both services require a paid subscription, and there are options for buying them separately or as a mix-and-match service.

Choices Abound

Streaming content is available through many Websites and apps and can expand the variety and use of your Internet experience. I strongly encourage you to explore and take advantage of the ever-expanding opportunities that streaming offers.

Strong Password

Lately, some websites requiring passwords have added a new feature to assess your password strength. As you create your password, a field of text may appear on the screen telling you if your password is weak, adequate or strong. The text might change color from red to yellow to green or even prevent you from creating a password that isn't considered strong.

But what exactly is a strong password and why do you need one? First, let's talk about why you need a strong password. According to Digital ID News, the average Internet user has 25 accounts, but only 6.5 passwords. In such a case, if a hacker can get access to one of your passwords, then that hacker can get into several of your accounts. And the weaker your password, the more likely it is a hacker can figure it out.

Many of us also like to use common passwords. Password expert Joseph Bonneau, in a recent interview with National Public Radio, said many people use "password" as a password or numbers in a sequence, like 123456. Nicknames like "princess" or common terms like "qwerty" get used often, too, making it easy for hackers to simply guess at your password.

A strong password is one that is uncommon and hard to guess. It should include a random combination of upper and lower case letters, numbers and special characters. Also, you should not reuse your passwords for numerous accounts.

Many experts recommend a sort of triage for your passwords. Your bank account should have a unique password with multiple characters in a random combination. A password for a site containing very little personal information won't need to be as strong.

Then, too, you also need to protect your passwords. One reason many of us reuse passwords or make them easy to remember is so that we can remember them. Some experts recommend keeping a password wallet or using a password app to keep track of all your passwords. If you use this, then you only need to remember the one password.

Take stock of your passwords. Are they strong? Will they protect you from hackers? If not, it might be time to give your passwords a workout and improve their strength in order to protect you.

Syncing

The term syncing is short for, and a synonym to, the word synchronizing. Synchronizing in the computer world is the process of matching up two or more copies of information, and updating all of them, so they are identical.

When all of your information is identical wherever you use it, it is in "sync."

Synchronization in the Olympics

If you've ever watched the summer Olympics, (I always try to) you might know two events scored on synchronization, synchronized diving and synchronized swimming. I'm not an Olympic event judge, but I know that higher scores are given for those teams that are better synchronized. This makes sense since the goal of the events is to have identical movement and positions for the team members.

For the diving event, it's two people who dive off a platform matching each other's movements, while for synchronized swimming, it's a team. Perfection is achieved when all the movements and positions are the same. Watching a whole team of swimmers go through their routine of synchronized motions and positions while is a challenge since so many team members are involved, and all of them need to be identical. Now let's move to the world of computers.

Synchronization for Computers

Your computer is an electronic device with some form or storage of information on it, like a hard drive or flash memory. It doesn't matter what the data or information is for our discussion, so it could be a set of contacts, or a list of products, or a document. If there is a copy of that information located on another computer, when one copy is updated or changed, the copies become out of sync, unless there is a way to update the information so it becomes identical again. The swimmers have a coach to help them stay in sync, and your data needs a coach too. The coach is a software program that performs the synchronization. Let's see how this is done.

Software Does the Work

Synchronizing two or more copies of information with each other requires software that can see the changes are on each copy, compare them, then update all the copies contain the same information.

For example, if your computer has a list of contacts with phone numbers, first and last names, and addresses, you might want to use that list of contacts on your smartphone or tablet, or even between a desktop and a laptop, or possible on all of these devices.

One way to synchronize the information is to use a cable to connect each device to the computer, then use software which will "sync" the data and match the two copies. This requires that each device be connected to your computer to do the sync. Here are some common ways you might even have done to sync data.

iTunes is a commonly used desktop software program that has been used with iPod music players for years to synchronize information between computers and iPods.

Adding More Devices for Sync

Just like with synchronized swimming, as you add more devices that you want to keep in sync with each other, the effort to do so can make it more difficult. One way is to connect your smartphone, tablet, MP3 player, and laptop to your main computer and sync each one by using a cable connection. Another way is to copy a file from one computer or device and move it to another using a flash drive. (I still have some floppy drives and Zip drives too).

But with modern mobile devices, data can be moved wirelessly using networks like WiFi and cellular. In order to move and synchronize data wirelessly, you still need to make a wireless connection between each device, so this would be the same as doing it by cable, except wirelessly. But, there is another way.

What a Master Copy Does

If you keep a master copy of your data or information on a computer that is always available on the Internet, then it's possible to use that computer to be your "master" copy of data for all of your devices. When your laptop, desktop, smartphone, or tablet connect to the Internet, each one checks in with the master copy of the information. Your device sends any updates and changes you made on it to the master copy, and the master copy sends any updates and changes it has to your device.

Using a master copy of data and information, and updating and changing it from each device, is one function of the cloud. When using a cloud service, you keep a master of your contacts, email, calendar appointments, photos, documents, files, and other information in one location. It's just that the master copy isn't on your desktop any longer, it's on a computer located on the Internet, or what is called the cloud. Your desktop becomes another copy of the data and information, but the cloud takes care of updating your desktop just as though it were any other device you use for a copy of that information.

T

Touchscreen

A touchscreen is a display surface that can interpret when something (usually a person's finger) touches it's surface. The act of touching the screen produces an electrical signal. This signal can be used just like a press of a key on a keyboard or a click of a mouse button. A touchscreen is different from other touch sensitive surfaces because it also includes a visual display that can display graphics and text.

Touchscreen Basics

Touchscreens have become the standard on smartphones and tablets and are also appearing in many other uses. Touchscreens offer greater versatility in product design by eliminating the need for a keyboard, mouse, and physical buttons. What makes touchscreens so versatile is not only the ability to respond to a touch, but to change the visual display that appears on the touchscreen surface.

If you've ever used a touchscreen device, you are already familiar with the fact that when you make contact with the touchscreen, your device reacts in some way. Your device might dial a phone number, change the visual display to show you new options, make a sound, snap a picture, or send an email. All of these are actions that occur as a result of some contact you made with the touchscreen. Your device's computer and software interpreted the contact you made with the touchscreen. You are using the touchscreen to send commands to your device using what are called "gestures."

Gestures

The software that runs on your device can interpret different ways you make contact with your touchscreen. What do I mean by contact? Human hands a pretty versatile and flexible and there are a couple of ways touchscreen engineers have figured out to take advantage of this. For example, a Tap is a common gesture on all touchscreen devices. It's used to start an app or give a command and it's similar to pressing a button. Did you ever wonder how your device knows it's a Tap? If so, read on.

Touchscreens can interpret where you make contact with the touchscreen. So if a button or command is in a particular position, the touchscreen will know that you are making contact in the location of a specific button. When you tap on a touchscreen keyboard, you are making contact with a specific character that you want to enter. I know that sometimes keyboards seem small on touchscreens, so you tap the wrong character and touchscreens are very sensitive about the position you made contact with it.

Your touchscreen can also interpret the duration of the contact you make with it, along with how many fingers you use, and if you move them while you are making contact with the touchscreen. So when you press your finger on the touchscreen and don't let go, your touchscreen knows that you are doing something different than a tap because of the amount of time you hold your finger on the touchscreen. Move your finger while touching it and you have what's called a "swipe."

All of these gestures are commands, and some gestures include using two fingers to "pinch" or "spread," which is how you can zoom in and out on web pages and maps. The touchscreen and software that interprets the gestures are able to give you a lot of control using just your hands. This eliminates the need for a bulky keyboard and mouse so you can use just the surface of your device to issues your commands. Touchscreens have made mobile computing possible by making smartphones and tablets self-contained devices.

How do they Display Information and Graphics?

Touchscreens are made in several layers of materials, that when manufactured, appear to be one solid surface. Most devices have a top protective layer to prevent scratches and damage. Beneath this is the touch sensing layer and beneath this layer is the display layer. The actual manufacture is much more complex and can include many more layers, but this is the basics.

These layers are all clear, except for the display layer at the bottom which is similar to what's inside the flat LCD (Liquid Crystal Display) computer display screen you might have for your computer. When your device is asleep, the screen display is off and doesn't respond to touchscreen gestures. That's why it's usually necessary to press a real physical button to wake up your device. Once your device is awake, the touchscreen is powered and is able to respond to your gestures.

Smartphone and tablet touchscreens respond to a light touch, but they aren't the only type of touchscreens. There are several types of touchscreens, which we'll learn about next.

Different Types of Touchscreens

There are two general types of touchscreens, ones that respond electrically, and ones that respond to pressure. And there are different touch options for them as well.

The common smartphone and tablet touchscreens respond to an electrical contact, and are called capacitive touch. Because the human body conducts electricity, when a finger makes contact with an electrically sensitive surface, a touchscreen can sense where your finger touched the screen. Capacitive touchscreens are very sensitive to touch and only require a light contact. Capacitive touchscreens don't work with non-conducting materials. This is why a ball-point pen doesn't work, and why there are stylus pens made with with conductive tips.

Capacitive touchscreens for smartphone and tablets are also referred to as "multi-touch." This means that they sense the duration and number of fingers when contact is made. While multi-touch screens respond to the widest variety of touch, there are touchscreens made that respond to a single touch and some that respond to two touch points. These are generally less expensive than the multi-touch type and are used in retail point of sale and industrial applications where multi-touch isn't required for the touchscreen.

The other general type of touchscreen is resistive touch. If you've ever used a card swiper at a checkout register at a retail store or a car GPS screen, you've probably used a resistive touchscreen. These types of screens are made with layers, but a touch occurs when pressure is applied at a point, creating electrical contact between two layers. This is just like pressing a physical button, but the visual display can change, and you can press any button created by the display.

Because resistive touchscreens use pressure, the surface is not the smooth clear glass you see on a capacitive touchscreen, but usually a frosted clear surface. Because resistive touchscreens don't use glass for their surface, they less likely to break or shatter so they are used for retail and other public locations.

What's Next?

Touchscreens have become so widely used for mobile computing devices that other types of technology are starting to use them. Microsoft's Windows 8 was designed from the ground up to work with a touchscreen computer display, with Windows 10 offering the same features. Apple's Magic Mouse, Touchpad, iPhone 6s models, and Apple Watch are touch sensitive devices made to use pressure sensitive gestures to control their computer or laptop. In the future, we'll see more devices using touchscreens that use buttons and keys.

Tweet

A Tweet is a posting made on the social media site called Twitter.

Twitter is a popular online social networking site used for microblogging through the use of Tweets, which are text based messages with a maximum of 140 characters. While registered Twitter users can send and read Tweets, unregistered users can only read them.

To join Twitter, go to twitter.com. You'll need to provide your first and last name, email, and choose a "handle" or username which is used by Twitter to identify you in your Tweets.

Other registered users can respond to Tweets by replying to the original posting. Allowing unregistered users to read a Tweet is part of what makes Twitter such a powerful social media tool. The registered user's message can easily reach hundreds or thousands of people. Tweets range from silly and mundane to profound and powerful, and can carry a lot of weight in today's world of real-time posting.

Why 140 characters?

The text based Tweets are limited to 140 characters because a text message can be sent with up to 160 characters, and the site reserves 20 characters for displaying the user's Twitter account name. Once a user has signed up on Twitter, they can follow the Tweets of people they'd like to hear from, and others can follow the user's original Tweets.

How to say more in 140 characters

It's possible to use the 140 characters for any combination of letters, numbers, and symbols, which allows Tweets to include links to websites in the message. Web services offer the ability to take a long website address and shorten it, like creating a code, so the link to the website can fit into fewer characters. Let's look at an example so you'll be able to recognize a short link.

Here's an example of a newsletter page link for last weeks newsletter on What is a Semiconductor?

http://www.bobology.com/public/What-is-a-Semiconductor.cfm

This link has over 50 characters, which would use up a substantial number of the 140 characters available in a Tweet. Using a service that shortens web addresses, the link to the web page in the Tweet is shortened to dlvr.it/4fk3HR, which is only 15 characters.

By using short web links, users of Twitter can say more in a Tweet than what 140 characters might allow them to say. Adding a web address link in the Tweet leads to more information such as a web page, photo, or video when a user clicks on the link contained in the Tweet. Of course, users can also use a full web address in a Tweet, it's just become a practice to use short ones.

349

Web sites that offer free web address shortening services include: tiny.url, ow.ly, bitly.com, and www.goo.gl (offered by Google) . Just copy and paste a long web address and the sites create a short one for you to use in Tweets, emails, and more.

Why Tweets travel widely

While Tweets are defaulted as public, meaning anyone can view them, there is a privacy setting that allows users to approve all followers and limit the viewing of Tweets to followers only. Users can also choose to "Retweet", or repost someone else's Tweet. These Retweets are usually indicated as such by using the letters RT and the original poster's Twitter account name along with the message.

While the first Tweet was posted on March 21, 2006, its popularity grew exponentially within the age of social media and networking. An estimated 500 million Tweets are sent each day, and roughly 75% of those come from users on a mobile smartphone. That number may seem surprising, but with over 230 million active users each month and many users who post several Tweets each day, it's easy to see how that number is reached. Twitter supports over 35 languages and a whopping 77% of its user accounts are based outside of the United States.

The use of Tweets has changed not only social lives of teens and young adults, but is known for changing the face of political communication. Now everyone from President Obama (with over 25 million followers) to your average citizen can share their opinion of political happenings, and it has created a new era of what is known as citizen journalists. Businesses have even benefited from Twitter through access to target markets via smartphones and the internet.

U

URL

URL stands for uniform resource locator. It's a text string of letters, numbers, and symbols that identifies a webpage, program, document, photo, or other resource found online.

How URLs Work

That didn't help much, right? Let's make it simpler. Imagine that you own a bakery. You want people to buy their bread from your bakery, but they have no idea where it's located. What can you do? Tell them your bakery's address, of course. Whenever they want to visit your bakery, they can just get in a cab and give the address to the driver. In turn, the driver will be the one to find the way and drop them off at their destination.

Now, let's say you have a website called Bobology. This website is out there on the Internet, just waiting to be visited. But aside from you, no one else knows where it is is, so it's in danger of getting lost amid the millions of other websites online. What can you do? Tell people your website's URL, which is http://www.bobology.com. This is what people type in the address bar of the browser they're using.

So in the above scenario, the URL is like the bakery's address, the address bar of the browser is like the cab, and the computer is like the driver. If you imagine it that way, it's easy to see how a URL functions. Interestingly, a URL is sometimes called Web address, which gives our analogy more sense.

A URL has three parts:

1. The URL protocol — These are the letters preceding the characters :// The URL protocol most people are familiar with is http://, which is used for websites. The http stands for HyperTest Transport Protocol, which helps the computers that run Internet understand how to send and receive information.

2. The address itself (or host name) — This is a name that separates a website from all the others. It should be a unique name. For Bobology, it's http://www.bobology.com. The www after the http:// stands for World Wide Web, which is used by the Internet computers to determine that the address is located on the World Wide Web, which is the Internet.

3. The location of the file or resource — A URL can lead to a specific location within a website. For example, the URL http://www.bobology.com/ public/Bobology-Blog-by-Bob-Cohen.cfm goes directly to Bob Cohen's blog within the Bobology website.

Knowing URLs Can Help Your Internet Safety

Knowing a little about how URLs work can help you avoid scams and fraud on the Internet. Sometimes you'll see an email that appears to come from a bank or other organization asking you to update some personal information, with a link to a URL in the text of the message. First of all, no financial organization ever asks for personal or login information in an email. They simply lock you out of your account if something is wrong.

Secondly, these emails, called "phishing" emails, are literally fishing for people who will click on the link in the email and provide the information requested and not bother to check the URL of the website before entering information. The link in the email doesn't take you to the correct website. It takes you to a website that may look like the bank, but isn't the bank's real Web site. To avoid this type of phishing scam, enter the URL you know for your bank or financial institution in your web browser by typing it in.

USB

USB, which stands for universal serial bus, is a component that allows devices to be connected to computers. A desktop or laptop computer, mp3 player and most smartphones feature the female port of a USB. A male USB connector is needed to connect these devices for usage or charging.

What Can You Do with USB?

A USB port on a computer allows you to connect things such as an external hard drive, mouse, or printer to your desktop or laptop. Devices which connect to computers are often referred to as peripherals, because they work with the computer. But USB can be used to connect all types of devices to computers, including cameras, and smartphones, all that's needed is a USB connector on both devices.

USB: Speed and Now More Power

All USB devices use a specific standard that allows them to function at a particular speed. The current standard for USB is 3.0, which offers transmission speeds of up to 5 Gbps. The previous standard, USB 2.0, provided speeds of only 480 Mbps. In addition to the USB connection speed, the standard applies to the size and shape of the USB connectors. USB can also supply power to a device connected to a computer or power adapter. --

Many smartphones and tablets use a charging cable with a USB connector that plugs into a charging adapter for power, and your computer supplies a little power to every device connected to it with USB. In fact, USB battery packs are now available that can even recharge mobile devices and range from small to very large capacity, like the one shown on the right.

In the case of smartphones, the USB technology is the same but the connector may be smaller: many such phones feature a mini USB port and come with cable connectors with mini USB male parts. This is most likely to accommodate the smaller size of a smartphone. It allows you to sync your phone on your computer and, through USB, you can easily add files from your hard drive, such as music and images, to your smartphone.

USB Industry Forum

Devices which use the USB description must meet an industry standard specification that's managed by the USB Implementers Forum, a non-profit corporation founded by a group of companies. The USB Implementers Forum Board of Directors includes representatives from Hewlett-Packard, Microsoft, Intel, and other global technology companies. The purpose of this organization is to support the advancement and adoption of USB technology through education, device testing, and marketing. The benefit to you, the consumer, is an extensive choice of devices which all work together with one common connector. While it's not necessary for a product to be certified as "USB," the USB Implementers Forum does have a formal product certification program. The new "certified" logo, shown below, can only be used by those products which have passed certification testing.

USB Makes Connections Easier

Before USB became a widely adopted industry standard, connecting devices to computers wasn't always easy. I remember a time when I needed a different cable, adapter, and connector for each peripheral I had connected to my computer. Some of you may remember terms like "parallel" cable, DIP switches, and IRQ's. If so, you can see how far we've come in making technology easier with USB, since to add a peripheral now is so easy almost anyone can do it.

Websites

USB Implementers Forum www.usb.org/

Username

A username is an identity created by the user of an account or online service in order to distinguish himself from other users. It can be the user's real name or a fictitious name that he creates. Other terms for username include sign-on name, screenname (screen name) and user nickname. The term originated in the late 1970s.

If you use any online service or Web site such as online banking or shopping, it's pretty common for you to see a screen that says "Enter Your Username." The username is the text that you enter to start the logon process. While it would be helpful if you could use one username for everything you do on the Internet with all of your accounts, sometimes that's not possible because not all Web sites and online services use usernames the same way. By the way, when I say "account," it refers to any Web, Internet, or mobile service that requires you to use a username.

If you're already using several Web sites and online services, you are probably already using several different usernames on the Internet. So of course, you have to figure out how to keep all of your usernames straight, so you enter the right one for the specific Web site you need to access. There's your email login username, your bank, your Apple ID, and maybe dozens more depending on how involved you've become in using online services. By the way, anyone with a Social Security Number can create an online account at any age and view reports on benefits and earnings. Often, if you don't want to wait on the phone for support, receive updates for the software you use, or avoid waiting in line for a "live" office visit, you're probably going to be using an online account with a username.

So why don't all these Web sites and online services use usernames the same way so you could use just one, and is it really a good idea to have one username anyway? First, let's look at what usernames really are used for by a Web site or Internet service.

Usernames Identify a Unique Individual

A username is unique to the user of an account, meaning that two people using an online account service cannot have the same username. Think of an example of two people who sign up for bank accounts at the same bank; under no circumstances will they ever be given the same account number. Similarly, usernames are always unique. If a user tries to create a username that is already being used, the software that runs the online service will not allow it.

Creating a username will generate a unique identity for you when using the services available from an online account. For example, the email service Gmail requires every user to create a username for her account, which also serves as her email address. Many people use their first and last name plus an initial. Because people's names are not unique (John, Mary, etc.) some people use combinations of their names and random numbers to create a username. Examples of usernames include johndoe, jdoe65, jdlovestofish, alwayssunnyinphilly.

Some online services allow you to create multiple accounts. A good example is Amazon, which is a popular shopping site. Amazon allows you to create multiple accounts, and uses your email address as your username. Use a different email address and you can create a new account. This type of approach allows a person to have one account for personal purchases and another for business purchases. Each account is completely separate from the other account, because it's a different username that's used to login for each account.

Ok, so now we know that a username allows an online service to identify a unique person who uses that service.

Why Can't I Use One Username for Everything?

Some Web sites and online services use an email address for your username and some don't. Technically, either approach works, but services that don't use your email address for your username require you to create a new username with letters and numbers. This becomes your username for the service and is what you use to login whenever you use the service. Sometimes the service limits the number of characters you can use for your username and sometimes they may require a minimum number of characters.

This all gets down to the way the people who created the online service. Some services use your email address and a password to logon, while others require you to create a unique username, and won't allow you to use your email. There are a few reasons why there's a difference.

One reason is that some online services identify you with an existing number or member ID. Things like a Social Security number, health care member ID, student ID, credit card number, auto-club membership, and bank account number are already used to identify someone or someone's account. As a result, sometimes a site will ask you to use that for your username. More often though, the service wants to keep your username more secure, and to do that they require you to create a new username that's different from your account, member, or ID number. Your new username is then used to access your online services.

Some services use your email for your username. The combination of your username and password is required to logon. In this case, your email address and your username are the same thing. Since your email address can be seen by anyone who receives an email from you, it's less secure than a separate username. Often, if a Web site or online service requires people to use something other than an email address for a username, it will discourage some users from signing up to use the service. As a result, Social Networking sites like Facebook, and shopping sites like Amazon let you use your email address for your username. Using an email address makes it easier to signup for the service since there are fewer steps to creating an account with the service.

What Happens to Usernames?

When you use a username to access or logon to a service, your Web browser will sometimes ask you if you want to save the username for that Web site. If your personal computer, phone, or tablet isn't used by anyone else, this is generally considered by security experts to be ok.

If you have saved usernames on your computer, anyone who can access your computer will be able to see and use your username. The best protection for this is to use a password for logging on to your computer. While it's not foolproof, it is a deterrent. Think of it like a lock on your home. A locked door isn't going to stop a determined robber from breaking in if they want to, but it will act as a deterrent, making it more difficult than an unlocked door or window.

Sometimes you may use a public computer or borrow someone else's. If you logon to any account and enter your username, your Web browser displays a pop-up message asking you if you want to save your username. If your borrowing anyone's computer or mobile device, always select NO so your username isn't saved. In this case, your password is your last defense.

It's surprising how many people still use the word "password" as their password, and I've included a link here to the newsletter article on passwords for you to learn more about them

V

Venmo

Venmo is a smartphone app that allows you to send and receive money from family and friends. You can easily bill someone, split the check, or send money using Venmo. Signing up and using Venmo is fast and easy, as well as free. Socially connect through newsfeeds on Venmo as well. See who's paying who, leave a comment, and "like" things.

Here are some reasons you might want to consider using Venmo:

- Send and receive money
- Request payments from friends
- Transfer funds from any bank to Venmo balance
- Pay people through Venmo balance or linked personal accounts
- Receive money from friends and send to your Venmo balance or your bank

How it works

Use Venmo to pay someone or request funds from them. The Venmo app is a place where you're able to create a balance of payments received, or you can set it up to send money and transfer funds directly from your bank. Venmo is also a social network with a newsfeed that allows you to see who paid or charged whom, and for what. However, you can change the privacy and sharing settings. Download the Venmo app to your phone. Once you've downloaded Venmo, it's time to get started! Sign up with Facebook, or your email. Then, start by finding friends searching their name or username. You can also invite some friends to join Venmo. Next, link your credit card or bank to your Venmo account.

How to send and request funds using Venmo

Your account needs to be connected to your bank or have a balance of money received to pay someone through Venmo. Send money by clicking on the small box in the upper right-hand corner of the homepage on the Venmo app. Choose a name, username, or phone number of the person you are paying, and add the amount, and a note. Then, finish paying by selecting pay. To request payment, follow the same steps, except select request at the end.

Venmo balance

You can consider your Venmo balance money in your purse. Add money to your Venmo balance through your personal bank, or receive payments to add to your balance. The funds in your Venmo balance can be used soon after getting paid to pay other's in Venmo, or sent to your bank account.

To my way of thinking

There are many uses for Venmo. You can easily add your accounts or debit/credit cards from almost any bank. People you go out with, friends who split the bill, or your roommate might find a good use for the app. It is fast and straightforward to use, and there are no additional charges to send and receive funds.

When you make a payment or request pay from a friend, you can do so straight from the Venmo app on your phone. It's like a virtual "wallet" that allows you to maintain a "balance" of payments received, as well as make a payment using those funds. You can also transfer money from "Venmo balance" to your personal account. Sending money from your bank through Venmo, and receiving payments from friends has never been easier!

Viral Video

Every now and then you will hear that a video went "viral." This term, as with numerous other words in this modern age of technology, has acquired whole new added meanings as it relates to the digital world. In a technological sense, people might presume that viral has something to do with a computer virus. But this is not the case.

When Does a Video Become Viral?

When a video goes viral it has simply become extremely popular. Its exposure on the Internet is growing by leaps and bounds as more and more people discover it and pass it along to other users. An image or an article can also become viral, and the meaning in those cases is the same.

So how many views, or hits, will classify a video, image or article as "viral?" There is no single specific number, but many videos, images or articles deemed to have gone "viral" gain more than a million views in a week or less. The classification is probably assigned more as a result of intensive activity and the rate of growth among users in a relatively short amount of time than of simply how many hits something receives.

How Do Videos Become Viral?

A video that has gone viral will likely be found on a video-hosting website, usually YouTube. Since so many people surf the Internet and enjoy viewing these videos, the news of a funny video travels fast. Some people spread the word by putting links on other websites or in forums, which receive a great deal of traffic. Some people just tell others about it. Those others, of course, will look for it, watch it and pass it along to someone else. Before you know it the page views of this video have skyrocketed, making the video very popular — and very viral.

Virus, Worm, and Trojan Horse

Virus, Worm, or Trojan Horse are terms used to describe different types of malicious software. If the word 'malicious" sounds bad, you're right, and you don't want any of these types of software on your computer.

Virus

A virus is a piece of software that installs itself on your computer and causes harm to your computer and data. With high-speed Internet connections, computers "catch" infections, most often when files are downloaded and as attachments to email. Viruses are created on a regular basis by computer hackers who sometimes use them as a challenge to see if they can get them to work or as a way to take control of a computer for some other purpose. Seldom do hackers have a constructive motive.

Running a current up-to-date anti-virus program will help prevent a virus from being installed by detecting any that appear in a file and sealing off the file to "quarantine" it, thereby sealing that file and preventing the virus from entering and contaminating your computer.

Before downloading any files, no matter what type, make sure you have anti-virus software installed and set to always be running so that it can do its job and protect you and your computer.

Worms

A Worm is another type of malicious software. A worm causes damage by copying itself over and over again to disrupt and eventually disable your computer.

Your anti-virus software typically checks for worms, which are also considered to be a specific type of virus.

Trojan Horse

A "Trojan horse" is named after the Greek legend. In this case, a malicious program is contained within a seemingly legitimate program. Just like in the Greek legend, malicious software is contained inside what looks to be a legitimate file, deceiving you, and potentially deceiving your anti-virus program.

What Can You Do?

Using and keeping your anti-virus software updated is critical for computer security and safety.

Microsoft Windows based computers, because they are the most commonly used, are also the most frequent target for malicious software. Microsoft includes an anti-virus program with the latest version of Windows, Windows 10.

Apple's Mac computers include anti-virus and other security software in the operating system provided by Apple, so no additional software is necessary.

And last, mobile devices like smartphones, tablets, and wearable devices all include software from the manufacturer. All that's necessary for you to do is to update your device's software when the manufacturer provides one.

Voice Recognition

Voice recognition is software that recognizes human speech and interprets the speech so it can be used by a computer. Voice recognition software can transcribe spoken words into text for voice dictation, identify a person from their voice, and use voice commands to perform specific actions on a computer.

Voice recognition software works by using a microphone on a computer or device to listen to someone's speech. Since a microphone converts spoken words into electronic signals, the software can analyze the signals. The voice recognition software then interprets the speech, and the voice recognition software uses the words.

Analyzing someone's voice can use a lot of computing power, but as computers have become smaller, faster, and less expensive, the computing power to do voice recognition is now available in almost every mobile or desktop computing device. In addition to the increased computing power available, the capabilities of voice recognition software have improved, so it has become faster and more accurate.

Depending on the application, a person's speech can be used in a variety of ways by voice recognition software, so let's take a look at some examples.

Applications of Voice Recognition Software

• Smartphones: Today's smartphones accept voice commands from users. You can talk to your smartphone to browse Internet, take notes, order pizza, make phone calls and change music stations. When you see a microphone icon on your keyboard or your screen, it's usually a sign that the application has voice recognition, and you can speak to your smartphone. Apple's SIRI feature uses voice recognition to accept commands for a wide variety of applications.

• Learning New Languages: Voice recognition software helps in learning a second language. The software helps with the pronunciation of new words and practice sentences in a new language.

• Air Traffic Control: Many airlines use voice recognition software to train Air Traffic controllers. The software acts a robotic pilot and helps with the simulation of real life flight traffic controls.

• Automobiles: Many new cars include voice recognition software to initiate hands free phone calls, change radio stations and play music from a connected smartphone.

• Healthcare: Many physicians use voice recognition software to dictate notes and prescriptions and can see their dictation typed, making corrections as they dictate and reducing errors.

• Court Reporting: Court reporters use voice recognition software to record lengthy and complex court proceedings.

Popular Voice Recognition Software

In addition to the built-in capabilities in smartphones and tablets, the latest versions of Apple Mac OSX and Windows 10 come with built-in voice recognition capabilities that accept commands and perform dictation. Many people find that using the built-in capabilities of the operating systems more than adequate for transcribing text and using their voice to issue commands to their computers.

In fact, voice recognition built-in to the operating system gives smartphones, tablets, and computers many accessibility features and can extend the use of these devices to people that need assistance.

For people looking to do more with voice recognition, Dragon's speech recognition software (available for both Windows, Mac, and mobile devices) is the industry leader and offers some additional capabilities which include higher accuracy for speech to text transcribing. One feature is the ability to "train" the software to recognize a person's voice, which increases the speed of transcription and interpretation of commands, since the software enables the creation of custom commands. Dragon's premium packages have the ability to transcribe a pre-recorded audio file and transcribe the text, which is used by many professionals who need extensive transcribing from dictated recordings.

To my way of thinking

Voice recognition is a powerful tool since it gives people the ability to communicate with a digital device using a more natural form of communication, the spoken word.

While it would be ideal if computers knew how each of use spoke, with our individual vocal range, pronunciation, and vocabulary, most competing devices don't our individual characteristics until we give them more information. Keep this need for the software to learn about you in mind when using voice recognition software, as your digital device may be capable of learning how you talk and become better at understanding you when you speak.

VOIP (Voice Over IP)

VOIP, an acronym for "Voice Over Internet Protocol," uses the Internet for telephone service rather than through traditional telephone lines. Voice conversations can be converted to a series of zeros and ones (which make them "digital"). Since the Internet uses digital signals, it's possible to use the Internet to send and receive voice conversations just like any other type of digital information.

Traditional phone calls

When we talk on the phone, a microphone converts our voice to electrical signals, while the speaker converse the electrical signals into a sound so we can hear. People's voices vary in volume and pitch, and the microphones and speakers convert these qualities into an electrical signal called "analog," since it varies continuously. There's another kind of signal that makes VOIP possible, and we'll get to that in a minute. While a microphone creates the signal, the speaker just does the opposite and converts the signal to sound.

Traditional telephone connections transmit and receive these signals over wires and switches that the telephone company owns and operates. When you dial a phone number, the number tells the telephone company how to connect your call and send the conversation. Since telephone companies connect to each other around the world, we have a global telephone network, with both wired telephones and wireless cellular telephones.

Digital voice technology

Unlike the continuous analog signal created from a microphone and speaker, a digital signal is made up of zeros and ones. An electrical circuit called an analog-to-digital converter takes the voice signal from the microphone and converts it into zeros and ones. A digital-to-analog converter does the opposite at the speaker end, converting the zeros and ones into an analog signal that a speaker can play.

Two things had to happen to make it possible to send and receive a live voice conversation using digital signals instead of analog. The quality and speed of converting the signals had to be comparable to traditional phone conversation, and the speed of the network had to be fast enough to send and receive the two sides of a conversation fast enough.

Improvements in electronics made the first part possible, so now we even have a small analog to digital converter in cellular phones. Faster Internet speeds made the communications side of this possible, and new devices made it possible to connect any phone to the Internet.

Connecting phones to the Internet

In order to connect a phone to the Internet, the phone needs have the capability to connect to the Internet, usually using an ethernet cable. VOIP phones have a built-in ethernet connection which connects to your home or office network, and for existing phones, there are converter boxes that have a standard telephone connector on one side, and an ethernet connector on the other. These adapters allow people to use their existing telephone equipment on the Internet.

Once your phone is connected to the Internet, a service is required which will connect your phone number back to the telephone network. Providing this service is where VOIP service companies come in, such as Vonage and Ooma, which provide connections from the Internet to the telephone networks around the world.

By using a VOIP service, the long-distance part of a phone call can be sent over the Internet, at a very low cost, and the phone call is only connected back to the local phone network in a location where the other number is located.

Saving money and increased options

As a result, VOIP can drastically reduce the cost of long-distance calls along with other types of calls that have traditionally been charged based on things like call-zones and minutes. VOIP has allowed many companies to enter the business of providing telephone service including cable television providers and VOIP services like Vonage and Ooma.

VOIP has become increasingly higher in demand in the past few years as it is much lower in cost than traditional telephone networks. Having a VOIP telephone line means that the user can place and answer phone calls through the Internet rather than rely on the telephone company provided line. Those who choose to have a VOIP service usually switch because of the low costs and high efficiency.

Some advantages of VOIP

In addition to the lower cost of VOIP phone service compared to traditional phone service, most VOIP services include additional capabilities that allow you to manage your phone using a web portal that the VOIP service provides as part of the service.

Using the provider's portal it's often possible to setup things that were previously an added cost or difficult to manage such as call forwarding, call blocking, and sending voice messages to an email address.

Business use of VOIP

The majority of large businesses now use VOIP telephone services because of the cost savings and often use their private computer network rather than the public Internet, but it's still VOIP since the phone call is being sent using the "Internet Protocol."

The services like Vonage and Ooma cater to home and small businesses and offer services which include multiple phone lines, fax, call routing menus and call recording (useful for customer service to keep records). If you have a larger organization, there are specialized VOIP service providers that handle converting and installing larger telephone installations.

If you run a business and haven't looked at the savings VOIP can provide, I definitely recommend it.

What about traditional phone service?

Most phone companies have stopped installing traditional telephone lines. In the past, these were dedicated wires (two for each phone line) that needed to be run to each residence or building for each phone. Office buildings are full of telephone cables that aren't used any longer as businesses have switched over to VOIP.

But in your home, you may think you have a traditional phone line, but it may, in fact, already be using VOIP run by the phone company. When Verizon started installing FIOS connections to their customers, they started disconnecting the old telephone wires wherever they installed FIOS and moved the telephone signals over to their digital FIOS network.

Cable companies that offer telephone service use VOIP, which is what allows then to connect your existing phones to the cable connection. While traditional phone companies don't put a VOIP converter box in your home, they do the conversion in their offices, so you don't need any converter box like Vonage or Ooma, but after they convert the analog signal to digital, it's a VOIP call just the same.

Phone Options and Porting

With the abundance of cellular phones, many people simply don't use a traditional telephone "land line" any longer and use their cell phone number for everything.

While services like Skype and FaceTime allow phone and video conversations, they aren't technically considered VOIP since they don't require a telephone number, but Skype has a low-cost plan that will give you a real phone number to use.

If you use a land-line, and want to keep the number and save money, consider the option of "porting" it to a VOIP service. Most VOIP services will let you move your existing phone number to their service for a small one-time fee.

To my way of thinking

With all the changes in pricing and costs, one issue that often gets lost is the value of support. If you have a land-line and cellular phone, your cellular service provider probably gives you better support than your land-line service company, so land-line support may bot be an issue. However, if you think you want 24-hour service by phone, expect to pay more for this with any phone service, which could be a reason for staying with your current phone company.

VPN (Virtual Private Network)

If you've wanted a way to use the Internet privately, so no one else can see what websites you visit, what's in your emails, or what you chat about with friends, a Virtual Private Network (VPN) can be a potential solution. A VPN creates a private, secure communications channel on a public network like the Internet. VPN's use software to establish a private, secure connection between computers. Like a private conversation, on a VPN no one can listen in on what you're saying, or in the case of computers, sending, to each other.

Basics of VPN's

The VPN software installed on your computer "scrambles" the data before it's sent out over the Internet. This scrambling is also called encryption, which makes it impossible for anyone to read or view the data. The receiving computer uses the VPN software to "decrypt" or unscramble the data so it can be opened by any software program on the receiving computer. VPN's create what's commonly called a tunnel on the public Internet.

Imagine cars are pieces of data that are moving along a road that connects one town to another. The road is open, and all the cars are visible from anyone standing on the side of the road or looking at them from above. Essentially, all the cars are public, as is the data that is traveling on the Internet.

Now imagine that someone adds a private lane on the road that hides the cars in that lane, similar to how a tunnel would conceal the cars traveling in a tunnel. There's the public pavement which anyone can see, and the private concealed one, which is similar to how a VPN uses the Internet to make data private.

Your home or office connection connects your computer to the Internet, which is a public network. You're using all of the publicly available cables that make up the Internet whenever you send or receive any information. But let's say you wanted a private connection with one person, for example, a family member.

Imagine if you could use a separate cable to connect you to your family member. You'd completely bypass the public Internet with your wired personal connection. But the problem for you and me is that it's expensive to string cables between buildings, much less cities. It's possible, however, and some large organizations do have their own cables, such as Google and government agencies.

But if you could use the existing cables of the public Internet, and create a private channel for communications, that would give you privacy, without the cost of your own wires. That's what VPN software does; it gives anyone who uses it the ability create a tunnel without the need for a physical connection, which makes the connection a "virtual" one.

What do you need to create a VPN

To create a VPN connection you'll need VPN software, and there are software solutions for consumers and businesses and organizations. Organizations use VPN's as a way for employees to communicate securely with company computers using the Internet, as in the case of a home office or employees that use laptops while they are out in the field. By using a VPN, the home or mobile worker can use commonly available Internet connections to establish a secure connection that keeps company communications private.

Consumers can use VPN's to create secure connections to the Internet. A consumer VPN uses a VPN service. The VPN service supplies the software or app you install on your computer. When you connect to the Internet, all of your communication is private and encrypted. They forward and receive the data to and from the public side, and make it private when sending it to or from you so only the identity of the VPN service is visible and not you.

To keep the communications secure and private, VPN's use a piece of information called a key to lock and unlock the encrypted information. When you start the VPN software on your computer, the software connects to the other end of the VPN to establish the secure link. The VPN software creates a unique key that is known only to the two computers that are communicating with each other. The key is added to all messages, then the data is encrypted and sent. The receiving computer uses it's key to unlock and decrypt the data. Only the sender and recipient can view the data whether it's an email message or a file.

Should I think about using a VPN?

If you're an organization, using a VPN gives you a private network while being able to take advantage of all of the public Internet access points and WiFi connections. It's like running a dedicated cable whenever you want to connect to any computer on the company or organization network.

For personal users using a VPN isn't as critical and is more a matter of the expense of subscribing to a VPN service, which charges monthly fees. If you want private communications, I've included some links to listings that rate VPN services. The reason individuals may not need a VPN is that there are other ways to encrypt data and create private communications. Health information is one area where privacy is important, and personal health data is protected by Health Insurance Portability and Accountably Act (HIPPA). HIPPA requires that all personal health information be kept confidential and secure. HIPPA is one reason medical services can't use email to communicate with patients.

An alternative solution exists in the case of HIPPA however, and that's a secure website. By using a secure website that requires a user to log in, the medical provider can provide medical information, such as a prescription history, on a site that requires a user to login with a username and password. Online banking is another example or secure communications using the Web.

In the case of online banking, banks, and financial institutions use what's commonly called a "secure" website. All web browsers have the ability to encrypt data when connected to a secure page, and you'll know you're connection is secure if you see a lock icon in your web browser or the web address in your browser begins with HTTPS instead of HTTP. The S indicates that the website is encrypting your communications and secure.

To my way of thinking

For an organization or for individuals that deal with sensitive information and want to keep their use of the Internet private and secure, a VPN offers a useful solution to obtain a high degree of privacy, security, and confidentiality. However, for the average person, the everyday tools to secure websites and private user accounts are usually more than adequate for you to use the Internet safely, so I don't recommend a VPN very often and you probably will never need one.

Websites

http://www.pcmag.com/article2/0,2817,2390381,00.asp

http://thesweetsetup.com/apps/best-vpn-solution-ios-os-x/

W

Wearable Technology

Wearable technology describes any type of device that you wear on your person and has the capability to communicate with some other technology, like a smartphone or computer.

As electronic devices become smaller and more portable, their capabilities are being placed in smaller physical packages that can be worn as easily as a watch, a pair of glasses, or a belt. The size and shape of the devices varies widely, but many on the market today are commonly made as a band that attach to a wrist, and might be called a smartwatch.

The advances in miniature electronics technology are making possible many smaller and more powerful devices, so manufacturers are designing and manufacturing more types of devices, and the broader and more general term, "wearable technology" is being used to describe this family of devices.

Using miniature electronic sensors, compact and lightweight wearable technology devices are capable of measuring movement, pulse, heart rate, temperature, and more. Using miniature wireless communications technology, usually Bluetooth, these wearable devices can send this information to another, more powerful device such as a smartphone, or store the data they collect to be transferred later.

Fitness Trackers

Other, more common wearable technology devices include sensors from brands such as Fitbit, Polar, or Nike+ activity tracker bands or clip on devices, or as low-tech as a simple pedometer. These devices are designed to be small and discreet, and can be slipped into a pocket, clipped onto a belt or bra, placed in a shoe, or worn on the wrist.

A basic pedometer, or step counter, contains an internal ball or other object that moves up and down with the person's movement and counts steps based on how much the body shakes. The shaking or movement of this internal ball signals a switch that causes the counter to click forward. Pedometers were first used in Japan during the mid-1960s to promote physical activity. Today they are a popular way to begin a physical fitness program and studies show that people who wear pedometers take more steps per day than those who set a goal to take a brisk, 30-minute walk each day. Step counters can be purchased as individual devices, though most smartphones now contain a similar device as a part of their hardware design.

Digital devices, like the Fitbit, Nike+, or Polar activity trackers, use more advanced programming to gauge a person's movement. They not only keep track of the daily number of steps taken, but can also be used to monitor stairs climbed, distance, calories burned, heart rate and overall activity level through the use of more complex motion sensors and altimeter technology. These high-tech devices can also be utilized to measure how well and how long a person sleeps. This information is logged wirelessly and can be accessed through a website or smartphone app. The user can access these logs to view quantitative data and comprehensive graphs that detail the results. Being able to view this information in real time gives users the ability to take their physical fitness tracking further than the basic pedometer has allowed.

More Advanced Types of Wearable Technology

Wearable technology also includes more expensive and versatile products such as Apple Watch, Google Glass or Samsung Galaxy Gear smartwatch, all of which offer software developers the ability to create custom applications. These devices include displays, cameras, touch sensors, and other features that were only available a short time ago only in smartphones.

In addition to all the buzz about consumer-focused wearable technology, commercial and medical uses of wearable technology are expanding rapidly. Companies are using smartglasses that display repair manuals, giving technicians the ability to have both hands free and pull up any documentation necessary when performing a task.

The Future of Wearable Technology

While people wouldn't necessarily want to walk around wearing a computer, people have been wearing technology for a long time, so wearing accessories isn't anything new. It's just that the accessories are changing with technology. Walking around with earbuds or headphones wasn't that common even a few years ago, and today, earbuds and headphones are a style accessory.

Since glasses and watches are two commonly worn accessories, both of which are socially acceptable, expect to see more advances in these two areas of wearable technology as manufacturers look for the right fit of price, style, and function that the consumer finds appealing. However, be prepared for some surprises that no one will be able to predict, including me!

Web Browser

The term "Web Browser" is used to describe a software application used for the purpose of viewing webpages from the World Wide Web. A web browser retrieves information such as text, photos, music, and videos and is the software that requests the information using the Internet. Once it has retrieved the information, a web browser will display it in a user-friendly form.

Why do you need a web browser?

All webpages are computer files that contain the images, text, and formatting of a webpage. When used on the World Wide Web, this information is included in an HTML file which stands for Hyper Text Markup Language. Your web browser is the application your computer or device uses to open and display an html file. Just like your word processor software opens a document file, it's your web browser that your computer or device uses to open an html file. Because HTML has standards set by the World Wide Web Consortium, HTML files can be opened and displayed properly by virtually any web browser.

Web addresses

In addition to locating and displaying a variety of information, a web browser can help a user navigate to various locations on the Web, using something called a Uniform Resource Locator or URL. The URL is the equivalent of a street address when sending someone a letter. It describes all the information needed for the web browser to locate a specific website and take you there and would display the information posted at that "address".

Types of web browsers

There are a number of web browsers available, and each has its fans and detractors. The most commonly-used browsers these days are Microsoft's Internet Explore , Mozilla'sFirefox, Google's Chrome, and Apple's Safari. Many of the functions in a web browser are the same across all web browsers since they all use the technology standards set by the Internet and World Wide Web.

World Wide Web consortium

An international standards organization called the World Wide Web Consortium http://www.w3.org/Consortium/ sets the standards for web technology. All of the companies mentioned above that build web browser software participate in this organization, led by Tim Berners-Lee, who invented the World Wide Web in 1989. Because we have technology standards, consumers and users of the web have many choices for a technology solution.

Common functions and features of web browsers

Although they are each different, they do have certain basic features in common. Their user interfaces all include a "Main Window" to view web content, "Forward" and "Back" buttons that allow you to view a previous web page, then move ahead. They each have an "Address Bar" where you can enter URL information in order to navigate to another website.

Most browsers include a "Search Bar" where you can enter a topic on which you would like more information. The search term is linked to a search engine and will return a list of websites that contain information on the topic you entered.

In addition to presenting information, a web browser will help you navigate to websites for other uses and applications. Webmail, social networks, ecommerce and the "cloud" are all resources typically available by using a web browser.

To my way of thinking

You might not have realized it, but your web browser is one of the most frequently used software applications on your computer or device. Whenever you "click" or "tap" to open a webpage or enter a web address, you're using your web browser application. If you think about how you use your technology, chances are that your web browser is one of your most valuable software applications, and it's usually included on any computer or device for free.

Webinar

A webinar is a seminar that takes place on the Web instead of in a physical location. A person can attend a webinar using their computer to listen and see documents displayed by the webinar presenter on their computer. Webinars are usually run by people or organizations and users are invited to attend by the webinar presenter.

Seminars versus Webinars

Seminars have been a common way of communication for some time. They are an effective way of communicating information to a group of people, instead of one person at at time. A seminar is generally a way to communicate information, not a work of fiction like a play or concert, although seminars often include performances to liven them up between presenters. One thing all seminars have in common is at least one person presenting information to a group of people.

As long as you can get information from one person to a group, The Web seems like a pretty good place to hold a seminar and webinar software has been developed just for that purpose. By using webinar software, a presenter is able to make a presentation from their computer to a group of people, who attend the webinar using their computers.

Webinar Services

To hold a webinar, the person or organization holding the webinar uses webinar software, usually from a webinar service company. The webinar service takes care of the technical side of sending one person's voice and computer screen, so all the attendees hear and see the presenter's material. The presenter can control what's displayed on all the attendees screens, so everyone sees the same information.

There are several companies who offer webinar services and some common ones are listed at the end of the article), and all the services have a few features in common. These features are an account with a webinar service for inviting and registering attendees, an audio conference capability, and a screen sharing capability.

Holding and Joining a Webinar

Webinar services provide the presenter with an account on their service for managing the webinar. Usually these accounts involve a fee, either one-time, monthly, or annual, and the pricing is based on how many people will attend the webinar. Using their account, the presenter is able to setup a date and time for the webinar. The presenter then invites attendees from the service, which sends out an email to the invitees. Invitees receive an email with a link to the webinar Web site, along with any username or passwords required.

When the time and date for the webinar comes around, the attendees join the webinar with a click on the Web link. Some webinars can be joined by invitation, others may require registration, it's very similar to a physical seminar registration only you'll attend over the Web and not at a physical location.

Audio Conference

Webinar services provide a way for attendees and the presenter to talk and listen to each other using an audio conference. You might have attended an audio conference, but if you haven't an audio conference is where multiple people can listen and speak to each other. Audio conferences can be the "classic" conference call set up with a phone and three-way calling, but when more people are attending, audio conferencing services are used.

Using an audio conferencing service an attendee dials in to a phone number (often toll-free) and uses a code, usually a few digits, to join the conference call. After entering their code, the attendee is connected to the conference call. Audio conferencing can be done independently of a webinar if there's no need to present any visual material.

Using an audio conference service gives the presenter the ability to control who on the conference can talk and who can listen. This is very useful to avoid noise when the presenter is speaking.

Almost all webinar services provide a way for attendees to dial-in using a standard phone. Many provide a way for an attendee to use their computer's microphone and speaker instead of using their phone.

Screen Sharing

Without screen sharing, webinars probably wouldn't exist. Screen sharing allows the presenter to share whatever is displayed on their computer screen with everyone attending the webinar. The webinar service uses it's software to take the display of the presenter's computer and broadcast it to everyone.

Using screen sharing, a presenter can bring up a document, presentation, and even draw on their computer screen, and all the attendees see the same documents, presentation, or drawings displayed on their computer screen.

By using screen sharing with audio conferencing, a presenter knows that everyone is seeing the same display and hearing the same words.

Some webinar services allow screen sharing to be passed around to different attendees. By using this feature, the presenter can invite attendees to draw on the presenter's computer screen just as though they were sitting next to the presenter. Passing around screen sharing also allows a webinar to have more than one presenter, with each presenter taking turns, just like a live seminar.

Why Use Webinars?

Webinars can save on travel expenses. Rather than having people travel to one location, people can attend over the Internet from their own location. This saves on travel costs. As a result of those cost savings, businesses have been heavy users of webinars for internal meetings and training. By using a webinar instead or paying for people to travel to a location, a business can save significantly on travel costs. But there are some other benefits of webinars.

Webinars make it easier for a presenter to share information to larger groups, without the need to worry about the size of a meeting room. Some webinar services are capable of holding webinars for thousands of attendees.

If you've ever missed a seminar, you know that they are seldom recorded. So if you don't attend, you don't get the information. You have to reschedule if it's even possible, or miss out. A webinar, however, can be recorded for playback at a later time by anyone who missed it or who wants to review the material. Most webinar services offer an option for the presenter to record the webinar so any invitee can click on the webinar link in the email and watch the recording. This often involves an additional fee, so not all webinars are recorded, it depends on the presenter and how they set up the webinar.

Some Additional Webinar Features

In addition to the audio conferencing, screen sharing, registration, and recording features, there are some other interesting webinar features that are available now.

Many webinar services offer video conferencing. The presenter and attendees can not only hear each other but see each other from a webcam (provided their computer is equipped with one). Usually there's an option to turn off the webcam feature if you don't want people to see you on their screens.

If you're wondering if it's possible to raise your hand in a webinar, it is. Some webinar services offer a chat tool where attendees can ask the presenter, or everyone, a question. The presenter sees that a question has come in from an attendee and can handle it just as though it was a live seminar. A common practice is for presenters to pause and invite questions at the end of a webinar, so your question may not get answered right away, and it depends on the volume of questions.

Mobile Webinars

With so many mobile users, many webinar services offer an app for tablets and smartphones. The apps are almost always free for attendees to use so they can attend a webinar from their mobile device, using the microphone and speakers or a headset for the audio. Some webinar services will work with the Web browser on a mobile device, but usually an app is required. Each webinar service uses their own mobile app. You'll need to install the app made by the specific webinar service company used by the presenter in order to attend on a mobile device. Some apps also allow the presenter to make presentations from their mobile device.

Drawbacks to Webinars

While webinars save money, allow for flexible attendance with recording, and can handle large groups without a meeting room, there are times when a live seminar is a better solution for communication.

A webinar doesn't give the presenter the ability to see the attendees and their reactions. Good presenters watch to see if attendees are paying attention and understand the information being presented. Webinar services have some tools that are used for this but they are not always effective and are not used often by presenters.

Attendees don't get the social experience of attending a live event. If location based events were dead, we still wouldn't have music concerts and art exhibitions, so this is not a generational issue. And people have different learning styles when absorbing new information and attending a webinar may not be the most productive for their style of learning.

Regardless of your own preferences, don't avoid a webinar if you see something worthwhile available by attending one. You might not get the first one, but the more you attend the more it will feel comfortable and familiar.

Webmail

Webmail is a type of email account which allows you to access your email from any computer or device with a Web browser and an Internet connection. The convenience of Webmail allows you to access and use your email from almost anywhere, even using someone else's computer and Internet connection. As long as you can open up a Web browser and reach the Internet, you can use a Webmail account.

Why is webmail so popular?

Webmail accounts don't require you to install or use an email application software such as Microsoft Outlook on your computer. You can read, send, reply, forward, organize your email into folders and save attachments.

The webmail service stores of all of your email on their computers and storage systems, and gives you a web page to use for accessing your email account. You login to your webmail account from the webmail service's web page using your email address and password.

What are some popular webmail services?

You might already have a webmail account, and common webmail providers include Google's Gmail, AOL Mail, Microsoft's Hotmail/Live/Outlook.com, Yahoo! Mail, and Apple's iCloud email. Many of the webmail services that are offered on the Internet are free but can include ads that display on the screen. An upgrade to a paid email plans will remove the ads.

Your Internet service provider may also provide you with access to webmail when you subscribe to their service so your existing email account may already be webmail capable. You might have to check with them to see if your account can be used as a webmail account, or, you may be able to change your account to a webmail account and keep the same email address.

Access from anywhere

One of the biggest advantages of webmail is that you can access it from anywhere with almost any device that can connect to the Internet. You don't need to carry your laptop with you just to check your email. Instead, you could check your webmail from your smartphone or even from an Internet café or public library. All your emails are stored on the providers' servers until you choose to delete them.

For those who do not regularly check their email on the same computer, do not have a computer or who frequently travel, webmail is a good option to access their email on public computers. Most webmail systems so you only need you to go to the provider's website, and then enter your username and password to access your account.

Are all webmail accounts the same?

Often webmail accounts are referred to as IMAP accounts, and while most webmail accounts use IMAP, not all IMAP accounts can be used with a Web browser. IMAP stands for Internet Message Access Protocol, which is a type of email account service. Many webmail accounts use this type of email protocol, which keeps a master copy of all email on the email service's computers. Webmail is the ability to access any email account using a Web browser, regardless of the type of software running the email service.

Microsoft Exchange is a common mail application used in business and government, but it's not IMAP. However, Microsoft Exchange does have a webmail option, called Outlook Web Access or OWA. I use Microsoft Exchange and pay for a single-user account, and I can use it with Microsoft Outlook on my desktops, the built-in email applications on my smartphones and tablets, and access it on the Web through any Web browser. I don't know of a free Microsoft Exchange email service, but you receive an Exchange email account with a subscription to Office 365, a paid service from Microsoft, which includes Microsoft Office applications.

Using webmail with computers and smartphones

While webmail works with a Web browser, it's also possible to setup your email account with a smartphone using an app or on a computer using a local application. Why would you do this you might ask since the point of webmail is to use it on the Web, right?

Sometimes the apps and applications included with smartphones and computers are designed to make using email easier and faster, and sometimes they add additional capabilities. For example, the Mail app provided on Apple iPhones, iPads, and the Mail app provided on Android phones are all designed to work with touch gestures.

While you could use your webmail account using the Web browser on your device, you would need to navigate around the screen using mouse clicks and keyboard commands designed for when you use a desktop or laptop. When you use your email account with the built-in apps on a smartphone or tablet, your email experience is optimized for a touch-screen device.

Whether it's a Microsoft Windows model or an Apple Mac, the built-in email application provides additional features and functions, and the built-in email applications usually work more like other applications on the computer, which can make them easier to use for many people.

For both smartphones and computers, using the built-in email application on the device with your webmail account lets you store a local copy of your email, so you can read and write emails while you're not connected to the Internet. When you connect to the Internet again, your new email messages will arrive in your Inbox, and your pending messages will be sent to their recipient.

One other advantage of using webmail with more than one device is that your email and folders stay up to date on all of your devices since a master copy is kept by the webmail service. Each device checks in and sends and receives updates whenever the device is connected to the Internet.

Are there any disadvantages?

If you only use webmail using a Web browser, in order to access your email to view or create an email, you must be connected to the Internet. Your email will not be saved locally on your computer. This means would also be unable to review your email later unless you have access to the Internet. Since Internet access is available with smartphones almost everywhere, this might not be a disadvantage unless you travel to places where cellular reception or WiFi access is not available.

Webmail users may miss some of the features that may be in the local email application software used on smartphones and computers. Users may be subjected to ads that are included by the webmail service with their emails, in addition to having to deal with the service's spam-filters that may be too efficient and mark some emails from people you know as spam.

To my way of thinking

Since virtually every type of smartphone and computer has an email application that is capable of connecting with a webmail account, and since webmail accounts are free, there's no reason not to be using a webmail account for your email.

Your email messages are stored, backed up, and you can keep your email up-to-date on all of your devices. As mobile computing is becoming the new normal, being able to use email anywhere, any time is a convenience you shouldn't be missing.

Webmaster

A webmaster is a person responsible for the management and operation of a website. As you use the Internet, you might come across this term when viewing a website and see an opportunity to contact the "webmaster" of the site. It's a real person, not a machine, that is responsible for making sure the site runs smoothly and is available on the Internet.

So what exactly does a webmaster do?

Responsibilities of a webmaster

The person who is assigned the role of a website's webmaster has complete control over the software that runs the site and the day-to-day management. Virtually all software has a role called the "administrator," which is the person who has complete control over the software, a webmaster is sometimes referred to as the administrator of a website.

For a small site, the webmaster is probably the same person who creates the content, answers the emails, makes changes to web pages, and pays any costs for the website. So if you're an individual or small business owner that runs your site, you are also the webmaster for that site.

Since the webmaster has to know how to run web software, it's common for a webmaster to have the skills to create and develop a website or perform web programming. But the skills and education background required to be a webmaster vary depending on the size and operating complexity of a website. For example, the webmaster of the Target store website has a much more complex job than the webmaster of bobology.com.

Responsibilities

Webmasters are expected to know how to manage the software that runs the website. It doesn't mean they have to know how to write programs, but a webmaster usually has some knowledge and expertise in HyperText Markup Language (HTML) which is used to format and layout web page content. There are some primary responsibilities for running a website so let's look them.

- Build or assist in the development of a website
- Install and verify the operation of any additional software for the site
- Manage the addition, change, or removal of any pages or content
- Create accounts for any users
- Verify the operation of the website
- Setup and manage security
- Manage the computer or computers that the website operates on
- Work with any vendors responsible for services
- Handle any incoming emails to the webmaster

The role of a webmaster may include additional responsibilities depending on the role and background of the person in that role. Some webmasters who know programming perform software development for the site while others who know graphic design take on layout and design roles.

Some webmasters are skilled in web marketing and conduct email marketing activities, social media and search engine marketing for the site. Still others take on managing any database software that is required to run the site. So the role and skill sets for an individual who's a webmaster can vary, and can become very specialized in large organizations who have a team of people running their site operations.

Education and jobs

Webmasters have a range of background and skill sets, so skills for any job might vary from organization to organization. Educational backgrounds vary as well and while there are job postings for webmasters, the skills required are most likely different from one job opening to the next. Some webmaster jobs require programming expertise while others require Internet marketing experience. Technical knowledge of the web is, however, a common skill set across all webmaster job openings. While there aren't many formal training programs for becoming a webmaster, knowledge of website software applications is valuable. Some of the more common website applications are WordPress, Drupal, Joomla, and Microsoft IIS.

To my way of thinking

If you run and manage your website now, you're the site's webmaster. Many personal and small business website solutions make it easy for you to operate a site with features and functions that are equal to many larger ones. For personal and small business use, I always recommend Google's Blogger solution. It's simple, free, and easy to learn and I cover it in my Blogging for Fun and Profit class and the companion workbook.

Once you learn how to run one website, learning how to run others becomes easier, and many features will be similar and familiar. Many webmasters are self-taught, and learned on their own, using their sites to demonstrate their skills for a job or even to run a web-based business. For others, an education in programming and software development has led them to a career in managing larger websites, since every organization is on the Internet today.

What's App

What's App is an instant messaging app for smartphones that allows users to send and receive messages without the need for a cellular company text messaging service and fees. Instead of using your cellular text messaging plan, What's App uses your Internet connection to transmit and receive messages.

What's App was in the news recently because Facebook agreed to pay $19 Billion, yep, that's right, billion, for the company. So here's how What's App works and what it does.

What What's App Does

What's App allows subscribers to send text messages, videos, pictures, voice messages, and share their location with other What's App users. It's called a cross-platform design because the app works on different brands of smartphones, iPhone, Android, Blackberry, Windows, and Nokia.

How to Start Using What's App

What's App is free to use for the first year, then 99 cents a year for continued use of the app on your smartphone when the free year is up. After downloading the app from an app store to your smartphone, you're prompted to create a username and subscribe to the service. Then What's App scans your contact list to see if any of your contacts are already What's App users, and if they are, automatically adds those contacts to your personal What's App contact list.

What's App History

Developed in 2009 by Brian Aston and Jan Koum, What's App grew quickly to over 200 million active users by February of 2013. Facebook acquired What's App in February of 2014 for the hefty sum of nineteen billion dollars. This acquisition is considered the largest purchase of a venture capitalist backed company ever seen in the business world. Due to Facebook's loose privacy policies, What's App actually lost many users after it was purchased by Facebook.

However, they also gained many users thanks to the media attention in places where What's App was not as well known. Shortly after the announcement of Facebook's acquisition of What's App users experienced a loss of service, which led to outrage throughout the world of social media.

Why What's App is Popular

In spite of the problems and questionable violations of privacy, What's App has allowed its users to stop paying their phone carrier for SMS service. Users pay What's App one dollar for a year of service, whereas most cell phone carriers charge around five dollars per month or more for a text messaging service.

What's App also adds some useful features that don't exist in cellular texting, like a distribution list, group chat, customization tools, and adding a location to a message.

Since most phone carriers charge higher rates for international messaging, What's App is a great way for people who travel or have family abroad to save money.

If you run a Social Networking company, say like Facebook, or a search website like Google, your biggest asset is the ability to continue to attract people to use your services so you can display advertising. Think of it like a television station that has to compete for ratings, and the prices they are willing to pay for the broadcast rights to major events like the Superbowl, the Olympics, or the World Series. These are events that attract millions of people and allow the TV station to make money from advertising.

Now think of what would happen to a TV station if a competitor won the broadcast rights to any of the events I mentioned above. The winning TV station not only gets the money from the advertisers, they also have the ability to run promotions for their own new shows during the event.

Keeping people tuned to your station is the idea, and if Facebook had let What's App fall into a

competitor's hands, then the competitor would have access to all the millions of What's App users, and while Facebook might not want to send them ads in What's App, Facebook can reach these users and connect them to their Facebook friends, and they have the time to figure out how to make more money with What's App without worrying about competitor buying the app.

Does this make a lot of sense to everyone? Maybe not, but if you look at all the people with smartphones in their hands and it kind of makes sense to have an app you own that so many people use every day.

WiFi

WiFi commonly refers to a wireless connection to the Internet. A WiFi connection to the Internet uses a wireless signal to transmit and receive Internet data between one or more computers or other devices such as a tablet or smartphone.

What Does WiFi Mean?

The term WiFi comes from the acronym for two words, wireless and fidelity. Wireless refers to the fact that an Internet signal is obtained without using direct wiring or cables. Like any wireless signal, an antenna is used to transmit and receive the WiFi signal. Your computer, tablet, smartphone, game console, TV, or other device needs a WiFi antenna to transmit and receive WiFi data. You may not see the antenna on the outside of your device, but if your device works with WiFi, it has a built-in antenna.

The Fidelity Part of WiFi

The second word of the acronym Wi-Fi is a bit more obtuse. Fi comes from the word Fidelity. This is a term that was previously used extensively in the business of recording and playback of music. Before there were computers, music was played on phonographs that picked up sound from a record. Early records had questionable quality and poor sound quality, or fidelity. Fidelity means the sound is as faithfully reproduced as current technology allows.

As records and phonographs improved, advertisers denoted some records and phonographs as High Fidelity. Thus, application of the term fidelity, as part of the acronym Wi-Fi, is accomplished by using the letters "Fi." So now that we know where the term WiFi came from, how does it work?

Using WiFi to Access the Internet

Your WiFi computer or device connects to another WiFi device, which is almost always a router. Routers are a specialized computer which does routing of data on networks. Most home and small business routers have a built-in WiFi antenna and if they have this antenna, they have WiFi capability. The router also has a wired connection to the Internet, usually to your Internet Service Provider (often your cable or phone company).

The router's antenna broadcasts a WiFi signal so your devices can locate it. For two devices to use WiFi, they need to recognize each other. WiFi networks use what's called a "handshake" before two devices can send and receive data to each other. It's like introducing two people to each other so they can start a conversation. Handshakes vary from one WiFi network to another since some don't require a password and some do, depending on how the WiFi network is set up to work.

Once your device has been introduced to the router and is on to the WiFi network using the "handshake," it can send and receive data using WiFi. The router communicates with devices connected to it using WiFi, using the WiFi side of the network. It then connects the WiFi side of the network to the Internet using the router's wired connection to your Internet Service Provider.

WiFi is a Radio Signal

WiFi networks commonly use one of two radio frequencies, 2.4Ghz and 5Ghz. These are radio frequencies managed in the U.S. by the Federal Communications Commission and around the world by the respective country's regulations.

Since WiFi uses radio signals, it can vary in signal strength based on distance, obstructions, and interference. These can all affect the reliability and speed of your WiFi Internet connection. Distance can affect your WiFi signal strength as you move further away from the antenna on your WiFi router. While many WiFi routers will broadcast a signal to most of a home, sometimes the distance is so far that the signal becomes too weak to use and you lose your Internet connection in certain locations.

This is why you can sometimes pick up the signal of your neighbor's WiFi router on one side of your home, although you would need a password to connect to it. If your signal is too weak in parts of your home, see if you can move your router to a location closer to the center. If not, you can add a router and cable to rebroadcast the signal to a new area of your home. This is how offices and schools create a signal that seems like it's available everywhere.

WiFi is a World Standard (for more techie types to read)

An international standards body called the Institute of Electrical and Electronics Engineers (IEEE) created the WiFi standard in 1997 and publishes the technical specifications so any manufacturer can build devices using the WiFi standard. The common term for the WiFi standard used for networks is called 802.11, and you may see this number on WiFi devices. The number comes from the group number at the IEEE that manages the standard. Technology companies, research organizations, and other organizations have volunteer IEEE members that serve on these standards groups.

Different WiFi Standards

As WiFi has developed, standards for it have changed to provide increased range and data. To tell what version of the standard your device uses, you'll need to know the number and letter of the WiFi standard it uses. These numbers all begin with 802.11, which is named after the IEEE group that manages the WiFi standard.

The 802.11 number will also have a letter after it, such as 802.11b, 802.11g, and 802.11n. As long as the two devices you want to connect to each other using WiFi have the same WiFi capability, they can connect with each other. Almost every device manufactured today includes support for 802.11b and 802.11g, so they will work with each other. Newer and higher priced routers may also include support for the latest version of the standard, 802.11n. The problem with 802.11n is that the standard isn't quite completed, so it's possible that two devices made by different manufacturers may not work together. However, all 802.11n routers also include support for 802.11b and 802.11g so they support almost every WiFi device made.

Technology Changes

As technology changes, updating one part of your technology may create issues with other parts. Our homes are becoming pretty sophisticated with desktops, laptops, tablets, smartphones, Internet TV, game consoles, and other Internet connected devices coming out like thermostats and light controls. As a result, it's sometimes necessary to upgrade an older part of your technology in order to work with something new. Often this is the case with WiFi.

If you have an older router, it may have problems connecting with newer devices like tablets, so often a router replacement which is usually under $100, will fix connection issues.

Often replacing technology is an easier, lower cost, and faster solution to trying to repair or fix a problem.

Windows 10

Windows 10 is Microsoft's latest version of the Windows operating system for personal computers, tablets, and smartphones. It will be available to the general public on July 29, 2015, and is a free upgrade for users of Windows 7 and Windows 8.

What's at stake for Microsoft

When Microsoft released Windows 8, the company tried to bring features of touch screen computing to the desktop and use a similar screen across all operating systems for Windows versions for the desktop, laptop, tablets, and smartphones. Microsoft was going to leverage the Windows customer base and partners (technical professionals with Microsoft certifications) from the desktop to attack the mobile marketplace. By designing an operating system that worked similarly from the desktop to the smartphone, Microsoft was hoping to get Windows desktop users to start buying Windows smartphones and tablets. Unfortunately, it has not been successful.

If you know anyone with a Microsoft Windows smartphone, you're the exception. Microsoft bought Nokia several years ago, deciding that it needed to gain ground against Apple and Android (Google) in the smartphone market. That purchase wasn't helpful to seeing more Windows phones.

But let's be realistic, people are using their smartphones more than their computers, so Microsoft made some management changes. The new management started to change direction from Windows 8 and prepared for Windows 10 (by the way Windows 9 is being skipped as a number; there was no Windows 9 operating system).

Many of the things people liked about Windows 7 are coming back into Windows 10, since may users of Windows 8 found it so different from Windows 7 or even Windows XP that it felt like using a new computer. Thus, Windows 10 is focused on the theme "it's familiar," which appears on Microsofts official Windows 10 website.

What's different about Windows 10

First of all, an upgrade from Windows 7 and Windows 8 to Windows 10 is absolute free. All you need to do to quality is to upgrade before July 29, 2016, which is one year from the official release of Windows 10. If you use Windows 7 or Windows 8, a small Windows icon should appear on the lower right of your screen in the taskbar. Click on the Windows icon and you should see information on how to reserve your upgrade.

In addition to being free, here are some of the main features of Windows 10

- Brings back the familiar Start menu that was removed in Windows 8
- Uses a new Internet Browser for viewing web pages called Microsoft Edge
- Allows four apps to snap into place on your desktop and create "virtual' desktops
- Integrates with the Windows Store for app and content purchases
- Introduces Cortana, a personal assistant that learns about you and how you work
- Includes apps like Maps, Photos, Mail & Calendar, Music and Video
- Includes Microsoft Defender anti-virus software standard
- Makes it easy to save all of your files and data in Microsoft's OneDrive cloud service

Let's take a closer look at the most significant new features.

Start Menu

The Start menu was removed from the desktop screen in Windows 8 making it difficult for many people to understand how to find a locate familiar menu items like apps and folders. Windows 10 brings back the Start menu to the desktop so you can use your familiar way of navigating or offers the option to use desktop icons.

Windows Edge

Windows Edge makes web browsing much easier on Windows. Internet Explorer came from Windows XP, and the web has changed a lot, and the web browser has become one of the primary apps we use daily. Edge has a feature that allows you to write on web pages you view with a stylus or type notes on the page, then save the page for later reference or to email to someone. A "reader" view is available that displays only the readable text on a web page for easier distraction-free reading, and Cortana, the personal assistant, is integrated with Microsoft Edge so you can use voice commands to search the web or other web browsing actions.

Windows Store

Like Apple and Google, Microsoft is now using a store on it's computers, tablets, and smartphones to users can install and purchase apps and content like movies, games and TV shows. Your purchases are stored by Microsoft using your Microsoft account, which you create when you install Windows 10. Purchasing and installing apps and content from the Windows store helps make installation safer and easier since Microsoft checks all the apps available from the store.

Cortana

Your personal assistant, Cortana, helps you by keeping track of your activity, like appointments and reminders, and will help create reminders automatically for you if you let it. For example, if you're using the calendar on your desktop, Cortana can remind you when to get ready to leave for an appointment and how long it will take to drive there. Cortana brings an artificial intelligence based personal assistant to Windows users who will be able to talk to their computer and use verbal instructions.

Windows OneDrive

Microsoft provides 15 gigabytes of free cloud storage service with their OneDrive cloud storage You can use this for storage of your documents, files, photos, and more. By using OneDrive for storing your documents and files, they are available to you from your OneDrive account on any Windows device you own and by using your OneDrive web account on any computer. Microsoft even has OneDrive apps for Apple and Android devices.

There are ways to increase your free storage capacity. For example, using OneDrive to store your photos will give you an extra 15 GB, and referring a friend who signs up will give you an extra 500MB. One terabyte of storage is included with a subscription to Office 365, which Microsoft's Office products (Word, Excel, PowerPoint, Outlook, Notes, etc.).

In case you were wondering, I already subscribe to Office 365 using a Home and Family plan, so five members of my family each can use Office and each receives 1 TB of personal OneDrive Storage. The Home and Family plan is the best deal at under $10 a month for all five users.

To my way of thinking

Whether or not you use Windows, Microsoft still has a big impact on the whole technology industry. When Microsoft does something like introduce a new Windows version, Apple, Google, Facebook and other technology companies all take notice.

Should you upgrade? Yes.

Windows 10 is much easier to use for people who struggles with the change from Windows XP or Windows 7 to Windows 8, and using Windows 10 will seem much more familiar. Windows 10 is more secure, with Microsoft Defender security software built-in, but if you already have a third-party security software installed Windows 10 will use your existing software.

Windows 10 has also been in use by millions of users during the development and test period. As a result, many bugs have been eliminated making it more reliable for the July 29th release. Microsoft used a new program called Windows Insider which allowed consumers the opportunity to participate in the development of Windows 10.

X, Y, Z

Intentionally left blank.

More Tech Terms for Free

Each week I explain a new technology term in my bobology newsletter. To subscribe visit **www.bobology.com** and use the email newsletter sign-up form in the upper right.

The free weekly newsletter describes a tech term every week. You'll be able to keep up with the ever changing language of technology.